The

Future

of

National

Urban

Policy

Marshall

Kaplan

and

Franklin

James,

Editors

Duke Press Policy Studies

Duke University Press

Durham and London 1990

© 1990 Duke University Press
All rights reserved
Printed in the United States of America
on acid-free paper ∞
Library of Congress Cataloging-in-Publication Data
The future of national urban policy.
Includes bibliographical references.
1. Urban policy—United States.   I. Kaplan, Marshall.
II. Franklin James.
HT123.U74655   1989   307.7′6′0973   88-33545
ISBN 0-8223-0908-4
ISBN 0-8223-0927-0 (pbk.)

Contents

Preface

In the lexicon of affirmative action Patricia Roberts Harris was a distinguished and exceptionally talented "twofer"—a black woman whose presence on an organization chart simultaneously enhanced both gender and race staff ratios. Indeed, such was her distinction that when a careless congressman at Harris's confirmation hearing as secretary of Housing and Urban Development wondered out loud whether or not she could empathize with the working class, she was forced to remind him with icy civility that her father was a Pullman porter. Her professional ability was demonstrated in assignment after assignment. A law school professor and dean, an ambassador and diplomatic delegate, and a U.S. cabinet secretary of two departments, she was committed to the needs of the often inarticulate poor: these were the special properties of Pat Harris's character.

She had particular need of these characteristics as the sixth secretary of HUD. Since its inception the department has always exhibited a split personality, carrying out the highly technical, almost arcane economic tasks of granting money subsidies to the volatile housing industry while purporting to speak for the urban poor and dispossessed. On one hand, the constituencies which cluster around HUD are well-to-do mortgage bankers, prosperous homebuilders, affluent real estate developers, and politically powerful mayors. On the other, the claimants are the homeless, the public housing tenants, hard-pressed community-based organizations in ghetto neighborhoods, and churches struggling to learn the intricacies of designing, funding, and building low-income housing. The trick for any HUD administration is not to be so bamboozled by the industry's interest groups—or overwhelmed by their statistical prattle of interest rates and secondary mortgage volumes—that one forgets the real needs of urban people, or the urgent claims of the core cities; the desperate plight of the overlooked American increasingly evident for twenty years now, since the long hot summer of 1967.

Pat Harris understood both roles. She was a special HUD "twofer" in the sense that with her lawyer's mind she could joust with the most sophisticated Gucci-clad lobbyist, but she never forgot what the department's main mission was—decent, affordable housing for everyone—and she persisted in that goal. So Urban Development Action grants may have appeared to be HUD's most visible program innovation during her tenure (1977–79, before she went on to become secretary of Health and Human Resources) but the attention to Section 8, the reform of the Community Development Block Grant program, and the renewed emphasis on fair housing were the real items on her agenda, if at times not blatantly outfront. They were the key provisions in the 1979 Housing and Community Development Act.

Harris left a department that undertook, in HUD's first Secretary Robert Weaver's words, "to unscramble the confused organization it had inherited and to make Housing Assistance Plans more effective," and that "revived the pre-1973 importance of supply-oriented housing assistance programs but permitted the Section 8 program to play an important demand-side role." So in the end, "The policy and program redirections in HUD during the Carter years were a refreshing break from the Nixon-Ford period."[1]

Budget constraints closed in toward the end of the Carter administration to be applied with savage force in the Reagan years. Yet the Congress refused to let the programs or the department go under, and Pat Harris's legacies are ready and waiting for revival.

Secretary Harris took from her national experience two important lessons that many of us learned there. The first is that whatever the ruffles and flourishes that accompany a cabinet appointment, the power is always—and rightly—constrained by the authority of elected officials. It is truly the pols who have the final say. The second is that if you want to truly know the good that government can do, you must work at the street level, and never more so than in urban programs.

Pat Harris learned both lessons and applied them in her campaign for mayor of Washington, D.C., conducted just before her death in 1985. She lost in her bid to become a street-level politician, but she tried valiantly. And her effort was testimony once again to her commitment to helping the majority of urban people, the homeless, the working poor, and the people in the neighborhoods—all those pieces of our cities on which our national economic prosperity and claims to urban justice ultimately depend.

Robert Wood
Former Secretary
Housing and Urban Development

Middletown, Connecticut
August 18, 1989

Introduction—A Response to Urban Distress: Challenge and Opportunity

Marshall Kaplan and Franklin James

Pat Harris would have liked this book. In the words of one of her colleagues, the "papers in it suggest the authors' commitment to cities. Pat probably would have disagreed with the analyses and conclusions in some of the papers. She would have welcomed a debate . . . she would have been a hell of a good advocate . . . she would have appreciated the need to find common ground. Above all, she would have applauded the book's intent to stimulate a needed dialogue concerning the well-being of Urban America."

For too long we have avoided a serious discussion about what role, if any, the federal government should play in helping maintain and enhance the health of American cities. Similarly, for too long we have been unwilling to entertain serious discussions concerning the federal ability to generate a comprehensive, strategic, or, indeed, any kind of reasonably cohesive urban policy. By the time this book is published a new set of leaders will have taken over the White House and, to some extent, the Congress. It can be hoped that their tasks will include the development of an effective federal approach to America's urban ills. Their efforts will be made easier by the willingness of the authors of this book to challenge past assumptions, to question present presumed urban problems, and to articulate realistic options for the future.

Federal Aid and Cities: Tales of Two Cities

Clearly, past federal initiatives aimed at cities proved useful to some cities. It helped them close the gap between their own limited revenues and their required expenditures for services. It assisted them in surviving downswings in the economy. It permitted them to provide threshold support to low-income households. It helped them generate the revitalization of selected neighborhoods.

Just as clearly, the critics of federal aid to cities have a case. Cities that appear healthy rarely attribute their vigor to federal assistance or federal policies. Most credit national or area economic trends. Some credit local public- and private-sector leadership. In this context many of our distressed cities suggest in effect two cities. Some among them illustrate booming downtowns and gentrified nearby residential areas fueled by market-driven variables and changing demography. Just short distances away, however, they reflect expanding ghettoes and deteriorating neighborhoods dependent for services on minimal public-sector dollars, including federal dollars. Their low-income, often minority, residents struggle to survive. Jobs are scarce. The availability of adequate health care, proper education, and decent housing is at best related to the luck of the draw and at worst nonexistent.

Whither or Whether a Comprehensive Federal Urban Policy

At this juncture we do not as a nation have a really good sense of the effect of past federal policies or programs on cities. Evaluations to date, despite the significant dollars spent on them, suggest conflicting impacts. Put two analysts in a room and you will likely get three, four, or more viewpoints concerning the effectiveness, efficiency, and equity associated with key federal initiatives undertaken over the last twenty years: initiatives such as urban renewal, Model Cities, the war on poverty, the Community Development Block Grant Program, and the Urban Development Action Grant effort.

We have heard and read that federal aid has been wasted because it has been too little too late, because it has been given to areas that do not have the competence to administer it, because it has rarely been provided for long enough periods to make a difference, because different federal initiatives often contain inconsistent objectives, because nationally imposed ground rules governing federal programs do not fit local conditions, and because it has been swamped or overwhelmed by national or international economic factors or other more powerful nonurban federal policies.

Many urban observers would argue that the inadvertent or unanticipated impacts of urban and nonurban federal policies and programs often had a more significant impact on cities than the specific sought-after results of federal urban aid. For example, some would suggest that the tremendous levels of suburban housing production in the fifties, sixties, and seventies

—production stimulated in part by the accessibility provided by federally supported roads and in part by federally provided housing insurance —fostered increased migration of whites from cities and the related phenomena of increased neighborhood blight and housing abandonment. And some would suggest that the growth of welfare payments and related in-kind services have muted the incentive of welfare recipients to secure jobs and have reduced their desire to move out of low-income areas.

Efforts to define a comprehensive urban policy have been limited, and none has been too successful. No administration has been able or willing to develop and articulate a comprehensive set of related goals and strategies concerning cities—goals and strategies that would specifically govern programs, budgets, and subsequent performance evaluations. The multiple and diverse social commitments of the Kennedy-Johnson administrations, while perhaps laudable in light of the minimal urban concerns of the Reagan administration, resulted in great numbers of "categorical" programs, or programs for every possible category of urban ill. Only after the fact and only with a lot of imagination can we sort out assumed administration goals concerning the revitalization of urban areas. Succinctly, the Kennedy-Johnson urban initiatives were driven more by events—political pressure, and the often changing perceptions of city problems of different agencies, congressional committees, and the president himself than by any broad-based set of policies.

Both the Nixon-Ford and the Carter administrations attempted to define comprehensive urban policies. The Nixon effort, responding to the congressional mandate to develop comprehensive urban-growth policies that would accommodate the then-anticipated tremendous growth of urban America and the related emptying out of rural areas, proved to be a limited one. It was long on analysis of demographic trends and their likely impact on metropolitan areas and cities and short on hard recommendations. Nixon-Ford programs were rarely guided by the mandated "biennial" reports to Congress. Rather, they were an outgrowth of the presidents' efforts to reform the diverse categorical program inventory, an inventory that neither the Feds nor the cities could strategically manipulate for their purposes. In securing enactment of block grants and revenue sharing, they led to significant changes in the way federal aid was delivered to cities.

The Carter administration's efforts to forge an urban policy were more notable for their vigor and their tenacity than for their success. In the end the administration produced a set of policies that focused only on distressed cities. They were aimed primarily at the targeting of limited federal dollars to troubled cities that, by and large, were losing their more affluent populations. Because President Carter committed to increasing the flow of resources to this one class of cities, the "Partnership for Urban America," as the policy was called, was bold in the context of the American political scene. Yet it was by no means comprehensive. Generally, even with respect to its client group—distressed cities—it emphasized economic over social initiatives and the revitalization of places ahead of expanded choices for people.

Can We Forge a Comprehensive Urban Policy?

Even assuming a continued decline of resources available to cities, the rationalists among us would likely argue for a comprehensive urban policy. After all, federal actions, whether consciously aimed at cities or not and regardless of anticipated budget constraints, will continue to have a major impact on the form, shape, and well-being of cities. Shouldn't these actions be guided by explicit political and substantively measureable goals and objectives? Given limited resources, wouldn't the Feds get more bang from their marginal dollar if we forced dollars to flow from articulated and articulate policies related to a priori analyses of likely cause-and-effect relationships?

Why haven't we responded to what appears to make eminent sense? As recorded in this book, federal efforts to define comprehensive policies appear to end in failure for several perceived analytical, institutional, and political reasons. According to the book's authors, some of the reasons are grounded in fact; others are premised on conventional wisdom which no longer is conventional or wise; some rest on myth and anti-city bias. In summary, these are some of the sets of reasons:

Analytical

1. We lack a firm understanding of city problems and the causes of city problems.

2. We lack the ability to anticipate with any degree of certainty economic, population, and social trends that vitally affect cities.

3. We lack the ability and/or the will to subject past and present federal actions affecting cities to thorough evaluation and to respond to negative evaluations.

4. We lack a consistent and compelling set of theories to guide the development of a comprehensive urban policy.

Institutional

1. Federal budget constraints make it difficult to provide the amount of aid to cities that would be essential if we developed a comprehensive urban policy.

2. Our federal system, or the relationship among and between federal, state, and local governments, cannot respond in a coordinated way to urban ills.

3. Federal agencies have disparate roles, missions, and client groups. They cannot initiate policies that benefit only one type of jursidiction.

4. States have little interest in helping cities. The constituent groups supporting the majority of their elected officials are nonurban.

5. Cities have too few resources and too many problems to mount a comprehensive set of policies or to join other levels of government in a comprehensive urban policy effort.

6. Cities do not have the competence or political will to initiate and maintain effective urban policies.

Political

1. Cities are losing their most politically powerful populations: affluent whites. They are left with the poor and/or minorities.

2. Growing, healthy areas of the nation do not want to help needy cities. National productivity objectives conflict with efforts to spend limited resources on distressed cities. We must focus on the economic winners.

The Book: Responding to Distress

The book is structured to respond to questions of urban need, to issues related to the effect of past and current policies on urban areas, and to the definition of possible future federal initiatives aimed at helping cities. Part 1 examines broad indicators of urban need or distress. Part 2 evaluates urban problems in key areas of concern such as education, infrastructure, housing, and poverty. It also provides a case study of one city whose schizoid social indicators point simultaneously to a great recovery and to continuing problems. Part 3 provides an evaluation of historical efforts at creating federal urban policies and a current status report concerning urban policies and federal aid to urban areas. Part 4 presents a critical evaluation of HUD, the federal agency assigned key urban policy responsibilities, and provides more optimistic evaluations of recent city hall, citizen, and nonprofit-group actions in response to urban ills. Part 5 provides an analysis of the attitudes of the American public toward helping the poor and, by implication, toward helping cities. It also contains a brief look at varied ways to generate an urban policy or policies. Finally, Part 5 contains a comprehensive set of recommendations for future federal policies that acknowledge current resource, political, and knowledge constraints. While they are not explicitly urban, the authors believe that if they are enacted they are likely to help troubled cities respond to their problems. It labels the proposed thrust "Toward a Nonurban Urban Policy."

Part 1: Urban Need and Distress—A Broad Overview

Franklin James's chapter provides relevant data concerning the status of large American central cities. He presents a policy-relevant set of indicators to measure urban distress and to evaluate the condition of cities over time. James concludes that many American cities are needy. More relevant from a policy perspective, he indicates that despite several years of national economic growth, many central cities that illustrated severe problems during the seventies and early eighties reflect severe problems at the present time.

The chapter by Roy Bahl, William Duncombe, and Wanda Schulman on the fiscal health of cities provides a bit more grounds for optimism than does James. Bahl and his colleagues suggest that cities may have benefited from the country's recovery from recession and the nation's ability to rein in inflation. Clearly, at least in the aggregate, the fiscal condition of cities looks better. But Bahl cautions us. He indicates that cities may have purchased improved fiscal health in part at the expense of deferred human and physical capital investment, higher tax rates, and lower urban service levels.

Part 2: Urban Problems—A Microscopic Look at
Key Areas of Concern

Frank Newman and his colleagues Robert Palaich and Rona Wilensky provide an important and concise look at the status of urban education. They frame their critical analyses within the context of statistics concerning poverty, particularly among increasing and disproportionate numbers of minorities that reside in central cities. Their analysis of education problems faced by central cities and their poorer residents is alarming.

Peter Edelman in his provocative chapter confirms the general and disheartening trends concerning poverty seen in central cities. He focuses on the increasing problems faced by Hispanics, blacks, the young, and female-headed households. He asks us to reevaluate past and present antipoverty strategies.

William Apgar's chapter presents an updated report card on the status of housing in America's metropolitan and urban areas. His analysis warns of increasing problems of affordability and housing conditions facing low- and moderate-income residents of cities. Low levels of production, housing abandonment, and relatively low incomes compared to costs have merged to escalate urban housing difficulties, particularly for renters. Contrary to conventional wisdom, Apgar notes that rents in metropolitan areas have risen rapidly since 1980.

According to Michael Pagano, America's cities illustrate significant unmet infrastructure needs. Water and sewer lines are literally crumbling. Bridges and roads are unsafe and/or often impassable. Pagano suggests that infrastructure problems generate from resource scarcity. City leaders face Hobbesian choices: either provide operations and services for residents or provide funds for capital investment and maintenance. Understandably, they often are required to sacrifice infrastructure for operations and services. As relevant from a policy perspective, local commitments concerning infrastructure investment appear not to be dependent on the amount of available federal aid.

Ian Menzies's chapter on Boston's assumed recovery points to an urban policy dilemma. While, as he notes, the vital signs concerning Boston's economic growth are healthy, the city remains divided along racial and income lines. Up to now the rising local economic tide has not floated all ships (neighborhoods) and all crews (blacks and poor people) equally. Racism, although less overt and vicious than during the seventies, remains an unfortunate fact of Boston's life.

Part 3: Developing a Comprehensive Urban Policy—
Maximum Hopes, Minimum Results

Marshall Kaplan provides a snapshot analysis of the changes that have occurred in the key economic, social, and institutional variables affecting the development of urban policy initiatives. He portrays the problems denying the nation a comprehensive urban policy. He notes the decline in the political fortunes and clout of central cities in Washington. Kaplan also calls attention to the absence of consensus concerning urban problems and the causes of such problems.

Charles Orlebeke traces the history of urban policymaking efforts in the Nixon-Ford and Carter administrations. He also describes the eclipse of urban policymaking efforts in the Reagan era. Orlebeke suggests that urban policymaking activities to date have had limited impact. He indicates that

President Bush would be wise to look at why past efforts at urban policy-making efforts have failed or been seriously flawed.

William Schambra questions in his chapter whether this nation can ever form a comprehensive urban policy. He suggests that liberals and not conservatives are to blame. According to Schambra's provocative thesis, liberals have never been able to reconcile two different perspectives concerning cities. The comprehensive-policy approach or "policy liberalism" reflected in President Carter's efforts is premised on a perception that effective federal initiatives must be based on an understanding of key cause-and-effect relationships and an understanding of significant social, economic, and environmental factors affecting city health and well-being. The program approach, or "national community liberalism," reflected in President Johnson's and President Roosevelt's efforts is premised on the development of individual programs responsive to different problems and a simple vision of America as a single community. The author indicates that liberalism and liberals have failed to choose between a politically effective but unsophisticated, and ultimately self-defeating, program approach to social problems and a sophisticated and comprehensive, but politically unpalatable, policy approach.

Kaplan's essay on neighborhood policy indicates that, at best, federal initiatives have generated uneven results. He traces the minimal impact of federal efforts to a maze of factors, among them: the absence of strong guiding neighborhood-development theories; the absence of consistent neighborhood strategies; the lack of understanding of cause-and-effect relationships in neighborhood change; and the varied perceptions Americans have of neighborhoods. He also blames the faddish policies often associated with federal intervention.

Robert Reischauer's chapter examines the rise and fall of national urban policy efforts in the context of allocated federal resources. He notes the significant decline in urban-related expenditures since the late seventies and suggests that, in light of the fiscal constraints facing the federal government, the increased role of the states, and the weakened political status of cities, it is unlikely that future administrations will try to emulate the past regarding large resource commitments to cities.

Peggy Cuciti provides an in-depth look at the Reagan administration's treatment of cities. She calls attention to the relationship of President Reagan's tax program and his defense priorities to cutbacks in federal aid. She also notes the urban effect of the administration's effort to shift or devolve responsibilities to the states. Cuciti indicates that distressed cities found their share of federal spending decreased between 1980 and 1986 relative to the nation as a whole and relative to a set of economically healthy cities.

Part 4: Institutions and Institutional Capacity

Robert Wood, former HUD secretary, and Beverly Klimkowsky offer an insightful and indeed very critical look at HUD and its role and mission. Wood reviews the relatively marginal effect the agency has had on cities. He also notes the conflict in the agency's role between its efforts to stimulate housing production in the suburbs and its efforts to revitalize older areas of cities. He asks a difficult question: Would efforts to assist cities be hindered if HUD were eliminated?

Since the mid-seventies, terms and phrases like "public-private sector partnerships," "community–city hall collaboration," and the important role of the "independent sector" have come to symbolize the increasing entrepreneurial activities of cities in generating "deals" to revitalize their older areas and the growing involvement of community development and nonprofit groups in renewal efforts. Bernard Frieden describes some of the successful examples of public-private sector partnerships. Concerning downtown development, he indicates that such partnerships hold promise in providing benefits to cities and their poorer residents. He provides data which indicate the positive contribution of service jobs to city residents, including low-income residents, and suggests that the substitution of service for manufacturing jobs could lead to some important pluses. But he suggests that cities must negotiate long-term agreements concerning jobs and training with private-sector developers if the benefits of downtown development and public-private sector partnerships are to help reduce poverty and expand the choices of the urban poor.

Langley Keyes notes the changes that have occurred in the outlook and operation of citizen groups in Massachusetts. His analyses indicate that citizen groups no longer want to remain in an adversarial posture regarding state and local governments. Rather, they desire to get in on the economic action. Most groups once hostile to government have found ways to become partners regarding economic growth and revitalization. While problems impeding cooperation remain, and while resources to foster joint efforts remain marginal, Keyes sees the Massachusetts experience as a prologue to a national expansion of citizen-initiated and citizen-developed partnerships that respond to varied urban problems.

Benson Roberts and Fern Portnoy corroborate Keyes's Massachusetts observations with national data and analyses. They note the significant growth of local community-development organizations and the unique relationships that have developed between national and local foundations and such organizations. To Roberts and Portnoy, the phenomenon is lasting and important. With federal assistance, community-development groups can generate neighborhood improvements, economic development, and jobs. It confirms the city as a laboratory for future urban policy initiatives.

Part 5: Looking to the Future: A Set of Nonurban Urban Policy Initiatives

James Sundquist's chapter lends cause for optimism to those who feel the nation must make a renewed commitment to its cities and its poor. His evaluation of public giving and public opinion over the last two or three decades suggests an American public that has not lost its social conscience. He perceives the public as ready to respond to leaders that request greater commitments to help distressed areas and people.

Paul Ylvisaker reviews some of the historical ways urban policies and urban initiatives have built national support, if not consensus, concerning their relevance. He calls attention to the intense urban problems that still exist and poignantly reflects upon the fact that their solution will likely require a spiritual revival and a spiritual challenge.

The final chapter in the book, written by Marshall Kaplan and Franklin James, weaves together the themes articulated by most of the authors. Kaplan and James focus on the absence of a consensus theory or theories to guide the development of urban policy initiatives. This fact, combined with the absence of agreement on the causes of city ills, the unfavorable politics facing city advocates, and continuing federal budget constraints, suggests that the days of comprehensive urban policymaking are over. According to Kaplan and James, urbanists—both scholars and practitioners—should look to key nonurban policy initiatives likely to be favored by the Bush administration and the 101st Congress. Many, if structured in a sensitive manner, would help respond to city problems in an effective way.

Part

1

Urban Need and Distress— A Broad Overview

1 City Need and Distress in the United States: 1970 to the Mid-1980s

Franklin James

Introduction

Many American cities are suffering from serious economic decline and from the loss of middle-class and affluent families.[1] In some cities the severity of such problems exceeds the capacity of either people or local institutions—business, government, or nonprofit organizations—to adapt to without experiencing significant hardship. In jargon which has come to be widely accepted in the United States, such cities are distressed.

Of course, cities are highly diverse. Some U.S. cities have dynamically developing economies. Some have been able to aggressively expand their municipal boundaries to enclose their suburbs. Some healthy cities, experiencing an economic resurgence, are a cause for hope that today's distressed cities with appropriate support and assistance may recover and regain their competitiveness for people or jobs. However, the healthy places should not distract us from the fact that urban distress has become more widespread and more severe since 1970.

The concept of distress was invented principally to meet national policy demands. The block grant programs created as a result of President Nixon's "New Federalism"—especially General Revenue Sharing and the Community Development Block Grant Program—distributed funds directly to cities and intended to allocate funds in proportion to need, or distress. The demands for need indexes multiplied with the creation of CETA, with the economic stimulus programs of the early Carter years, and with the increased concern with urban economic development programs. Academics and federal agencies responded to those programmatic needs with an efflorescence of indexes, sometimes fine-tuned to reflect particular program objectives and structures.[2]

The continuing relevance of distress needs to be constantly evaluated.

The political wisdom of the concept has been marginal at best. Targeting to distressed cities was a principal theme of the Carter urban policy.[3] The articulation of the policy goal in 1978 contributed to an uproarious political debate, the result of which was a standoff that stalled subsequent efforts to target funds to urban distress. The concept has even less political relevance today as a result of the hostility of the Reagan administration to direct federal aid to local governments and its indifference to any special claims distressed areas may have for federal assistance.

It will be argued here that the concept of distress retains its relevance for two basic reasons. First, appropriate conceptual and empirical indicators of distress help chart basic trends in the well-being of cities and their residents. This analytic function offers insight into the priority of urban claims for federal and state resources. Second, distress indicators are useful for evaluating the distributive impacts of federal and state policies, whether they be explicitly urban initiatives or nonurban ones with urban impacts. In this second function, distress is related to the urban impact analyses started during the Carter years.

This chapter aims to provide useful insight into current patterns of urban distress by developing a refined city typology. This typology is used to reexamine urban change during the 1970s and to develop preliminary information on social and demographic trends in various types of cities during the 1980s. The new typology requires only standard census data so that it can be estimated on generally comparable terms in both 1970 and 1980. This permits unique insight into how the severity of city distress changed in individual cities as well as groups of places during the decade.[4] The empirical analysis will focus on big cities with 1980 populations in excess of 250,000. This focus is dictated by resource constraints. However, the patterns of change found among these large cities are not unique. Many smaller communities are undergoing very similar transitions.

It may not commonly be recognized how much distress worsened among America's big cities during the 1970s. The city typology developed here implies that not one big U.S. city was distressed in 1970, yet one in four such cities was distressed, using plausible criteria, by 1980. With respect to trends since 1980 there is a widespread but largely wrong impression that many big distressed cities of the late 1970s have turned the corner and are healing despite the neglect of national urban policy during the Reagan years. The quantitative analysis suggests that urban distress has been lessened in some cities and is worse in others, but there is no strong evidence that city distress has significantly ameliorated on average.

Rationale for the Community Typology

We are focusing on conditions in municipalities—that is, cities. For much of its history the United States left urban problems and urban policies to the states. By and large, states left these problems and policies to local governments: municipalities and, sometimes, counties. For example, until the 1930s local governments had the major responsibility for welfare and education policies designed to help the urban poor. It is only comparatively recently that states and the federal government have assumed much of the local government responsibilities for welfare and school spending.

Similarly, land use controls such as zoning laws and growth management ordinances are major shapers of patterns of urban development, population mobility, and neighborhood change in urban areas. While the legal power to enact such laws lies squarely within the states, states (with the exception of Hawaii) have delegated this responsibility to municipalities and counties.

This heavy reliance on municipal and county governments has made the capacity of these governments to solve their problems a critical concern for national urban policy. Municipal limits are powerful shapers of the nature of urban problems. They delimit the availability and quality of public services and the breadth and height of local taxes. As a result, city limits warp the location decisions of both people and employers. In a nutshell, frequently arbitrary and obsolete municipal boundaries are more important for some types of urban policy considerations than are more economically meaningful metropolitan limits or socially meaningful neighborhood areas.

Very many indexes of city "distress," "hardship," "need," and "stress" have been developed during the past decade.[5] This diversity reflects the fact that distress has several dimensions. Peggy Cuciti has argued, for example, that urban distress results from a confluence of socioeconomic hardship among city residents, fiscal inadequacy of public sector institutions, and city growth or decline in economic and/or demographic terms.[6]

These conceptually distinct dimensions of distress are linked through powerful cause-and-effect relationships, however. Great concentrations of people disadvantaged by poverty or structural unemployment can impair local public institutions and in extreme cases can render them incapable of ameliorating people's problems. High taxes, poor services, and concentrations of disadvantaged population can undercut business investment and job creation, thus leading to economic decline. When this occurs, both fiscal and socioeconomic distress are exacerbated. Distress can also obviate the adjustment of individuals to economic opportunities and can encourage destructive adjustments.[7]

The urban typology developed here has two dimensions: *resident need*, a function of poverty rates, unemployment, and per capita income growth; and *population change* during the previous decade.

As its name implies, resident need measures the economic resources and status of people in cities. Resident need is similar in concept to Cuciti's "socioeconomic hardship." Resident need is clearly relevant for targeting federal or state resources to cities. Cities with high resident need are appropriate targets for programs, such as employment and job-training assistance, delivering aid directly to disadvantaged people and for programs, such as community and economic development assistance, seeking to help such people through improving the environment in which they live. Resident need also reflects the fiscal capacity of municipal governments because income, sales, and property tax bases are in part a function of the level and distribution of income among city residents.[8]

Population change is inherently a more ambiguous indicator and is more closely related to the problems of places than of people. Population loss can exacerbate many social and economic problems of cities. Out-migrants from cities tend to be of above-average socioeconomic status. The loss of such people reduces both the purchasing power of city residents and the fiscal capacity of cities. Because many costs of running a city are fixed and not readily reduced in the face of falling demands or needs (such as infrastructure reinvestment costs), population loss can increase the costs of services to people and businesses remaining in the city.[9]

At the same time population loss is frequently an element of the adaptation of older, densely built-up cities to contemporary life-styles and technologies. Population and housing loss can permit more spacious conditions for people and businesses remaining in the city.

Because of its ambiguous relationship to the needs of people, city growth and decline are introduced as a second dimension of the typology, independent of resident need. It is to be expected, however, that cities are most distressed when resident need is high and population loss is rapid.

The community typology helps highlight communities which are successfully adapting—that is, declining cities in which resident need is relatively low. The typology also helps identify declining cities where inadequate adaptation is producing severe distress—that is, declining cities with high needs. Differences among these cities may provide useful clues for future policy.

Measuring Resident Need

Resident need combines several indicators to measure the economic well-being of persons in cities: their access to jobs and employment; the adequacy of their incomes to afford decent (above poverty) standards of living; and the pace of improvement in their average standard of living.

In empirical terms resident need is a composite index of three specific economic indicators: poverty rates, changes in real per capita income, and unemployment rates. Poverty rates are among the best and most widely accepted indicators of economic deprivation and are heavily weighted (by 40 percent) in calculating resident need.[10] Change in per capita income is a good indicator of the rate of improvement or decline in the average economic status of residents in a city and was weighted equally with poverty (40 percent). Unfortunately, unemployment rates are not a highly reliable indicator of job shortages or of structural unemployment. Indeed, rapid job growth, immigration, and frictional movement of people among jobs can result in high unemployment in economically healthy communities, whereas high unemployment rates in distressed cities generally mean frequently long-term or structural unemployment among people in need of work. Because of the ambiguities inherent in the unemployment rate indicator, it was weighted lower than poverty or income change: 20 percent.[11]

To measure trends in resident need over time the same general indicators were used to compute the resident-need index for 1970 and 1980. In the 1980 index poverty and unemployment rates are those reported in the 1980 census. Change in per capita income is measured between 1969 and 1979. In the 1970 resident-need index poverty and unemployment rates were those reported in the 1970 census for the cities; changes in real per capita income were measured between 1959 and 1969. *To provide a context within which to interpret the findings, the index has been normalized so that a value of 100 indicates resident need in the nation as a whole.* This approach facilitates analysis of how the economic well-being of residents of these cities has shifted relative to the economic well-being of the U.S. population as a whole.

Neither poverty rates nor measures of per capita income have been corrected for geographic differences in life-styles or in costs of living. On average, the costs of living are higher in big cities than in smaller communities or in rural areas. Thus, a given rate of poverty indicates generally greater actual deprivation in a big city than in a small community. A given level of per capita income has on average greater purchasing power outside big cities than inside them. In the 1970 and 1980 analysis big cities where the index took a value of 100 or less were classified as "relatively low" need. Cities where the index took a value of over 130 were classified as having "relatively high" need. Other cities were classified as having "moderate need."

Measuring City Growth and Decline

The community typology uses population change rather than employment or economic change to divide cities into growing, declining, or stable places. Population change is useful for this purpose because it is highly correlated with other potential indicators (the correlation coefficient between job change and population change between 1970 and 1980 in the seventy-four cities with population in excess of 200,000 was almost 0.90);[12] and high-quality population estimates are provided frequently, permitting regular updating of this component of the typology.

The cities were ranked according to population growth. Three general groups were defined: *decreasing population*: Cities that lost 10 percent or more of their population between 1970 and 1980; *stable population*: Cities whose population gain or loss between 1970 and 1980 was less than 10 percent; and *increasing population*: Cities that gained population by 10 percent or more between 1970 and 1980.

A 10 percent population change in only a decade represents a rapid rate of change. Nevertheless, 60 percent of large central cities showed population losses or gains of more than 10 percent from 1970 to 1980. This gives some indication of how rapidly population change is proceeding in the nation's central cities. Exactly the same categories were used in describing population change between 1960 and 1970.

Cities by Type in 1980

Table 1.1 lists the fifty-six biggest American cities by their levels of resident need in 1980 and the pace of their population growth or decline over the previous decade. Table 1.2 summarizes the results of applying the city typology to the fifty-six biggest cities in 1980.

The diversity of these big cities is apparent. One in four is classed as having decreasing populations and relatively high levels of resident need. These high-need, declining cities are located in all major regions of the United States. However, not all high-need cities experienced population loss during the 1970s. Five high-need cities had reasonably stable population levels during the 1970s. They include Miami, Memphis, and New

Table 1.1 Big Cities by Type: 1980

Resident Need 1980	Decline − 10 Percent or More		Stable		Growth + 10 Percent or More	
			Population Change, 1970–1980			
High (1.3+)	Atlanta	1.689	Birmingham	1.418	El Paso	1.392
	Baltimore	1.578	Miami	1.451		
	Boston	1.326	New Orleans	1.515		
	Buffalo	1.565	Oakland	1.395		
	Chicago	1.461	Memphis	1.379		
	Cincinnati	1.361				
	Cleveland	1.580				
	Detroit	1.839				
	Louisville	1.391				
	New York	1.430				
	Newark	2.173				
	Norfolk	1.364				
	Philadelphia	1.509				
	St. Louis	1.468				
Moderate (1–1.3)	Kansas City (Mo.)	1.009	Columbus	1.118	San Antonio	1.272
	Milwaukee	1.103	Indianapolis	1.010	San Diego	1.009
	Pittsburgh	1.199	Jacksonville	1.111	Tucson	1.041
	Washington, D.C.	1.239	Long Beach	1.069		
			Los Angeles	1.191		
			Sacramento	1.224		
			San Francisco	1.044		
			Tampa	1.196		
			Toledo	1.263		
Low	Minneapolis	.733	Dallas	.957	Albuquerque	.973
	St. Paul	.892	Denver	.970	Austin	.912
			Fort Worth	.967	Charlotte	.923
			Nashville	.939	Honolulu	.850
			Oklahoma City	.897	Houston	.888
			Omaha	.911	Phoenix	.912
			Portland, Ore.	.974	San Jose	.805
			Seattle	.866	Virginia Beach	.859
			Tulsa	.780		
			Wichita	.797		

Source: See text.
Note: The figures following the city name are the index of resident need for the city in 1980.

Table 1.2 Classification of 56 Big Cities by Resident Need and Population Change: 1980 (Number of Cities with Populations of 250,000 or More)

Resident Need 1980	Population Change, 1970–1980			
	Decreasing – 10 Percent or More	Stable	Increasing + 10 Percent or More	Total
Relatively High	14	5	1	20
Moderate	4	9	3	16
Relatively Low	2	10	8	20
Total	20	24	12	56

Source: See text.

Orleans, southern cities with relatively high poverty rates. One high-need city experienced marked population growth: El Paso. Population growth in El Paso is significantly boosted by high levels of natural increase and immigration of Hispanics with low earning power. The data suggest that several of the twenty cities experiencing rapid population losses may be adapting somewhat successfully to change. Four such declining cities showed moderate (rather than high) levels of resident need in 1980. Two—Minneapolis and St. Paul—showed low levels of resident need.

While the cities are diverse, it is equally clear that strong relationships link city growth or decline and resident need. Most growing cities also showed relatively low levels of resident need (eight out of twelve). Most declining cities showed high levels of resident need (fourteen out of twenty). The fourteen cities classified as experiencing both decreasing population and high resident need are identified in most studies as among the most troubled in the nation. For example, a recent study by the U.S. Department of Housing and Urban Development (HUD) ranked cities on the basis of a distress index which incorporated measures of poverty, crime, unemployment, and aged housing. Of the fifteen cities identified in that study as most distressed, thirteen are listed in table 1.1 as relatively high-need cities with decreasing populations.[13] Similarly, cities identified as least distressed in this HUD study are generally classified here as relatively low-need cities with growing or stable populations.[14]

Table 1.3 presents three "hardship" ratings reported for the fifty-six cities in a recent Brookings Institution study: *distress*, which reflects *levels* of unemployment, crime, and poverty rates in cities, as well as housing age and per capita income; *disparity*, which reflects *city/suburban differences*

Table 1.3 Relationship Between the City Typology and Recent Ratings of City Distress, Disparity, and Decline by the Brookings Institution

Brookings Institution Ratings	Cities with Relatively High Resident Need		Cities with Relatively Low Resident Need	
	Decreasing Population	Stable Population	Stable Population	Growing Population
Average Distress Rating[a]	−3.3	−0.4	1.3	2.1
Average Disparity Rating[b]	−3.9	−2.2	0.8	2.9
Average Decline Rating[c]	−1.6	0.2	1.2	1.5

Source: Katharine L. Bradbury, Anthony Downs, and Kenneth A. Small, *Urban Decline and the Future of American Cities*. (Washington, D.C.: Brookings Institution, 1982).
[a]Distress ratings range from −5 (most distressed) to +5 (least distressed). Distress is a function of 1975 unemployment rate, 1975 violent crime rate, 1969 poverty rate, percent of 1970 housing built before 1940, and city/SMSA tax disparity, 1971.
[b]Disparity ratings range from −5 (greatest disparity) to +5 (least disparity). Disparity is a function of city/SMSA differences in 1975 unemployment rates, 1975 violent crime rates, percentage of 1970 housing units built before 1940, and city/SMSA ratios of 1974 per capita income and 1969 poverty rates.
[c]Decline ratings range from −4 (greatest decline) to +4 (least decline). Decline is a function of change between 1970 and 1975 unemployment and violent crime rates, change between 1971 and 1975 in city government debt, and change in per capita income between 1969 and 1974.

in unemployment, crime, and poverty rates, as well as differences in housing age and per capita income; and *decline*, which reflects *recent trends* in unemployment, crime, per capita income, and city fiscal well-being.[15]

For each of these ratings hardship is indicated to be greatest when the index is negative and least when it is positive. As can be seen, these Brookings Institution indexes uniformly indicate that the greatest hardship exists among the fourteen cities experiencing relatively high resident need and rapid population losses. The three indexes also suggest that hardship is lowest among cities with relatively low resident need and increasing populations.

The three Brookings Institution indexes of city hardship described above were estimated on data from the mid-1970s, or on the basis of trends from the start to the middle of the seventies. A review of the indexes shows that the fourteen higher-need, declining cities suffering from the greatest distress in 1980 were also experiencing the most rapid rate of decline (or increase in distress) as of the mid-1970s. One of the major determinants of trends in city hardship or distress is the ability of a city to compete with suburbs for people, business investment, and jobs. As indicated by the Brookings disparity index, the fourteen high-need, declining cities were least able to compete with their suburbs: so, they suffer the greatest disparities.

It should be emphasized that cities classified as having low resident need are those in which resident need was lower in 1980 than it was in the nation as a whole. These include eighteen cities with growing or stable populations. These are generally located in the Sunbelt. They also include Minneapolis and St. Paul, two cities which appear to have mastered the art of growing old gracefully. As a group, these low-need cities generally face smaller social and economic problems and have greater resources than does the average community in the United States. They thus have a relatively marginal claim on national assistance, assuming such assistance was available. By contrast, the high-need cities, especially those with declining populations, face relatively large problems. These cities have strong claims on available federal aid designed to redistribute resources to either needy individuals or to their communities.

Changing Patterns of City Need
During the 1970s

In order to better understand patterns of change in cities during the 1970s, this essay's city typology was estimated for 1970. Because the 1970 typology is defined and estimated in exactly the same manner as in 1980, it offers unique insight into changes in city distress during the 1970s.[16]

The 1970 city typology is described in table 1.4 for the same fifty-six cities examined above. Two striking differences are apparent between the listing here and that presented earlier: (1) 1970 resident need is classified as high (at least 1.3 times more severe than in the United States as a whole) for only three cities—New Orleans, Newark, and El Paso. By contrast, twenty of these fifty-six cities had high levels of resident need in 1980; (2) only six of the cities experienced rapid population loss during the 1960s; strikingly, none of these declining cities were classified as having relatively high resident need in 1970. By contrast, twenty of the cities experienced rapid population loss during the 1970s, and three-fourths of these suffered from high levels of resident need.

At base, the biggest cities of the United States appear to have entered the

Table 1.4 Big Cities by Type: 1970

Resident Need 1970	Decline − 10 Percent or More		Stable		Growth + 10 Percent or More	
	Population Change, 1960–1970					
High (1.3)	None		New Orleans	1.43	El Paso	1.308
			Newark	1.46		
Moderate (1.3+)	Birmingham	1.28	Atlanta	1.190	Albuquerque	1.116
	Buffalo	1.14	Baltimore	1.170	Jacksonville	1.058
	Cleveland	1.185	Boston	1.052	Los Angeles	1.136
	Pittsburgh	1.087	Chicago	1.051	Memphis	1.199
	St. Louis	1.275	Cincinnati	1.136	Miami	1.247
			Detroit	1.172	Sacramento	1.234
			Long Beach	1.012	San Antonio	1.247
			Louisville	1.096	San Diego	1.090
			New York	1.042	Tucson	1.019
			Norfolk	1.203		
			Oakland	1.255		
			Philadelphia	1.047		
			Portland, Ore.	1.038		
			San Francisco	1.093		
			Seattle	1.021		
			Tampa	1.148		
			Washington, D.C.	1.070		
			Wichita	1.063		
Low (4)	Minneapolis	.877	Denver	.971	Austin	.935
			Kansas City, Mo.	.946	Charlotte	.960
			Milwaukee	.935	Columbus	.959
			St. Paul	.835	Dallas	.924
					Fort Worth	.974
					Honolulu	.745
					Houston	.952
					Indianapolis	.856
					Nashville	.828
					Oklahoma City	.959
					Omaha	.854
					Phoenix	.924
					San Jose	.973
					Toledo	.901
					Tulsa	.988
					Virginia Beach	.869

Source: See text.
Note: The figures following the city name are the index of resident need for the city in 1980.

Table 1.5 Big Cities with the Highest and Lowest Levels of Resident Need: 1970 and 1980

	10 Highest Need		10 Lowest Need	
Rank	1970	1980	1970	1980
1	Newark	Newark	Honolulu	Tulsa
2	New Orleans	Detroit	Nashville	San Jose
3	El Paso	Atlanta	Indianapolis	Wichita
4	St. Louis	Cleveland	Virginia Beach	Houston
5	Birmingham	Baltimore	St. Paul	Virginia Beach
6	Sacramento	Buffalo	Omaha	Seattle
7	Miami	Philadelphia	Dallas	Honolulu
8	San Antonio	New York	Minneapolis	Austin
9	Oakland	Chicago	Toledo	Charlotte
10	Cleveland	St. Louis	Austin	Denver

1970s in relatively good economic shape. Half were experiencing rapid population growth. The important linkage between population loss and residential need perceived during the 1970s was tenuous during the 1960s. *If distressed cities are limited to those suffering from both high resident need and rapid population loss, then no big U.S. city was distressed in 1970.* Indeed, a principal goal of national urban policy during the late 1960s and early 1970s was to foster the decentralization of population away from big cities to smaller places and to free-standing new towns.[17] While the economic future was recognized by experts as uncertain for most and bleak for many of these big cities, their generally low or moderate levels of resident need reflected their traditional role as centers of economic growth for the U.S. economy as a whole.[18]

The rapidity of change in city conditions during the 1970s is underscored in table 1.5, which lists the ten cities with the highest and lowest levels of resident need in 1970 and 1980. Only three cities appear on the lists of the neediest cities in both 1970 and 1980. These are Newark, St. Louis, and Cleveland. Reflecting regional patterns of economic change, seven big cities of the South and West which were among the ten neediest in 1970 were supplanted in 1980, mostly by big cities of the North.[19] Similarly, only three cities were ranked among the ten lowest-need big cities in both 1970 and 1980: Honolulu, Virginia Beach, and Austin. Cities supplanted from this low-need list during the 1970s are disproportionately from the North.

As Nathan and Dommel have previously pointed out, the range of need grew markedly among big cities during the 1970s.[20] In 1970 the maximum value of the resident index was 1.47 for Newark, and the minimum value was .75 for Honolulu. By 1980 the minimum index value had hardly changed (it was .78 for Tulsa), but the maximum value had surged to 2.27 in Newark, a city which remained steadfastly at the top of the list. Put another way, Newark's 1970 resident need was 50 percent higher than in the nation; by 1980, that figure had risen to almost 220 percent. Perhaps more important, increasing economic disparities among big cities were not produced by "rich" (low-need) cities getting "richer" (though some did, such as Houston). For example, the average resident need score for the ten cities with lowest resident need in 1970 *rose* during the decade, from .85 in 1970 to .95 in 1980. Rather, mounting disparities in resident need were the result of surging resident need among the neediest cities. The average value of the resident need index was 1.63 in the ten cities with highest levels of need in 1980; this was almost 40 percent higher than the need levels in these same cities in 1970 (1.17).

The urban distress indexes created during the 1970s were designed to compare one city with another, or with its suburbs. These indexes tracked the *relative* decline of distressed cities with a good degree of accuracy.[21] However, these indexes provided no point of reference. Given traditional American values, it is not surprising that discussions frequently concluded that low-need cities were winning a competitive struggle with less efficient or capable distressed cities. The resident need index used here makes it clear that less-needy cities were not doing better (they were not "winning"). Rather, residents in some distressed cities were suffering from rapidly diminishing opportunities and rising needs. From another vantage point the massive economic transformations going on in most big cities during the 1970s were leaving people in *some* cities without sufficient economic opportunities commensurate with their skills and experience. Even among highly distressed cities, some had what were clearly vibrant economic futures, given their great capacity to adopt new economic functions and thereby to maintain their productivity. Examples include major national and regional economic centers such as New York, Boston, and Philadelphia. The task then for urban policy was to help people and cities adapt to rapid change. Unfortunately, the logic of urban policy discussions of the 1970s made aiding distressed cities and their residents seem like shoring up losers.

Absolute changes in individual economic indicators dramatize the deterioration of economic conditions that occurred in many cities during the 1970s (table 1.6). In the table cities are divided into types on the basis of their characteristics in 1980, and the data also describe changes in the

Table 1.6 Average Changes in Population, Unemployment, Poverty, and Per Capita Income, by 1980 City Type[a]

	Cities with Relatively High Resident Need		Cities with Moderate Resident Need		Cities with Relatively Low Resident Need	
	Decreasing Population	Stable Population	Decreasing Population	Stable Population	Stable Population	Growing Population
City Population Change (percentages)						
1960–1970	− 6.6	4.2	− 2.9	33.6	26.2	46.5
1970–1980	− 16.3	− 2.2	− 14.3	0.1	0.1	34.2
Poverty Rate (percentages)						
1969	13.3	16.7	10.2	10.3	8.9	9.4
1979	18.5	18.5	11.9	11.7	8.8	8.5
Unemployment Rate (percentages)						
1970	5.1	5.5	4.3	5.3	4.8	3.9
1980	10.5	7.9	7.4	7.4	4.6	4.8
Per Capita Income (1969 dollars)						
1969	3,010	2,750	3,360	3,500	3,300	3,310
1979	3,180	3,285	3,940	3,700	4,100	4,030

Source: U.S. Bureau of the Census.
[a]Both resident need and population changes are those used in the 1980 typography.

various types of cities during the 1960s and 1970s. As can be seen, average poverty and unemployment rates rose markedly between 1970 and 1980 in cities which in 1980 exhibited either moderate or relatively high levels of resident need. Strikingly, the average unemployment rate almost doubled during the decade in relatively high-need cities with declining populations; unemployment rates hardly changed in cities in which resident need was relatively low in 1980. Similarly, poverty rates rose by 40 percent during the 1970s in cities with relatively high resident need and declining populations, while they fell in cities with relatively low resident need. Real per capita income rose very marginally in high-need, declining cities (up 5.6 percent from 1969 to 1979), but burgeoned by almost one-quarter in cities with relatively low resident need.

Such trends are the result of many forces. The cities experiencing marked increases in resident need during the 1970s differed from other big cities in that they tended to be surrounded by incorporated suburbs and therefore unable to annex new areas; i.e., their populations tended to make up a small proportion of overall metropolitan populations; they tended to be located in metropolitan areas where populations grew slowly or declined during the 1970s; and they tended to be located in metropolitan areas with weak economies, as indicated by high unemployment rates.

These differences should come as no surprise. Cities surrounded by incorporated suburbs such as Atlanta and Boston are easily cut off from growth taking place in their suburbs in either jobs or middle-income households. Relative to cities with aggressive annexation policies (such as Houston or Indianapolis), cities surrounded by legal jurisdictions can compete for a relatively small spectrum of metropolitan economic activities. By contrast, they tend to bear a disproportionate share of metropolitan economic decline. Moreover, the overall economic health of metropolitan areas circumscribes the opportunities available for central cities. City fiscal, social, and economic policies can shape city futures to only a limited degree. When economic distress is most widespread in a metropolitan area or region, the likely success of city policies for ameliorating distress is most limited.

Urban Trends in the 1980s

The evidence from the previous sections shows that the impetus for a new national urban policy during the 1970s rose from mounting problems in the cities, not from evanescent political concerns. While the policies themselves proved fragile and short-lived, the distress which gave rise to them has proven to have staying power.

Unfortunately, it is impossible to trace post-1980 economic trends in a comprehensive manner, even in big cities. Data series are too fragmentary. Economic and demographic trends in cities since 1980 have been powerfully shaped by the recession of 1981 and 1982 as well as by a continuation of the secular trends of the 1970s. The information in table 1.7 shows that the onset of recession in 1980 and 1981 resulted in widespread erosion of living standards. Between 1979 and 1983 the real purchasing power of average per capita income fell by 2 to 6 percent in all types of big American cities. However, real per capita income had generally recovered by 1985. In that year real income levels were higher on average for every group of cities than they had been in 1979. Average unemployment reached a peak of over 12 percent in 1982 in cities with high resident need. Average unemployment rates have declined significantly since then. Average unemployment rates were generally lower in 1987 than they had been in 1980. Cities where this was not the case were frequently though not always

Table 1.7 Trends in City Economic Conditions: 1980–1984

City Population	Cities with Relatively High Resident Need		Cities with Moderate Resident Need		Cities with Relatively Low Resident Need	
	Decreasing Population	Stable Population	Decreasing Population	Stable Population	Stable Population	Growing Population
Percentage Change 1980– 1986	−0.7	1.8	−4.1	7.8	5.0	11.5
Per Capita Income (1969 $)						
1979	3,180	3,290	3,880	3,660	4,140	4,030
1983	3,008	3,220	3,630	3,590	3,990	3,830
1985	3,258	3,263	3,925	3,892	4,230	4,175
Unemployment Rate Percent[a]						
1980	9.3	7.8	7.1	7.0	5.3	5.2
1982	12.1	12.8	10.9	10.0	7.8	7.0
1983	11.5	12.4	11.8	10.1	7.9	7.0
1984	9.4	10.4	8.4	7.9	6.2	5.0
1987[b]	7.8	8.8	6.2	6.2	6.8	5.7

[a]Source: U.S. Bureau of Labor Statistics, *Local Area Unemployment Statistics*. Note that these data are not necessarily consistent with unemployment rates derived from the 1980 Census.
[b]1987 unemployment data are estimates based on trends in unemployment between May 1984 and May 1987.

communities whose economies relied heavily on oil or other extractive industries. They included New Orleans, Austin, Dallas, Denver, Fort Worth, Houston, Oklahoma City, and Tulsa. These were generally (except for New Orleans) cities in relatively good economic shape in 1980. Declines in unemployment rates have been truly remarkable in several cities classified as distressed in 1980. Most strikingly, 1987 unemployment rates were 5 percent or lower in New York City, Boston, and Norfolk, all of which were high-need cities at the start of the decade.

Trends in the index of resident need since 1980 can be estimated in eleven cities. These are cities for which crude 1983 poverty data are available. Per capita income figures are available for these cities in both 1979 and 1985. Unemployment rate data are available for 1980 and 1987. Thus, resident need can be calculated for 1980 and for the mid-decade. Trends in only eleven cities are not necessarily representative of general national trends, but they are suggestive.[22]

Conditions in these eleven cities are described in table 1.8. Both high-need and relatively low-need cities are included among the eleven. As can be seen, estimated poverty rates increased in every city between 1979–80 and 1983. The biggest increases occurred in Chicago, where poverty surged from 24 to 34 percent, and in Miami, where it increased from 32 to 42 percent. Poverty also rose in Honolulu, Houston, Denver, and other low-need cities. Unemployment remained somewhat higher in 1987 than it had been in 1980 in a bare majority (six of eleven) of these cities. Finally, per capita income rose in purchasing power (constant 1969 dollars) in six of the eleven cities. Thus, even in simple absolute terms, it cannot be argued that the 1980s have ushered in fundamentally more positive economic trends in these big cities. Rather, economic conditions have improved in some of these eleven cities—notably New York—and deteriorated markedly in others.

Perhaps more important, trends in the resident need index imply that economic conditions have deteriorated in most of these cities relative to conditions in the rest of the country. Resident need is measured *relative* to indicators of need in the United States as a whole. Between 1979 and mid-decade resident need held constant or rose in ten of the eleven cities listed in the table. The rise was most rapid in Houston, Louisville, and St. Louis. Need also rose very rapidly in Chicago and Denver. The index of resident need *fell* only in New York City, where a remarkable economic recovery seems under way. Clearly, there is no evidence that the decline of many big cities into economic distress has stopped or slowed. At base, economic conditions appear to have been worse relative to the rest of the United States in a number of ways at mid-decade than they had been in 1980. This is true in all major groups of cities.

Conclusions and Implications

The 1970s introduced a striking and abrupt change in resident need and in population trends in the big cities of the United States. Resident need frequently surged upward; population fell rapidly. By the end of the decade about one in four cities suffered from both high levels of resident need and rapid population loss; these cities were clearly distressed.

The abruptness with which city distress rose during the 1970s helps explain the lag in U.S. policy response. City economic distress was not

Table 1.8 Trends in Resident Need Between 1979 and the Mid-1980s: Selected Cities

	Poverty[a]		Unemployment[b]		Per Capita Income[c] (1969 dollars)		Resident Need[d]	
	1979/80	1983	1980	1987	1979	1985	1980	Mid-1980s
High Need, Declining Cities								
Baltimore*	30	35	9.1	7.2	2,970	3,050	1.28	1.26
Chicago*	24	34	9.0	9.5	3,500	3,410	1.17	1.26
Louisville	32	37	7.7	8.8	3,170	3,220	1.19	1.29
New York City	31	32	8.6	6.7	3,670	3,950	1.23	1.08
St. Louis	36	39	6.4	8.9	2,970	3,110	1.21	1.31
High Need, Stable								
Miami	32	42	6.9	7.6	3,070	3,140	1.23	1.29
Low Need, Stable								
Denver*	22	24	5.9	9.0	4,320	4,410	.97	1.06
Portland, Ore.*	24	27	7.1	5.6	4,090	3,800	1.06	1.03
Seattle*	22	26	5.8	6.2	4,690	4,560	.99	1.04
Low Need, Growth								
Honolulu*	14	17	4.8	3.9	4,520	4,040	.82	.79
Houston*	17	21	4.5	10.2	4,440	4,280	.81	1.08

[a]Source: U.S. Bureau of the Census, *Annual Housing Survey*. Poverty was defined as follows:

  1979: household income under $7,000
  1980: household income under $8,000
  1983: household income under $10,000

In these years official poverty thresholds for a family of four were $7,400, $8,400, and $10,200, respectively. Note that the estimates presented in the table do not control for family or household size. An asterisk indicates the poverty data are from 1979. Otherwise, they are from 1980.
[b]Source: U.S. Bureau of Labor Statistics, Local Area Unemployment Statistics. Note that these data are not necessarily consistent with unemployment rates derived from the decennial census.
[c]Source: U.S. Bureau of the Census.
[d]Source: See text.

placed on the domestic policy agenda in the U.S. until 1978, with the release of President Carter's first report on urban policy.[23] Two years later concern with city economic distress was swamped by the election of Ronald Reagan as president. Since 1980 the congress and the president have been largely unable to agree on major initiatives to reduce urban distress.[24]

Recently, some analysts have heralded economic readjustments in troubled urban economies.[25] However the actual situation is more ambiguous. If city distress is deepening in many cities, as the fragmentary post-1980 data presented above suggest, then current national policies may be creating significant fiscal and economic pressures. These pressures will re-emerge during the next national recession just as they did in the recession of 1974–75. At a minimum this uncertain situation calls for frequent, careful monitoring. Each of the components of the city typology are updated regularly in the United States, with the exception of poverty rates. It is to be hoped that the development of need indexes will continue to be addressed by urban scholars.

2 The New Anatomy of Urban Fiscal Problems

Roy Bahl, William Duncombe, and
Wanda Schulman

In 1975 American cities seemed ready to take the fall. New York City had defaulted and a few other places were close, the move to the Sunbelt was in full flower, and city economies in the North were hurting, bond ratings were coming down, retirement systems were in trouble, city-suburb disparities in tax effort and service levels were too wide, and the quality of infrastructure and current government services in many inner cities was badly deficient. Policy discussion focused on a national development bank, a targeted employment tax credit, reform of welfare financing, and amending the big federal urban aid programs—CETA, ARFA, and Local Public Works. In fact, federal policy in the 1980s has taken a decidedly different path—all but ignoring the "urban problem"—and yet the dire straits predicted for the fiscal condition of cities never materialized. What happened?

In this chapter three explanations are offered.[1] The first is that the basic problems were recession and inflation, and with the strong recoveries of the late 1970s and mid-1980s and the lower rates of inflation in most of the past decade, cities were able to outgrow their problems. The second hypothesis is that the urban fiscal problem was essentially poor planning and management, and during the last decade cities have found a way to live within their means and still provide adequate services.[2] The third explanation is that cities avoided their fiscal problems by passing them on in the forms of deferred human and physical capital investment, higher tax rates, and lower urban service levels. The first two explanations suggest that cities have entered the era of less federal assistance and the new U.S. income tax code in reasonable shape to compete. The third explanation contradicts the first two.

This essay is presented in four sections. First, it provides an update on the measures of health which are typically used to gauge the fiscal condition of cities and state and local governments. Second, it discusses the implications of the changing U.S. economy and changing federal policy for the economic strength of large urban areas; how have the urban economies benefited from the national policies of the 1980s? Third, it focuses on the fiscal response of large urban governments to these economic and federal policy changes, with an eye to determining whether real retrenchment has been the order of the day. Finally, based on data and analyses developed in previous sections, it considers the three hypotheses suggested above concerning urban fiscal problems and explores their implications for the future.

Trends in Fiscal Condition

There is no generally accepted measure of the fiscal health and distress of state and local governments.[3] Nevertheless, three general indicators of financial health seem to have held the floor during most of the 1970s. These are the general surplus of the state and local government sector as recorded in the National Income Accounts (NIA), Philip Dearborn's studies of city budget conditions, and the comparative, statistical studies of fiscal and economic distress. The question we raise here is how these indicators of fiscal health and distress—which were read in the 1970s to indicate severe financial problems—have tracked during the 1980s.

The NIA Surplus

The most used (and misused) measure of fiscal conditions is the general surplus of state and local governments as reported in the NIA.[4] An increase in the surplus—a measure of the excess of current revenues over total expenditures—may result because of economic growth or increased government efficiency, but one may also get to a larger surplus by raising taxes to exorbitant levels, reducing essential expenditures, or deferring infrastructure maintenance. Still, the surplus measure provides some indirect evidence about fiscal health. It measures the extent to which current revenues can cover total expenditures and contribute to further improvements in public service levels, lower tax rates, and repay debt. Movements in this surplus roughly indicate the direction of state and local government sector budgetary movements.

The size of the surplus in the mid-1980s indicated a positive fiscal situation for state and local governments. There was a positive general account surplus from the second quarter of 1983 until the fourth quarter of 1986, averaging $19.8 billion in 1984 (4.2 percent of total state and local government expenditures), $16.0 billion in 1985 (3.1 percent of expendi-

Figure 2.1   General Account Budget Surplus, State and Local Governments,
1969–87

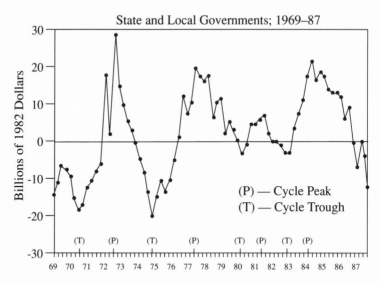

Source: U.S. Department of Commerce, Bureau of Economic Analysis, *National Income and Product Accounts of the United States, 1929–82*, and *Survey of Current Business*, July 1986 and 1987 and March 1988.

tures), and $7.4 billion in 1986 (1.3 percent of expenditures). This surplus position and tax reductions by state governments suggested that state and local governments had discretionary funds with which to support public service levels and to generally deal with fiscal problems.

The question rises as to whether this surplus is a signal that the fiscal situation of state and local governments had become fundamentally more sound than it was in the 1970s. The answer is no. The favorable budgetary position was due to stronger national economic growth. Moreover, there was nothing that unusual or different about the size of the general surplus in the 1983–86 period; it followed the business cycle in much the same way that it did during other recent contractions and expansions (see figure 2.1). Relative to total state and local government expenditures, the surplus has stayed in the same range as in past business cycles (see table 2.1).

There are, however, three important differences about the performance of the surplus in the 1980s (versus the 1970s) that may indicate a stronger fiscal position. The first is that the state and local government surplus has reacted less to the business cycles of the 1980s. To demonstrate this, we

Table 2.1 General Account Surplus of State and Local Governments: Trends and Cyclical Swing

Year:Quarter	Amount (in billions of 1982 dollars)[a]	Percent of Total Expenditures
1970:IV(trough)	−18.7	−5.32
1972:IV(peak)	28.6	7.57
1975:I(trough)	−20.2	−5.07
1977:III(peak)	19.5	4.73
1980:II(trough)	−4.0	−0.95
1981:III(peak)	6.5	1.55
1983:I(trough)	−3.9	−0.93
1984:II(peak)	21.1	4.90

Cycle[b]	Cyclical Swing (in billions)		Net Accumulation (in billions)	
	In Current Dollars	1982 Dollars[a]	In Current Dollars	1982 Dollars[a]
1969:III−1973:IV	5.8	13.9	−2.1	−8.0
1973:IV−1980:I	8.3	13.6	8.6	7.9
1980:I−1981:III	6.9	7.7	3.5	3.7
1981:III−1987:IV[c]	7.8	7.1	38.5	34.8

Source: Department of Commerce, Bureau of Economic Analysis, *National Income and Product Accounts of the United States, 1929–82*, and *Survey of Current Business*, (March 1988 and July 1986 and 1987).
[a]Deflated using the implicit GNP deflator for state and local government purchases.
[b]From the beginning of one contraction to the end of the following expansion.
[c]The latest data available at the time of this writing.

have calculated a kind of cyclical swing in the general surplus: the difference in the *average* quarterly general surplus in a contraction against the surplus in the following expansion. The greater the swing, the more sensitive the surplus to a particular business cycle. For example, the average quarterly surplus swung from a negative $4.58 billion to a positive $1.19 billion during the 1969–73 business cycle, a difference of $5.77 billion (table 2.1). When these data are deflated and computed across business cycles, the conclusion emerges that the surplus has been less cyclical in the 1980s than in the 1970s. This indicates a more conservative fiscal behavior on the part of state and local governments, perhaps because of painful lessons learned in the 1970s.

A second important difference is that state and local governments have fared better over the business cycle in the 1980s than in the 1970s; recessions have hurt the state and local government budgetary position much less than expansions have helped. This may be shown by taking into account the average duration of the business cycle and calculating "net accumulation;" that is, by how much did the state and local government sector recover the deficit it incurred during the recession *and* accumulate reserves during the expansion? A larger net accumulation implies that the state and local government sector financial position was helped more by the recovery than it was hurt by the recession. This was the case during the 1973–80 cycle when state and local governments added about $8 billion (in 1982 dollars) more to their surplus during the twenty quarters of expansion than they drew down during the five quarters of recession, and it is true of three of the four cyclical periods studied here. During the present business cycle that began in the third quarter of 1981, state and local governments have accumulated a real surplus of nearly $35 billion. This is the largest real accumulation in the last four business cycles, and, moreover, it has occurred in a time when the growth in federal aid has been sharply curtailed. This would seem to be evidence of a new fiscal strength of the state and local government sector in the 1980s.

Third, the period since 1987 shows a different response than in the 1970s. Despite continued expansion in the economy, the state and local government sector has incurred a deficit averaging $7.7 billion (1.3 percent of expenditures). Levin expected this deficit to increase to $10 billion by 1988.[5] Even this deficit, however, can be interpreted as a sign of fiscal strength. State and local governments have been drawing on their substantial surplus accumulation by making new long-term borrowing commitments in 1984–86 (which reduced the size of the NIA surplus) and by cutting income tax rates in 1986 and 1987. The ensuing slowdown in revenue growth, reductions in federal aid, and a continued poor revenue performance by some oil states (where fiscal health is not the rule) led to the deficit. State and local governments reacted to this by slowing the real growth in expenditures, particularly on structures, rather than by increasing taxes. It is too early to argue convincingly whether the 1987 deficits are a temporary pause in the growth of the surplus or a turning point in the general fiscal health of the sector.

Where Is the Surplus?

What we do not learn from these trends in NIA data is how these surpluses (deficits) and accumulations are distributed across the fifty states and 30,000 local governments. In particular, we do not learn what we most want to know: how the large urban area governments have fared during the most recent expansion. The National Income Accounts are not disaggregated below the national level, and no complete disaggregation of the surplus is done. There are, however, three analyses that go some way toward answering our questions. The Bureau of Economic Analysis (BEA) does a periodic division of the surplus among state versus local governments;[6] the National Conference of State Legislatures tracks the surplus of state governments;[7] and Philip Dearborn follows the budgetary position of a sample of large city governments.[8]

From these more disaggregated data we can learn three important things about the changing fiscal health of state and local governments during the past decade. The first is that local governments as a class have fared better than state governments throughout the period. Local governments show smaller deficits during recessions and larger surpluses during expansions. On average, local governments maintained a real surplus ($2.1 billion) and state governments a real deficit ($1.9 billion) during the 1970s. In the 1980s the average real local government sector surplus was $7.3 billion, compared with a $0.9 billion deficit for state governments. As a percentage of expenditures, local surpluses have averaged 2.8 percent in the 1980s, which is close to the highest levels achieved in the 1970s. Although Levin and Peters conclude that this is partly due to anomalies in the surplus measure, it is unlikely that such high surpluses are purely artificial.[9] More impressive is the fact that the stronger surplus position in the 1980s was built without an increased emphasis in state budgets on aid to local governments.[10]

The second finding, drawn from the work of the National Conference of State Legislatures, is a very dramatic shift in the size of balances held among states. At various times in the 1970s and early 1980s oil states such as Texas and Alaska accounted for a substantial proportion of cash balances held by the states. By the mid-1980s, the situation had changed dramatically, and the large balances were held by northern states, while the farm-belt and energy-belt states were feeling serious budgetary pressures.[11] Not only were the fiscal responses different in the 1980s, but the balance of fiscal power among the regions had changed.

The third lesson is that large cities have built a reasonably comfortable financial position in recent years. Dearborn provides some direct evidence about how larger cities have fared. His most recent results are particularly interesting because they suggest that large central cities have found a way to share in the growing sector surplus. It should be noted that his thirty-city sample is a good representation of growth and decline settings: twenty lost population between 1971 and 1984, and the population of the entire sample shrank by 4 percent; five cities lost more than 20 percent of their populations; and five had a gain of more than 20 percent.

His analysis focuses on liquidity position, fund balances, and the gap between general fund revenues and expenditures. One clear result of his tracking is that large city budget deficits are cyclical, usually occurring in the fiscal year following a national recession. Thirteen of his thirty cities ran a deficit in 1976, nineteen in 1980, ten in 1981, and sixteen in 1983. But in 1984, only six cities showed an operating deficit. Moreover, he finds the improvement in fiscal position to be generally widespread, as may be seen in table 2.2. General fund balances as a percentage of revenues more than doubled between 1976 and 1984. These results lead Dearborn to conclude that large cities were "in perhaps the best financial condition they have been in since 1971, as judged by their success in balancing budgets and maintaining balance sheet surpluses and liquidity."[12]

The National League of Cities does not reach so upbeat a conclusion as does Dearborn, but their survey of the actual and prospective fiscal condition of 660 cities from 1984 to 1986 indicates a surprising fiscal strength. Their results show that more than half of all cities began 1986 with a general fund surplus in excess of 6 percent of total expenditures and with a revenue growth rate in excess of 6 percent during 1985.[13] Nearly 60 percent of the cities surveyed expected to use part of their existing balances to finance 1986 operations. The results of their 1987 survey are not as optimistic, indicating generally slower revenue growth and declining cash balances.[14]

Fiscal Distress

In the 1970s there was an outpouring of studies on fiscal distress. These studies, really designed more to rank than to measure the fiscal and economic strain on cities, were stimulated by the use of federal assistance to support urban finances in the early 1970s and the need to find objective indicators of urban distress to include in the grant formulae. But perhaps more important, these studies attempted to show that changing U.S. federalism and the changing structure of the economy had left some cities unable to provide their citizens with either jobs or an adequate level of public services.

The comparative approach focuses on urban areas, usually large cities, and attempts to measure relative economic, social, and fiscal health. The comparison usually considers more than budgetary position in trying to get a fix on the balance between resources available and service level "needs." The specific measurements used are sometimes flawed and always debatable, but the intent of most of these studies is to identify cities whose populations have heavy concentrations of high-cost, low-income families. Despite the very great differences in approach, there has been substantial consistency

Table 2.2 Selected Major Cities' General Fiscal Condition, Balance (or Deficit)[a] as a Percentage of Total Revenues

	1971	1976	1981	1984
New York	−9.2	−31.1	−0.5	0.1
Chicago	−47.5	−24.8	−10.5	−8.5
Los Angeles	—	—	3.1	—
Philadelphia	−6.1	−10.2	4.4	1.8
Detroit	−3.7	−5.6	−16.2	−3.1
Houston	10.8	7.4	15.5	3.7
Baltimore	2.4	8.1	2.7	0.7
Dallas	4.3	6.7	6.9	5.9
Cleveland	−16.6	0.2	−7.4	−0.9
Indianapolis	4.5	2.7	3.8	6.1
Milwaukee	12.3	21.8	18.6	6.8
San Francisco	15.8	9.5	23.5	21.8
San Diego	7.3	8.3	8.6	9.5
San Antonio	5.7	−3.9	10.0	6.8
Boston	13.4	−10.7	−7.5	−6.0
Mempis	6.7	2.7	5.0	9.3
St. Louis	−2.9	1.2	−0.7	0.8
New Orleans	−1.2	4.5	8.4	2.3
Phoenix	4.4	3.0	0.1	4.4
Columbus	3.3	3.4	−0.2	4.3
Seattle	22.9	1.3	6.3	12.3
Jacksonville	26.3	11.9	11.4	6.6
Pittsburgh	7.9	5.6	1.1	0.7
Denver	8.2	6.4	5.1	3.1
Kansas City, Mo.	1.2	4.5	9.6	6.5
Atlanta	17.3	25.0	17.5	18.2
Buffalo	2.1	−15.0	−0.3	−0.03
Cincinnati	0.9	2.7	10.6	5.9
Nashville	6.3	16.9	6.3	4.2
Minneapolis	12.9	6.6	15.7	14.4
Unweighted Average	3.8	2.0	5.0	4.7

Source: Dearborn, Philip. Fiscal Conditions in Large American Cities. Paper prepared for National Academy of Sciences, July 1986.

[a]Because of deficiencies in financial reporting, especially in 1971 and 1976, many balances or deficits are not in accordance with generally accepted accounting principles. Pro forma adjustments were made to reported balances and deficits in some cases to make them more compatible with accepted accounting principles. For 1981 and 1982 balances, the undesignated fund balance was generally used, but in some cities it was referred to as unrestricted.

in the findings. Nearly all lists of cities in trouble in the 1970s included the large cities of the North and Midwest and few in the South or West.[15]

Bradbury has attempted to determine whether the distressed cities of the

1970s realized an improved or worsened position by 1980.[16] She finds, essentially, that their relative position has not changed. Her quantitative rankings show that the "distress position" generally worsened between 1975 and 1980 for cities that had declining populations, smaller shares of metropolitan populations, and for cities located in the North. Ladd, Yinger, et al. also see a worsening of fiscal distress over time.[17] They find that the expenditure needs–revenue gap of central cities has been increasing over the past two decades and that the fiscal condition of the largest cities is far worse than that of middle- and smaller-sized cities. Even Dearborn's generally optimistic conclusions include a flag about the continuing fiscal disadvantage of northern cities. He finds continuing fund deficits, low liquidity, and/or severe revenue expenditure imbalances in New York, Chicago, Philadelphia, Detroit, Boston, Cleveland, St. Louis, and Buffalo (see table 2.2). This leads him to conclude that cities with balance sheet problems had a hard time improving their condition, while those in a healthy condition continued to improve.

Cities and the Changing U.S. Economy

Much has been made of the relationship between national economic performance and the economic condition of cities. Some see the issue in terms of the very straightforward proposition that a rising tide lifts all boats. Others think that some sectors of the economy do not share adequately in national growth and would put central cities in this class. The first question to ask, then, is how have central city economies performed in the first half of the 1980s?

The national growth in income, employment, and prices is only one dimension of the changing economy which can have an important impact on city finances. It is also important to consider the effects of discretionary policy, particularly reductions in federal and state aid. Another set of potentially significant impacts relates to changes that are outside the direct control of governments: the tax-limitation sentiment, the Sunbelt shift, and the increasing concentration of the poor and elderly population.

The Economic Base of Urban Areas

The 1970s were a rough period for urban economies. For the first time several metropolitan areas were losing population, urban unemployment rates were up, and the most rapid growth was outside of metropolitan areas. The problem came to a head with the recession of the mid-1970s, which had a particularly devastating effect on the economies of many large central cities in the older industrial region. These declining urban areas—and there were a great many of them—did not keep up with the rest of the nation in the economic recovery of the last half of the 1970s. As a result, many large cities entered the 1980s in a quite different way than they had entered the 1970s: their per capita income advantage over the rest of the nation had fallen or disappeared, their national employment and population shares were greatly diminished, and they were looking at the prospect of more decline as the recession of 1980 began to set in.

Since fiscal collapse never came, the question we want to address here is whether or not the expected urban economic decline materialized in the 1980s. We cannot survey all cities; moreover, it is well-known that reliable employment and personal income estimates are not available below the county level. We can, however, report the results of an analysis of the economic performance of U.S. counties and regions in the 1980s and then turn to our own analysis of large city-counties.

Daniel Garnick's analysis of BEA's employment data series gives a good account of the transition from the 1970s to the 1980s.[18] His results show that employment in metropolitan-core counties grew at a rate well below the national average between 1969 and 1979.[19] The same pattern was true in the more slowly growing Mideast, Plains, and Great Lakes regions, and core-county employment actually declined in the Mideast. The first part of the 1980s, plagued by two recessions, has shown a slower overall national growth and an even slower growth in core counties. Employment in core counties declined in the Great Lakes and Plains regions. However, the story is quite different in New England, the Far West, and the Sunbelt, where core counties have exceeded total regional growth in total employment. Core areas in the Mideast region have done better in the 1980s than they did in the 1970s, but they have not done well. In the Great Lakes and Plains regions they have done significantly worse.

These county data do not describe central *city* economies and cannot be matched with fiscal data. This shortcoming leads us to study the employment growth pattern of ten large city-counties, a sample that gave some good insights in an earlier (1978) work.[20] The sample has some diversity in population size and in regional location with five northern, three southern, and two western cities.

One might begin such an analysis by studying the pattern of employment growth in the labor market areas—approximately the metropolitan areas—as described in table 2.3. All except New York grew during the 1970s, but the northern areas grew more slowly. Denver, Jacksonville, and Nashville were the only cities experiencing employment growth during the recession of the

Table 2.3 Percentage Change in Total Nonagricultural Employment in
Ten Metropolitan Areas: 1972–1986

Metropolitan Area	1972–80	1980–81	1981–83	1983–85	1985–86
Baltimore	2.1	−0.2	−0.2	3.3	2.7
Denver (Boulder)	4.6	3.8	1.8	3.5	−1.4
Indianapolis	2.6	−2.2	−1.2	4.4	4.0
Jacksonville	2.8	3.3	2.5	6.7	4.0
Nashville (Davidson)	3.3	2.9	1.4	6.8	3.7
New Orleans	3.8	2.9	−1.5	0.0	−2.5
New York	−0.7	1.6	0.1	2.2	1.6
Philadelphia	0.8	0.3	−0.2	3.2	2.4
St. Louis	1.4	−0.1	−0.2	3.5	2.3
San Francisco (Oakland)	2.9	1.3	−0.8	2.5	0.5
United States	2.6	0.8	−0.5	4.0	2.6

Source: Department of Labor, Bureau of Labor Statistics, from "Employment, Hours, and Earnings" tape.

early 1980s. As the recovery began, all areas except New Orleans experienced growth after 1983, but the northern areas generally grew more slowly than the southern and western areas. The story here is that employment growth in the metropolitan areas of large cities in the North has long lagged behind the rest of the country and this lag has continued into the 1980s.

Cities fared even worse than their metropolitan areas in the 1970s, as indicated by the data for these ten city-counties (table 2.4). Four of the five northern-core counties suffered an employment loss during the 1970s; of the entire sample only Nashville had a growth rate above the U.S. average, and every county's share of employment in its metropolitan area declined. The performance of these urban economies in the first three years of the 1980s was similar. Except for Jacksonville, employment in these central counties declined, with the northern cities generally losing the most jobs. With the economic recovery after 1983 there were significant employment increases in many of these counties, with less of a clear regional pattern.

The declining dominance of these counties in their own metropolitan areas is perhaps the most dramatic change described in this table. By 1985 half of these counties accounted for less than half of metropolitan area employment, compared to 1972 when they represented close to 70 percent of employment in most cases.

Table 2.4 Employment Growth in Ten Metropolitan Central Counties: 1972–1985[a]

	Annual Percentage Change			Central County/Metropolitan Area Employment Ratio			
	1972–80	1980–83	1983–85	1972	1980	1983	1985
Baltimore	−1.91	−3.07	7.59	59.33	43.91	40.28	40.46
Denver	2.61	−0.84	3.50	69.70	55.39	51.46	49.47
Indianapolis	2.37	−3.09	5.68	87.13	84.01	82.78	81.91
Jacksonville	2.37	2.17	7.32	92.39	88.03	86.89	85.89
Nashville	3.49	−0.75	7.91	78.70	74.93	74.08	72.66
New Orleans	0.01	−2.86	−0.45	70.43	53.77	50.80	49.18
New York City	−0.98	−0.18	n.a.	91.21	88.41	88.14	n.a.
Philadelphia	−1.62	−2.11	1.35	49.56	38.57	36.42	34.37
St. Louis	−2.50	−4.34	2.49	54.99	37.63	33.99	32.03
San Francisco	2.83	−0.54	4.40	67.34	62.64	62.41	61.14
United States	3.23	−0.84	5.44				

Source: U.S. Department of Commerce, Bureau of the Census, *County Business Patterns for 1972*, 1980, 1981, 1983, and 1985.
[a]1983 metropolitan boundaries were used for all years.

Federal and State Aid Policy

Another event of major importance in the late 1970s and early 1980s is the substantial slowing of growth in federal grants to state and local governments. The Advisory Commission on Intergovernmental Relations (ACIR) places the beginning of the slowdown about 1978. Since then, real federal grants have fallen from $108.7 billion to $82.8 billion in 1987, and from 3.4 percent of GNP to 2.3 percent. The result of this decline is that state and local governments have become much less dependent on federal aid: from 34 percent of revenues generated by local taxes and fees in 1978 to 21 percent in 1987.

The most important direct urban aid programs—CETA, ARFA, and Local Public Works—disappeared by the early 1980s, and general revenue sharing was soon to follow. As may be seen in table 2.5, big city governments had become greatly dependent on federal assistance in the 1970s. For example, Baltimore, Buffalo, Cleveland, and Detroit among this group all received at least forty cents in direct federal aid for every dollar raised from own-sources in 1977. On average, the reliance on federal aid in these fifteen large cities went from one-third to less than one-seventh of total local revenues in ten years. The drop in dependence on direct federal aid was especially severe after 1983 as the Reagan administration continued to redirect grants to the states. Federal aid per capita has been cut almost in half since

Table 2.5 Direct Federal Aid as a Percentage of Own-Source General Revenue, Selected Cities and Fiscal Years, 1967–1986

	Fiscal Years, Percentage				Per Capita[a] Real[b] Federal Aid		
	1967	1977	1981–83[c]	1984–86[c]	1977	1982	1986
St. Louis	1.0	27.5	29.6	12.9	$166	$155	$118
Newark	1.7	31.9	21.0	21.3	208	44	90
Buffalo	2.1	87.6	59.6	25.8	428	326	190
Cleveland	8.3	56.9	30.8	18.8	220	187	136
Boston	10.0	21.4	15.5	10.1	265	151	97
Unweighted Averages	4.6	45.1	31.3	17.8	257	172	126
Baltimore	3.8	45.5	29.2	11.8	306	160	138
Philadelphia	8.8	30.1	20.3	7.9	205	156	85
Detroit	13.1	46.7	67.3	14.5	241	337	117
Chicago	10.9	30.2	40.6	16.7	119	153	81
Atlanta	2.0	13.9	16.3	15.7	76	94	119
Unweighted Averages	7.7	33.3	34.7	13.3	189	180	108
Denver	1.2	21.1	13.1	8.8	158	117	61
Los Angeles	0.7	24.3	18.0	9.1	114	78	47
Dallas	0.0	15.8	13.6	9.0	68	56	25
Houston	3.1	14.4	15.1	5.6	57	71	45
Phoenix	10.6	37.9	29.9	19.4	110	95	78
Unweighted Averages	3.1	22.7	17.9	10.4	101	83	51
Unweighted Averages of 15 Cities	5.2	33.7	28.0	13.8	$183	$145	$ 95

Source: U.S. Department of Commerce, Bureau of the Census, *City Government Finances in 1966–67, 1976–77, 1980–81, 1981–82, 1982–83, 1983–84, 1984–85,* and *1985–86;* and U.S. Department of Commerce, Bureau of Economic Analysis, *National Income and Product Accounts, 1929–82,* and *Survey of Current Business,* July 1986 and 1987.
[a]Based on 1975, 1980, and 1985 population figures.
[b]Deflated to 1982 using the implicit GNP deflator for state and local government purchases.
[c]Unweighted average.

1977. For certain cities, and particularly some of those in the declining region, the losses were very great. The question to be asked is whether, and how, these revenue losses were replaced and with what consequences for local public services.

Urban governments are also affected by the discretionary policies of state governments. In particular, state assistance to local governments was reduced during the early 1980s, with real per capita state aid only recently reaching levels achieved during the late 1970s.[21] In 1979 cities received $73 in state aid for every $100 of general own-source revenue, with this ratio dropping to $54 by 1986.

Other Changes in the Economy

Other important changes in the U.S. economy may have affected the fiscal performance of cities in the 1980s. The sense of fiscal despair that had set in during the 1970s may have been lifted by the many announcements that the economic shifts to the Sunbelt that so dominated the 1970s were over. This may have been psychologically important, even though it is probably not a true assessment. Certainly, Garnick's analysis, based on BEA data, does not support this argument. The Mideast and Plains regions are growing at rates below the national average; the Great Lakes region is in decline; and the Southeast, Southwest, and Far West continue to grow faster than the rest of the nation. Some of the steam may have been taken out of Sunbelt growth by the recessions of the early 1980s and by falling oil prices, but a reversal in the pattern of regional shifts has not occurred.

Another major factor affecting state and local government budgets in recent years is the aftermath of the tax-limitation movement. There have not been a succession of Proposition 13 and 2-½ programs in the 1980s, but the message of the limitation movement does not seem to have been lost. This recognition of voter sentiment against higher taxes has probably been a major reason for the more conservative expenditure policies of the 1980s, and it may explain some of the budgetary strength that cities have shown.

The changing structure of the U.S. population has important implications for city finances. The increasing concentration of the elderly is pretty well-documented, but their impact on city budgets in the 1980s is not easily sorted out. On the one hand, the elderly pump a good deal of money into the economy—witness the increasing share of transfer payments in personal income—but they are not easily reached by local property taxes and are exempt from some portion of local sales taxes. It does seem true that it costs more to supply services to the aged, but much of this assistance is supported by federal funds. The net effect on local budgets, and how this has affected the performance of the city fisc in the 1980s, is simply unclear.

Still another major factor is the question of poverty. The evidence points to a heavy and increasing concentration of the poor in central cities. Kasarda notes that minority population in central cities in the Northeast grew from 33 percent in 1975 to 41 percent in 1985 (and from 28 to 36 percent in the Midwest) and that the average, national central-city poverty rate had grown from 12 percent in 1960 to nearly 20 percent by 1983.[22] There has been a pronounced growth in the number of households headed by black females —prime candidates for continued poverty—and 64 percent of such households now live in central cities. The growth in this concentration of the poor seems incongruous with the budgetary health reported above.

Fiscal Responses in the 1980s

How have urban governments adjusted their budgets in response to the changing economy and the retrenchment in external aids in the early 1980s? They had a number of options: reductions or expansions in the size of the public employment work force and in the rate of public employee compensation; increased or decreased tax rates; and reduced borrowings and shifts from one type of expenditure to another. The one response in which we are most interested, that of changes in the quality of public services, is not directly measurable, but we may get some idea of this from other indicators. In the sections below we consider first the response of state and local governments in aggregate and then turn to the response of local governments in large urban areas.

State and Local Governments

As noted above, the state and local government sector has reacted to the economics of the 1980s by running a general account surplus during much of the period. It apparently has done this by some combination of increasing tax rates and slowing the rate of growth in expenditures. To better understand how this has happened, we have compared the fiscal outcomes of the 1970s and the 1980s, as shown in the top panel of table 2.6. A first finding is that while the rate of increase in real personal income fell off slightly in the 1980s as compared with the 1970s, real taxes grew at an increasing rate. This growth appears to be at least partially in response to declining federal aid, particularly for municipalities where aid declined by close to 7 percent per year from 1980 to 1986. This finding squares with Gold's report that there were significant tax increases in 1982 and 1983, mostly by state governments, in the aftermath of the recession of the early 1980s. The very rapid growth in the general account surplus during 1983 is explained by these fiscal actions. Between 1984 and 1987, however, many of these temporary tax increases were rolled back and the surplus began to moderate.[23]

On the expenditure side, state and local governments appear to have slowed the growth in real expenditures from 1980 to 1983, due entirely to a sharp drop in capital expenditures. Municipal government expenditures continue to grow slower than those of state and other local governments, although

Table 2.6 Average Annual Percentage Change in Fiscal Indicators: 1970–86
(1982 dollars)[a]

	1970–80	1980–83	1983–86	1980–86
All State and Local Governments				
Personal Income	2.96	1.22	4.28	2.74
Federal Aid	5.62	−3.73	3.32	−0.26
Taxes	1.59	1.59	4.78	3.17
Direct Expenditure	2.88	2.46	3.63	3.04
Capital	−0.36	−3.81	5.30	0.64
Other	3.56	3.45	3.40	3.42
Current	3.64	2.45	3.80	3.12
Assistance and Subsidies	−1.55	−0.41	2.77	1.17
Interest on General Debt	4.57	10.92	10.10	10.51
Insurance Benefits and Repayments	6.06	10.61	−4.85	2.59
All Municipalities				
Federal Aid	13.97	−6.87	−6.88	−6.88
Taxes	0.41	1.86	3.63	2.74
Direct Expenditure	2.12	1.85	3.34	2.59
Capital	0.42	−1.31	3.30	0.97
Other	2.54	2.50	3.35	2.93
Current	2.85	2.05	2.73	2.39
Assistance and Subsidies	−5.55	−1.38	0.66	−0.37
Interest on General Debt	2.09	9.85	10.97	10.41
Insurance Benefits and Repayments	3.11	3.46	4.12	3.79

Source: Department of Commerce, Bureau of the Census, *City Governmental Finances, in 1969–70, 1979–80, 1985–86*, and *Governmental Finances in 1969–70, 1979–80, 1985–86*; Bureau of Economic Analysis, *National Income and Product Accounts, 1929–82*, and *Survey of Current Business*, July and August 1987.
[a]Personal income deflated using the implicit GNP deflator for total GNP and the rest deflated using the implicit GNP deflator for state and local government purchases.

capital expenditures did not decrease as sharply. This pattern has turned around since 1983, with total and capital expenditures growing by more than 3 percent per year from 1983 to 1986. As pointed out by Levin, much of this capital spending has been financed with debt, explaining the sharp growth in interest payments and the drop in the general surplus since 1980.[24]

Employment

Since employee compensation represents 60 percent of local expenditures, it is important to consider employment and compensation trends. Often overlooked in the study of expenditure patterns is the mix in the labor-cost changes between employment and average rate of compensation. An analy-

Table 2.7 Employment (Full-Time Equivalent) of Private Industry and Government (annual percentage change)

Calendar Year	All Industry	Private Industry	Federal Civilian	State and Local Government
1972−75	1.2	1.1	0.6	3.5
1975−80	2.9	3.4	0.8	1.8
1972−80	2.3	2.5	0.7	2.4
1980−82	−0.6	−0.6	−1.1	−0.7
1982−84	2.9	3.4	1.3	0.8
1984−86	2.2	2.4	0.1	2.0
1980−86	1.5	1.7	0.1	0.7

Source: U.S. Department of Commerce, Bureau of Economic Analysis, *National Income and Product Accounts, 1929–82*, and *Survey of Current Business*, July 1987, table 6.7.

sis of public employment trends indicates that after the early 1970s, when the state and local government sector grew at a rate above that for private industry, a retrenchment took place (table 2.7). Growth rates were slower than in the private sector in the post-1975 recession period, and this trend carried over to the 1980s. In both 1981 and 1982 state and local government employment actually decreased. Since 1982 the employment rolls have again begun to expand, but at a rate well below that in the private sector. The implication is that there was a kind of structural break in the last half of the 1970s, probably less due to national economic policy than to a legacy of the recession: a new hesitancy to make the longer-term commitment implied by expanding the employment level.

Even more extreme than this retrenchment in state and local sector employment is the curtailment in job growth for municipalities (see table 2.8). For the twenty cities studied, municipal employment declined by 1.2 percent per year from 1972 to 1984, with the sharpest decline occurring in the early 1980s. The increase of 2 percent in 1985 was an important reversal of this trend and is consistent with the pattern for all state and local governments reported in table 2.7. Although it is difficult to draw strong conclusions on regional patterns, it appears that the older northern cities experienced sharper employment decreases in the early 1980s and stronger employment growth in 1985 than the southern and western cities. From 1980 on (with the exception of 1981 and 1982), employment in these cities generally moved in the same direction as total municipal employment. It appears that the turnaround in the mid-1980s is primarily due to employment expansions in medium-sized municipalities, specifically cities with populations between 300,000 and 1 million.

Table 2.8   Employment (Full-Time Equivalent) of Large Cities, 1972–1985

	FTE Employment in 1985		Average Annual Percent Change in FTE Employment			
	Total	Per 10,000 Population[a]	1972–80	1980–82	1982–84	1984–85
Baltimore[b]	29,260	383	0.95	−10.27	−3.92	−0.85
Boston	20,572	360	0.12	−13.56	1.21	7.68
Chicago	—	—	−0.06	−1.31	—	—
Cleveland	8,472	155	−3.90	0.02	−4.09	2.91
Dallas	—	—	0.91	0.33	1.92	—
Detroit	19,304	177	−2.63	−3.36	−5.90	9.52
Honolulu	8,307	103	1.75	−2.98	−0.85	2.17
Houston	20,649	121	5.45	5.19	0.23	8.48
Indianapolis	11,047	156	7.18	−5.14	−0.67	6.46
Los Angeles	42,046	136	−0.56	−1.08	2.30	1.29
Memphis	18,589	287	−0.14	−1.19	2.36	−15.21
Milwaukee	8,673	140	−0.18	−2.38	−0.52	0.89
New Orleans	10,987	197	1.69	−10.13	5.37	−0.63
New York[b]	339,487	474	−1.95	2.53	−0.09	6.62
Philadelphia	31,196	189	−1.83	0.63	0.01	−1.45
Phoenix	8,898	104	4.91	−3.91	3.39	2.91
San Antonio	12,068	143	0.89	3.47	4.53	4.08
San Diego	7,688	80	0.34	−0.87	3.09	7.29
San Francisco	24,804	348	0.08	−0.69	7.30	3.70
Washington, D.C.[b]	39,417	633	−2.14	−2.72	0.57	3.36
Average	33,073	209	−0.94	−0.47	−2.83	2.01

Source: U.S. Department of Commerce, Bureau of the Census, *City Employment in 1972,* 1980, 1982, 1984, 1985.
[a]Based on 1984 population.
[b]Includes data for city-operated institutions of higher education.

Compensation

This story of employment retrenchment and slow growth leads us to question whether austerity also was the order of the day on the compensation side of the wage budget. The answer is that it was not. State and local governments may have had limited growth in employment and total spending in the 1980s, but they did not slow the rate of compensation increase.

A first step in exploring this issue is to ask whether the growth in public-employee compensation levels is somehow out of line with private sector-employee compensation. The data in table 2.9 show that average wages and salaries were 2 to 3 percent above those in the private sector in the

Table 2.9 Average Annual Real Employee Compensation[a] by Type Per Full-Time Equivalent Employee by Sector

	Average Annual Growth Rate (in percentages)			
Calendar Year	All Industry	Private Industry	Federal Civilian	State and Local
Wages and Salaries				
1972–75	−1.49	−1.38	−2.10	−1.82
1975–80	−0.99	−0.74	−1.85	−1.90
1980–86	0.75	0.57	−0.11	1.82
Supplements to Wages and Salaries				
1972–75	4.67	3.98	8.22	5.82
1975–80	2.34	2.33	1.28	3.68
1980–86	1.18	0.72	4.46	3.25

	Percentage of Private Industry			
	Wages and Salaries		Supplements	
	Federal Civilian	State and Local	Federal Civilian	State and Local
1972	146	103	127	98
1975	143	102	144	104
1980	135	96	136	111
1986	129	104	170	128

Source: U.S. Department of Commerce, Bureau of Economic Analysis, *National Income and Product Accounts, 1929–82*, and *Survey of Current Business*, July 1987, tables 6.5 and 6.7; and U.S. Department of Labor, Bureau of Labor Statistics, unpublished CPI data and *CPI Detailed Report*, January 1987.
[a] Deflated using the Consumer Price Index.

early and mid-1970s but had fallen to 4 percent below by 1980. However, in the 1980s state and local government wages caught up to and again exceeded those in the private sector. The difference in the annual growth rates reported in the top panel of table 2.9 for 1980 to 1986 are startling, showing average real gains three times greater in the state and local government sector than in the private sector.

There are many possible reasons why wages paid to state and local government workers have grown faster in the 1980s than those paid elsewhere in the economy. One possibility is that because of shrinking population bases in the cities, it was necessary to raise wages to be competitive in the marketplace. Another is that unions and state and local governments may not have adjusted their agreements or their expectations to the realities of a lower rate of inflation. Yet another is that some of the wage growth implied in the averages is an illusion. To the extent that governments add fewer new employees or reduce the size of the work force, there is likely to be a disproportionate impact on younger, lower-paid employees. By the nature of arithmetic averages, it is quite possible to reduce the size of the work force and to grant no wage increases to remaining employees and still end up with a higher average wage for the work force. Most likely, the growth in average compensation is attributable to all three of these effects.

If large cities were harder pressed fiscally than were states or other local jurisdictions, it might be expected that city-employee wages would have grown at more modest rates than wages for other state and local government employees. This appears to be generally the case, with thirteen of twenty cities analyzed experiencing slower growth in earnings than the state and local sector as a whole (see table 2.10). Most of the older cities in the North experienced a decline in compensation, although Baltimore and New York City were notable exceptions.

Employee compensation includes much more than wages. Fringe benefits such as pensions, Social Security coverage, and health and hospital insurance add considerably to state and local government expenditures. The costs associated with providing such supplements to employees have been growing faster than wages in private industry and in federal, state, and local governments (see table 2.9). The nonsalary cost per employee in the state and local government sector is approximately $5,158, equivalent to about 23 percent of average earnings and up from around 12 percent in 1970. Fringe benefits, therefore, are a significant item in state and local government budgets.[25] Not only has fringe-benefit compensation to state and local government workers grown in real terms since 1980, but the gap with private-sector workers has widened considerably (see table 2.9).

Large Cities

What has been the response of the largest cities in the United States to the new economics of the 1980s? Has it differed from that of all municipalities? If so, what have large cities done differently since the 1970s that explains Dearborn's findings of a relatively sound budgetary position, and Ladd, Yinger, et al.'s finding of a growing gap between expenditure needs and available revenues? We have studied the fiscal response of overlapping local governments in the twenty-seven largest Metropolitan Statistical Areas (MSAs) and can give some description of their fiscal response. The picture is one of a rather dramatic retrenchment in most fiscal variables.

The procedures we have used in computing this response are important

Table 2.10 Average Annual Earnings[a] Per Full-Time Employee[b] in Large Cities: 1972–1985 (1982 dollars)[c]

	1972	1980	1985	Average Annual Percent Change	
				1972–80	1980–85
Baltimore	16,903	15,896	17,694	−0.8	2.2
Boston	20,877	17,185	17,302	−2.4	0.1
Chicago	25,032	22,229	20,475	−1.5	−1.6
Cleveland	22,710	20,685	20,586	−1.2	−0.1
Dallas	17,910	20,756	19,531	1.9	−1.2
Detroit	26,426	26,238	22,012	−0.1	−3.5
Honolulu	21,368	19,849	19,742	−0.9	−0.1
Houston	18,632	21,237	19,270	1.6	−1.9
Indianapolis	17,032	15,556	15,424	−1.1	−0.2
Los Angeles	29,600	25,587	28,097	−1.8	1.9
Memphis	14,942	17,228	18,577	1.8	1.5
Milwaukee	25,910	23,107	22,353	−1.4	−0.7
New Orleans	14,735	13,020	16,087	−1.5	4.3
New York	24,800	21,110	23,387	−2.0	2.1
Philadelphia	24,465	22,824	22,223	−0.9	−0.5
Phoenix	20,155	21,492	23,568	0.8	1.9
San Antonio	18,529	18,163	18,849	−0.2	0.7
San Diego	24,594	25,119	22,273	0.3	−2.4
San Francisco	27,561	24,949	26,500	−1.2	1.2
Washington, D.C.	20,181	24,170	22,464	2.3	−1.5
Total State and Local Government Sector	18,761	18,135	18,447	−0.4	0.3

Source: U.S. Department of Commerce, Bureau of the Census, *City Employment in 1980, 1985*; *Local Government Employment in Selected Metropolitan Areas and Large Counties: 1972*; Bureau of Economic Analysis, *Survey of Current Business*, July 1986, and *The National Income and Product Accounts, 1929–82*.
[a]Equals October earnings multiplied by 12.
[b]Includes all employees other than instructional except for total state and local employees, which excludes education employees.
[c]Deflated using the implicit GNP deflator for state and local government employee compensation.

because they aid in understanding these results and because the approach taken here is different from what is usually done. First we include the fiscal actions of all overlapping local governments in these metropolitan areas. Second, we make the time-series consistent by relying on the narrowest definition of the MSA, that is, if only three counties are common to an MSA throughout the period, we have used only those counties in computing the fiscal responses.[26] Third, we report results for four time-periods in table

Table 2.11 Changes in Selected Fiscal Variables: Unweighted Averages for 27 Cities (1982 dollars per capita)[a]

	1970–75	1975–79	1979–81	1981–83	1984–85
Absolute Changes					
Taxes	12.28	2.16	−34.32	28.89	23.28
Expenditures	149.07	24.81	−32.29	3.98	39.22
Expenditures Excluding					
Public Welfare	142.12	38.39	−26.23	5.71	31.64
Real Debt Outstanding	13.49	−68.45	−56.60	56.43	106.99
State Aid	82.68	15.25	−9.73	−11.73	27.97
Federal Aid	63.12	50.85	−16.66	−22.65	−9.51
Average Annual Percentage Change					
Taxes	0.5	0.1	−3.5	3.0	4.4
Expenditures	2.8	0.5	−1.4	0.2	3.3
Expenditures Excluding					
Public Welfare	2.9	0.9	−1.2	0.3	2.8
Real Debt Outstanding	0.2	−1.3	−2.2	2.2	7.4
State Aid	5.2	1.0	−1.3	−1.6	7.5
Federal Aid	20.7	10.5	−5.5	−8.6	−8.7

Source: Department of Commerce, Bureau of the Census, *Local Government, Finances, in Selected Metropolitan Areas and Large Counties: 1969–70*, 1978–79, 1980–81, 1982–83; *Local Government Finances in Major County areas: 1983–84*, 1984–85; *Current Population Reports*, Series P-25, No. 739, 873, 957, Series P-26, No. 82-1-SC, 65-52-C, 78-4; Bureau of Economic Analysis, *National Income and Product Accounts, 1929–82*, and *Survey of Business*, July 1986.
[a]Deflated using the GNP deflator for state and local government purchases.
[b]Due to changes in the Census publications it was not possible to obtain complete data for some of the cities for 1984 and 1985. Those counties where published data exist are presented. The results for 1984 and 1985 are not strictly comparable to earlier years. Population estimates for 1984 are used for both 1984 and 1985.

2.11: 1970–75, a period of fiscal expansion; 1975–79, the aftermath of the recession and the height of the tax-limitation movement; 1979–83, a period of two short recessions and the beginning of economic expansion; and 1984–85 to capture the effects of that expansion.[27]

On the revenue side between 1970 and 1975 these data showed the largest increases in federal and state aid, with minimal growth in taxes and debt. These resources funded a substantial increase in real expenditures of close to $150 per capita (a growth of 2.8 percent per year). During the last half of the decade the real increase in federal aid growth continued, albeit at a lower rate; local governments scaled back their borrowing, hiring, and spending; and taxes rose more slowly. It would appear that the real increase in per capita expenditures that took place in the last half of the decade, as well as the tax reductions and net debt retirement, were financed by federal and state aid. It seems pretty clear that urban governments were making a definite choice to reduce the size of their activities. It is also important to remember the setting of the late 1970s. Many cities were not recovering quickly from the 1975 recession, and this was a period when tax limitations were in vogue.

When the real increments in federal and state aid turned negative in the years from 1979 to 1983, local governments responded first by cutting real per capita taxes and net borrowing during the 1979–81 period. But between 1981 and 1983 they substantially increased both real per capita taxes and borrowing. The increases in compensation for local public employees during 1980–83, then, seem to have been financed by reductions in the number of employees, reductions in other current expenditures, and increased taxes in 1983. During the ensuing recovery, taxes and debt in these cities continued to grow rapidly. These, combined with a sharp increase in state aid, have financed a strong growth, particularly in capital expenditures and transfer payments.

Of course, there is variation across urban areas in this fiscal response, as is described in table 2.12. However, the general conclusion seems to hold. Most cities have suffered major reductions in federal aid during the early 1980s, which forced them to reduce expenditures. With the economic recovery and large discretionary tax increases since 1982, growth in expenditures has continued. Those cities experiencing slow expenditure growth after 1984 appear to be primarily northern industrial cities, which lends credibility to the hypothesis that they still operate under difficult fiscal conditions.

Conclusions

This analysis helps to explain why severe urban fiscal crises have not materialized in the 1980s. The first hypothesis is that national economic growth has buoyed up local government revenues and that low rates of inflation have made it possible to control expenditures: that is, cities simply grew out of their fiscal problems. The evidence, however, is mixed. BEA data show that the economies of core metropolitan counties in the older industrial regions have done little better in the 1980s than in the 1970s; yet employment data for the ten largest city-counties are more consistent with the hypothesis that the economic base of large central cities has strengthened in the 1980s.

The second proposition is that urban governments have become more able to cope with the realities of limited resources. They have lived better within their fiscal means in recent years and have managed to do this while providing an adequate level of public services. The first part of this proposition is certainly true. City budgets are more austere in the 1980s than in the 1970s. In the shadow of the tax-limitation movement and faced with large federal aid cuts, local governments have slowed the rate of growth in their expenditure budgets and have cut real-tax and borrowing rates. This austerity has led to some measure of fiscal health. Not only have there been no major crises, but the local government aggregate surplus grew steadily in the mid-1980s, and most large cities found themselves with cash balances. Perhaps the best proof of this new austerity is that state and local government budgets were less affected by the business cycles of the 1980s than by those of the 1970s. But is this truly a structural break in state and city finances or just a temporary departure? The evidence shows that local governments have moved to a higher rate of spending since 1983.

The third hypothesis is that budget austerity has been accomplished at the expense of reductions in the quality of public services. Because we cannot measure the quality of public services directly, this hypothesis cannot be easily tested. Yet there is some indirect evidence that public-service levels have been compromised. Public employment has not grown, and to the extent that public-service levels are directly related to public-employment levels, the new fiscal conservatism may have diminished the quality of services that the government provides. Moreover, an examination of fiscal outcomes shows that state and local governments in aggregate emphasized a relatively high growth in public-employee compensation that was financed by slowing the growth in nonlabor expenditures, reducing the number of public employees, and increasing taxes. A not unreasonable conclusion, then, is that the new austerity of the 1980s has involved a reduction in the quality of urban public services.

Table 2.12 Real Revenues and Expenditures in Selected Cities[a] (Average Annual Percentage Change)

City	Taxes	Federal Aid	Expenditures
		1975−79	
Baltimore[b]	−0.24	11.46	−4.14
Cleveland[b]	−0.34	21.66	2.36
Chicago	−1.04	17.96	−0.24
Detroit[b]	9.06	10.66	1.36
Milwaukee[b]	−2.44	7.36	1.56
Minneapolis-	−7.54	−7.54	−7.54
St. Paul	1.06	−1.04	11.16
Philadelphia	2.66	2.86	1.16
Dallas[b]	2.56	14.36	3.66
Denver	6.26	8.86	2.36
Atlanta	1.06	21.36	3.06
Boston	−0.74	22.06	2.16
Washington	3.66	2.86	−0.04
Pittsburgh	1.76	5.16	5.66
Seattle	−0.94	24.36	1.66
Miami	4.56	16.26	3.86
Houston[b]	8.86	8.56	11.36
Indianapolis[b]	−5.64	15.66	−0.04
Los Angeles	−12.94	17.86	−1.14
Memphis[b]	−0.54	5.76	−0.64
San Francisco	−12.64	1.16	−1.14
Tampa	4.66	22.56	4.66
Honolulu	0.46	18.46	−2.44
New Orleans[b]	4.86	14.36	2.66
New York	−1.14	5.06	−6.84
Phoenix	5.86	11.16	5.26
San Antonio[b]	1.56	12.06	4.36
San Diego	−8.74	12.26	2.66
Unweighted Average	0.43	12.27	2.01

Source: Department of Commerce, Bureau of the Census, *Local Government Finances in Selected Metropolitan Areas and Large Counties: 1969–70, 1978–79, 1980–81, 1982–83; Local Government Finances in Major County Areas: 1983–84, 1984–85.*
[a]Deflated by taking the difference between the compound growth rate for the nominal value of the indicator and the inflation rate (implicit GNP deflator for state and local government

able 2.12 (continued)

	1979–83			1984–85	
Taxes	Federal Aid	Expenditures	Taxes	Federal Aid	Expenditures
0.96	−14.64	0.46	5.10	−3.40	−6.10
0.46	−8.24	−0.94	1.70	12.10	0.90
3.26	0.36	−0.04	0.20	−21.50	−15.70
1.76	−5.44	−1.74	−1.50	2.60	0.10
1.76	−7.04	0.16	8.20	15.60	11.80
−7.74	−7.74	−7.74	−5.00	−5.00	−5.00
−0.04	1.96	−12.04	0.90	−13.30	2.20
−1.74	5.76	−0.94	1.50	−9.90	1.80
4.76	−7.64	5.46	16.90	4.20	7.90
2.56	−13.14	2.46	10.40	−26.30	9.00
2.66	−17.04	0.76	2.30	−14.70	3.10
−8.14	−3.64	−5.84	0.10	−20.30	−0.30
2.46	−6.84	−0.44	4.50	2.10	5.10
2.86	10.46	−0.94	−1.00	7.50	4.40
−0.84	−14.54	1.56	3.20	−8.10	1.10
3.76	10.66	3.16	8.90	−7.90	3.50
7.76	2.16	9.06	6.10	−5.30	1.70
−1.14	−14.44	0.76	7.10	−20.00	−3.10
1.86	−8.94	1.96	6.50	−4.80	6.00
1.06	5.16	1.86	2.10	−54.40	−4.40
1.36	−7.84	1.06	5.40	8.60	6.20
8.46	−13.64	5.76	5.80	−5.00	5.20
3.16	−17.44	0.96	1.70	−10.20	2.20
7.46	−6.74	4.96	−2.20	−12.10	3.10
0.96	−3.34	−0.34	6.00	−3.60	5.00
−3.94	−4.44	4.16	8.40	−11.90	12.90
4.06	−7.14	4.46	19.30	−9.00	14.70
5.06	−10.54	3.36	9.60	−8.30	10.60
1.95	−5.79	1.08	5.08	−8.05	3.29

purchases).
[b]Due to changes in the Census publications it was not possible to obtain complete data for some of these cities for 1984 and 1985. Those counties where published data exist are presented. The results for 1984 and 1985 are not strictly comparable to earlier years.

Part

2

Urban Problems—
A Microscopic Look at Key
Areas of Concern

3 Reengaging State and Federal Policymakers in the Problems of Urban Education

Frank Newman, Robert Palaich,
and Rona Wilensky

It is no secret that the quality of education in urban areas of this country has suffered during the past twenty years. The impact on young people who live in urban centers has been devastating. The web of policy support for young children that characterized the adoption of the Elementary and Secondary Education Act at the federal level and the increasing state role in the funding of education during the sixties and early seventies quickly gave way to a splintering of the coalition and a new, multilayered bureaucratic response. This process led to the interpretation that problems in urban schools were too great to solve and that investing additional money was a waste. In the end this interpretation kept federal and state policymakers from launching new initiatives in urban areas, leaving the urban school districts to care for the students that remained.

In this time of growing fear that a large number of students will never enjoy a productive life and will jeopardize this country's international competitiveness and standard of living, it is time for state and federal policymakers to rethink their position vis-à-vis urban youngsters and once again to become players in the effort to design an effective policy response. Unfortunately, this is not an easy or well-defined job. Breaking the link between poverty and school success, and between minority status and middle class is not easy. In the past, well-intentioned policies have often exacerbated the problems of urban education rather than solved them. The political risk of involvement often outweighed the political payoff. In addition, there were no assurances that the money set aside for urban education initiatives ever had a significant effect on the supposed targets of the policy —the students.

The first section of this essay presents a brief overview of the current state of affairs in urban education. At present, policymakers are faced with the choice of doing nothing and seeing another generation slip into the underclass category or seizing the leadership and policy initiative to attack this difficult policy area. The intergovernmental system of this country, a natural setting for experimentation, has produced many successful local and state intervention strategies based on new ideas and approaches. The second section of this chapter organizes these efforts into a handful of categories and describes some of the more prominent success stories. This effort follows in the footsteps of several outstanding national reports, including the Institute for Educational Leadership study, *Dropouts in America*; the Committee for Economic Development study, *Children in Need*; the National Governor's Association report, *Making America Work*; the Hudson Institute's report, *Workforce 2000*; and the W. T. Grant Foundation report, *The Forgotten Half*.[1] However, these efforts are best described by Judith Viorst in the foreword to Lisbeth Schorr's new book on breaking the cycle of disadvantage, *Within Our Reach*: "Many of us, who yearn for a safer society for ourselves and a solid, reasoned basis for helping others, have thrown up our hands in despair and declared, Nothing works! But anyone reading this book . . . will be left with a vision of hope and life-transforming possibilities that are . . . within our reach."[2] Enough is known about how to make specific programs work, and the time has come to create an environment that supports those programs and to muster the political will to make it happen.

However, knowing that positive outcomes are possible for urban youngsters does not define a role for any particular actor in the policy environment. The complex nature of school governance exacerbates an already difficult situation. In the final section of this chapter we select the actors — state and federal government — and examine their potential role in raising the quality of education found in urban schools.

Education in Urban America

The Cities

There is no single image of American cities that captures their racial, ethnic, and economic diversity. The composition of the population in urban centers varies, both among cities and within their boundaries. Neither is the crisis uniformly felt within or among the cities or their neighborhoods. The collapse of many urban neighborhoods is a process driven by complex historical, regional, and economic factors. But regardless of where or why it occurs, the process of community collapse is characterized by extreme concentration and isolation of racial minorities and the poor. This concen-

tration is both a result of economic and social change and a primary cause
of further deterioration.

In 1980 forty million people, representing almost one-fifth of the U.S.
population, lived in cities with at least 250,000 residents.[3] Contrary to the
popular image, central cities on average are predominantly white. In 1980,
64 percent of all central-city residents were white, 22 percent were black,
11 percent were Hispanic, and 3 percent fell into other racial or ethnic
categories. Still, this represents a significant concentration of racial minorities in cities. While only 24 percent of whites live in central cities, 58 percent of blacks make their home there as do 50 percent of Hispanics.[4] Looking at individual cities, one finds enormous variations in their racial and
ethnic composition. Some, such as Atlanta, Baltimore, Detroit, New Orleans, Oakland, and Washington D.C., have a majority of minority residents; while others, like Seattle, St. Paul, Portland, and Minneapolis, are
overwhelmingly white. Few are adequately described by the national
average.[5]

Because there is a direct connection between race, ethnicity, and poverty,
cities with large minority populations face radically different problems when
compared with their predominately white counterparts. According to the
1980 census, only 8 percent of white central-city residents had family
incomes below the poverty level, while the figures for blacks and Hispanics
were 27 percent and 25 percent, respectively. The racial and ethnic imbalance is more pronounced if one considers both poor and near-poor families:
in 1980, 11 percent of central-city whites had a family income of 125
percent of poverty level or less, while 34 percent of black families and 32
percent of Hispanic families in the central city lived at this income level.[6]

Central cities are home not only to the majority of minority-group citizens who experience poverty disproportionately, but they are also home to a
disproportionate number of families headed by female single parents with
children under the age of eighteen who bear the brunt of contemporary
poverty. In 1980, 32 percent of all such white families, 66 percent of all
such black families, and 65 percent of all such Hispanic families lived in
central cities.[7]

The concentration of the poor into isolated communities has been most
clearly shown in William Julius Wilson's studies of the nation's five largest
cities—New York, Chicago, Los Angeles, Philadelphia, and Detroit—
which by themselves accounted for half of the total poor population of the
fifty largest cities in 1980. In these five metropolises the number of poor
grew by 22 percent between 1970 and 1980, while the number of people
(poor and not poor) living in poor neighborhoods (census tracts with at

least 20 percent poverty) grew by 40 percent. In the neighborhoods with at least 30 percent of their residents in poverty, total population grew by 69 percent, while in neighborhoods with poverty rates of at least 40 percent the total population grew by 161 percent.[8] In these same cities the number of poor people living in poor neighborhoods grew by 58 percent overall, by 70 percent in neighborhoods with at least 30 percent poverty, and by 182 percent in neighborhoods with at least 40 percent poverty.[9] These concentrations of the poor are also concentrations of racial or ethnic minorities. Overall, only 2 percent of these cities' non-Hispanic whites lived in extremely poor neighborhoods.[10] In Wilson's words: "It is the growth of the high and extreme poverty areas that epitomizes the social transformation of the inner city, a transformation that represents a change in the class structure in many inner city neighborhoods as the non-poor black middle and working classes tend to no longer reside in these neighborhoods, thereby increasing the proportion of truly disadvantaged individuals and families."[11]

This concentration of poverty in isolated communities within the metropolitan area is evident in all cities, but it is most acute in the largest cities. It is a trend that is fundamental to understanding those who are permanently mired in poverty. The Urban Institute has defined an underclass neighborhood as a census tract with extremely high concentrations of people in each of four categories: female-headed families, high school dropouts, families on welfare, and working-age men who do not regularly work. In 1980 there were 880 underclass tracts, with a total population of 2.5 million and a poverty population of 1.1 million. The number of children under age nineteen in these areas was 844,000. The racial composition of these tracts was 28 percent white, 59 percent black, and 10 percent Hispanic.[12]

Comparing these tracts to the U.S. average the following differences stand out.[13] In the underclass tracts families with children headed by a woman account for 60 percent of all families; the U.S. average is 19 percent. In underclass tracts 36 percent of young people age sixteen to nineteen are not enrolled in high school and are not high school graduates; this compares to 13 percent as the U.S. average. Of underclass tract households 34 percent receive public assistance as compared to 8 percent of all U.S. households.

Moreover, government policies intended to relieve the worst effects of poverty have intensified the patterns of concentration. Public housing projects within these poor neighborhoods have further isolated minorities and concentrated poverty. The human cost of concentrating poverty is found in Wilson's descriptions of the Robert Taylor Homes and the Cabrini-Green Homes of Chicago:[14]

The official population of the Robert Taylor homes in 1980 was almost 20,000 but there were an additional 5,000 to 7,000 non-registered adults. All of the registered households were black and 69 percent of the residents were minors. The median family income was $5,470. 93 percent of the families with children were headed by a single parent. 83 percent of the non elderly headed families with children received AFDC. Unemployment was estimated to be 47 percent in 1980.

With .5 percent of Chicago's more than 3 million people, the Robert Taylor homes were the location of 11 percent of the city's murders, 9 percent of its rapes and 10 percent of its aggravated assaults. (These figures refer, of course, to reported crimes.)

In the Cabrini-Green homes 13,000 people, almost all black, were officially registered. Minors were 66 percent of the registered population. 90 percent of the families with children were headed by women; 83 percent of the households were on welfare and 81 percent received AFDC in 1983.

In a nine week period beginning in early January 1981, ten Cabrini-Green residents were murdered; thirty-five were wounded by gunshots, including random sniping and more than fifty firearms were confiscated, "the tip of an immense illegal arsenal" according to the Chicago police.

Educators and policymakers have accepted the view of poverty as a handicap for the individual student, but the extraordinary concentration of poverty and the resulting deterioration of communities present a different problem. Again, William Julius Wilson provides insight into the dilemma this sets up for students and schools:

A perceptive ghetto youngster in a neighborhood that includes a good number of working and professional families may observe increasing joblessness and idleness but he will also witness many individuals regularly going to and from work; he may sense an increase in school dropouts but he can also see a connection between education and meaningful employment; he may detect a growth in single-parent families, but he will also be aware of the presence of many married-couple families; he may notice an increase in welfare dependency, but he can also see a significant number of families that are not on welfare; and he may be cognizant of an increase in crime, but he can recognize that many residents in his neighborhood are not involved in criminal activity.

However, in ghetto neighborhoods that have experienced a steady out-migration of middle- and working-class families . . . the chances are overwhelming that children will seldom interact on a sustained basis with people who are employed or with families that have a steady breadwinner.

The net effect is that joblessness, as a way of life, takes on a different social meaning; the relationship between schooling and post-school employment takes on a different meaning. The development of cognitive, linguistic, and other educational and job-related skills necessary for the world of work in the mainstream economy is thereby adversely affected. In such neighborhoods, therefore, teachers become frustrated and do not teach and children do not learn. A vicious cycle is perpetuated through the family, through the community, and through the schools.[15]

The problems of poor and minority students, for example, in the Five Points area of Denver and those in the Cabrini-Green neighborhood of Chicago, cannot be treated similarly. Size of the city and degree of poverty concentration are important factors. Both cases deal with poverty, racism, underachievement, drugs, teenage parenting, violence, and unemployment. In the most isolated poverty neighborhoods employment opportunities are scarce.[16] Even in plants completely surrounded by poor neighborhoods, word of job opportunities is most likely to follow those already employed there home to their neighborhoods rather than to reach the streets immediately outside the plant. All of this contributes to the differences in the communities' internal resources for addressing these problems and requires policies that take into consideration extreme concentrations of poverty and unemployment. The policy challenge is to reforge the relationships which sustain community life when they no longer occur in certain inner-city neighborhoods, because they are replaced by gang life and other forms of "antisocial" behavior.

The School Systems

The process of concentrating racial and ethnic minorities and the poor is continued in the urban public schools. In 1980 the public school systems of U.S. central cities served 19 percent of all the white public school students, 56 percent of all the black public school students, and 48 percent of all the Hispanic public school students.[17] Most school systems serving minority students in America are large. In 1984, 58 percent of black students and 49 percent of Hispanic students were served by districts with over 19,000 students, while 44 percent of black students and 37 percent of Hispanic students were served by districts with more than 40,000 students.[18] And many of these large urban districts serving minority students are incapable of meaningful integration. Recent projections indicate that within the next few years just seven of the nation's twenty-five largest city school systems will have white enrollments greater than 30 percent.[19] In short, urban minority students, like urban minority residents, are concentrated and isolated within urban public school systems.

A useful profile of some of the nation's largest urban school systems is found in "The Condition of Education in the Great City Schools: A Statistical Profile, 1980–1986," which reviews information on thirty-seven urban districts, the smallest of which, St. Paul, served 31,670 students in 1985–86. According to the report:

> In 1984 these districts served 32.3 percent of the nation's black students, 26.8 percent of the nation's hispanic students, 20.1 percent of the nation's Asian students and 4.3 percent of the nation's white students.[20]
>
> Between 1980 and 1984 white enrollment in Great City schools declined 17.6 percent, black enrollment declined 4.5 percent, hispanic enrollment increased 17.0 percent and Asian enrollment increased 36.2 percent.[21]
>
> In 1980 whites accounted for 30.8 percent of all Great City school students, while in 1985 the figure was 26.1 percent. In these same years hispanic enrollment increased from 18.8 percent of the total to 22.7 percent. Black enrollment fell slightly from 46.5 percent of the total to 45.8 percent.[22]
>
> In 1984 minority students accounted for 29 percent of all U.S. students. In that same year minority students accounted for 73.1 percent of all Great City school students.[23]

Indeed, after more than a decade and a half of busing and other court-ordered remedies there has been little overall change in the isolation of black students. Since 1972 the major change has been a dramatic increase in the isolation of Hispanics. The following summary of the research by the University of Chicago's Metropolitan Opportunity Center demonstrates the national extent of segregation:[24]

> In 1984, only 18.3 percent of New York State's black students attended predominantly white schools. In Michigan the figure was 16.2 percent and in Illinois 16.0 percent. In the same year, 85 percent of the Hispanic students in New York State attended predominantly minority schools. Fifty-nine percent were in intensely segregated schools that were 90–100 percent minority.
>
> In Texas, with a student population that is 28 percent Hispanic, 78 percent of the Hispanic students attend majority nonwhite schools and 40 percent attend intensely segregated schools.

Three-fourths of California's Hispanic students and 68 percent of those in Florida attend schools where less than half the students are white. These levels represent significant increases in the degree of Hispanic segregation since 1972.

Achievement

The levels of achievement in predominantly minority schools are significantly lower than those in predominantly white schools, and the likelihood of high dropout rates is much greater. A study of five thousand California schools shows that more than two-thirds of black and Hispanic third-graders were in schools with test scores below the national norms. The lowest quartile of California schools, ranked by test scores, were 67 percent black and Hispanic and had only 28 percent white students. The top fourth of the schools, in contrast, were 85 percent white, 7 percent Hispanic, and 2 percent black. By grade three, about five of every six black and Hispanic students were in below-average schools, while 60 percent of whites were in above-average schools.[25]

Similar patterns were found in the Chicago schools. Using graduation and dropout rates to gauge success, the Chicago Panel on Public School Policy and Finance, an independent research group, found:[26]

The overall dropout rate in the Chicago public schools in the class of 1982 was 43 percent, for Hispanics 47 percent, for blacks 45 percent, for whites 35 percent, for Asians 19 percent. For Hispanic males the rate was 54 percent, and for black males, 53 percent. For that same class, 47 percent of the graduates came from just 21 schools (approximately one-third of the City's High Schools) and only one quarter of the students from these schools dropped out. Of these schools, 18 graduated more than ⅔ of their 1978 entering class. Five schools graduated more than 80 percent of their students.

Of the students entering these successful schools 72 percent read at, or above, normal rates. Few students (13 percent compared to 26 percent system wide) entered high school overage. The racial distribution of these students was disproportionately white (34 percent), with fewer blacks (57 percent) and half the average rate of hispanics (6 percent). At three of these schools more than 80 percent of the entering class was white and eight had a majority of white students in the entering class.

On the other hand, the 21 schools with the highest dropout rates all had more dropouts than graduates and together they account for 49 percent of all dropouts from the system. Together these schools had 56 percent of their entering students drop out.

More than one third of the students entering these schools entered overage. Seventy percent of the students entering these schools had below normal or missing reading scores. Two schools had more than ⅘ of their students in this category. The students at these schools were 76 percent black, 18 percent hispanic and only 6 percent white.

The authors of the study concluded that Chicago operates a two-tiered public high school system which concentrates dropout-prone students into inner-city black and Hispanic high schools.

Unanticipated Consequences

Further, even policies intended to make a portion of the urban schools attractive to middle-class families of all races have the effect of concentrating poor students, most of whom are minority, within schools where underachievement is rampant, thereby accelerating the momentum toward failure. When magnet schools and other elite programs recruit and screen students, they ensure success for the few at the expense of the system as a whole. For example, the screening process in Milwaukee magnet schools effectively eliminated poor minority students from the program. Although each of these special schools had to have at least 44 percent minority pupils, the students getting through the screening were overwhelmingly non-poor. Magnet schools in other large cities also tend to have relatively few low-income students.[27]

The Schools

The process of concentrating and isolating poor and minority students is continued within the walls of the schools as tracking, ability grouping, and remedial pullout programs create internal segregation.[28] Perhaps more important, these practices, combined with the pedagogy of discipline, directly contribute to the culture of failure that exists in the schools and the urban communities from which they draw.

Tracking and Ability Grouping

Virtually every American school separates students into ability groups in the lower grades and differing tracks in high school.[29] This practice is pernicious, not only because it continues the process of concentration previously described, but also because it creates new pressures for failure. Within virtually every school in the nation the poor and members of minority groups are again disproportionately concentrated in classes at the lowest track levels, while children from upper socioeconomic groups are consistently overrepresented in higher tracks.[30] This isolation of minority students into lower-level classes has been carried to its greatest extent by the tendency to place disproportionate numbers of minority students in special-needs classes.[31] Conversely, minority students are drastically underrepresented in the upper-echelon programs.[32]

More important, assignment to a lower track or academic ability group is a life sentence for continued failure since lower-level students are never taught the same material as upper-track students and are subjected to the least effective pedagogical strategies.[33] Schools assume that "disadvantaged students begin their schooling with a learning gap in those areas valued by schools and mainstream economic and social institutions." This leads to a second assumption: that these students "will not be able to maintain a normal instructional pace without prerequisite knowledge and learning skills." While on the surface this approach appears rational and compassionate, it is not. As Henry Levin explains:

> First, it stigmatizes them with a mark of inferiority and reduces learning expectations both for them and their teachers. Such students are viewed as slow learners and treated accordingly with negative consequences for student esteem and performance. Second, by deliberately slowing the pace of instruction to a crawl, a heavy emphasis is placed on endless repetition of material through drill and practice. The result is a school experience that lacks intrinsic vitality, omits crucial learning skills and reinforcement and moves at a plodding pace.
>
> These two characteristics mean that the disadvantaged child gets farther and farther behind the educational mainstream, the longer that he or she is in school. That is, the very model of remediation is one that must necessarily reduce educational progress and widen the achievement gap between advantaged and disadvantaged children.[34]

Pullout Remedies

Separate from tracking but closely related in its effect on student performance are the remedial programs which pull out students and disrupt their normal educational agenda. Suzanne Soo Hoo, an elementary school principal in Cerritos, California, suggests what happens when the pullout model is used:

Take a minute and imagine what happens to a [special needs] student and his day when he qualifies for more than one program. . . . Each service requires approximately 20 to 60 minutes of instruction from a specialist trained to deliver specific instruction. Essentially all the programs are "pull outs" where a student is pulled out of his/her regular classroom setting for instruction someplace else. Consequently, the student misses parts of the basic program like reading, language, math, social studies, health, p.e., music or art in order to get speech, Adaptive PE, Chapter I services etc.

Curiously there exists expectations that this student should receive all those services rightfully due him, to assist with any disadvantages he is presumed to have, even if it means visiting six to eight specialists in a day. This is the state's attempt to respond to the needs of marginal students and equalize some of the social inequities.[35]

The inequity inflicted in the name of equity in both tracking and pull-out programs is made worse by the fact that, again according to Levin, "schools do not focus on the gap per se. There is no time limit established for closing the achievement gap and bringing disadvantaged youngsters into the educational mainstream. Rather the interventions tend to be procedural and mechanical without clear goals."[36]

Retention and Suspension

Closely related to these structural barriers to knowledge is the way in which school discipline and advancement policies are applied with disproportionate results for urban minority students. While grade retention and school suspension undoubtedly are justified in some cases, the reliance on these extreme measures is disruptive and alienating to the students. Furthermore, there is little real evidence that the frequent use of these measures is beneficial for the students who are affected or those who remain.

Minority school populations generally have retention rates three to four times higher than those of majority school populations, and some research has pointed to recent increases in nonpromotion that fall most heavily among minorities.[37] There is little evidence, however, that retention improves the achievement of students in either the short or long run. Instead, for most students, being held back results in stigma, low self-esteem, a lack of interest in extracurricular activities, and waning motivation.[38] Furthermore, it is one of the strongest factors explaining school dropout rates.[39]

The problems stemming from suspensions are twofold: they tend to take students who are already at risk out of school and thus increase their alienation from schooling; and because of the way they are dispensed they often discriminate against minorities. Suspensions tend to be used three times as often with black students as with white students, and black males are especially vulnerable. In 1982 blacks accounted for 16 percent of student enrollment, but received 31 percent of suspensions and 28 percent of instances of corporal punishment.[40] Research suggests that most suspensions are not a consequence of serious offenses but rather of a school professional's reaction to the behavior of minorities.[41] An example of the disparity in the way white and black students are treated is offered by Michelle Fine: "Within four months, two similar incidents occurred. Rodney, a black, low income minority adolescent was suspended from his school and escorted into the juvenile justice system for the same charge that Perry, a white middle class boy was verbally chastised by local police. Rodney spent the night in a juvenile facility, acquired a 'record' and was placed on probation. Perry was warned in the presence of his parents by local police, half winking, half serious, that this *could* lead to trouble, but that he and his friends would be let off this time."[42]

There are serious questions about the goals of suspension and retention policies. If the goal is to maintain order in classrooms for students who remain in them, then such policies may be of some benefit to those students. The only impact of the policies on the person suspended, however, is to force them out of the school building. These policies make no attempt to engage the offending student in any learning activity.

The Students

An ethnographic study by John Ogbu shows how, from a student's point of view, a sense of alienation from the dominant culture contributes to school failure in Stockton, California:

> The [black] children diverted most of their efforts away from school work into nonacademic activities. Other observers report similar findings. These observations have led me to believe that the poor school performance of black children is partly a result of not putting enough time, effort and perseverance into their schoolwork. . . . [These] children know what is required in order to do well in school. In my research interviews in Stockton, black children explained that one of the reasons Chinese, Japanese and some white students do well in school is that they expend more time and effort on their school work than black students.[43]

In answer to the question of why inner-city black children fail to give adequate time, effort, and perseverance to their schoolwork, Ogbu concludes:

"One [reason] is that blacks, from generations of experience, realize that they face a job ceiling; therefore, they develop a variety of coping responses that do not necessarily enhance school success (such as joining the culture of the street). The other is that the fact of segregated and inferior education has resulted in an abiding antagonism and distrust between blacks and the schools."[44]

This lack of trust sets in motion a dance between the school and the student in which the system does not believe that the students can perform and the students react to those expectations. This in turn promotes an alienation that leads students to withhold from themselves and the system what they could do if school were not seen as their enemy. As a consequence, high levels of underachievement, low esteem, inflated truancy, and dropout rates, which we take to be the hallmarks of urban schools, result. The ultimate irony can be found in Michelle Fine's conclusions on the personalities of dropouts and non-dropouts. "The dropout profile was of a student relatively non-depressed, critical of social injustice, willing to take initiative, and unwilling to mindlessly conform. "Good students," those who persisted, were relatively depressed, self blaming, teacher dependent, unwilling to take initiative in response to a mis-grade and endlessly willing to conform."[45]

The complex role of expectations, class background, and pedagogy is explored in Jean Anyon's 1979 study of fifth-grade classes at five different New Jersey schools.[46] Three schools were located in an industrial city, and two were in one of its affluent suburbs. Summarizing her work, Anyon found:

As the social class of the community increased . . . the following increased: the variety and abundance of teaching materials in the class-room; the time reported spent by the teachers on preparation; higher social class background and more prestigious educational institutions attended by teachers and administrators, more stringent board of education requirements regarding teaching methods, more frequent and demanding administrative evaluations of teachers; teacher support services such as in-service workshops; parent expenditure for school equipment over and above district or government funding; higher expectations of student ability on the part of parents, teachers and administrators; higher expectations and demands regarding student achievement by teachers, parents, and administrators; more positive attitudes on the part of teachers as to the probable occupational futures of the children; an increase in the children's acceptance of classroom assignments; and cultural congruence between school and community.[47]

This picture of pedagogical inequity is rounded out by Michelle Fine's description of a South Bronx high school in which she found that students need to *earn* the opportunity to be critical, to participate, and to work collectively. She observed that "smart kids" get to participate, "remedial kids" get to memorize; smart kids get to work in groups, remedial kids are accused of cheating; smart kids are creative, remedial kids are right or wrong.[48]

Perhaps most telling was her finding of the image of good school behavior internalized by ghetto youngsters. She asked high school dropouts if, when they were younger, they were the kind of kids who participated in class a lot. She found herself not understanding their answer, "Not me, I was a good kid," until she had heard it repeated over and over again.[49]

We are left, then, with a portrait of an environment so unresponsive to the real needs of children that it drives out those with energy and enthusiasm and consigns them to a future in which little else but the street awaits them. In conclusion, to understand the role of social isolation in the pathology of school failure for urban youngsters, it is important to look at both the concentration of poor and minority youngsters in certain schools and the school practices that further segregate students from learning. Further, lowered expectations of ability and achievement appear to be endemic to schools which serve poor and minority students in urban areas. When schools approach large numbers of poor and minority students, they see failure in the making. In treating them as failures they seal their fate.

Strategies That Work

There seems to be a developmental sequence to restructuring schools to meet the needs of students in poor urban communities. The first step is to reforge the sense of trust between the school and the student and their parents and community. It is clear to the students we have talked with that they believe school personnel do not care about what is going on in the lives of the students. In the poorest of urban neighborhoods it is quite possible that the schools are the only traditional social institution remaining. This places a large responsibility on the schools since they are the institution that stands between the youngster and gangs or other antisocial activities.

The second step is to ensure that all students experience success in academics. It is not enough for schools to become the social center of the community and find ways to earn the trust of the parents and students. This step requires that schools understand their students and their learning styles. It requires school professionals to use this knowledge to tailor how they present material to the individual students in their classrooms and rethink how they use their time throughout the school day. They need to be tracking the progress of each student on basic skills, critical thinking, and motivation. In simple language, each teacher must become less of a presenter of material and more of an academic coach. Lack of improvement in this area has dramatic consequences. If students believe that no person in the school thinks they can succeed, they will "vote with their feet" and drop out of school.

The final step is that students must see a relationship between working hard in school and some future goal. Richard De Lone described best the concept of a small future.[50] There are two key components to the concept: the length of time one attaches to the future, and the strength of the relationship between present actions and future outcomes. If the primary concern is immediate survival, the time frame is likely to be measured in weeks and months rather than years or decades. When one's future is measured in weeks and months, formal schooling and learning in general are often not terribly relevant. Even if one has a future measured in years, if the adults with whom one comes into contact have high school diplomas but remain unemployed, the connection between work in school and future outcomes is eroded.

Given the development sequence described here, what general strategies seem to be effective in reaching poor students in urban school districts? Recently the Education Commission of the States (ECS) convened several working groups to discuss this question.[51] From these discussions consensus emerged on five broad categories of intervention: *early intervention*, *parent involvement*, *mentoring*, *school restructuring*, and *collaboration*. If public policy is to have an impact on the success of urban education, strong efforts must be made in each of these areas.[52] The five categories are described in further detail below, and selected examples are provided to illustrate their power.

Early Intervention

Under the category of early intervention, several different but related services are found. At its core, early intervention focuses on child care, early childhood education, and training new parents to help their children learn. Two themes are evident in the research. First, an expanded view of the early years is necessary. Studies show that the prenatal period as well as the first nine years of life are crucial to successful social and educational upbringing. Second, those who come to school ill-prepared quickly fall behind and are likely to stay behind. Further, the research indicates a number of steps should be taken to meet the needs of children and parents, including adequate, day-long day-care programs; early education programs for three- to five-year-olds; and a comprehensive program of health, counseling services, social services, and day care for poor families. Although these programs exist in some form in many locations, the demand for such services outstrips their availability.[53]

Two policy approaches are gaining popularity today; the development of state initiatives modeled after the federal Head Start program and a growing interest in parent education programs. Head Start, the federal early childhood education program established in the 1960s, is cited by experts and policymakers alike as one of the finest examples of high-quality early childhood care and education. States across the country, including Florida, California, New York, Massachusetts, Oregon, New Mexico, and Minnesota, have implemented and refined programs based on the federal model.[54] A great deal is known about the impact and effectiveness of early intervention programs. What is needed are more programs to increase the number of children served and a system of governing these efforts that remains responsive to parent and community needs and works closely with the schools that serve the student once the program is completed.

Parent Involvement

Parent involvement is on everyone's list of practices to make schools more effective, to help families create more positive learning environments, to reduce the risk of student failure, and to increase the likelihood of student success. The research identifies five types of parent involvement that lead to a comprehensive school-family partnership.

—Schools involve parents in learning about their children's health and safety, preparations of children for school, and conditions that support school learning and behavior.
—Schools are obligated to communicate with parents about school programs and child progress.
—Schools involve parents as volunteers who assist teachers, administrators, and children in classrooms or in other areas of school life.
—Teachers ask parents to assist their own children at home on learning activities that are coordinated with the children's classwork.
—Schools involve parents in school governance and advocacy via

decisionmaking roles in the PTA/PTO, advisory councils, or other committees or groups at the school, district, or state level.

In the past the emphasis has been on the second, third, and fifth activities listed. The research on the impact of schools' active involvement in the first and fourth areas is very promising. From her studies in Maryland, Joyce Epstein was able to draw several exciting conclusions. They include the following:

Teachers who are leaders in the use of parent involvement in learning activities at home were able to involve parents with all educational backgrounds, not just well-educated parents.

When parents were involved by teachers in learning activities at home, they reported that they knew more about their children's instructional programs; received many ideas from the teacher about how to help at home; believed that the teacher wanted them to help their children; and rated the teacher higher in interpersonal skills and overall teaching ability.

Teachers tended to involve the parents in reading activites at home with their children, more than in other school subjects. . . . and, our research showed, students gained more in reading achievement from fall to spring if their teachers frequently involved parents.

Teacher leadership—not parent education or marital status—made the difference in whether parents improved their knowledge about the school and about helping their children, and whether the children improved their reading scores.[55]

The connections between teacher practices, parent responses, and student achievement in reading suggests that if teachers helped parents understand how to help their children at home in other specific school subjects, more children would improve their mastery of those subjects. This is especially true for students who need extra learning time to practice or review basic skills. The interest in parent education programs is relatively new. A number of states, including Oregon, Arkansas, Minnesota, and Missouri, have initiated statewide parent education efforts. Typical activities associated with these efforts include parents reading to their children (and working on their own reading skills), teaching parents how to teach reading, writing, and math skills to their children, and sensitizing parents to the learning habits of their children.[56]

Because teachers and administrators play the key roles in including or excluding parents from their children's education, all policies targeting at-risk youngsters should have a component that builds teachers' and administrators' capacities to engage parents in practices that make a difference in academic success for their children.

Mentoring

Mentoring, a one-on-one relationship that encourages and guides personal growth and development in an individual, is another effective way of helping at-risk youngsters. The need to develop and maintain mentoring programs is great. According to a recent Commonwealth Fund report, students who receive mature and caring human support are more likely to graduate from high school, more likely to become and remain employed, and less likely to repeat pregnancies. As Margaret Mahoney wrote in a Commonwealth Fund annual report, "whether or not young people succeed depends in large part on individuals who help them establish values and who inspire effort. Youngsters lack and need the direct intervention in their lives of mature individuals who provide the one-on-one relationship that can reassure each child of his innate worth, instill values, guide curiosity, and encourage a purposeful life."[57]

Mentoring relationships can be devoted to personal growth, academic skills, career development, friendship, and athletic or artistic growth. For example, a recent ECS/Campus Compact survey of campus-based community service programs reveals that many institutions have active service programs designed to help at-risk younger people in their communities. Such programs range from tutoring to coaching athletic teams. In a majority of these activities students are paired in a one-on-one relationship with younger children. These and other mentoring programs must be designed to identify and reach at-risk youth to assist them in both personal and academic development. Such goals require time, commitment, and training on the part of the mentor and the support of and close collaboration with local schools, community-based organizations, volunteer organizations, and state policymakers.

The goal of such a relationship is to increase children's motivation to stay in school by increasing their academic and critical-thinking skills, building their self-confidence, and enhancing their sense of what the future holds for them. Such relationships can be built at many levels, as the following examples illustrate. In many middle, junior high, and senior high schools, school-age mentors are working with their peers, especially in the areas of academic tutoring and suicide prevention; at many higher education institutions, college students are working as mentors in a wide variety of capacities; and, finally, adults are working as mentors in many successful programs such as Big Brother or Big Sister programs, the Career Beginnings program developed at Brandeis University, the "Working Coach" model of England's Grubb Institute for Behavioural Studies, and the "I Have a Dream" Foundation programs of philanthropist Gene Lang.

What is needed is an increase in volunteers to establish a long-term relationship with at-risk young people. Through that relationship each youngster can get the feeling that the outside world wants them to succeed. Thereby youngsters can establish their own codes of social responsibility. Policymakers can encourage this process in two ways. The first is to mount an aggressive leadership campaign that increases the number of volunteers, and the second is to decide whether additional incentives should be implemented to encourage mentoring efforts.

School Restructuring

Why must schools restructure? How does restructuring benefit at-risk urban students? The case for restructuring has grown more compelling over the last decade. The flaws of the comprehensive high school and the elementary and middle school/junior high structures that support it have become increasingly clear as shifts in social and economic forces as well as rapid changes in technology have occurred in this country. From the point of view of the working professional, the schooling system often forces talented, competent teachers into narrow, compromised situations. Teaching professionals need an environment that allows them to define and follow through on challenging assignments, to thoroughly know and understand the progress of every student, and to constantly improve their understanding of the material they teach. In the vast majority of schools today such opportunities do not exist.

When one examines schools that profess to be restructured, it is clear that no two good schools are precisely alike. Their strength derives from the imagination and energy of their staffs, the communities that they serve, and the personalities and motivation of the students they enroll. Thus no standardized model exists, although good schools share some common characteristics. The Coalition of Essential Schools has identified the following nine principles:

— An intellectual focus. Schools should focus on helping adolescents to learn to use their minds well.
— Simple goals. Schools' goals should be simple: that each student master a limited number of essential skills and areas of knowledge.

—Universal goals. The schools' goals should apply to all students, while means to achieve these goals will vary as the students themselves vary.

—Personalization. To the maximum extent feasible, teaching and learning should be personalized to student needs. Control over specific pedagogies must be unreservedly placed in the hands of principals and staff.

—Student-as-worker. The practical metaphor governing day to day life in the school should be student-as-worker, not teacher as deliverer of instructional services.

—Student exhibitions. High school students should be awarded a diploma only after successfully completing a final demonstration of mastery—an exhibition.

—Attitude. The tone of the school should explicitly and self-consciously stress the values of high expectations, of trust and of decency and fairness.

—Staff. Principals and teachers should perceive themselves as generalists first and specialists second.

—Budget. Ultimate administrative and budget targets for high schools should include: total student loads per teachers of 80 or fewer pupils, substantial time for collective planning by teachers, competitive salaries for staff and a total per pupil cost not to exceed by 10 percent that of traditional schools.[58]

As was stated, no model of a restructured school exists that can be exported from site to site because each restructured school builds its practices from its unique mix of professional staff, students, and interests. In practical terms, however, there are several standard assumptions regarding school structure including the following: the optimal size of the school unit; serious reexamination of how students are placed in groups; a shift from the goal of controlling students to the goal of increased learning for all students; and a comprehensive effort to track student progress not just in basic skills but also in critical-thinking skills and in motivation to learn. These assumptions, along with many others, will receive close scrutiny in a restructured setting.

To successfully implement such a program at a particular site, district, state, and federal policymakers must agree to provide adequate levels of technical assistance, some financial aid, and such regulatory waivers and/or adjustments in federal, state, and district practices as are needed by the site. Some may interpret these policy actions as capitulating to those who have caused the problem. As anyone knows who has ever tried to change the vision of a company, an organization, or a team, however, "reluctant folks make poor adventurers." Education staff and students must be allowed to shape life within their workplace. To encourage this to happen in individual sites across the country, policymakers must find ways to advance the following principles: work to build a shared vision; organize educators in creative ways; use appropriately varied strategies for change; share leadership and responsibility; build in collaboration and flexibility; promote information that moves educational change forward; and restructure with high regard for the people in the process.

Collaboration

Those interviewed in a recent ECS survey of state policies to serve at-risk youngsters defined collaboration as an ongoing meeting between and among schools, state agencies, state and local governments, and community organizations to resolve a common problem. With respect to the at-risk youth issue, there is general agreement that collaboration makes sense, that it should be stimulated and encouraged. Yet it is as complicated in practice as it is elementary in theory.

Collaboration concerns relationships among people—how organizations as well as individuals relate to one another. The experiences of people running effective schools serving at-risk youth suggest that faculty in such schools are more likely to share personal motives and common goals. Also, the laying of common objectives with clear direction, set stages of implementation, and measured outcomes is easier when the faculty is empowered to make decisions. This kind of situation naturally lends itself to collaborative decisionmaking within a school.

Before effective programs can be implemented, the barriers to collaboration must be addressed. The structure of state agencies, mind-sets, time constraints, limited resources, and inflexible policies are some of the roadblocks to collaboration reported by state program directors. One common complaint is that agencies serving youth (for example, education, health and human services, and juvenile justice) do not always offer comprehensive programs for youth at risk. This sometimes results in duplicate services or no services at all.

In a recent ECS report examining collaboration entitled *Community of Purpose* the authors identified the pros and cons of collaboration and the reasons why it must be tried.

Collaboration is crucial because service-providers often are unaware of the resources available in the community to help them help kids.

Programs that consider the whole child have been found to be most effective. The issue can be teen pregnancy, substance abuse or youth suicide but the approach must be multi-dimensional and therefore involve collaboration.

Collaboration does not place the burden of problem-solving solely on the schools. It involves the *entire* community working together to provide services or resolve problems for at-risk youth.

The momentum is maintained by leaders from every political level who have global understanding of the problem and are committed to search for solutions through systemic change.

Collaboration encourages creativity and risk-taking. When adults organize themselves in new ways, they can create a positive learning environment enabling students to acquire the expanded range of skills, knowledge and attitudes they need. The perspectives and approaches of diverse groups are essential to create this positive environment.

What are the Barriers to Collaboration? Many. Long-term benefits of collaboration are far less visible than the short-term costs. Slow starts, institutional posturing, external interference, "turf" disputes and entirely new layers of stress are some of the front-end costs reported by different collaborations.

[The authors conclude] first, collaboration does *not* mean the abdication of individual responsibility. Whether a governor, a state schools chief or district superintendent, a department head or a school principal, it comes with the job. The leader who goes out on a limb should expect to take the heat. But collaboration and the collective ownership that results from it is a formidable power against special interests.

Second, collaboration does *not* mean relegating leadership duties to an indecisive politburo. "I learned to appreciate the benefits of shifting control to teachers and becoming comfortable with the few knowns and the greater uncertainties that typifies renewal," says Principal Suzanne Soo Hoo. "A large part of my job is to be the chief worrier about the culture of our school that would foster these talks."

And finally, collaboration *can be* a force greater than the sum of its parts. . . . Many agencies are often times dealing with the same types of problems. By gathering together the different people who are working on common issues, a structure can be created to select a common goal, a common plan, a *real* agenda.[59]

In many ways, encouraging collaboration may be the easiest category for policymakers to influence. In most cases the agencies that must collaborate report directly to elected officials. Policymakers must seriously consider whether existing patterns of oversight are consistent with their goals for agency collaboration and cooperation.

The Role of State and Federal Policymakers

Three distinct strategies are available to state and federal policymakers to respond to the needs of urban education. First, change the operating assumptions currently held by those participating in urban public education. Second, ensure that all new comprehensive reform efforts incorporate elements of the five categories identified above. Third, recognize that appropriate interventions in central cities and urban neighborhoods are not alike.

Change the operating assumptions. For public education to better serve at-risk urban youngsters, the school system itself must change many of the assumptions on which the current system is built. Change of this magnitude is extremely difficult. The first operating assumption must be a belief that all children can learn. This is a significant change from the current practice of categorizing students described earlier. It is also clear that successfully changing this assumption will change the way learning occurs throughout the school system.

The second challenge is to develop an enhanced methodology for evaluating student progress. Virtually all assessment efforts at present evaluate different levels of basic skills with some additional emphasis on problem solving. Unless a greater emphasis is placed on assessing critical-thinking skills and motivation, we may never engage at-risk students in the learning process. The third challenge is to develop an investment strategy that encourages risk-taking and causes the school system to respond. These challenges focus on assumptions that underlie the assessment of student progress and the financing of public schools. Without these two mechanisms available to support the local response to the new assumption that all students can learn, efforts on the part of parents, students, school professionals, and the school system will be severely hampered.

Unfortunately, even if these changes in the education system were to occur, it is unlikely that the outcome would immediately change for a large percentage of young people. The final challenge is to change the operating assumptions held by these youngsters and their families. They must be convinced that education will play an important role in their future, and, therefore, that it is worth investing time and resources in schooling. Further, the schools must re-earn the trust of the urban minority and poor community and thereby become agents of opportunity rather than of separation and isolation.

Convince educators and the public, through success stories, that all children can learn. No simpler statement describes why education is so important and why it attracts people to the field. Virtually everyone believes in the abstract that "all children can learn." When the conversation turns to the discussion of a particular child, however, the firmness with which the belief is held begins to waver. If the child's progress does not conform to the learning pattern assumed by the standardized test, problems result for both the system and the student. The school and the system are criticized for lower standardized test scores, while the student is most often referred to special classes in which a very limited curriculum is taught in a narrow pedagogical style. The mismatch between the child's progress and the results of the standardized test is driven by many factors, only one of which is a child's ability to learn. Other factors include motivation to learn, the school's curriculum, learning style, previous preparation, and the matchup among several of these in a particular case. Only the child's ability and previous preparation, however, are assumed to be the problems.

The typical school and district response to this situation has been to place additional barriers between these students and their access to the more complete curriculum and the more interesting pedagogical techniques. The now institutionalized response of public school systems is definitely a major contributor to the mix of forces that limits the success of poor, urban, and minority youngsters.

To change the assumption to a belief that all students can learn, state and federal policymakers must take action on the leadership and policy fronts. By asking the right questions, policymakers can reshape the discussion and thereby change the assumptions underlying it. The central line of questioning concerns outcomes for all students. There are two major themes. The first is to use testing information currently collected more effectively, and the second is to challenge schools and districts to prove that they are doing an effective job with these youngsters. Regarding currently administered test results, the role for policymakers is to constantly ask how minority and poor students are performing relative to the test medians for the school and district. The second step is to monitor how individual students do throughout their schooling. Finally, it is the role of the policymaker to convince the public that a broader use of test score results is needed. The second theme is the urgent need to identify and recognize programs, schools, and districts that are doing an effective job with poor, urban youngsters. Without effective recognition, these local efforts are likely to be only temporary.

Two efforts must be undertaken by policy initiative to make the transition between assumptions. The first focuses on developing staff capacity. A growing literature exists on learning styles, restructured schools, and classroom management techniques that assist in reaching at-risk youngsters. The problem is that these resources are not widely used by educators as they rethink their school environment. Unless teachers and principals believe that all students can learn and unless they have command of the literature and pedagogical techniques necessary to implement that vision, attacking wrong assumptions will be futile. An investment in developing staff capacity is essential for policymakers. The second policy initiative is the development of a mix of incentives for schools and districts who work effectively with at-risk urban youngsters.

Enhance the capacity of the education system to measure the progress of its students. Currently, most schools and districts are at a loss to explain the rates of progress (or lack thereof) that poor and minority students make through the school system. In part this is due to the fact that we do not organize the assessment information we currently collect to answer this question for at-risk youngsters. In larger part it is due to the fact that current assessments of student progress focus only on basic competencies and are only beginning to include the assessment of critical-thinking skills, while motivation and attitudes toward learning are not even measured. In addition, information that might explain why an individual did not do well is rarely collected. As the situation exists today, assessment information does not help the teacher understand why a student does not know a particular set of factual information; neither does it help the public or parents understand why the schools are not working for their children.

A quantum leap is needed in the state of assessment practice. The first need is to expand assessment coverage from basic competencies to critical-thinking skills and attitudes toward learning. Some attention is currently being given to critical-thinking skills, but a much greater effort is required. In contrast, little attention has been given to understanding attitudes and motivation toward learning. Expanding assessment in these two areas is essential to hold schools and school systems accountable for serving at-risk youngsters.

The second need is that assessment information as it typically exists often answers questions for aggregated units, such as districts, states, or even federal policymakers, but does not help those who provide education services to kids. For assessment results to become a unifying force, information collected must be of use to the teacher first and then aggregated so that the appropriate larger units can use the information to answer their accountability questions. This is a major research-and-development effort that the federal government should lead and support. Fortunately, this is not such a risky investment since all but a handful of states test their elementary and secondary school students at stages along their career, and there is a pent-up demand for new assessment technology.

Stimulate innovation through strategic investment. It is widely assumed by all involved that dollars invested in education in urban areas are dollars that will never reach the youngster whose needs the money was meant to address. Depending on the particular urban area, the chief culprit could be the janitors, the principals, the teacher unions, or the bureaucracy. The bottom line is that state and federal policymakers are afraid that a large-scale investment in urban education is a complete waste of money. Compounding this lack of confidence in the urban district to administer such an influx of dollars is the uncertainty over what the dollars should pay for.

Given this lack of confidence and uncertainty as to whether one type of program should be implemented, the competitive grant-financing mechanism has been tried in several states as a vehicle to fund at-risk programs. This financing mechanism has several advantages including the funds bypassing all the bureaucratic compromises and contracts, reaching the target population, and stimulating new approaches and collaborative ventures. There are two observed negatives to the approach. It is much more difficult for the state to determine what it got for its money and whether or not there are real winners and losers in the competition for a relatively small amount of money.

In our judgment this is the first of a new generation of incentive-financing mechanisms whose goal is to push new funds toward targeted student populations. Given the dissatisfaction with and the costliness of formula-driven funding mechanisms, the new financing mechanisms will be thoroughly explored.

Convince children and their parents that in the future skills acquired through education will be more closely associated with successful adulthood than at any time in the past. In the world of the inner-city poor the evidence is to the contrary. People with high school diplomas are often shut out of the legal economy, while those employed by the "street" economy are significantly better off. Within the school itself the values and the message to inner-city youngsters is clear: Don't waste your time and ours. The question is whether individual schools can reshape that message as they respond to the challenge that all students can learn. Not only do schools have to rethink and implement a new way of doing business, but they must sell their approach to the students and parents in their attendance area.[60]

Such an effort will require leadership, public support, and many adult volunteers to make it happen. It will also require school professionals to gain the trust of the community they serve. At the very least, state and federal policymakers need to be partners in the leadership team that guides this public relations effort to call for full participation. Policymakers should also consider financially supporting the outreach effort required of these schools.

Incorporate the five components of programmatic success. A great deal is known about effective components of programs for youth at risk. In our opinion the states and federal government should not design and run programs for improving urban education. Cities, districts, neighborhoods, and schools should be in that business. Nevertheless, state and federal government will be called upon to finance such efforts. It is, therefore, very important that state and federal policymakers be familiar with the general components of effective programs and choose financing mechanisms that put discretionary money behind those efforts. Early intervention, parent involvement, mentoring, school restructuring, and collaboration are all powerful ideas to invest in. It is also true that investing in multiple categories can yield even greater results.

Responding to Urban Differences

The increased isolation of the poor and minorities is a trend in every urban center of this country. Across urban centers, there is substantial variation in the degree to which this isolation is a problem. Cities like Denver and Minneapolis have a time before the isolation of their poor communities catches up with that of New York, Chicago, and Los Angeles.[61] Further, in certain neighborhoods, independent of what city they are found in, the isolation of the urban poor has also reached dangerous proportions. This implies a two-pronged effort on the part of state and federal policymakers. The first focuses on attacking the growth of this trend in communities where isolation is not nearly as acute. In these cities and neighborhoods the state and federal response is adequately described by focusing on changes in the underlying assumptions and making sure that new programs implemented have adequately taken into account the five components of a successful youth-at-risk strategy.

A second type of effort is required in the most isolated communities. This is direct intervention in the schools with technical assistance, additional funds, and community outreach, and reestablishing the schools as a viable institution in the poorest neighborhoods of the largest metropolitan areas. Efforts to assist urban education in these neighborhoods may also need to be linked to welfare, housing, employment, and other policies required to put the community back on its feet. Even though such an intervention is a complex undertaking, the cost to society of not reaching those youngsters prevents us from balking at the task.

In conclusion, state and federal policymakers need to rejoin the battle for quality education in urban areas. Their options for action range from focusing attention on the problem through leadership and program implementation to direct intervention in schools in certain neighborhoods. Unfortunately, for youngsters caught in this situation, time is short. Action is needed now.

4

Urban Poverty:
Where Do We Go from Here?

Peter Edelman

On March 20, 1988, two days before the presidential primary election in New York had begun but many months after the start of the presidential campaign, the *New York Times* ran a front-page story featuring the headline, "Candidates Turn to Problems of Cities in New York Race." The story explained that the Democratic candidates were only then starting to focus on urban issues in their stump speeches because "in the early primaries, the candidates were appealing to largely rural and suburban constituencies;" "a number of urban issues are widely considered intractable;" and "with the nation facing a record deficit, few local officials are expecting a large infusion of federal aid."

For those whose particular concern is urban poverty, the story was good news and bad news. The good news was that urban poverty had, at least implicitly, made its way back onto the list of campaign issues. The *New York Times* listed each candidate's stance on drug abuse, housing, health and welfare, education, and crime. Each of these issues is an area of particular interest to low-income people. After nearly a decade of the politics of antigovernment, the story implied that there was renewed interest in a role for government in solving pressing social problems, especially those of low-income people.

The bad news was that urban issues in general and urban poverty in particular had not come into the campaign discussion until very late in the game, and even then had only arrived in the form of generalizations, except for what Jesse Jackson was saying. If we seem to have awakened from the years of being told it was morning in America, our own morning was not beginning with a particularly hearty breakfast.

Nonetheless, we are about to turn a new page. One can hope that the preelection presidential timidity was only a campaign-induced pathology and that some limited new initiatives will be possible even as deficit-reduction measures are pursued. So the question rises, if we are going to have a new emphasis on dealing with urban poverty, what will it involve? What policies will we want to pursue and what actors will need to play a role? Which aspects of urban poverty need to involve the federal government or at least need to be part of a national agenda, and which do not? Which will need to deal with people in ways unique to the fact that they live in cities, and which will be nonspatial, aimed at people in need regardless of where they live?

These observations are offered from the perspective of the author's experience based on study of the issues and work as a practitioner. The thoughts expressed emanate from years as a Senate staff member and state official and an equally long period teaching, writing, and consulting about poverty issues.

The Changing Face of Poverty

Poverty in 1989 was different in remarkable and important ways from its composition in the 1960s and earlier. First, the elderly used to be disproportionately poor and are now, as a group, less poor than the population as a whole. The indexing of Social Security and the enactment of the Supplemental Security Income (ssi) program in the early 1970s have added up to an enormous social-policy success for the elderly (although elderly women and minorities remain disproportionately poor). The trend lines crossed in 1982, and since then a lower percentage of the elderly has been poor than is the case for the general population.

Second, children as a group are now much poorer than the rest of the population. This is largely due to the increased incidence of female-headed families, which has spelled economic disaster for millions of women and children. The increasing number of low-wage jobs in general and the continuing barriers women confront in getting good jobs mean that working women with children and no husband are more likely to be poor than they used to be. Further, welfare benefits have been steadily deteriorating in real terms for nearly two decades so that transfer payments do not lift families who are unable to work out of poverty.

Third, the weakness in the economy that has persisted since 1973 has brought an increase in the number of families in which someone works full-time but is unable to earn enough to get the family out of poverty, and a corresponding increase in the numbers of those who work part-time because they cannot find full-time work and are in poverty as a consequence. The working poor are a much clearer target for policy attention in 1988 than was the case two decades ago.

What are the numbers? In 1987 there were 32.5 million poor people in America, representing 13.5 percent of the population.[1] We had made fairly steady progress in reducing poverty from 1959, the year we started keeping the statistics, until 1973. In 1959, 22.4 percent of Americans were poor.[2] In 1973 we reached our all-time low of 11.1 percent.[3] We held about steady until 1978 and then started to climb again, reaching 15.2 percent in 1983.[4] The 1987 figure of 13.5 percent, 1.7 points below the recent high and 2.4 points above the "all-time" low, might seem to represent pretty good recent progress (although the underlying numbers are that 8 million more people were poor in 1987 than in 1978),[5] except for the trends within the poverty population. "Only" 12.2 percent of the elderly were poor in 1987, while 20.6 percent of children were poor.[6] Forty percent of the poor people in America are children.

Minorities remain disproportionately poor—blacks at 33.1 percent and Hispanics at 28.2 percent in 1987[7]—but the even more shocking numbers are what we have recently learned about the relation between family structure and poverty. Children in female-headed families were poor at a rate of 54.7 percent in 1987.[8] Children in Hispanic female-headed families were poor at a rate of 70.1 percent.[9] And 68.3 percent of the black children in female-headed families were poor.[10]

To be born into a female-headed household is a sentence to poverty—62 percent of children born into female-headed families are poor for the entire first ten years of their lives, whereas only 2 percent of those born into two-parent families are poor for such a long time.[11]

Why so much poverty, especially in single-parent families? The causes are multiple and certainly include bad preparation for the labor market and, for some, poor motivation, but there are two fundamental causes above all others. One is weakness in the labor market, and the other is weakness in the framework of income maintenance.

A very large number of nonelderly poor adults work when they can and are still poor. About 2 million work full-time and are unable to get their families out of poverty.[12] Another 6 million work part-time or only part of the year,[13] often because they are unable to find full-time work or unable to accept it due to lack of adequate available child care. The minimum wage produces $6,880 for the whole year. The poverty line in 1987 was $11,611 for a family of four and $9,056 for a family of three. The minimum wage has lost 31 percent to inflation since the last increase went into effect in 1981.

The labor market has been a problem for fifteen years. In the 1970s we created 24 million new jobs, a good performance, but so many baby-boomers, women, and immigrants entered the market that unemployment went up nonetheless. Now we are finally getting the benefit of fewer new entrants coming into the labor market, with a consequent reduction of unemployment below 6 percent for the first time since 1974 and a resultant tightening of wages at the low end in those regions with "hot" economies. Unfortunately, however, we have a new problem. The new jobs being created are not nearly as good as the ones they are replacing. Over half the new jobs created between 1975 and 1985 offer wages in the lowest third of the wage structure. The gap in pay between younger workers and older workers has widened substantially, making life particularly difficult for young families.

If the higher unemployment and weakened wage structure of the late seventies and eighties have contributed to poverty, so has the failure of benefits to keep pace. Welfare and food stamps combined (the latter is indexed, the former is not) have lost 22 percent of their real value to inflation since 1970. In only one state—Alaska—does the combination of the two bring a family up to the poverty line. In two states the two combined do not bring a family even up to half the poverty line. And in nearly half the states two-parent families do not qualify for welfare at all.[14]

Not surprisingly, therefore, the poor are getting poorer. About 40 percent of the poor, or about 13 million people, now have incomes below *half* the poverty line.[15] For a family of four this means trying to exist on less than $5,800 a year, and for a family of three we are talking about less than $4,500 a year.

The squeeze goes two ways. Not only has income not kept pace but the cost of living—in particular, the cost of housing—has skyrocketed. A quarter of all American households now pay over 30 percent of their income for housing, and 5 million households pay over 60 percent. No wonder the ranks of the homeless rise daily.

The geographic map of poverty is bimodal: disproportionate numbers of the poor in rural areas and in central cities, fewer (but not a trivial number) in the suburbs. Persistent poverty, which is a far more serious problem than is generally acknowledged, is similarly bimodal, concentrated rurally and in inner cities.

These facts having been stated, it might be useful to dispel a number of common myths about poverty. Nearly two-thirds of poor people are white. Blacks and Hispanics together make up less than 35 percent of the poor.[16] The majority of poor people do not receive welfare in the sense of cash assistance, so poverty is far from synonymous with welfare. More poor people live in families headed by married couples or men than in households headed by women. Only a small minority of the poor live in the highly concentrated poverty areas of inner cities. And the vast majority of the poor move in and out of poverty.[17]

What Have We Learned?

If the years have produced too little progress against poverty, they have at least produced some greater understanding of what we should do if we are to make a stronger effort. This greater understanding adds up to a number of lessons:

—Self-sufficiency for all of those capable of it should be the fundamental and central aim of antipoverty policy.

—The general health of the economy is highly relevant to the level of poverty. At the same time a healthy economy, either nationally or locally, will not put everyone to work. Specific strategic, structural interventions are needed, too.

—Antipoverty policy can be understood in terms of a series of concentric circles, with the broadest being macroeconomic policy, the next being generalized "prevention" that seeks to produce educated and healthy citizens, the next being targeted prevention efforts that relate specifically to populations identified as being at risk, and with the smallest concentric circle being programs and services directed at people already experiencing poverty or particular problems that typically eventuate in chronic poverty or living in environments with similarly impacted outcomes.

—A full, three-dimensional antipoverty program must involve a multitude of disciplines and areas: education, health care, new bridges to the job market, child care, housing, community economic development, law enforcement, anti-drug initiatives, social services of various kinds, and income maintenance. Moreover, an array of actors and institutions must play a role and take a measure of responsibility in ameliorating poverty: government at all levels, the business community, the nonprofit community in all of its manifestations, schools, churches, neighborhood organizations, civic leaders, and the individuals who are actually experiencing poverty.

—A newly sophisticated definition of federalism in relation to antipoverty policy produces a clearer view as to which items might be viewed as part of a national agenda and which local and, as to the national agenda, which should be nationally administered and which merely the subject of federal funding with the primary activity and even detailed agenda setting to occur locally.

—As the concentric circles narrow, policies and programs will need to sharpen in focus, both in terms of defined groups of people, especially age-specific definitions, and in geographic or spatial terms. Nearly every area of policy development, whether it be education, health care, or housing, will involve some group-specific and place-specific aspects.

—We need to be in the game for the long pull, and we need to understand that the problems go far beyond the need for added funding to include deep concerns about the performance of institutions and bureaucracies.

Self-sufficiency is the name of the game. This should be obvious but it is not obvious enough, either historically or in the activity of current politicians who pay lip service to self-sufficiency but do not propose or endorse measures that broadly promote self-sufficiency, and do not support income assistance that enables survival in the absence of adequate opportunities for self-sufficiency.

The hypocrisy or, to be more charitable, inadequacy of current talk about self-sufficiency inheres in the present wave of welfare reform. In currently pending federal legislative proposals, self-sufficiency is an explicit policy goal only for current welfare recipients, with far too little emphasis on the programs and policies that are necessary to keep people from the welfare rolls in the first place, and a fatal lack of investment in job creation or work experience slots in states continuing to experience high unemployment. On the other hand, programs such as ET in Massachusetts, GAIN in California, and REACH in New Jersey are far more sophisticated, serious efforts to promote self-sufficiency for current welfare recipients than anything ever tried before. That is all to the good, even though these efforts do not constitute a full antipoverty strategy.

A healthy economy featuring available jobs at good pay is the best antipoverty strategy, although it is not a sufficient strategy by itself. This is another obvious proposition, but it does seem to have become clearer in recent years as some labor markets have tightened around the country. The availability of jobs affects the poverty rate very directly. On the other hand, available jobs do not employ many people who lack basic skills, cannot find child care, would lose health coverage, or are not geared up to look for work for one reason or another. ET in Massachusetts and a number of other welfare-to-work endeavors around the country show that "hot" economies do not sop up structural unemployment without added initiatives. In addition, massive attention should be given to schools with concentrations of poor children and to their initial transition into the labor market so that they go to work when everyone else does and do not end up on welfare or in the street.

Concentric circles are an image that captures how we might think about antipoverty policy. The largest circle would be the overall health of the economy. The second, and an extremely important one, would be prevention. We need to focus on how our mainstream institutions—schools and health care, primarily—function to prevent poverty. This second circle includes targeted prevention on populations at risk, which will need to involve both the mainstream institutions and other, more specialized agencies. Thus, we might think of prevention as beginning with prenatal care, but to target and reach low-income pregnant women and especially pregnant teenagers we will need special financing in the form of Medicaid expansion and outreach efforts. The same would be true of neonatal care. Early childhood development would be a next stage of prevention. Here, we should emphasize expanding Head Start very substantially. Prevention then moves on to the schools, and there is a major agenda of school improvement for schools that serve disproportionate numbers of poor schoolchildren. As children get older, prevention acquires a labor market dimension. Schools serving large numbers of non-college-bound youth will need to take special steps to identify students at risk of dropping out and provide them with particular support, including job-readiness skills and part-time paid work experience during the school year that connects to the summer job program to offer year-round attention to the at-risk youth.

The third and most specialized concentric circle is really two: intervention in families with particular problems, including out-of-home care for children when family preservation cannot be accomplished; and intervention in highly impacted communities where what is done with the schools, health care, law enforcement, housing, and economic development must somehow be added into a whole that transcends the sum of its parts and becomes a community strategy, if that is possible.

A full antipoverty strategy must involve a wide array of areas and actors. We now know more than we ever have about how many factors and activities bear on poverty and about the impossibility of accomplishing sufficient progress by choosing to rely solely on either government or the private and nonprofit sectors by themselves. We seldom live up to our rhetoric, but it is at least true that, more and more, our rhetoric now captures the complexity of this matter, including the need for individuals to take a fair measure of responsibility for themselves as part of the bargain.

An antipoverty policy for the nineties will feature a new clarity about the sorting of national agendas and local agendas. The income side of the agenda, for example, needs to be much more national than it is at the present time. This has been accomplished for the elderly by the indexing of Social Security and the enactment of ssi (although it is still up to the states to decide how much to supplement the ssi minimum). But we have a long way to go for the nonelderly poor. For the working poor, national action is needed to raise the minimum wage and offer wage supplementation in the form of an enhanced Earned Income Tax Credit or otherwise. For those among the nonelderly poor who are not working, national action is needed to establish an income floor, coverage for all who are in need, and appropriate incentives and supports to encourage self-sufficiency. The idea of a national minimum is of course controversial, but to me it is obvious that a decent society must offer cash support even to people who are able to work if it is not going to offer enough jobs to go around. There are many design issues, to be sure, but I can think of no good reason to have fifty-one different welfare systems and fifty-one different payment levels as we have now.

So transfer payment policy is largely a national agenda. So is civil rights. Other aspects of antipoverty policy will involve different mixes, with action from Washington appropriate in some measure, accompanied by other contributions.

Education is a good example. The federal government provides Chapter 1, which helps disadvantaged children with basic skills, and Public Law 94–142, the Education of All Handicapped Children Act, which contributes to the education of children with special needs. Even if fully funded, though, these proven programs are not a panacea. Schools must change and school systems must change, and larger numbers of our most talented young people must be attracted to teaching. All of this requires state and local leadership and funding from both the public and private sectors. Especially needed is a strong, continuing message from the business community that it wants to hire the graduates of inner-city schools and their General Education Diploma counterparts. We need a thousand Eugene Langs who will say to inner-city high school and even younger students that if they graduate their college education will be assured. Pell Grants and low-tuition public colleges — policies of government — may send the same message, but it has a concreteness and a human dimension when a Eugene Lang sends it. And similar, strong, continuing messages are needed from black and Hispanic leaders and role models.

Low-income housing is another good example. Federal subsidy of some kind will be needed to support a public, nonprofit, and private triad of activities, but the local developers and trade unions and construction companies and foundations and churches and civic groups will have to play a role, too, and it should be done in a way that creates jobs for the residents of the community.

The question of encouraging self-sufficiency for current welfare recipients is still another good example. National policy should set standards as to minimum packages of transition services, and provide a fair share of funding. But the required package will vary from city to city. One extremely important variant is the rate of unemployment. Putting people to work is easier and cheaper in tight labor markets where private sector jobs are fairly easily available. In labor markets with high unemployment, public job creation will be a necessity rather than an option if our aim is genuinely and sincerely to put people to work. Even in tight labor markets, however, special efforts will be needed. Problems with education and training, child care, health coverage, and transportation still block employment for many even when jobs are available. So do problems of ignorance and motivation. Outreach and transition services are critical to ensure the broadest possible distribution of opportunities in tight labor markets. That is the lesson of ET, the welfare-to-work transition program in Massachusetts. ET is successfully promoting the transition to private employment for people who would otherwise not be reached. The issue is not whether to make such efforts. They are long overdue. The question is what kind of work-experience or job creation programs to add to them in cities where overall unemployment remains high.

What we now know about family structure and about geographic structure suggests some group-specific and some place-specific policies. The newly emerging facts about the devastating consequences of being born into a female-headed household suggest the need for intensive efforts to prevent that from occurring. Without any reduction in prevention efforts geared to younger children, adolescence needs a new emphasis. Pregnancy should be prevented not merely by education and family planning, but more fundamentally by bolstering the life chances of adolescents, young women and young men. This is an age-specific or group-specific emphasis, but it will also be place-specific because the young people who are at greatest risk of passing their poverty on to the next generation also happen to live in the inner city.

We are entering a period of special opportunity on these problems. The demographics are finally on our side. There is going to be a decrease in the availability of entry-level workers, although minorities will constitute a higher percentage of the pool. We are already seeing fast-food chains having to bid up wages in some locales in order to attract workers. But, sad to say, right now in all the inner cities I know about there are too many young people —though far from all—who will not participate even if jobs do become more available. Some who now end up dealing dope will seize legitimate opportunities but others will not. Bill Moyers was right at the same time that he was wrong. He was wrong in not emphasizing the current shortage of jobs and he was wrong in not emphasizing the large numbers of inner-city people who work extremely hard, often for very low wages. But he was right that there is a "culture" and an ethos in these disorganized neighborhoods, these shells where most of the middle class moved out and left behind a population which disproportionately includes the least stable and the least able.

If we are to break the cycle of poverty for the persistently poor, we are going to need a massive and sustained effort. If we are to convince young men to participate in the legal labor market, if we are to convince young women that having children in their teens is exactly what they should not want to do, the messages are going to have to be delivered over and over, and yet again. Exhortation will not suffice. The promise of the possibility of full participation in the society and its economy must be palpable and continuing, and the education necessary to fulfill the promise must be available and of clear and demonstrable quality. This endeavor will have to involve place-specific and group-specific policies.

A long-term commitment must be made to working on the problem, and the effort must extend to the malfunctioning of institutions and bureaucracies. The overtone of the sixties, the connotation, the music if not the words, was, money from the government will solve it. Putting aside the fact that the government never invested enough to come close, there was never a real sense of the complexity of the problems. Too few people saw that nearly every one of the institutions that was supposed to serve the poor was flawed in its capacity to deliver. And there was certainly a quick-fix mentality. If a program did not show results in a year, it was designated a failure and the critics called for new ideas. We are going to have to be in this one for the long pull, and we are going to have to pay attention to the performance and the competence of the institutions and agencies that are supposed to serve the poor.

Where Do We Go from Here?

Underlying an antipoverty agenda for the next four years are seven premises:

—Restoring a federal commitment to antipoverty policies
—Maximizing the overall number of jobs in the economy
—Promoting and enabling self-sufficiency and individual responsibility
—Preventing poverty
—Focusing on strategically important age-specific groups
—Providing adequate income support for people for whom work is not available or feasible and
—Encouraging and supporting new state and local roles and private sector involvement

What, then, is the antipoverty agenda for the Bush administration and the 101st Congress? I suggest the following:

—Fiscal and budgetary policies that make limited new federal spending possible while also reducing the deficit
—Doubling of Head Start over a four-year period (it now reaches about one in five of those eligible)
—Continued expansion of Medicaid until it mandates coverage for all mothers and children living in poverty and offers reimbursement to states which decide to cover all mothers and children with incomes somewhat above the poverty line, an agenda on which surprising progress has already been made over the past eight years
—Comprehensive child-care legislation that would assist in the establishment and funding of quality child care on a sliding-scale fee basis, with the specific design and provider mix to be determined locally
—A new low-income housing initiative that would provide assistance for public, nonprofit, and private involvement in increasing the supply of low-income housing
—Welfare reform legislation to create a national minimum benefit, mandated assistance to two-parent families, and a full package of transition services for employment, including job creation and work experience in areas of high unemployment
—An Adolescent Life Chances Act to encourage schools, employers, and social service agencies to work with at-risk teens on work experience, job readiness, and teen pregnancy prevention
—Tough anti-drug and anti-gang law enforcement activities and increased

emphasis on drug education and treatment efforts
—Increased funding for programs that work, like Chapter I in the area
  of education, WIC (the Women, Infant, and Children Special Nutrition
  Program), and foster-care prevention services.

This is far from a complete list of what should be done over a period of
time. It is a feasible agenda for the very short run.

Beyond the specifics, however, we need national leadership. We need a
president who tells the American people this is important. We will need
money from Congress. But in addition to being a national agenda, it is an
agenda that needs to involve actors and actions going far beyond the national government. Dealing with the persistent poverty in our cities is certainly a national agenda, but it is also, far more than we ever recognized in
the past, a local agenda, bound up and tied up with the leadership and the
institutions of each and every city in America. So a president who will lead
us is vitally important. We need to do our very best. A president who cares
and communicates his caring regularly and repeatedly is critical to a revitalization of real national concern about poverty in America.

5

Rental Housing in the United States: A Focus on Metropolitan and Urban Areas

William C. Apgar, Jr.

The emergence of the growing rental payments problem and the growth of homelessness has caught many policy analysts by surprise and spurred the nation to rethink the national commitment to the national goal of decent and affordable housing. As part of this reexamination, this chapter presents a newly developed price index for residential rents and relates observed patterns of rent increases to changes in housing supply-and-demand conditions in the nation's metropolitan areas.

The chapter suggests that some broad generalizations go a long way in explaining the observed patterns of rent trends over the past two decades. For much of the 1960s and early 1970s the movement of population and jobs away from the core of the nation's large metropolitan areas combined with the construction of a large number of subsidized rental units in core areas to create an excess supply of rental housing in many market areas, especially the low-quality housing submarkets serving low- and moderate-income households. As a result, for much of this period increases in real rents were modest, and disinvestment and abandonment of low-cost existing rental stock was high.

Since 1980 the supply-and-demand situation in residential rental markets has shifted dramatically. Having lagged behind national trends for decades, population and employment growth accelerated in metropolitan areas in the early 1980s. Key to this turnaround is the apparent stabilization of the employment base in the core counties of the largest metropolitan areas. With the diminished supply of low-cost rental units that resulted from the high levels of abandonment in the 1960s and 1970s and the added demand pressure that resulted from rapid increases in the number of households using Section 8 Certificates, Housing Vouchers, or other types of demand subsidies, the situation was ripe for a rapid increase in rents in metropolitan areas.

This chapter begins with a discussion of recent trends in residential rents and continues with a detailed analysis of the likely determinants of these rapid rent increases. The third section presents some brief comments on the effect of growing rents on the nation's poverty-level population. The chapter concludes with some observations about the difficult policy choices that must be made if the nation is to address the growing rental-payments burden of many of its most economically disadvantaged citizens.

Historical Trends in Residential Rents

A casual assessment of the residential rent component of the Consumer Price Index (CPI) suggests that in the 1970s rents fell sharply in real terms. Detailed analysis of rent trends now ongoing at the Joint Center for Housing Studies suggests that the residential rent component of CPI presents a distorted view of recent rent trends. The Bureau of Labor Statistics (BLS) estimation procedures do not control for changes in the quality of the dwelling unit due to depreciation. As a result, the widely used BLS residential-rent component of the CPI is not a true price index because it traces rent trends for units not of a constant level but rather of a gradually decreasing quality.

This section briefly describes the BLS estimates of residential rents and presents estimates of a residential-rent index adjusted to account for deterioration of the housing inventory. These estimates suggest that properly measured real rents move with the business cycle, falling during periods of declining housing-market activity and increasing during periods of cyclical increase. Real rents did fall slightly in the early 1970s, but since 1981 they have increased by nearly 16 percent nationwide and now stand at their highest levels in more than two decades.

Renter Costs: Biased Data Distort
Historical Analysis

Numerous studies of housing trends over the past two decades examined the residential-rent component of the CPI prepared by the BLS and concluded that real rents are rising modestly now, but have yet to return to peak levels achieved in the late 1960s. (Note: For a summary of these studies, see John C. Weicher, Kevin E. Villani, and Elizabeth Roistacher, editors, *Rental Housing: Is There a Crisis?* (Washington, D.C.: Urban Institute Press, 1981).

Despite a sophisticated data collection effort and an equally sophisticated series of adjustments performed by the BLS, CPI data present a distorted view of recent rent trends. As first noted by Ira S. Lowry of the RAND Corporation, the CPI rent component is derived from information obtained for a sample of residential dwelling units, which are resurveyed each year. For units continuing in the sample, adjustments are made only for major changes in the level of services provided by the property owner or changes in the level of rent subsidy. As a result, changes attributable to depreciation of the dwelling unit are not accounted for; neither are cost increases on utilities paid directly by the tenant. (For further discussion, see Ira S. Lowry, "Inflation Indexes for Rental Housing," Working Note N–1832–HUD, Rand Corporation, Santa Monica, California, 1982. See also William C. Apgar, Jr., "The Leaky Boat: A Housing Problem Remains," in Peter D. Salins, editor, *Housing America's Poor* (Chapel Hill: University of North Carolina Press, 1987.)

The failure to adjust the CPI rent index for depreciation produces a systematic downward bias in the estimate of residential rents relative to the prices of other components of the CPI. A true price index tracks the price of a particular good or service of constant quality and characteristics. The BLS has found no practical way to adjust the index of residential rent changes for the deterioration in housing quality that inevitably occurs as a dwelling unit ages. Based on a review of the work of Lowry and others, I assume that deterioration or obsolesence reduces the amount of housing services provided by the property owner by three-quarters of 1 percent (.0075) per year and use this assumption to estimate a revised residential rent series. (Note: A study by William C. Randolph reviews alternative empirical estimates of the likely magnitude of the bias. See "Housing Depreciation and Aging Bias in the Consumer Price Index," U.S. Department of Labor, Bureau of Labor Statistics, Working Paper 166, April 1987.)

In addition to concern about the ability of the CPI to correctly measure residential rents, there has been concern about CPI measures of homeownership costs. Prior to 1983 the CPI homeowner's cost measure was based primarily on the cash cost of homeownership, where the cash cost is defined to be the sum of several ongoing expenses (including outlays for mortgage interest payments, fuel and utility costs, maintenance and repairs, real estate taxes, and insurance) less the income-tax savings associated with owning a home.

For much of the 1970s such cash-cost measures substantially overstated the total cost of homeownership, particularly to the extent that equity buildup (increases in the value of owner-occupied housing) served to offset high cash costs. Since homeownership costs were a major element in the overall

CPI for all urban consumers, the biased measure of homeownership costs yielded not only a distorted view of the trends in homeownership costs, but a biased view of the aggregate cost of living for all urban consumers.

In 1983, after several years of experimentation, the BLS introduced an improved measure of homeownership costs based on the concept of rental-cost equivalent. The measure was chosen from among several alternative methods for estimating the total cost of homeownership, where total cost includes ongoing cash expenses adjusted for the tax consequences of owning a home as well as the indirect savings realized by the homeowner from house price appreciation and the resulting equity buildup. The new measure was termed CPI–UX, with the "x" included to distinguish the new measure of homeowner costs from the earlier flawed measure. Properly measured (adjusting for increases in the homeowner's equity), the index of prices for all goods and services purchased by all urban consumers increased by 99 percent from 1970 to 1980, which is noticeably slower than the 113 percent increase recorded by the old CPI measure.

While the above discussion is somewhat technical, it has an important bearing on historical analysis of trends in real rents, where real rents are defined as the price of rental housing relative to the price of all goods and services. Prior to 1983 BLS-based measures of real residential rents were distorted by the failure to account for depreciation of rental units and by the overstatement of the aggregate price increases of all goods and services resulting from the overstatement of the homeowner's cost. As indicated in figure 5.1, the adjustment to the measure of residential rents and the adjustment to the measure of total CPI combine to produce a radically different view of long-term trends in real residential rents. In figure 5.1 the BLS Rent Index uses the unadjusted measure of residential rent and is deflated by the all-items CPI measure that was in effect prior to 1983. By contrast, the "Revised Rent Index" employs the measure of residential rents adjusted for depreciation deflated by the revised price index for all goods and services, the CPI-UX.

The difference between the two measures of real rents is striking. Note that while the old index implies that real rents fell by close to 16 percent for the period 1967 to 1981, the revised index shows a more modest decline of 7 percent. Both the old and new indices show increases in real rents since 1981. Unlike the old measure, however, the new measure implies that real rents have increased by nearly 16 percent since 1981 and now stand at their highest levels in two decades.

Figure 5.1   Alternative Measures/Residential Rents (1977 = 100)

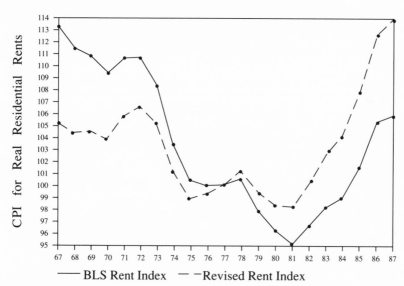

——— BLS Rent Index   — —Revised Rent Index

Revised Estimates of Real Rents

Figure 5.2 presents estimates of real gross and contract rents for a representative unit with the characteristics of the median-priced rental unit in 1977. Contract rent is equivalent to the BLS concept of residential rent —the monthly payment to the property owner for housing services. Gross rent includes not only contract rent but payments for fuel, water, sewage, and other utilities.

Real rents (adjusted for inflation) tend to move with the business cycle, falling during downturns and rising during expansions. Despite a sharp jump in rental vacancies, since 1981 contract rents have increased 16 percent faster than the rate of inflation and now stand at their highest levels in more than two decades. Gross rents have moved up as well but somewhat more modestly because of the slowdown in energy-price inflation. Nevertheless, the rise in gross rents is still pronounced: up 14 percent from 1981 to 1987.

Gross rent is seemingly the more comprehensive measure, but note that changes in contract rent have considerable analytical significance. Gross rent, for example, can change as a result of shifting energy prices or other factors that have little to do with the long-run cost of housing capital. Policy analysts should note, however, that the persistent increase in contract rent during a period of substantial new construction suggests that there has

Figure 5.2   Rental Costs

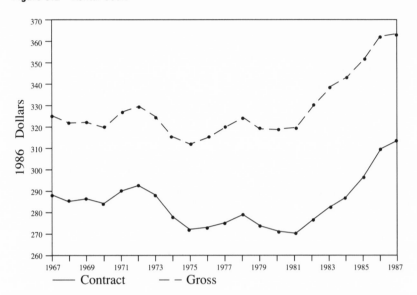

been a long-term increase in the rental price of housing capital. Unlike a run-up of energy costs, such a long-term trend is not quickly reversed. Over the past six years the cost of supplying rental housing appears to have drifted upward, a movement that can only point to continuing high rent levels in the years ahead.

The broad national price trends presented in this essay mask the complex price movements that take place in distinct housing submarkets. As indicated in figure 5.3, the Northeast and the West, areas of vigorous economic expansion, have witnessed the sharpest rent hikes during the decade. From 1981 to 1987 real gross rents in the West increased by nearly 19 percent, while those in the Northeast rose approximately 17 percent. More modest rent increases occurred in the Midwest and South.

In addition to these broad regional trends the Joint Center for Housing Studies is now assessing rent trends for selected metropolitan areas and different housing-quality submarkets. As indicated in table 5.1, real rents in Boston increased by 25.4 percent from 1981 to 1986, while rent increases for the same period in Buffalo were a more modest 12.3 percent. In the West real rents advanced in San Francisco by 36.3 percent, far in excess of the 15.6 percent increase recorded for Denver. Despite these variations, significant real rent increases were recorded in sixteen of the seventeen metropolitan areas depicted in table 5.1. Only in Houston, a metro-

Figure 5.3   Regional Rental Costs

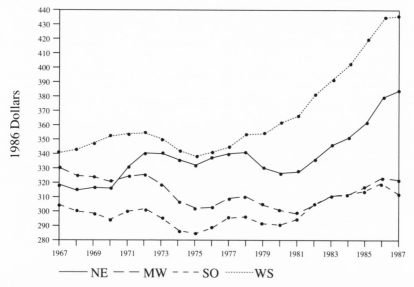

politan area noted for substantial overbuilding of rental housing, have real
rents held at or slightly below their 1981 levels.

Substantial variations in rent increases also exist within any given metropolitan area. Available data suggest that sharp as it has been, the growth in
median rents understates the rent increases experienced at the low end of
the market. New construction and major rehabilitation have added to the
housing supply at the upper end of the market, while housing disinvestment
and abandonment continue to drain units away from the bottom. The result
is a pattern for most market areas of modest rent increases for the best-
quality housing but substantial rent increases at the low end of the market.
(Note: For further discussion, see William C. Apgar, Jr., with Ruijue Peng
and Jennifer Olson, "Recent Trends in Real Rents," Working Paper W87-5,
Joint Center for Housing Studies, Harvard University, 1987.)

Housing Market Dynamics and Metropolitan Area Rent Trends

Recent growth in residential rents has caught many analysts by surprise. Yet
in light of the shifting fortunes of the core areas of the largest metropolitan
areas, these trends are perfectly understandable. For much of the 1960s
and early 1970s the movement of population and jobs away from the core
areas of the nation's largest metropolitan areas and the construction of a

Table 5.1 Percentage Change in Real Residential Rent for Selected
Metropolitan Areas: 1981–1986

Northeast		Midwest	
Boston	25.4%	Chicago	18.0%
Buffalo	12.3	Cleveland	12.6
New York	17.9	Detroit	11.1
Philadelphia	24.3	Kansas City, Mo.	19.2
Pittsburgh	12.3	Minneapolis/St. Paul	16.8
West		South	
Honolulu	17.7%	Atlanta	24.2%
Denver	15.6	Dallas	18.4
Los Angeles	29.4	Houston	−1.4
San Francisco	36.3		

Source: Joint Center for Housing Studies Estimates based on data from U.S. Bureau of Labor
Statistics.

large number of subsidized rental units in core areas created somewhat of
an excess supply of rental housing in many market areas, especially in the
low-quality housing submarkets serving low- and moderate-income households. As a result, for much of this period increases in real rents were
modest and, as noted earlier, disinvestment and abandonment of central-
city housing was high.

By contrast, rental markets in the 1980s were dominated by a different
dynamic. Starting in the late 1970s, the shifting emphasis in federal housing assistance efforts toward demand-oriented programs added purchasing
power to the low end of the rental market. Growth in metropolitan area
population and employment, and particularly growth in the high-density
core metropolitan areas, further added to demand pressure. Combined with
the continued selective abandonment of dwelling units in low-quality neighborhoods, these shifts in demand appear to be the root cause behind the
shift from rent declines in the 1970s to rent increases in the 1980s. This
section examines the underlying shifts in supply-and-demand factors before
turning to a more detailed assessment of the implications of recent rent
increases on the well-being of the nation's low- and moderate-income
households.

The Decline of Metropolitan Areas in the 1960s and 1970s

The decline of major metropolitan areas in the United States during the 1960s and 1970s, particularly in the high-density core areas of the nation's largest metropolitan areas, is well documented. While some analysts focused on the revitalization and gentrification of selected inner-city neighborhoods, the reality for central cities of major metropolitan areas was a steady loss of population and jobs to the suburbs of older metropolitan areas in the Northeast and Midwest, to the newly growing metropolitan areas of the South and West, and to nonmetropolitan areas across the country.

Since 1980 metropolitan areas have experienced noticeable improvements in population and employment growth. While the shifting fortunes of individual cities and metropolitan areas are not well understood, the resurgence of economic activity in the central portions of the nation's largest metropolitan areas appears not only to have slowed the long-term decentralization process but also, and more important, has added to the pressure on the price of rental housing.

Figure 5.4 seeks to place recent trends in metropolitan population growth and decline into an appropriate historical framework. Using population es-

Figure 5.4   Annual Population Growth Rate

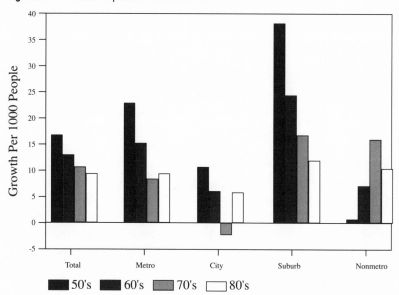

Table 5.2 Decade Gross Loss Rate for Conventional Inventory,
1960–1970 and 1970–1980 (Loss as Percentages of Initial Period Stock)

Region	Central City		Suburban	
	1960–70	1970–80	1960–70	1970–80
Northeast	10.6	11.9	5.4	3.6
North Central	13.0	10.9	7.0	4.0
South	15.6	8.1	10.2	6.1
West	12.3	6.1	8.9	3.2
Total	12.9	9.4	7.5	4.2

Notes: Conventional inventory is total year-round units less mobile homes. Estimates for the 1970s derived from AHS data for period 1973–1980.

timates from the 1950, 1960, 1970, and 1980 censuses and Census Bureau estimates for 1984, the figure provides estimates of the annual rates of population growth from 1950 to 1984. In addition to total population growth, figure 5.4 also presents growth-rate estimates for the central-city and suburban portion of metropolitan areas as well as for nonmetropolitan areas. In each instance the growth rates in figure 5.4 are based on the central-city and metropolitan area definitions that were in effect in 1970, approximately the midpoint of the period under consideration. (For further discussion of these data, see William C. Apgar, Jr., "The Decentralization of Population and Employment: 1950 to 1984," Working Paper W86-5, Joint Center for Housing Studies, Harvard University.)

As figure 5.4 illustrates, the recent increases in rates of growth for metropolitan areas result from an increase in the growth rate of central-city populations that more than offsets a decline in the rate of suburban population growth. Despite the movement of manufacturing and other basic employment out of central cities in the 1950s and 1960s, the strong flow of migrants from rural to urban areas—particularly the movement of rural blacks—allowed central-city populations to grow in the 1950s and 1960s at modest rates, although they were below the national average.

During the 1970s, continued population gains recorded by smaller central cities throughout the nation and by the larger central cities of the South and West were unable to offset the substantial population declines experienced by the largest central cities in the Northeast and Midwest. As a result, the nation's central cities lost nearly 1.6 million people during the 1970s.

Table 5.2   (continued)

Non-SMSA		Total	
1960–70	1970–80	1960–70	1970–80
6.7	6.6	7.8	7.3
9.8	9.1	10.2	7.9
13.1	11.5	13.3	9.0
15.2	9.8	11.5	5.5
11.3	9.4	10.7	7.6

Source: U.S. Bureau of Census, *Components of Inventory Change*, 1960 to 1970; U.S. Bureau of Census, *Annual Housing Survey*, 1973–1980.

Metropolitan Decline and Housing Disinvestment

The massive loss of population had a devastating effect on central-city housing markets. While there is no precise method for measuring the extent of housing disinvestment that occurred in the 1960s and 1970s, there can be no doubt that massive disinvestment occurred. Simple economic theory suggests that the level of maintenance expenditures and investment in the existing inventory for a given unit depends on the cost of maintenance relative to the expected return. In depressed inner-city neighborhoods experiencing high vacancy rates and little growth in real rents, there will be little incentive to provide even routine maintenance, let alone major improvements. As the unit deteriorates, the probability that it will be lost to the inventory grows. As maintenance slips, the unit becomes uninhabitable and is either demolished, abandoned by the owner, or closed down by public authorities as being in violation of local health and safety codes.

Table 5.2 presents estimates of gross decade loss rates for conventional housing inventory for the 1960s and 1970s. Here, a decade loss rate is defined as the proportion of conventional housing (total housing less mobile homes) that is removed from the housing inventory (abandoned, destroyed, converted to nonresidential uses, or otherwise removed). The table reveals the persistently high levels of inventory loss in the 1960s and 1970s. During the 1960s some 6.4 million housing units were lost from the conventional housing inventory, a loss of 10.7 percent of the total stock of conventional housing at the start of the decade. Though the loss rate fell during the 1970s, in absolute terms inventory losses remained high, with some 5.3 million units lost. (For a further discussion of inventory loss rates, see William C. Apgar, Jr., H. James Brown, George Masnick, and

John Pitkin, *The Housing Outlook: 1980– 1990* (New York: Praeger Publishers, 1985.)

The data in table 5.2 are consistent with the pattern of metropolitan development discussed earlier. Throughout the 1970s losses remained high in central cities in the Northeast and North Central regions, as the housing market in these areas continued to adjust to the loss of population and economic base. Particularly hard-hit were older residential neighborhoods, as evidenced by the high rates of loss among dwelling units built before 1950. In the 1970s, 12.5 percent of all units built before 1950 were lost. In Northeast and Midwest central cities, areas that contained the largest share of this older housing, loss rates of the pre-1950 stock jumped to 15 percent.

Metropolitan Revitalization in the 1980s

No sooner were analysts coming to grips with the cause and the extent of the decline of housing and economic activity in major metropolitan areas than the growth of metropolitan areas began to accelerate. As heralded in the *Washington Post* on September 22, 1984, "after a decade of fleeing to small cities and rural areas, Americans are moving back to the cities again, setting off a new round of growth in the nation's metropolitan areas." Whether the renewed growth was a result of expanded numbers of in-migrants or the result of an increased ability of metropolitan areas to hold on to their existing population remains to be seen, but there can be little doubt that the 1980s saw a resurgence in metropolitan area growth. Compared to the annual average growth rate of 8.5 people per thousand of the 1970s, metropolitan population growth averaged 10.3 persons per thousand for the first six years of the 1980s. Annual data suggest, moreover, that the growth of metropolitan areas is gathering momentum, with annual average metropolitan growth averaging 11.8 persons per thousand from 1984 to 1986.

A recently completed analysis by Nancy McArdle of the Joint Center for Housing Studies presents a clear picture of the nature of the rebound in metropolitan area growth. Using population and employment data for each of the nation's approximately 3,100 counties, McArdle examines growth trends for counties classified both in terms of metropolitan and nonmetropolitan status, but also by density. As McArdle observes, metropolitan classification is useful for some purposes but can bring misleading conclusions. Counties defined as metropolitan are a heterogeneous lot, ranging from Kings County, New York, with a population of 2.2 million people to Los Alamos County, New Mexico, with a population of just 17,599 people.

Table 5.3 Total Metropolitan County Population and Employment Growth by Density Class (Annual Average Growth Rates per Thousand, 1970–80, 1980–86)

Metro County Density Class	Number of Counties	Total in Thousands			Growth	
		1970	1980	1986	1970–80	1980–86
Metro Population						
Class 5 (High Density)	36	40,184	37,645	37,925	−6.5	1.2
Class 4	52	39,662	42,530	45,240	7.0	10.3
Class 3	144	37,973	43,620	46,640	13.9	11.2
Classes 1 and 2 (Low Density)	226	22,797	29,293	32,994	25.1	19.8
Total	458	140,616	153,088	162,799	8.5	10.3
Metro Employment						
Class 5 (High Density)	36	20,581	21,242	22,836	3.2	12.1
Class 4	52	17,977	23,444	26,622	26.6	21.2
Class 3	144	16,610	21,829	24,780	27.3	21.1
Classes 1 and 2 (Low Density)	226	8,915	12,740	14,656	35.7	23.4
Total	458	64,083	79,255	88,894	21.2	19.1

Source: Joint Center for Housing Studies, Harvard University, County Data Base.

Recognizing these problems, the Joint Center County Data Base also classifies counties by density class, ranging from density class 1 (the 2,268 counties with less than sixty-seven persons per square mile in 1970) to density class 5 (the thirty-seven counties with more than 1,730 persons per square mile). Though high-density counties are more visible, the 2,268 low-density counties had roughly the same total population in 1970 as did the thirty-seven high-density counties. (For discussion, see Nancy McArdle, "Population and Employment Decentralization Trends as of 1986," Working Paper W88-5, Joint Center for Housing Studies, Harvard University.)

Analysis of data for individual counties demonstrates that the rebound in growth in the aggregate figures for all metropolitan areas is intricately linked to the stabilization of population and employment in the largest, most densely settled metropolitan areas. As indicated in table 5.3, the highest-density metropolitan counties have shifted from losing 6.4 persons per thousand annually to gaining 1.4 persons per thousand annually from 1980 to 1986.

Table 5.4 Regional Metropolitan County Population and Employment by Density
Class (Average Annual Growth Rates per Thousand, 1970–80, 1980–86)

Metro County Density Class	Northeast		Midwest	
	1970–80	1980–86	1970–80	1980–86
Metro Population				
Class 5 (High Density)	−9.5	0.9	−8.1	−2.1
Class 4	1.3	1.7	3.7	3.4
Class 3	5.3	3.5	6.1	3.1
Classes 1, 2 (Low Density)	6.2	3.2	14.6	4.8
Total Population	−2.5	1.8	1.6	1.6
Metro Employment				
Class 5 (High Density)	−4.5	14.2	2.2	5.6
Class 4	19.0	23.0	20.5	16.3
Class 3	14.9	16.2	20.5	10.2
Classes 1, 2 (Low Density)	13.7	20.3	24.0	11.9
Total Employment	6.4	17.4	13.5	10.1

Source: Joint Center for Housing Studies, Harvard University, County Data Base.

More impressive was the rebound in employment. While all metropolitan
areas showed a small slowdown in total employment growth resulting from
heavy employment losses in the recession years of the early 1980s, annual
employment growth in high-density counties expanded from a meager 3.2
percent increase per thousand workers in the 1970s to a 12.1 percent increase in the 1980s. While these high-density core metropolitan counties
still display below-average growth, the resurgence of growth implies that
these areas are no longer the drag on the total metropolitan economy that
they were in the 1970s.

Renewed growth in high-density areas is found in all regions of the country,
but nowhere is the phenomenon more striking than in the high-density
counties of the Northeast. As indicated in table 5.4, having lost population
at a rapid rate in the 1970s these counties are now holding their own and
even experiencing some slight population growth. While population growth
is not enough to suggest that the long-term process of decentralization has

Table 5.4   (continued)

	South		West	
	1970–80	1980–86	1970–80	1980–86
	− 3.1	2.2	15.6	15.9
	14.1	18.0	7.8	14.7
	19.8	15.9	23.1	20.0
	29.1	24.7	31.9	26.4
	17.9	17.3	19.5	20.1
	9.7	13.7	38.3	23.3
	36.6	26.7	27.1	17.0
	32.4	25.7	40.9	29.3
	35.6	23.8	46.4	29.1
	31.4	24.4	36.6	23.9

been reversed, it is sufficient to suggest that these areas are now able to hold on to a larger share of their population. Key to this turnabout in the Northeast has been steady employment growth. While each of the county groupings in the Northeast depicted in table 5.4 experienced growth, acceleration of employment growth in the high-density counties is truly remarkable. After losing some 4.5 jobs per thousand annually in the 1970s, employment growth in the 1980s soared to 14.2 jobs per thousand.

The Changing Orientation
of Housing-Assistance Efforts

These changes in population and employment growth trends were matched by equally pronounced changes in the level and nature of housing-assistance efforts targeted to households living in metropolitan areas. Historically, housing-assistance efforts in the United States relied upon the new construction of units for low- and moderate-income occupancy. More recently, housing policy in the United States has come to rely more heavily on housing subsidies provided to tenants living in existing, privately owned housing units. Use of demand-side subsidies has grown steadily since the Section 8 program was established in 1974. Following the recommendations of the President's Commission on Housing report in 1982, the demand-side approach was central to the housing policy pronouncements of the Reagan administration.

In his review of the policy implications of the increased use of demand-side subsidies, John Weicher notes that the use of demand subsidies raises several potential problems, including the possibility that added demand subsidies will generate rent increases not only for participants but also for all low-income households in metropolitan areas. Weicher begins with a review of the Experimental Housing Allowance Program (EHAP), a major demonstration project conducted in the mid-1970s to assess the likely market impacts of a universal housing-demand subsidy program. Weicher also compares the EHAP findings with the results of modeling efforts conducted by the Urban Institute and U.S. Department of Housing and Urban Development. Weicher concludes that even a universal housing allowance program would result in a rent increase of no more than 5 percent, and that increases of this magnitude would occur only in those market areas where initial housing quality is low and the program-induced demand increases are focused on a smaller supply of decent housing. (John C. Weicher, "The Voucher/Production Debate," a paper prepared for the Housing Policy Project of the Center for Real Estate Development, MIT, Cambridge, Mass., April 1988.)

Weicher's estimates of the rent increases that are likely to result from greater reliance on housing-demand subsidies is arguably low. He concedes that his estimates of the modest rent increases relate to long-run changes in rents, that is, changes over a period of five to ten years. According to his paper, in the short run no housing program "works" well in a tight market with limited supplies of housing that meet program standards. Sudden program-induced expansion of housing demand will drive rents up until supply responds to meet the demand change. Yet, as Weicher correctly observes, housing suppliers are slow to respond in the face of observed rent increases. Thus even Weicher concedes that in the short run, a housing-allowance program could trigger sizable increases in selected market areas.

These later comments by Weicher are broadly consistent with the view of housing market dynamics represented in the modeling work of John Kain and William C. Apgar, Jr. Their assessment of the effect of the market effects of housing allowances suggests that a universal housing-allowance program might trigger significant rent increases for both recipients and nonrecipients, as well as encourage disinvestment and abandonment of units that do not meet program standards. These results flow directly from a model that explicitly represents housing market dynamics as a disequilibrium process. The Kain/Apgar model further recognizes that the responsiveness of housing investment to changes in rents is complicated by the presence of a number of market imperfections, ranging from inability of property owners to secure financing for projects in blighted neighborhoods to neighborhood externalities that link the profitability of any given housing investment to a range of neighborhood amenities beyond the control of individual property owners. In effect, this modeling approach builds on the notion that the housing market is best viewed as a series of short-run supply adjustments that by their very nature tend to lag behind the underlying shifts in demand. (For a more complete discussion of the modeling approach, see Kain and Apgar, *Housing and Neighborhood Dynamics* [Cambridge, Mass.: Harvard University Press, 1985].)

As these comments suggest, while the long-run consequences of a housing allowance may be minimal, the short-run effects may be substantial. Housing economists will undoubtedly continue to debate the effect on market rents of the shift to greater reliance on housing-demand subsidies. It is striking to note that the areas with the most substantial increases in residential rents in the early 1980s had the profile that the Kain/Apgar and other models suggested would make them most vulnerable to demand-subsidy program-induced rent increases. Following a history of abandonment and disinvestment, and limited capacity to produce new units, the core areas of major metropolitan areas in the Northeast were particularly ill-suited to absorb the additional demand pressure that resulted from the greater reliance on housing-demand subsidies. It seems more than likely, therefore, that the rapid expansion of housing-demand subsidies in these areas in the late 1970s was a contributing factor to increases in rents.

New Construction and Rent Levels

If the effect of housing subsidies on rent levels is difficult to assess, so is the effect of new construction on rents. One thing does seem clear: despite high levels of apartment construction, real rents have moved up sharply since 1981. In explaining the phenomenon of high levels of apartment construction, growing vacancies, and rising rents, it is important to note that much of the increase in vacant units is concentrated in selected housing submarkets. As widely reported, the most rapid buildup in rental vacancies has been in the South. In addition, vacancies have tended to cluster in new

Figure 5.5   Rental Vacant Units by Current Rent, United States, 1981–1985

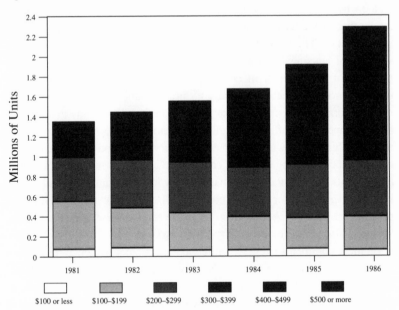

Rental Vacant Units by Real Rent, United States, 1981–1988 (1985 = 100)

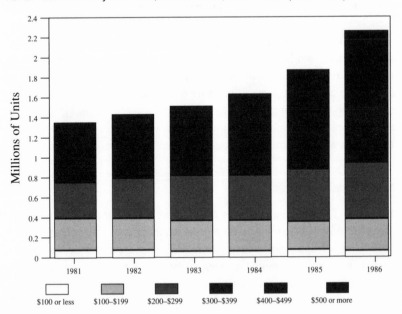

Source: U.S. Bureau of the Census, Current Housing Reports, Series H-111, *Vacancy Rates and Characteristics of Housing: Annual Statistics*, 1981–1986.

housing units as opposed to older ones. Finally, since much of the new rental construction is in developments with five or more units, much of the increase in vacancies is in buildings with five or more apartments. Since 1981 rental vacancies have grown from 1.54 million to 2.66 million. Of this increase, 719,000 or 65 percent resulted from increased vacancies in structures with five or more units, and 837,000 or 75 percent were in units built since 1970.

In theory, submarkets with high vacancies may draw households away from other submarkets, and the vacancy rate will tend to equalize across submarkets. The data presented in figure 5.5 suggest that this has not happened. Rather than reduce rents in order to expand occupancy, many vacant newly constructed units remain on the market at relatively high rents. Measured in current dollar terms, all the increase in rental vacancies for the past five years has been for units renting for $300 per month or more. Even measured in real terms, 90 percent of the increase in vacant units has occurred in units renting for more than that price.

These data confirm that the high rate of new construction of apartment units in the past several years has done little to expand the supply of units available at low and moderate rents. Since much rental construction is focused in particular metropolitan areas, and within metropolitan areas in large apartment complexes serving the high-rent submarkets, high rates of aggregate vacancy have only a limited effect on checking increases in median residential rents. The result is a period of both increasing aggregate vacancies and increasing median rents.

The Declining Supply of Low-Cost Units

Despite the recent high levels of apartment construction, the supply of low-cost units continues to shrink. Even adjusting for inflation, the number of units renting for less than $300 per month dropped by nearly 1 million between 1974 and 1983; the number of units with rents above $400, in contrast, increased by 4.5 million to 10.2 million.

The loss of low-rent units involved two distinct dynamics. Some fell into disrepair and were removed from the stock. In selected urban neighborhoods, excess supply conditions still prevail, and the resulting depressed market rents are simply insufficient to cover the costs of operation and maintenance. Yet the revitalization of core-area economies and the added purchasing power provided by expanded housing-demand subsidies imply that other formerly low-cost units—especially those located in the stronger housing markets of the Northeast and West—are being lost to a second dynamic as

Figure 5.6   Total Rehab Expenditures by Unit Type (Billions of 1987 Dollars)

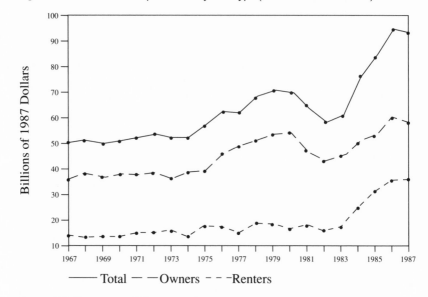

Source: U.S. Department of Commerce, Construction Reports, Residential Alterations and Repairs, Series C-50.

they are upgraded to serve subsidized tenants or to attract higher-income occupants. (Note: The finding concerning the decline in the stock of low-rent units has been confirmed by a number of analysts. See, for example, Cushing N. Dolbeare, "Low Income Housing Needs," Report Prepared for the National Low Income Housing Coalition, Washington, D.C., 1987.)

It is difficult to measure the extent to which low-cost housing continues to be abandoned, on the one hand, or to be revitalized and upgraded, on the other. Recent data on expenditures for rehabilitation suggest, however, that the extent of rental rehabiliation is significant. As indicated in figure 5.6, after virtually no growth in real terms from 1972 to 1982, rental rehabilitation expenditures (as measured by the U.S. Bureau of the Census) more than doubled from 1982 to 1987. Rental rehabilitation expenditures increased in all regions of the country, but particularly sharp percentage increases were recorded in the Northeast. Apparently, the growth of employment in core areas and associated growth in real rents has made investment in private-market rental rehabilitation profitable again in many metropolitan areas, a fact that can only serve to further diminish the supply of low-cost rental housing in the years ahead.

Rental Housing and the Poor

Over the past two decades slower real income growth and higher real housing costs have exacerbated the problems of low- and moderate-income households. Gross rent as a share of income rose sharply from 1974 to 1987 and remains at historically high levels. Even though they pay a large share of their incomes for rent, many residents still live in poor-quality housing. Moreover, most of these households must face the growing rental payments burden alone: available rental assistance is simply inadequate in light of the growing number of low-income renter households.

This section begins with a discussion of the changing composition of renter households and continues with an assessment of changes in rent burden. It concludes with a discussion of recent trends in federal housing-assistance efforts and the extent to which current subsidies are sufficient to shield poverty-level renter households from the ravages of high and growing residential rents.

Changing Composition of Renter Households

Rental housing is increasingly the home of the nation's lower-income households, while higher-income households increasingly choose to own a home. Since 1974 the homeownership rate fell for households with incomes less than $10,000 (again measured in 1986 dollars). By comparison, the number of homeowners with real incomes above $50,000 grew by 4 million over this period and the homeownership rate increased from 86.2 to 89.1 percent.

The growth in the number of low-income renter households has widened the income gap between owners and renters. Between 1972 and 1982 the median income of renters fell by 21 percent, from $18,000 to $14,000. With the economic expansion of the mid-1980s the median renter income improved slightly but not enough to reduce poverty among renter households. From 1983 to 1987 the number of poverty-level renter households increased by 300,000 to 7.5 million. By contrast, the number of poverty-level owner households fell by 500,000 to 4.5 million. Thus, by 1987, 63 percent of all poverty-level households lived in rental housing.

As a group, renter households, then, are younger and poorer, while homeowners are older and richer. From 1974 the median income of renters aged twenty-five to thirty-four fell by 18.5 percent (table 5.5), while the median income of renters aged twenty-five or less was 25.8 percent lower than real incomes of young renters in the mid-1970s. Rental housing is also increasingly becoming the home of the nation's children. Between

Table 5.5 Number of Households and Household Income by Age, Tenure, and Household Type

	Owner			
	Number (in Thousands)		Median Income (1986 Dollars)	
	1974	1987	1974	1987
Household Head under 25				
Single	81	142	13,099	14,307
Married with Children	658	270	23,231	17,822
Married No Children	507	250	26,715	26,196
Single Parent with Children	48	52	11,523	8,920
Other Households	83	119	21,721	16,099
Total	1,377	833	23,419	18,934
Household Head 25–34				
Single	300	895	24,160	22,604
Married with Children	5,695	5,489	31,362	32,839
Married No Children	1,073	1,658	38,563	41,126
Single Parent with Children	446	646	16,954	17,302
Other Households	116	549	29,461	28,769
Total	7,630	9,237	31,220	32,006
Household Head 35–44				
Single	269	933	23,312	27,512
Married with Children	6,765	8,020	37,055	40,146
Married No Children	723	1,603	37,169	48,020
Single Parent with Children	692	1,312	22,525	22,902
Other Households	204	639	28,913	33,114
Total	8,653	12,507	35,284	38,044
Household Head 45–64				
Single	1,955	2,642	12,974	15,691
Married with Children	5,750	4,047	37,402	40,186
Married No Children	8,771	10,944	32,755	37,454
Single Parent with Children	688	681	21,493	20,462
Other Households	1,426	2,090	23,231	23,369
Total	18,590	20,404	30,965	33,168
Household Head 65 or Older				
Single	3,312	5,230	7,434	8,997
Married	5,070	7,421	15,603	18,982
Other Households	1,211	1,621	15,184	15,807
Total	9,593	14,272	12,730	14,962

Source: Joint Center Tabulations of U.S. Department of Housing and Urban Development 1974 Annual Housing Survey and U.S. Department of Commerce March 1987 Current Population

Table 5.5   (continued)

Renter			
Number (in Thousands)		Median Income (1986 Dollars)	
1974	1987	1974	1987
1,055	1,110	11,732	12,437
1,051	659	18,608	13,690
1,318	659	22,325	17,879
492	780	7,248	4,581
750	1,156	11,906	11,279
4,666	4,364	15,828	11,737
1,510	2,963	20,623	17,817
2,673	3,234	24,160	20,899
1,195	1,412	32,059	29,028
1,157	2,213	10,965	7,271
507	1,444	20,908	19,098
7,042	11,266	22,340	18,199
694	1,709	19,282	19,934
1,452	1,853	26,715	23,793
332	566	30,200	29,749
724	1,389	12,665	12,988
210	679	16,999	19,288
3,412	6,196	21,963	20,357
2,091	2,223	11,615	10,341
912	687	24,406	21,662
1,592	1,302	26,170	25,092
421	404	12,013	9,961
715	1,057	15,565	14,333
5,731	5,673	18,216	15,814
2,572	3,281	6,300	6,409
1,124	984	12,379	13,766
464	462	11,160	10,457
4,160	4,727	8,485	8,336

Survey.
Note: Income data as of prior year.

Figure 5.7   Rental Costs Burden

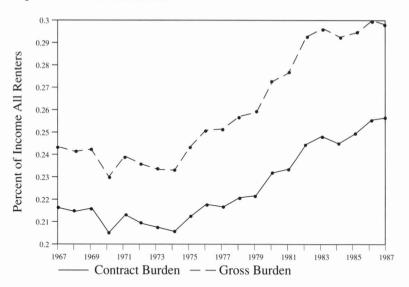

1974 and 1987 the number of renter households with children grew more than four times faster than the rate for all households. In contrast, the number of young homeowners with children actually fell over the past decade and a half.

Rental Cost Burden

The growth of low-income rental households in the face of rapidly rising rent increases is a clear prescription for trouble. Increased rental payments burdens have strained the resources of low-income families and have undoubtedly contributed to the growing indigence of homelessness observed in recent years. Figure 5.7 presents estimates of the constant-quality rental-cost burden, where rent burden is the annual contract or gross rent as a percentage of the median income of renter households. The rental-cost burden measure used in this report is for a unit with constant characteristics. To the extent that high renter costs force households to select units of lower quality, tracking actual rent burden (that is, actual rent paid divided by household income) will understate the growth in rent burden.

The constant-quality rental-cost burden—measured as either annual gross rent or contract rent for the representative unit as a percentage of median renter income—also remains relatively high (figure 5.7). The gross rent burden fell slightly from 1967 to 1974 but has moved up sharply since that time. What is striking is that the strong economic recovery that began in 1982 did nothing to alleviate the rental-cost burden: increases in real rents have steadily outweighed growth in real income.

Rental Payment Burden by Family Type

The incidence of high rental burdens has increased, particularly among the young. In 1974 the gross rent burden (estimated as the ratio of median rent to income) for households with heads aged twenty-five to thirty-four was 18.7 percent; by 1983 the burden had reached 25.4 percent (table 5.6). Households with heads under the age of twenty-five experienced even sharper increases.

As noted earlier, rental housing is increasingly becoming home to low- and moderate-income families with children, especially single-parent households. From 1974 to 1987 the number of married couples aged twenty-five to thirty-four with children who rented their housing increased from 2.7 million to 3.2 million (table 5.6). At the same time the number of single-parent families (primarily women with children) nearly doubled from 1.2 million to 2.2 million.

Table 5.6 makes clear why the rental payments burden is increasingly a problem for young households: the median income of young single-parent renter households with children fell 34 percent from $10,965 in 1974 to $7,271 in 1987. With shrinking incomes and growing rents, the increase in rent burden for this type of family is unavoidable. The rent burden for young single-parent families with children thus increased from 34.9 percent to 58.4 percent over this period.

Elderly households continue to devote relatively high shares of their incomes for rent but, unlike their younger counterparts, the real income of elderly renters has not declined sharply over the period. Indeed, elderly married-couple households enjoyed a slight increase in real income thanks to the indexation of Social Security payments against inflation.

Moreover, since the homeless are not counted as households by the Census Bureau, the data in table 5.6 may actually understate the current payments problem. While there are no reliable national figures on the homeless, their number appears to have grown in recent years, especially among families with children. While further investigation into the causes of homelessness is clearly warranted, the data in table 5.6 should leave little doubt that the rising rental payments burden is a major contributing factor.

Table 5.6 Rent Burden by Age and Family Type

Age and Family Type	1974 Income	1987 Income	1974 Rent	1987 Rent	1974 Burden	1987 Burden
					(percentages)	
Household Head under 25						
Single	11,732	12,437	287	318	29.3	30.7
Married with Children	18,608	13,690	292	324	18.9	28.4
Married No Children	22,325	17,879	329	365	17.7	24.5
Other Households with Children	7,248	4,581	279	309	46.2	81.1
Other Households No Children	11,906	11,279	367	407	37.0	43.3
Total	15,828	11,737	312	348	23.7	35.6
Household Head 25–34						
Single	20,623	17,817	331	367	19.2	24.7
Married with Children	24,160	20,899	344	382	17.1	21.9
Married No Children	32,059	29,028	382	424	14.3	17.5
Other Households with Children	10,965	7,271	319	354	34.9	58.4
Other Households no Children	20,908	19,098	395	438	22.7	27.5
Total	22,340	18,199	347	385	18.7	25.4
Household Head 35–44						
Single	19,282	19,934	325	360	20.2	21.7
Married with Children	26,715	23,793	363	403	16.3	20.3
Married No Children	30,200	29,749	359	398	14.3	16.1
Other Households with Children	12,665	12,988	319	354	30.2	32.7
Other Households No Children	16,999	19,288	325	360	22.9	22.4
Total	21,963	20,357	343	375	18.8	22.1
Household Head 45–64						
Single	11,615	10,341	257	285	26.6	33.1
Married with Children	24,406	21,662	348	386	17.1	21.4
Married No Children	26,170	25,092	350	388	16.0	18.5
Other Households with Children	12,013	9,961	310	343	30.9	41.4
Other Households No Children	15,565	14,333	294	326	22.7	27.3
Total	18,216	15,732	306	333	20.1	25.4
Household Head 65 or Older						
Single	6,300	6,409	203	225	38.6	42.1
Married No Children	12,379	13,766	302	335	29.4	29.0
Other Households No Children	11,160	10,457	257	285	27.5	32.8
Total	8,836	8,540	238	257	32.4	36.0

Note: Both income and rent are in 1986 dollars.

Low-Income Housing Assistance

Housing assistance efforts have done much in the past to improve the housing situations of low-income households. Eligibility varies from one program to the next, but in general federal rental-assistance programs aid households with incomes at or below 80 percent of the area median. It is surprisingly difficult, however, to obtain estimates of the characteristics of households actually served by these programs. HUD data suggest that in 1988 there were approximately 4.3 million units of public or otherwise federally subsidized rental housing, but provide no demographic data describing characteristics of the households living in these units. In the absence of detailed HUD data, this essay uses survey-based estimates that differ slightly from the HUD estimates of total households served, but have the advantage of providing needed information on the characteristics of the households living in subsidized rental units. (Note: For a discussion of trends in the number of HUD-assisted rental dwelling units, see Cushing Dolbeare, "Low-Income Housing Needs.")

By any measure, the Housing and Community Development Act of 1974 sparked a major expansion in the number of households receiving rental assistance. According to the March 1987 Current Population Survey, 3.8 million households (consisting of 8.9 million persons) lived in public housing or rental housing otherwise subsidized by the federal government. While this growth has virtually stopped in the past several years, the 1987 figure is up nearly 73 percent from the figure of 2.2 million recorded by the 1974 annual housing survey.

Much of the increase in housing-assistance resources has gone to aid the poorest households. Among renter households with real incomes below $5,000, the proportion living in subsidized housing nearly doubled between 1974 and 1987 (figure 5.8). Households with incomes in the $5,000 to $10,000 range experienced somewhat more modest gains in the share subsidized.

Nevertheless, existing programs serve only a small fraction of eligible low-income households. According to the Current Population Survey for 1987, just 11.8 percent of all renter households received housing assistance. Even among renter households with incomes below $5,000, less than one-third received subsidies. Of those with incomes in the $5,000 to $10,000 range, less than one-quarter were assisted.

Whether or not these data reflect appropriate targeting of resources is, of course, a political judgment. It is clear, however, that the growth of housing-assistance resources has failed to keep pace with the growth of low-income

Figure 5.8   Rental Assistance by Household Income as Percentage of
Rental Households

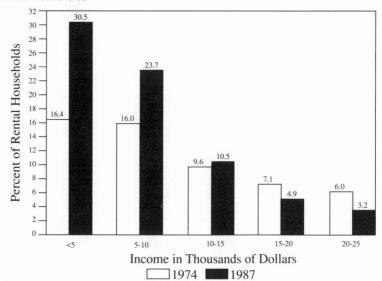

renter households. In 1974, 2.2 million renter households with incomes
below $5,000 received no housing assistance. By 1987 this pool of eligi-
ble but unassisted renter households had grown to 3.2 million. Among
households with incomes in the $5,000 to $10,000 range, the number of
households receiving no rental assistance grew from 3.8 million to 4.5
million over the same period.

Given the variation in housing requirements of households of different
types and ages, income alone is a poor measure of the ability of a household to secure adequate housing in the private nonsubsidized market. Federal poverty definitions establish the income required by various types of
households to consume adequate levels of housing, food, and other neces-
sities. By this measure, only 2.1 million (or 28 percent) of the nation's 7.5
million poverty-level renter households lived in public housing or other
subsidized rental housing last year. Among the near-poverty-level renters
(households with incomes above the poverty level, but less than two times
that level), participation was only 19.8 percent.

Concluding Comments

Despite the evidence presented in this chapter, there persists a sense that
the rental-housing problem is overstated. For example, as recently as 1982

the Report of the President's Commission on Housing concluded that the rental-cost burden had not increased dramatically since 1974. The commission argued that real rents had declined in the past decade. Any growth in rental payments had to represent, in the opinion of the President's Commission, the fact that households were choosing to consume rental units of better quality. High rent burdens were not the result of higher costs for a unit of given quality, but rather the result of higher levels of housing consumption.

This chapter presents an alternative view of metropolitan rent trends, a view that builds from an empirically sound measure of the price of rental housing of constant quality and a theoretically sound assessment of housing market dynamics. It suggests that some broad generalizations go a long way in explaining the observed patterns of rent trends over the past two decades. For much of the 1960s and early 1970s the movement of population and jobs away from the core areas of the nation's large metropolitan areas combined with the construction of a large number of subsidized rental units in core areas to create an excess supply of rental housing in many market areas, especially in the low-quality housing submarkets serving low- and moderate-income households. As a result, for much of this period increases in real rents were modest, and disinvestment and abandonment of low-cost existing rental stock was high.

Since 1980 the supply-and-demand situation in residential rental markets has shifted dramatically. Having lagged behind national trends for decades, population and employment growth accelerated in metropolitan areas in the early 1980s. Key to this turnaround is the apparent stabilization of the employment base in the core counties of the largest metropolitan areas. With the diminished supply of low-cost rental units that resulted from the high levels of abandonment in the 1960s and 1970s and the added demand pressure that resulted from rapid increases in the number of households using Section 8, Housing Vouchers, or other types of demand subsidies, the situation was ripe for a rapid increase in rents in metropolitan areas.

If this view is correct, there is little reason to suggest that rents are likely to fall sharply in the near future. The depressed rents of the 1970s represented a special combination of events that is unlikely to be repeated in the years ahead. The continued growth of metropolitan area economies and the recently enacted tax-reform legislation should continue to exert upward pressure on rent levels. With current programs able to serve only one in four poverty-level households, many families will find their available resources stretched to the limit as they struggle to obtain decent housing.

Public officials charged with setting the future direction of housing policy face an equally bleak set of choices. The high cost of subsized new construction makes it difficult for these programs to reach a large number of the very poor. Yet the continued reliance on the less-expensive, demand-oriented strategy threatens to add to rent pressures in many already over-heated urban markets, further undermining the situation of the vast number of nonsubsidized poverty-level households.

In the absence of federal-level commitment to a universal entitlement program for low-income housing assistance, policymakers must seek to walk a careful line that continues to add to housing-demand subsidies, while at the same time working to develop the new construction and the rental rehabilitation programs that are needed to help offset potential rent increases. Achieving such a careful balancing of supply-and-demand ap-proaches is admittedly difficult, but the growing rent burden of many of the nation's most vulnerable households makes this a task well worth pursuing.

6 Urban Infrastructure and City Budgeting: Elements of a National Urban Policy

Michael A. Pagano

The ebb and flow of public opinion in the last decade has moved the urban infrastructure issue alternately to the fore of public debate and then to the back burner. Splashed across newspapers, magazines, and the nightly TV news, the popular media flash pictures of cars being swallowed up by collapsed streets, flooding caused by water-main breaks, bridges crashing into rivers and ravines, and other infrastructure-related disasters. Policymakers at all levels are pressed to join those calling for more infrastructure spending. Analysts and academics armed with the jargon of gerontology recommend a broad range of government and private-sector activities for rejuvenating the "aging" infrastructure and preventing further "decay" and "deterioration."

The first major infrastructure alarm was issued at a 1978 conference in which George Peterson (1978) concluded that urban capital needs were escalating, urban capital investment was not, and new forms of capital assistance must be found. The issue was popularized a few years later by the now-famous tract *America in Ruins* (Choate and Walter, 1981). A decade after Peterson's warning, the National Council on Public Works Improvement sounded a nearly identical alarm—a concession that little had changed. The final report from the Council to the President and Congress concluded: "Measured in 1984 dollars, state and local capital investment peaked in 1972 at $34 billion; annual federal outlays for capital, however, peaked at $25 billion in the late 1970s" (1988: 7) (see figure 6.1). As a percentage of gross national product, gross public investment in public works declined from 2.3 percent in 1960 to 2.0 percent in 1970 to 1.12 percent in 1985 (1988: 47). The council's major finding: "After two years of study the [council] has found convincing evidence that the quality of America's infrastructure is barely adequate to fulfill current requirements,

Figure 6.1 Government Capital Outlays for Public Works

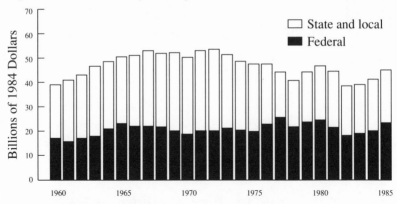

Source: National Council on Public Works Improvement, 1988, p. 7.

and insufficient to meet the demands of future economic growth and development" (1988: 1).

Clearly, we are facing an infrastructure crisis of immense proportions. The crisis is particularly acute at the local level. Cincinnati, a city long respected for professional management of its capital facilities, projected a revenue shortfall in 1987 between needs and resources of nearly $13 million per year for streets, parks and recreation facilities, public buildings, and solid-waste facilities. Unmet street and bridge needs in Louisiana's cities and towns approached $62 million annually in 1984, while in Florida the figure for unmet city-street needs was $50 million, and it was $180 million for California cities (National Infrastructure Advisory Committee, 1984). An Urban Institute study of the condition of the urban infrastructures of sixty-two cities found that as of 1980 nearly 25 percent of streets in Wilmington, Delaware, were in poor condition, 22 percent of the streets in Sioux Falls were poor, and 17 percent of Louisville's and Miami Beach's streets and 15 percent of Pittsburgh's were classified poor (Peterson et al. 1984). The report further classified more than half the bridges in Buffalo, Charlotte, Independence, Miami Beach, New York City, Rochester, and Shreveport to be either structurally deficient or functionally obsolete in 1980. Oakland, according to data compiled for the Urban Institute study, averaged (between 1978 and 1980) 608 sewer breaks per 1,000 miles of sanitary sewers each year. Houston averaged 571 breaks, Everett 352, and Baltimore 328. New York City and New Orleans averaged over 4,000 sewer backups per 1,000 miles of sanitary sewers annually, Garland and Scranton averaged over 3,000, Boston over 2,000, and Chicago and Baltimore over 1,000. Ogden and Billings experienced over 700 water-main failures per 1,000 miles of pipe annually between 1978 and 1980. The failure rate in Dallas was 591, Phoenix's was 459, and Detroit's 393. According to a 1986 comprehensive review of national and regional infrastructure-needs studies of the past fifteen years, the overwhelming evidence suggests that unmet needs for airports, highways and bridges, mass transit, water supply, wastewater, and water-resource facilities exceed billions of dollars (Apogee, 1986).

Urban resources are scarce, problems are not. The question, then, is not whether or not the nation's cities can respond to the urban infrastructure challenge, but rather why they have not and how they can. In this chapter we propose first to identify very briefly local officials' perceptions of constraints on increased infrastructure spending. Second, we offer a framework for understanding the trade-offs in the local capital decisionmaking process and the influences of federal grants on that process. The next three sections discuss urban and federal strategies. After a discussion of prominent city government infrastructure strategies, we outline two broad strategies for federal government involvement in addressing the urban infrastructure crisis. One encourages a federal infrastructure block grant; the other outlines features of a national infrastructure maintenance policy.

Constraints

After nearly a decade of public activism on the urban infrastructure issue, the problem remains. Infrastructure spending is too low by anyone's standards. And yet the question remains: if the "infrastructure crisis" is so acute, why do not policymakers respond? The simplistic response is that elected officials do not have the political will to make the hard decisions. If the electorate demanded more infrastructure spending, city officials would address the problems. Although appealing, this does not answer the obvious questions of what constrains that decision-making behavior or of what is valued more by key local decisionmakers.

A recent survey of key local officials asked respondents to identify the important factors that in their views constrained capital spending levels.[1] Three primary constraints were identified by nearly one-third of the respondents: their city's tax base had declined; operating costs required more revenues, reducing funds for capital projects; and tax rates and user charges were inadequate (see table 6.1). Borrowing and state-imposed restrictions were mentioned by very few respondents. Even "taxpayer opposi-

Table 6.1 Constraints on Capital Spending

	Percentages[a]
Hampered local tax base growth	37.2
High operating costs	30.3
Inadequate tax rates and user charges	29.5
Taxpayer opposition	19.7
Capital needs adequately addressed	16.5
State restrictions on constraints on revenues and expenditures	6.8
Borrowing restrictions imposed by city ordinances	1.1
Other	13.5
	N = 468

[a]Percentages do not total 100 due to possibility of two responses per respondent.

tion" was identified by less than 20 percent of these key local officials. More important, only 16.5 percent felt their cities' capital needs were adequately addressed.

These same local officials responded to two other questions concerning constraints on issuing additional general obligation (G.O.) and revenue debt for infrastructure purposes. Their responses to the G.O. question revealed a fear that taxpayers would disapprove (35.9 percent) and that, since G.O. debt would raise general taxes, economic growth would be affected (26.5 percent). These same general concerns were raised in their response to the revenue debt question; namely, that economic growth would be adversely affected (30.8 percent) and that users would not approve (19.4 percent) (see table 6.2).

In other words, local officials view infrastructure needs as just one set of unresolved and constrained urban issues chasing scarce local resources. Local officials' perceptions of constraints on their options to raise revenues through purposive government action indicate that they certainly acknowledge underfunding of urban infrastructure. But unless current conditions change radically, local officials will continue to point to the underfunding as a result of several factors. One of those constraints identified in table 6.1 is a budgetary concept related to the notion of scarcity. Resources to fund either operating or capital needs result in trade-offs between maintaining service-delivery levels and meeting infrastructure needs. The concept of trade-offs is identified explicitly in the following section.

Table 6.2   Reasons Why More G.O. and Revenue Debt Not Issued

Local officials indicated these reasons why their city does not issue more G.O. debt for capital purposes or more revenue debt for capital purposes:	G.O. Debt (Percentages)[a]	Revenue Debt (Percentages)[a]
Taxpayer/user disapproval	35.9	19.4
Resulting higher taxes or user charges make city less attractive for economic growth	26.5	30.8
Capital needs are adequately met	20.5	29.9
Need to protect credit rating	15.6	7.7
Capital projects should be financed through current revenues	11.3	12.4
Interest rates are too high or change too frequently	4.1	4.9
City at its debt limit	3.8	NA
Other	16.0	16.5
	$N = 468$	$N = 468$

[a]Percentages do not total 100 due to possibility of two responses per respondent.

Trade-Offs in the Decisionmaking Process

Macrobudgetary Decisions

Radical disruptions to cities' fiscal environments require a search for options to address the problem.[2] The urban fiscal crises of the past decade represent one such disruption (see Levine and Rubin, 1981; Bradbury and Ladd, 1985; and Bahl, 1984); and the federal aid cutbacks of the 1980s represent another (see Ellwood, 1982; Nathan and Doolittle, 1983; and Warren, 1985). Responses to these disruptions are made in the budgetary process by city officials. These officials are confronted with the first "hard choice," or the first macrobudgetary decision. This hard choice is premised on whether the use of local (own-source) revenues should be allocated for capital spending purposes or for operating activities of city government. Operating budgets generally finance service delivery, personnel costs, and regular day-to-day activities of the cities (recurring costs); capital budgets finance construction, rehabilitation, and major repair of cities' infrastructures (nonrecurring costs).

In this framework city officials agree to a minimum level of operating needs that can be financed with local revenues *before* they decide to allocate local funds to meet a minimum level of capital needs. (For a similar macrobudgetary decision argument, but at the federal level, see Fischer and Kamlet, 1984; and Cusack, 1986.) In other words, projects funded through the capital budget are expected to be more sensitive to shifts in total city revenues than are the day-to-day operating needs of the city. The capital budget, then, is more revenue-elastic than the operating budget. If the revenue shift results in fewer city revenues, Wolman (1983:256) argues that "expenditures will be cut in a manner which *minimizes* visible service reduction."

Should spending not reach minimum levels of capital needs, cities issue debt to help cover the difference—unless prohibited by state law. As a result, any new own-source revenues will be allocated to either operating or capital spending needs, depending on the relative demand or preference for those two macrobudgetary categories. Because debt issuance also requires repayment through local revenues, cities unable to meet their minimum capital spending levels with local revenues and debt search for options that would shift the burden elsewhere. Issuing debt, however, involves the same type of competition between operating and capital needs as allocating current revenues. Debt must be amortized over many years. Annual debt payments drain off revenues that could be used for operating purposes. Because these revenues are dedicated for debt retirement, and are also own-source revenues, the total amount of own-source funds available for meeting minimum operating needs is reduced. Competition then proceeds over what remains in the total pool of own-source revenues after the dedicated revenues are deducted. *The first response to disruptions in cities' fiscal environments, then, is to protect the operating budget and adjust the capital side.* (For supporting empirical evidence, see Levine and Rubin, 1980; Levine, Rubin, and Wolohojian, 1981; Wolman, 1983; and Reid, 1988.)

Results from a recent survey are suggestive of this revenue-elasticity hypothesis. Two simulation-type questions were presented to a sample of chief budget officers in U.S. cities.[3] One asked how they would expect their city to allocate revenues if total city revenues from all sources declined by a catastrophic 25 percent; the other asked them to predict changes in outlays if total revenues surged by 25 percent. When compared, the two responses —although not reflective of past decisions, but rather indicative of their a priori expectations as informed observers of their cities—paint a very rough and impressionistic picture of the responsiveness of operating and capital programs to changes in revenues. And while the technique is admittedly imprecise, this attitudinal approach to measuring the revenue-elasticity of city operating and capital budgets complements econometric studies of state and local fiscal behavior (see, inter alia, Inman, 1979).

The simulation questions allowed respondents to be placed in one of three groups: those who believed that their city could tend to support capital spending levels at all costs (regardless of, say, a radical drop in revenues); those who believed that their city would tend to support operating programs at all costs; and those who believed that their city would allocate increases and decreases evenly to both operating and capital budgets. Obviously, this type of question cannot segregate budgetary responses according to changes in a specific revenue source; neither can it identify how specific functional categories would respond to revenue shifts.[4] The revenue-source issue is important because some revenues are used only for certain functions, while others are more fungible in nature. By not specifying the revenue source, respondents were asked to analyze the *total* capital spending plans rather than the parts—an artifact of the questionnaire. Nevertheless, the purpose of this simulation question is not to identify functional preferences but to compare the aggregate of capital spending with the aggregate of operating spending as a means of identifying the "macrobudgetary decision."

For the *revenue reduction scenario*, nearly two-thirds (62.7 percent) of the chief budget officers predicted that their cities would protect operating spending and reduce capital outlays, while less than 10 percent predicted the across-the-board reduction option. Only 27.5 percent believed their cities would both reduce operating spending substantially and maintain capital spending near current levels. The second scenario, which presented a *revenue increase* for cities, resulted in nearly half the respondents (49.0 percent) predicting that their city would increase capital spending significantly while holding the line, or only modestly increasing, operating spending. Almost one-third (31.4 percent) predicted the increased operating-spending response, and 19.6 percent believed both capital and operating spending would increase by the same proportion.

To the extent that the responses of these budget officers reflect the values and priorities of their cities, there seems to be a clear indication that capital spending is more revenue-elastic than operating programs. Radical disruptions to the city's revenue stream will probably be felt most clearly on the capital side rather than on the operating side.

Federal Influences on Budgetary Decisionmaking

Econometric studies of state and local fiscal behavior argue that through the political process, residents express preferences for consumption of both public (government-provided) and private (market-provided) goods. As total income of a community rises, consumption of both types of goods increases, but not necessarily at the same rate. If each resident's preference function (which depends on income, cost of service output, tax price of services, and other variables) could be calculated and summed, public-service provision would match residents' demands.

The fiscal behavior studies incorporate federal aid as a variable that affects the financing of and preferences for public-service provision. City behavior is assumed to be "responsive" to the grants. A matching grant "requires that the government receiving the grant match it with own-source revenue in accordance with some, fixed matching rate. . . . Whether own-source financing increases or decreases depends upon the price elasticity of demand for public expenditures" (Stine, 1985: 228). Local governments can be stimulated to spend more own-source revenues on the aided function if demand is price-elastic. As the price declines, more will be demanded. Conversely, if demand is price-inelastic, own-source financing will decrease; that is, local governments will substitute federal aid for own-source revenues. A nonmatching grant is predicted to have an income effect, thus reducing own-source spending on the aided activity. That is, it is viewed as additional income to the community and therefore will result in higher consumption of both public and private goods. A matching grant effectively reduces the price of a project to the recipient community (see Inman, 1979). Federal matching grants either substitute for local revenues or stimulate some additional spending on the aided activity above the level the locality would have spent in the absence of the grant, depending on the preferences for that service by the city's residents. Although there is considerable empirical disagreement on the "response" to matching grants —some view it as stimulative, others substitutive—there is more empirical agreement on the "response" to nonmatching grants. Predicted to have an income effect, studies indicate nonmatching grants induce a "flypaper effect"—money sticks where it hits (Gramlich and Galper, 1973). In other words, the nonmatching grants stick to the public sector for its use rather than satisfy *both* public and private preferences as predicted.

The public budgetary decisionmaking framework presented here modifies the fiscal behavior model and purports to explain the observed "flypaper effect." In other words, we expect "money to stick where it hits," but, unlike the assumptions made in the traditional fiscal behavior literature, we do not assume a price or income "response" by cities (or city officials) to federal aid; neither do we assume that city officials perceive their primary decision criterion as one of selecting between private and public preferences.

Exogenous aid (federal and state aid) is perceived by local officials as a means to maximize the number and volume of projects a city can undertake. Because the stock of projects from which a city can select always exceeds available revenues ("infrastructure needs" are always greater than revenues), the additional funds are used to build more projects. Due to the competition between capital and operating needs, any additional funds to the city (additional to those over which the city has control) allow for more needs to be met. According to fiscal federalism studies, the decision calculus of weighing public preferences against private preferences assumes that the primary allocative concern for public officials is to allocate resources efficiently to meet those preferences. Our assumption is that city officials make choices about taxing and spending efforts on the basis of an *acceptable tax burden* and of a responsibility to satisfy both operating and capital needs. Since the taxpayer's *local* tax bill is not increased because of the federal grant, local officials perceive aid to be costless.[5] There is no need, then, for local officials to rebate some of the aid to satisfy private wants. Federal aid sticks to the public sector to satisfy public wants because those wants (or "capital needs") are viewed as important by local officials and because they do not affect a city resident's tax burden (Pagano and Moore, 1985).

Moreover, local officials do not perceive federal aid as a stable source of revenues. The political volatility of aid availability encourages local officials to exert control over fiscal matters which they can control (local taxes) rather than over exogenous, noncontrollable factors, such as federal aid. To rebate aid to consumers (in the form of lower taxes) in one year in which federal aid is augmented only makes future tax decisions more difficult and more visible once federal aid is reduced or abolished. As a result, any exogenous aid is perceived as supplementary or "additive" to the volume of projects already scheduled for construction or repair.

Federal grants do not *cause* communities to readjust resources—depending on preferences for private and public services—because they are viewed as completely external to the macrobudgetary decision calculus. Grants may affect which projects are selected, but they are not expected to influence a city's local commitment of revenues. Distortion in city behavior as a result of federal involvement, then, is not expected at the macrobudgetary level of local commitment, but rather at the micro level of specific project selection. Once a city has decided how much it is willing to divert from its own revenues for capital purposes (or, its local commitment), projects are selected that will maximize total capital spending. Thus, projects eligible for federal funding will be selected ahead of projects ineligible for federal funds until all federal dollars are leveraged (for empirical evidence of leveraging, see Pagano, 1986).

A second, and singularly important, impact of federal aid is at the "bottom line." Without federal involvement, total capital spending would be considerably lower. The implication is that federal aid realistically cannot be expected to alter local commitment to capital spending regardless of the matching ratio and the nature of the grant. Nevertheless, it most definitely raises total capital spending and distorts project selection.

Home Base: Measuring Local Commitment

After the city allocates its own-source revenues to operating and capital needs, those levels of spending become the base for the next round of spending decisions in the subsequent year. Recalculation of the minimum level is not expected to be undertaken because of the costs of that activity. Rather, last year's decisions, which resulted from interactions and compromise by numerous key decisionmakers, now stand as the politically legitimate precedent (or home base) upon which this year's negotiations proceed (see Larkey, 1979).

The argument we are making is that *local commitment* to capital spending —that is, local revenues diverted directly to capital projects plus local revenues dedicated to debt repayment—will change only marginally from year to year. Capital expenditures are affected directly, immediately, and in many cases substantially, but local commitment is altered incrementally. *The base, then, upon which future decisions build is not the level of spending but rather the level of local commitment.*[6]

Local commitment for meeting capital and operating needs is expected to increase incrementally from one year to the next. This outcome does not result from key decisionmakers weighing and comparing all possible uses of current revenues, but rather from beginning with a precedent and calculating an incremental set of minimum needs for the present year. If own-source revenues are adequate to address minimum levels of operating and capital needs, then local commitment for capital spending should be increasing constantly. If revenues are inadequate, the minimum level of operating needs will drain revenues from capital spending, resulting in a declining trend unless more debt is issued.

An Illustration

To illustrate the importance of the local commitment concept in explaining local fiscal behavior, raw data on city expenditure and revenue patterns were collected and tabulated from Dayton, Ohio.[7] The extraordinary difficulty in collecting and reconstructing needed data made it impossible to do so for other cities. Even though the local commitment and federal aid data from Dayton do not span twenty or thirty years, they do cover a volatile twelve-year period when federal grants first increased and then decreased (1975–1986). As a result, the data illustrate local commitment responses not only to federal aid increases—the norm for fiscal impact studies—but also to federal aid cutbacks.

Figure 6.2 presents the data from Dayton. In current dollars local commitment increased rather steadily between 1975 and 1984, then rose dramatically in 1985 due almost entirely to a one-time, permanent increase in the city income-tax rate (from 1.75 percent to 2.25 percent). Because a portion of the income tax is reserved for the capital budget, we expected (local commitment to capital spending was expected to rise in 1985 at a rate slightly faster than the previous years and then to stabilize at that level in 1986 and beyond. Furthermore, it was expected that) the 1986 base would become the base for decisions on the division of current revenues for meeting the minimum levels of capital needs in subsequent years.

In constant (1967) dollars Dayton's local commitment to capital spending increased at a fairly stable rate over the period, reaching its peak in 1986 at about 130 percent of its 1976 level. Federal grant contribution to Dayton's capital spending pattern fluctuated considerably over the twelve-year period, generally increasing until 1981 and then generally decreasing until 1986. In current dollars, federal grants for capital spending purposes peaked at $11 million in 1980 and 1981 and dropped nearly to its 1975 level by 1986.

While Dayton's *local commitment* to capital spending increased at a fairly steady rate during the period under study, there appears to be no response in local commitment to federal grants for capital purposes between 1975 and 1986.[8] The data from Dayton provide tentative support for the perspective that cities do not adjust their local commitment of revenues for capital spending on the receipt of federal aid. Federal grants appear to be fairly unrelated to Dayton's local commitment. Instead, local commitment for Dayton increased *incrementally* over the study period, while federal aid fluctuated considerably.

Figure 6.2

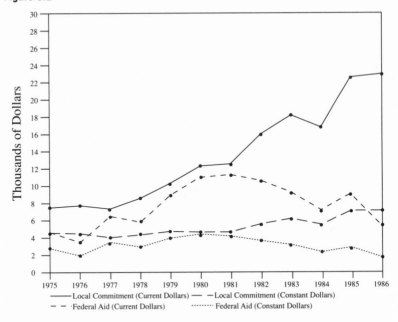

Survey Data

Additional financial data are unavailable from a larger sample of cities due to the extremely difficult nature of data collection. A survey of local officials was tapped for corroborative purposes.[9] When asked how they would expect their city to respond to a 25 percent decrease in federal aid for infrastructure, two-thirds of the local officials responded that local commitment would change slightly, if at all. The most frequent response (36.9 percent) indicated that local commitment would not be altered, and the next most frequent response (26.4 percent) was that the change would be marginal (defined as less than a 10-percent increase in local commitment). One-fourth of the respondents indicated that local commitment would increase substantially, implying a perception that federal aid can be replaced by local revenues. The remaining 11 percent said their cities would decrease local commitment, implying that federal aid induces a response in local commitment (see table 6.3).

The prediction of an overwhelming majority of local officials implies that federal aid availability has little impact on their local commitment. Furthermore, their response did not correlate with any other factor selected for investigation. City size, region, perception of constraints on capital spending, revenue-source reliance for capital spending, perception of con-

Table 6.3   Local Responses to a Decrease in Federal Grants

Faced with a 25 percent reduction in federal grants for capital purposes, the percentage of local officials who predict their city's commitment of local revenues for capital outlays would:

increase local commitment to cover at least 10 percent of reduction	25.5
increase local commitment to cover less than 10 percent of reduction	26.4
not alter local commitment much at all	36.9
decrease local commitment	11.1
	$N = 450$

straint on debt issuances, and other factors were not found to be associated with this response.

When asked how they would expect their city to respond to a 25 percent increase in federal aid for capital purposes, the majority (48.3 percent) responded that local revenues would not be altered at all, and another one-quarter of the respondents replied that local revenues would be increased only "moderately." Less than 5 percent adopted the response that local revenue would increase "substantially," and over one-fifth responded that local revenues would actually decrease (see table 6.4).

No factor was significant in explaining the responses to the federal aid increase question. Respondents who selected the options to either decrease or increase local commitment substantially did not respond to the other inquiries in a manner that would indicate significantly different perceptions or revenue experiences compared to others.

Conclusion

City capital spending is in constant tension with city financing of recurring activities funded through the operating budget. Consequently, to require cities to address their own infrastructure needs, or to assume that they would if public demand were more visible, misses an important behavioral element of budgetary decisionmaking. Capital spending decisions are incremental; attempts to radically realter or realign a city's trade-off between operating and capital needs will in most cases fail.

Federal aid does not induce a change in local commitment by the recipient community. Total capital outlays are affected substantially, but own-

Table 6.4   Local Responses to an Increase in Federal Grants

Faced with a 25 percent increase in federal grants for capital purposes, the percentage of local officials who predict their city's commitment of local revenues for capital outlays would:

not be altered at all	48.3
increase moderately	25.1
increase significantly	4.9
decrease	21.7
	$N = 447$

source contributions to a city's capital investment plan are not. Consequently, declines in federal (and state) aid in most cases will not be covered by local revenues.

City Strategies

Cities have pursued a number of strategies over the last decade to address the urban infrastructure crisis. The constraints identified earlier restrict the number and type of options that have been tried or considered. Cities have pursued one strategy quite vigorously. Instead of radically readjusting historical trade-offs between operating and capital needs, cities respond to infrastructure demands by shifting the costs of infrastructure provision to individuals and developers and away from the general taxpayer. This cost-shifting response has been accomplished by imposing fees on consumption, levying development or impact fees, and developing "creative" or "innovative" finance schemes for urban infrastructure.

Fees and Cost-Shifting

Proposition 13 and taxpayer revolts nationwide ushered in a new era of "pay-for-it-yourself" local fiscal policy. Public services provided in discrete quantities and sold in marketable units should be charged a "market-like" fee. A fee structure should encourage more rational consumption behavior; consumers would demand only what they could afford and would not rely on nonbeneficiaries to subsidize their needs. As a result, fees and other user charges have been the fastest-growing revenue source for local governments. In 1978, the last year before the tax revolt, user fees amounted to only 29.8 percent of city own-source revenues and 18.1 percent of total city revenues (the total includes intergovernmental revenues). By 1986 the Census Bureau reports that fees and charges surged to 40.1 percent of city own-source revenues and 27.9 percent of total city revenues (U.S. Department of Commerce, Bureau of the Census, 1988).

Development fees, another popular option pursued by cities, are fees assessed on commercial and residential developers for the costs of requisite infrastructure (Stegman, 1986). Rather than require the city to issue debt and underwrite the costs of street development, sewer- and water-line extensions, and sidewalk and lighting installation, a development fee places the cost of infrastructure provision squarely on the users. Not only does this strategy shift infrastructure costs to the user, but more important it provides a financial cushion to the city because it can use its debt capacity and revenues earmarked for capital outlays on other projects. Without this finance tool, cities presumably would have to choose between providing infrastructure to the newly developed areas or maintaining adequate replacement and renovation of existing infrastructure in established areas of the city, but not both.

Impact fees require developers and builders (particularly in dense central business districts) to pay the city a premium for the privilege of building or redeveloping (Porter, 1986). Impact fees are premised on the observation that commercial development frequently, if not always, has an adverse "impact" on employment, housing, and infrastructure. Cities that have adopted linkage fees, such as Boston, San Francisco, and Santa Monica, recognize that new development often displaces older, substandard housing, leaving the occupants with few options and the city with the responsibility of finding adequate housing (Keating, 1986). These cities also understand that most of the jobs created as a result of development require higher skills than those possessed by the surplus labor pool in the city. New employment may be created, but the city's chronically unemployed or underemployed and low-skilled or unskilled tend not to benefit. Again, the city is left with the responsibility for these unemployed. Furthermore, as in the case for development fees, these cities will experience increased demand for infrastructure services (streets, parking, traffic control) because of the development. The impact fee is one means of providing housing, job training programs, and infrastructure for the city's residents without raising taxes, issuing additional debt, or diverting capital projects from other areas.

Widespread use of linkage fees is inhibited by two developments. One is legal, the other demand-constrained. Washington state's supreme court ruled that linkage fees are unconstitutional because they constitute a discriminatory exaction for the benefit of others (see Keating, 1986). Other cities are reluctant to impose linkage fees for the same reason, namely, that they are a tax rather than a fee and may be ruled unconstitutional by their states. A more dominant restriction on the use of the impact fee, however, is that it probably cannot be considered a viable revenue-raising device in cities without hyper-demand for specific real estate. The cities that have successfully enacted and implemented impact fees are those same cities in which developers are tripping over each other to have a piece of the action. High demand for those sites means developers will probably pay any price, agree to any demand, and provide any service, just to be granted the authority to redevelop.[10]

Creative Finance

Creative finance is a term, like beauty, that is defined by the beholder. Much of the early literature on creative finance focuses on debt instruments and cash management. Peterson and Hough (1984) and Hamilton (1983), for example, encouraged local governments to consider what were then deemed exotic debt options: zero coupon bonds, variable rate bonds, put options, warrants, and tax-exempt commercial paper, to name a few. Debt instruments were a likely target for innovations after the passage of the 1981 Economic Recovery and Tax Act (ERTA) in which new tax laws altered the composition of holders of debt and made the tax-exempt bond market less lucrative compared with the taxable bond market than it had been in the past. Further, investment of bond proceeds, arbitrage, advanced refunding, and returns on idle cash became all-consuming tasks of city finance officers (see Miller, 1986; and Galper and Toder, 1983). The first wave of creative finance techniques, then, primarily centered on cash management or debt management.

Subsequent to ERTA, the federal government slashed federal aid to local governments—eliminating the General Revenue Sharing program in 1987—and established a radically different tax code in 1986. The implication of both events is that local governments were motivated to consider innovative or creative financing techniques other than cash management or debt instruments. The second wave of what is called "creative" or "innovative" finance today really is not as new as the names imply; rather, the terms refer to infrastructure financing techniques that have been used infrequently by local governments or that need to be implemented more broadly. The emphasis of these techniques shifted from cash management and moved toward marketlike strategies. As cities nationwide have shifted their revenue reliance from general taxes to user fees and charges, most of the creative finance techniques of the late 1980s share a common feature of match-ing facility costs with identifiable users. A recent study of innovative infra-structure finance identifies some fairly standard techniques, such as expan-sion of special assessment districts or tax-increment financing for public facilities (roads, central business district improvements, stormwater dis-tricts), developer exactions, equity participation by both the local govern-ment and private firms, and creation of utility or development districts (Apogee, 1987). Each of these creative financing techniques attempts to shift the burden of infrastructure finance from the general taxpayer and move it closer to the beneficiary.

It is difficult to judge the extent to which any of these creative financing techniques have been adopted nationwide. Developer exactions, for exam-ple, are not reported as separate revenues for city government finance data as collected by the U.S. Bureau of the Census. Nor is it possible to separate general or revenue debt issued by a city from debt issued for special assess-ment or tax-increment districts. Nevertheless, it appears that the popularity of many of these techniques is increasing rapidly. Cities have fewer federal dollars for infrastructure finance, the 1986 Tax Reform Act appears to have a greater impact on infrastructure projects than any other local government activity, and local commitment of own-source revenues for infrastructure projects cannot be expect to increase radically. As a consequence, cities have every incentive to continue pursuing appropriate innovations to meet their infrastructure needs.

A Digression

An inference should not be made that operating spending should be re-duced as a means to buttress or augment capital spending (the trade-off issue). Robbing Peter to pay Paul may be ill-conceived as a mechanism to address the urban infrastructure problem. Closing down homeless shelters or charging homeless people a fee so that a residential street can be resur-faced may solve one city problem but would most likely worsen the city's quality of life. The trade-off requires analysis of a complex web of deci-sions. If a city contemplates a trade of an operating program for an ex-panded capital program, it needs to assess the issue of who bears the bur-den of the operating program's elimination as well as who bears the burden (and receives the benefits) of the capital facility. In other words, local officials might consider financing market-type goods and services on a fee-for-consumption basis so long as groups of individuals are not excluded from consuming the "public" good.

Federal Strategies

The impact of federal aid must be recognized in designing new infrastructure programs.[11] Although the argument above suggests that federal aid did not substitute for, nor stimulate, local revenues for capital spending, federal aid did and does allow cities to construct more and better public facilities than they otherwise would have. And federal aid did generally improve the quality and performance of capital facilities. Cities would not have invested at those levels without outside assistance because in part, as the analysis has indicated, local efforts to raise taxes significantly for infrastructure provision are perceived as a threat to the city's economic growth potential. Federal assistance for infrastructure reduces that threat and allows higher total levels of capital spending, without altering local commitment to capital spending. Consequently, cities have built larger, and a greater quantity of, public facilities than they would have if left on their own.

Federal Grants and Institutions

In light of these observations an important federal strategy to pursue is to preserve what currently exists. The primary urban programs that should be preserved include the Wastewater Treatment Grants (Section 201), Community Development Block Grants, and Urban Development Action Grants. Federal programs have played an important role in helping cities build fixed assets that otherwise would most likely not have been constructed or certainly would not have been constructed as soon as they were. The level of construction activity would not be maintained by localities if federal involvement were reduced. Cities will not significantly alter their local commitment to capital spending. Only at the federal level can revenues be raised that reduce the problem of cities' unwillingness to jeopardize economic growth by raising taxes for capital projects.

A new infrastructure program that should be considered by the federal government is an infrastructure block grant. An infrastructure block grant would allow localities the discretion to choose appropriate investment levels for a variety of infrastructure facilities. The impact, however, would not be to alter local commitment. Rather, total capital spending would be increased by the amount of the grant. A block grant would give cities the autonomy to spend the funds on projects they believe are worthy rather than on those the federal government deems meritorious. If all federal categorical capital grants were consolidated into a block grant and more funds were made available, a survey of local officials suggests that more capital spending would probably be realized on streets, bridges, and public buildings, and less of an increase on fees for other functional areas (parks and recreation, museums, libraries, or senior citizen centers). Capital spending on water and sewer facilities, according to the survey respondents, would probably remain unchanged.[12]

Indeed, an infrastructure block grant would be more preferable, it seems, than the creation of new institutions (such as a national infrastructure bank) because a block grant represents a new infusion of money and allows local governments the autonomy to identify their own needs. For example, the National Infrastructure Fund (NIF) proposed in 1984 was designed as a $30 billion, interest-free, revolving loan program to help support state and local capital spending. Besides the exclusion of maintenance activities as a legitimate use of these proceeds—an argument to be pursued below—the proposal would not have altered local commitment. These government loans would only have encouraged cities to reduce their debt payments because the interest on NIF loans would be considerably less than the interest costs of borrowing in the tax-exempt market. The NIF loan program, then, probably would have raised total capital spending by the amount of interest the localities would have spent in its absence. However, there would not have been any discernible impact on cities' commitment of local revenues to capital spending.

Senator Daniel Patrick Moynihan's recent proposal would also have no effect on local commitment. The "National Infrastructure Development Act of 1988" establishes a National Infrastructure Corporation that will provide assistance to state and local governments. Similar in design to the NIF, it would provide low-interest loans to state and local governments for infrastructure projects. Again, the amount of local capital spending, we suspect, would increase only by the amount of the subsidized borrowing rate—a small gain. New institutional arrangements, such as an infrastructure bank or a bond bank, cannot be considered a panacea to the urban infrastructure crisis, for their ability to alter local commitment is diminished.

The noteworthy accomplishment of such institutions is their ability to reduce the market rate of borrowing and to allow previously excluded jurisdictions the opportunity to borrow. These accomplishments should be acknowledged; but whether cities borrow from these new institutions or from Wall Street, the difference in capital spending will be marginal. They represent transfers of borrowed debt, not a new infusion of capital. An infrastructure block grant would provide local governments the fresh infusion of capital.

The current federal budgetary climate with Gramm-Rudman, domestic program reductions, and congressional unwillingness to reverse the funding decline for urban programs strongly suggests that creation of a new urban infrastructure block grant program or the expansion of existing federal grants would be exceptionally difficult, if not outright impossible, to accomplish. More probable and certainly more politically palatable for the nation would be action on some old recommendations, such as the modification of federal mandates and engineering design standards. Both have been identified as costly, sometimes prohibitively costly; and both should be reconsidered. Mandates require local governments to pay for the costs of achieving national objectives—a lofty goal, but an expensive one to local governments strapped for fiscal resources. Engineering design standards are in many cases inflexible and inappropriate for low-demand facilities (see National Infrastructure Advisory Committee, 1984; and National Council on Public Works Improvement, 1988). Nevertheless, the abolition of mandates and a reduction in engineering design standards mean that local governments will devise and implement their own policies—which may or may not coincide with national objectives. The risk that thousands of different design standards and mandates might result from this action may mean that nothing is changed.

A National Infrastructure Maintenance Policy

One overlooked dimension of this debate on federal interference with local government infrastructure provision should be pursued. It is a dimension that would directly address the real problem of infrastructure decay, and one that would not challenge the federal government's prerogative of imposing uniform standards and mandates: a federal policy designed to *maintain existing capital facilities in good condition* (see Pagano, 1984; and Leonard, 1986).

The National Council on Public Works Improvement reports that while capital spending declined over the past three decades, spending for operations and maintenance increased (see figure 6.3). The implication to be drawn, it seems, is that governments are investing more in the maintainenance of their facilities than they had previously. Other studies focusing on only maintenance expenditures in sixteen cities demonstrated a reverse trend between 1957 and 1977 (Peterson et al., 1980–82; and CONSAD, 1980). The disparity between the two sets of reports rests on the "operations" outlays component. Because no aggregate data exist that separate "maintenance" from "operations," the council's report indicates a positive trend, while the other reports—which are case studies that segregate main-

Figure 6.3   Government Operations and Maintenance Outlays for Public Works

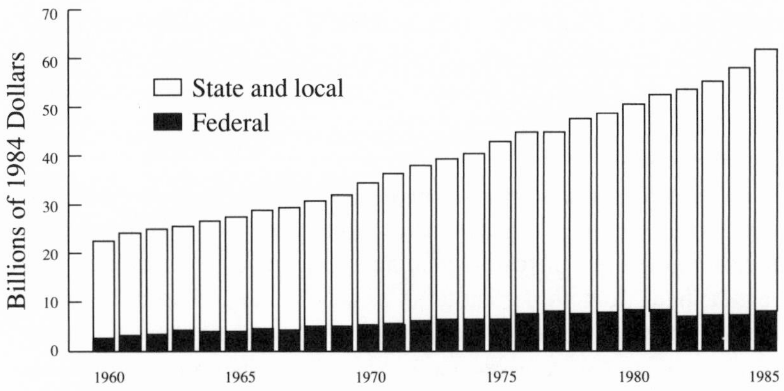

Source: National Council on Public Works Improvement, 1988, p. 7.

tenance outlays from operations—argue that maintenance had suffered.

If the urban infrastructure crisis is a product of not just inadequate capital spending but also inadequate maintenance spending, then one mechanism by which the federal government can help arrest the deteriorating condition of urban infrastructures is to *eliminate antimaintenance biases in federal programs*. For example, the Federal-Aid Highway Act's 3R program in 1976 was created in recognition of the growing need to repair the nation's federal-aid highways. Rehabilitation, resurfacing, and restoration were reclassified as "capital" projects and eligible for federal funding (the fourth R, reconstruction, was added in the 1981 reauthorization). Consequently, federal recognition of this antimaintenance bias has been beneficial to the physical condition of federal-aid highways. If "maintenance" (defined as activities that allow, rather than prolong, the useful life of a facility to be reached) could also be classified as "capital" for federal funding purposes, the antimaintenance bias in federal programs could be effectively removed. This provision should be attached to all federal "capital" programs. An infrastructure maintenance policy would also be relatively costless; no new programs, no additional funds, and possibly less administrative overhead would be needed.

Arguments against this proposal basically state that if the benefits of a program do not exceed a one-year period, then the beneficiaries or users ought to shoulder the entire burden. Only by standard definitions does maintenance benefit the immediate users, and not the future users. The immediate users, therefore, should pay. However, if the benefits extend to future generations, then there seems to be some basis for allowing federal funds to defray project costs (for "eligible" projects only). Indeed, maintenance programs benefit future users also; without it, a facility's design life will not be met. Benefits of a sound maintenance program exceed a one-year period.[13] If the concern of a federal infrastructure policy is to reverse the decline in infrastructure condition, then *maintenance* ought to be the focus of such a policy.

Furthermore, the *unrestricting* of federal aid may have efficiency benefits. A study by the Congressional Budget Office (1985) argues that the reduction in the EPA matching grant for construction of wastewater treatment facilities from 75 percent to 55 percent in 1984 reduced the overall costs of secondary treatment plants by some 30 percent. Although no empirical analysis exists to assess the increased efficiency and reduced costs of a maintenance program—studies thus far have examined the effects of changing the matching ratio for capital investment—the following inferences appear reasonable. First, cities use their *own* resources more efficiently than federal and state monies; and second, cities will probably select more efficient use of federal money if given the discretion to use those funds for either construction and rehabilitation or maintenance and minor repair. More efficient use of public funds should result.

In exchange for loosening the restrictions on federal grants for urban infrastructure, a "maintenance fund" ought to be required in all city capital budgets, where maintenance activities are typically funded, for repair and maintenance activities and should not be part of the operating budget. Infrastructure maintenance activities, because of their recurring nature and, to a lesser extent, their monetary size, are included in operating budgets. Capital budgets, by definition, exclude maintenance and operating outlays. *The primary cause of "infrastructure decay" is not inadequate capital investment but inadequate maintenance spending.* Structures deteriorate because maintenance has been deferred too long. At that point, then, massive infusions of funding are required, and at that point the problem can be defined as inadequate capital investment. But the cause at first is inadequate maintenance. One reason for maintenance deferral is that maintenance is easy to cut because its effects are not visible immediately and sometimes, if maintenance is underground, never visible.

The maintenance fund for non-fee-supported infrastructure should be financed much like an enterprise fund. Rather than collect funds from "fee-like" activities, this fund (which must generate an annual surplus) should require transfers from general fund revenues annually. Annual maintenance cost estimates for the design life of each project should be calculated by public works and budget officers. Because those costs should be close to zero for the first few years and escalate rapidly thereafter, an average amount should be calculated and deposited in the maintenance fund each year for the design life of the facility. As the surplus grows in the first few years, it will be drawn down during the years in need. This budgetary activity would aid in managing the local government's maintenance program. Instead of needing a large infusion of maintenance dollars in, say, a facility's fifth or tenth year and finding the funds unavailable—which appears to be the general problem today—the funds for that facility would have been accumulating in the maintenance fund since the first year of operation. Therefore, they should be adequate in the facility's fifth or tenth year. This maintenance fund would be similar to a debt service fund in its operation.

If current revenues fund both operating and capital programs, creation of a maintenance fund might appear to be a drain on revenues for operating programs such as social and environmental programs. A maintenance fund need not be viewed as another attack on urban social programs funded through a city's operating budget. Instead, it should better enable cities to manage and plan for future capital facilities. Future maintenance costs would have to be considered in the city's decision to construct facilities, unlike the current practice of considering only the initial construction costs. Total long-term construction and maintenance costs should encourage cities to construct facilities more carefully. An overbuilt and undermaintained city could be avoided with a national infrastructure maintenance policy.

A national infrastructure maintenance policy has to be justified in terms of national impact. If congress has already agreed that "environmental protection," "national transportation networks," and "economic development" are *national* in character and that construction cost subsidies for those purposes are legitimate, then there is no logical reason why federal subsidies to maintain those facilities could not be accorded the same justification. After all, it is highly problematic whether cities would have (or could have) constructed such facilities without federal aid; the physical size of local infrastructure, as a result, is considerably larger than it would have been in the absence of federal intervention. Now that those federally aided facilities have been constructed, cities are saddled with rapidly escalating operation and maintenance costs. A national maintenance policy could move these national objectives of providing a sound transportation network, a safe environment, and economic development opportunities in the right direction.

For city governments that are not expanding the physical size of the infrastructure, a national maintenance policy could generate immediate benefits. For the growing cities this policy might preempt an infrastructure crisis. In all cities there ought to be support for this policy, especially if the benefits of this policy not only exceed the current year but also enhance the development prospects of the nation.

Conclusion

The deteriorating condition of urban infrastructures and the incapacities of local governments to meet escalating infrastructure demands require the concerted effort of all levels of government, the private sector, and users. Based on the analysis presented above, several predictions about the future state of urban infrastructure can be advanced.

First, city governments cannot be expected to substantially raise their local commitment to infrastructure spending. Any increases will be incremental and long-term, not immediate and drastic. City officials responsible for making those decisions not only feel constrained about raising infrastructure spending because of their perception that higher taxes and fees make their city less attractive to taxpayers and businesses, but also they are cognizant of the trade-off between operating and capital needs. The pressing demands of operating-budget needs combine to hold down rapid increases in capital spending.

Second, federal and state aid will not alter a city's local commitment of resources for infrastructure. Although the volume of projects will be affected, cities cannot be stimulated to spend more on infrastructure from their own pockets than they would in the absence of federal aid. Federal program designs intent on altering local commitment cannot be expected to meet much success. Infrastructure banks also will only lower local borrowing costs, not raise local commitment.

Third, the costs of constructing and maintaining urban infrastructure can continue to be shifted from the general taxpayer to users and developers. In their quest to find adequate revenues for urban infrastructures, user fees, development and impact fees, "creative" financing, and a host of other finance mechanisms premised on the benefits principle will continue to be analyzed and adopted by cities. Not only are general tax rates kept down as a result of such actions, but taxpayers can take refuge in the fact that only if they consume public facilities will they pay for them. Against the backdrop of taxpayer rebellions, the policy of shifting infrastructure costs to users may be viewed as a godsend by policymakers.

Fourth, just as the urban infrastructure problem of the late 1980s is not significantly different from that of the late 1970s, without a major change in federal policy toward urban infrastructure, such as the infrastructure block grant proposal and the National Infrastructure Maintenance Policy, reports from 1998 will sound the same alarm as those from 1988 and 1978. Bridges will continue to collapse, urban infrastructures will decay, crumble, and crash; the sky will continue to fall! And the federal government should do something. Because cities' tax policies are in competition with each other, individual cities will not adjust their tax policy radically in accordance with their infrastructure needs. Only the federal government can impose uniform tax rates across all taxpayers and cities.

The National Council on Public Works Improvement recommended increasing infrastructure spending immediately by over 100 percent. The policies for federal involvement in urban infrastructure recommended above cannot realistically be expected to approach the council's suggestions but, together with local strategies designed to more clearly target fees to beneficiaries, a critical step may be taken in the direction of resolving the problem. However, without substantial and radical changes in current federal infrastructure policies, the geriatrics ward of national urban policies will continue to be filled with decrepit and dying public facilities.

7

Boston—An Urban Policy Prototype or a Continuing Urban Policy Problem?

Ian Menzies

Boston during the seventies was an urban policy disaster, a city torn asunder by school desegregation, a city lacking "common ground" between its rich and poor, its blacks and whites, between neighborhood and neighborhood. Today Boston is perceived as an urban-policy paradigm. Its strong economic growth is helping pay for neighborhood and housing revitalization programs. Its private sector is increasingly involved in efforts to expand job and educational opportunities for minorities. What is the real urban policy significance of Boston in the eighties?

To have been born in Boston is not necessary to know the city, or to understand it. The outsider who adopts it is much more likely to appreciate its richness, its history, and its unique dynamic than is the native. As a writer and editor for the *Boston Globe* for almost forty years, it has been fascinating to observe the city's evolution. It has been a remarkable one.

Boston today is a youthful, vibrant city; a world-class city within a new world frame. It can be passionately Olympian, espousing great causes, or embarrassingly parochial: a city of learning, the arts, of entrepreneurial and technological initiatives, but at the same time a city of ethnic neighborhoods, group turf, and racial tensions.

Jan Morris, that most sensitive chronicler of cities, describes it as the only metropolis she knows that has enjoyed "a true renaissance." She is right. In the boardrooms of London, Paris, Tokyo, Zurich, and Rome, as well as Montreal and Toronto, developers talk glowingly of Boston. To them it is the place to be, America's current "in" city, a regional capital in which to profitably invest.

In fact, more than $1 billion a year is currently being spent on development in Boston—two-thirds of it foreign or out-of-state money—and this investment will continue for at least the next five years. Developers are lined up with proposals, to the degree that the Boston Redevelopment Authority (BRA) can virtually dictate its own terms.

Even so, we must ask whether this revival, this enormous boom—fifteen new high-rise office buildings in ten years, ten new hotels in eight, plus multiplying numbers of luxury condominiums—is overwhelming the city's downtown area. Can Boston continue to absorb $1 billion a year in development, as projected for another five years, without jeopardizing its character and grace? Are we creating a socially divisive city of rich and poor?

The physical problems are obvious—twenty-one towering tubes and boxes over 400 feet high with more to come. Not so obvious are other problems, some related to the booming economy, some not; among them a tragically inept Boston public school system, a critical lack of affordable housing, persistently high street crime, sporadic racism, worker shortages, and horrendous traffic congestion.

Growth, in the form of sun-blocking, wind-funneling high rises, has most certainly diminished Boston's historic legacy of human scale, its delightful walkability. On the other hand, and in all fairness, is today's threat of over-building any worse than yesterday's threat of abandonment, bankruptcy, and unemployment?

It is easy to forget that between the two world wars and even into the early 1950s, Boston was a dying city, an urban backwater. For a period of thirty years, not one major new building rose in the city. Boston was a shabby, broken-down, bluestocking, politically corrupt city, a subject of satire and national ridicule. Many of its finest buildings, including some designed by Charles Bulfinch, New England's greatest architect, and Alexander Parris (the Quincy Market buildings), were hidden by signs, billboards, and false fronts. The city's streets were dirty, something that hasn't changed; its buildings blackened by soot, grime, and age, something that fortunately has. The city was physically depressing.

This, as it turned out, was not all bad. As America's outstanding urbanist, the late Lewis Mumford, once said: "Boston was saved from the first onslaught of modernity by its own backwardness." Developers did not discover Boston until Boston rediscovered itself; until in 1959, the same year John F. Kennedy was mounting his drive for the Democratic nomination for president, its power-money men, facing a city heading for bankruptcy, formed a sixteen-member committee to "save the city." The committee was nicknamed "The Vault" because it met in the inner sanctum of the late Ralph Lowell's Safe Deposit and Trust Company.

The Vault threw its support behind a new mayor, John F. Collins (although it had supported his opponent John E. Powers), and Collins, in turn, hired Edward J. Logue, then rebuilding New Haven, Connecticut, to head

Boston's urban renewal program. Under Logue's skillful management, Boston cornered more federal renewal money than any other major city its size. And by the mid-1960s what was then called the New Boston had begun to take shape. The city had the beginnings of a new and exciting skyline. Bostonians began to feel better about themselves, their city, and their future.

To match the new mood and excitement came, in 1968, a new mayor, Kevin H. White, with an upbeat panache and a team of whiz kids—Barney Frank, Ira Jackson, Fred Salvucci, Kathy Kane, Jim Young—to parallel the city's rising skyline. White, for sixteen consecutive, impressive, tumultuous, and latterly confrontational years, held on to the mayoralty chair, even through the trauma of school busing—a record unmatched by any prior Boston chief executive, including James Michael Curley.

Meanwhile, out along Route 128, known as the Golden Semicircle, a new space-age computer-based technology had sprung up. Catalyzed by the bright young researchers who during World War II had been working on radar bombsights, fiber optics, and advanced electronics at Harvard, MIT, and Boston University, the explosive growth of suburban technological firms along Route 128 drew worldwide attention to Massachusetts. That attention, in turn, triggered the interest of international investors, thus reinforcing the physical revival begun under the 1960 renewal program.

Boston could have improved its physical and economic image to some extent with federal money alone, but it could never have become the highflier it is today without the powerful spin-off from its first-rate academic institutions and research hospitals. Federal defense money that flows into Massachusetts at a per capita rate higher than any other state in the nation—$8.6 billion in 1986—has an ironic twist considering that the city-state moralizes more than most against war, nuclear power, and defense spending.

Boston's strength, more accurately a metropolitan strength, comes from its tremendous academic depth: fifty-six degree-granting colleges and universities within twenty miles of the city's downtown center, and 260 if one includes New England. Nowhere in the nation or the world is there a larger per capita grouping of academic institutions. And it is this academic base, attracting innovative entrepreneurial minds, that has enabled Boston to spring back into national prominence and economic contention following eras of depression. As Stephen Coyle, director of the Boston Redevelopment Authority, likes to criticize Boston's current downtown growth as too overwhelming, "One has to remember the bad years to appreciate the good . . . employment versus unemployment . . . congestion versus stagnation."

Today the boom shows no signs of abating. Between now and the end of the century Boston will benefit from an estimated $20 billion investment in private-public development and improvement projects alone.

Unemployment should remain low, although James Howell, chief economist of the Bank of Boston, warns that the computer industry trend toward automation could cause some unemployment in that industry. And that could affect Boston's service industries. "Every industry has a growth cycle," says Howell, "and I'd expect a certain lumpiness—ups and downs—in the computer industry between now and the year 2000." But the size of Boston projects now in the pipeline or about to enter it would seem to guarantee a positive growth pattern for years to come.

There is, for example, the $1.1 billion Fan Pier/Pier 4 development, largest ever undertaken in Boston, virtually a new town, in-town, that will add nearly 5 million square feet of new high-rise offices, hotels, condominiums, and rental housing to the South Boston waterfront—a development equal to five Prudential towers or two and a half International Places. An additional $1.1 billion is slated for expansion along Northern Avenue and at the World Trade Center.

Then there is the Third Harbor Tunnel and depression of the Central Artery, $4 billion; Boston Harbor cleanup, $6.1 billion; renovation of Prudential, $500 million; renovation of Lincoln, Lewis, Battery, and Sargent wharves, $450 million; a new stadium, hotel, offices, and condominiums at North Station, $632 million; Dudley Square, Roxbury, $500 million; Charlestown Navy Yard, $500 million; Columbia Point, $200 million; plus new office and housing construction at scattered sites, $3 billion to $4 billion.

Not only are the economic indicators strong but so are the demographics. Boston's population, which dropped to 562,994 in 1980, is now up to 601,000 and, according to BRA Research Director Alex Ganz, the city has gained 96,000 jobs since 1976, raising the total number of jobs to 610,000, of which two-thirds are filled by suburbanites.

And it is not just the quantity of jobs; the quality also has risen. The overall annual average wage now approximates $23,000, putting the personal income of those who work in the city higher than the average for Greater Boston, the state, or the nation. Offsetting that a bit, however, is the latest cost-index figure for U.S. cities which shows Boston to be the most expensive city to live in, in almost every category—groceries, health care, housing, utilities, and transit.

Ganz, explaining the rise in average income, says it results from larger firms with over five hundred employees moving their staffs into "back office" space in suburbia on the basis that it makes little sense to house

$15,000-a-year employees in downtown office space costing $30 and more a square foot. While this outward movement has reduced by 7 percent the number of employees working in Boston for large firms, it has been more than offset by a rise in employees working for medium-sized firms (fifty to five hundred employees) at higher-salaried positions.

Boston's population, again due to its academic base, is also one of the youngest in the nation, with an average age of twenty-nine, compared with thirty-four in San Francisco, thirty-three in New York, thirty-two in Philadelphia, and thirty in Los Angeles. And its minority population, among major cities, remains relatively low at 34 percent. Only Seattle (20 percent) and Minneapolis (11 percent) have smaller minority populations.

And what Ganz calls "quite astonishing" is the in-migration of whites into the city since 1980, a complete turnaround from the 1970–80 period when almost a third of the white population left for suburbia. The dramatic impact of this turnaround reveals that one-third of all heads of households in the city moved to Boston within the last five years and 45 percent within the last ten years. Newcomers are close to becoming the city's new majority, which will inevitably bring change.

Since 1980 of those moving into Boston either for the first time or as returnees, 38 percent have been white, 30 percent Hispanic, 14 percent black, and 18 percent Asian and other. Currently, the Asian and Pacific Islanders have had the greatest proportional increase, 65 percent. But they still make up only 4 percent of the city's overall population. Whites still constitute 66 percent of Boston's population, blacks 23 percent, and Hispanics 7 percent.

Ganz maintains that Boston's population would increase even more rapidly if affordable housing were available. The number of housing units increased from 232,000 in 1970 to 250,000 in 1985, but most have been in the higher price ranges. A city ordinance does protect the handicapped, elderly, and low-income people from eviction as a result of condominium conversion, and even tougher, broader legislation is proposed.

There are other very positive indicators. Last year the city hosted 8 million visitors who, according to Robert Cummings, president of the Greater Boston Convention & Tourist Bureau, spent an estimated $2.5 billion. If one includes secondary benefits, tourism had a total economic impact of $5 billion. It also provided Boston with $25 million in tax receipts and the state $110 million. Tourism, which supports 47,000 jobs in Greater Boston, is now the state's second largest industry. Education, health care, and hospitals come first.

Cummings, who believes tourism will be the largest industry in the United

States by the year 2000, predicts an annual growth rate in tourism in Boston of 5 to 10 percent. Asked what the city should be doing to encourage tourist growth, Cummings said, "improve transportation within the city, especially to and from the airport, insist on better quality cabs and more informed drivers, clean up the harbor and improve the public access to the waterfront." He also feels that services to aid overseas visitors, not all of whom speak much English, are needed, including facilities to change money.

Other observers with a stake in tourism feel the condition of some of the city's historic tourist attractions, such as Faneuil Hall, the Old State House, and some in-town cemeteries is "scandalous." It is estimated that $5 million is needed to restore Faneuil Hall and $6 million to prevent the collapse of the Old State House, both wards of the National Park Service. They would also urge Mayor Ray Flynn to demand that city streets be kept clean. Boston, like New York, is known as a dirty city, a national soubriquet it does not need.

But we should not forget the national impact of, on the one hand, Boston's always-contending professional sports teams and on the other, its continuing stream of Nobel Prize winners. And, though it may seem a bit absurd, a city's national standing can in part be calculated by the number of TV sitcoms sited in its streets, hospitals, police precincts, and barrooms. Boston is doing well. Even movieland is finding the city and its surrounding suburbs an exciting backdrop.

Is it reasonable, therefore, in the light of such positive numbers and such a positive image, to find a downside to the Boston story?

Yes, because, like the mountaintop, it's there.

It is at the same time, however, only fair to say that most, but not all, of the negatives found in Boston are as readily found in every major city in the nation. Some negatives are peculiar to Boston or at least more apparent or, as in the case of school busing, more publicized.

There are, for instance, those who firmly believe that downtown Boston is already overbuilt; that the nation's most walkable big city—packed into two square miles—has been irreparably damaged; that because of the inhuman scale of blank, precipitous walls rising from narrow sidewalks, creating shadowed wind tunnels while entrapping noise and pollution, the city no longer provides the strolling pleasure it once did.

It is fair criticism. Boston's early redevelopment planners simply failed to recognize that because the city is not built on a grid, ensuring street-end views of sun and sky, hills or harbor, skyscrapers built on cowpath streets would eventually create huge semicircular barrier walls.

It is also clear that four-term mayor Kevin White (1968–83), although warned, failed to restrain his BRA developers and refused to appoint a public design review committee. In 1979 White, who deserves great credit for the Faneuil Hall marketplace as well as other innovative city initiatives, in effect admitted that development got away from him. "In the next 10 years the Boston skyline will change more than it has in all its history," he stated, adding "it scares me more than busing."

What about Mayor Flynn, who, unlike White, seldom speaks about design or particular projects or leastwise isn't asked by the media? Flynn readily admits to concern about over-building. "It must be held in check," he says. "We can't afford to be run by developers and planners who are just in it for the economics."

The Mayor considers BRA Director Stephen Coyle's height limit plan "a bold step, but a necessary one," one that falls in line with Flynn's aim to make Boston "a desirable place for people to live in . . . with affordable downtown housing," but he adds this warning: "If the city is not kept in the hands of those who love it, it will lose its character and become someone else's city."

Critics suggest this may already have happened and that fifty years from now architects, planners and developers will admit they designed buildings for an urban environment without considering the consequences, just as they built highrise public housing that in many instances was so unlivable it had to be either blown up, thinned out or partially abandoned.

BRA Director Steve Coyle, the most innovative of the city's long line of redevelopment bosses and the most articulate, speaking of bulk, says "there'll be no more New England Lifes, no more International Places," which he ad-libs, "has more Palladian windows than in all of Italy."

Coyle is not enamored of some of the buildings that preceded his arrival in Boston in 1984 and, in retrospect, he chides himself for not being tough enough with those that, though already in the pipeline, he could have "restrained," International Place being one he specifically mentions.

Although Coyle has outlawed 600-foot-plus buildings (John Hancock-Prudential size) through temporary zoning regulations, he is still prepared to approve buildings up to 350 feet in height in the North and South Station areas and up to 400 feet around Bedford and Essex streets in the old leather district. Strictly speaking, the high-rise love-in is not yet over, something both Flynn and his new Civic Design Review Committee, chaired by John de Monchaux, dean of MIT's School of Architecture, might wish to review.

Coyle firmly believes that his approach to cooling off high-rise pressure by gradually establishing height limits— a restriction foolishly discarded by Boston in 1965—will work better than San Francisco's moratorium on new development. He may well prove right. There is no question that Coyle has been innovative with his parcel-to-parcel linkage program—the pairing of publicly owned development sites to leverage community benefits—which is now under way.

Using his Interim Planning Overlay District (IPOD) approach, Coyle says, "I'll have the entire city rezoned, including the neighborhoods by 1989." The IPOD approach, which sits well with Mayor Flynn, is designed to allow comprehensive planning and rezoning of a neighborhood by the community, thus ensuring that the rezoning will meet the community's needs. It is, however, a slow process, involving countless meetings among the community, the BRA, and other city agencies.

High-rise building is having, and will continue to have, its most devastating effect, whether downtown or in neighborhoods, on traffic, city congestion, noise, and air pollution. "Gridlock," says Douglas Foy, executive director of the Conservation Law Foundation (CLF), "is the single greatest threat to Boston's continued economic growth." This is one of the principal reasons that CLF has questioned the size of the proposed Fan Pier/Pier 4 project in South Boston, a high-rise spillover from the downtown area.

"This project alone," says Foy, "will generate 17,000 additional automobile trips a day—enough to fill an entire lane of the Central Artery bumper to bumper all day long," a criticism that has led directly to the city proposing a new Fan Pier station on the Red Line.

Coyle is sensitive to the problem but disagrees with Foy that traffic is the city's major problem, believing that if good jobs are available, people will accept some commuting hardships. Those hardships, says Foy, will mean that new commuters will spend four years of their lives sitting in traffic jams going to and from work.

Will a third harbor tunnel and depressing the Central Artery resolve the congestion? No, says State Transportation Secretary Fred Salvucci, whose Herculean persistence has made both projects possible, but it will hold off gridlock.

In the North End, where opposition to the Central Artery project is strongest, Joseph Matara, president of the Haymarket Pushcart Association, calls the expense "incomprehensible" and feels the solution should be a second airport and mass transit. North-Enders' fear for their businesses is legitimate. But Salvucci, whose Italian heritage is on the line on this one, swears he will do everything possible to minimize the impact of construction work. And he does not disagree with Matara as to mass transit being an important component toward a solution. The problem is to get people to use mass transit in sufficient numbers to reduce the congestion.

The answer, of course, is to make mass transit as attractive as possible. The two most productive approaches, as measured by current commuter interest and rising ridership, are commuter rail and water ferries; which is not to say that an improved and more reliable MBTA service with expanded suburban parking is not equally important. Also critically needed is fast three-hour rail service between Boston and New York to reduce both air and ground congestion at Logan Airport.

To some, such as Foy, traffic is the greatest threat to Boston's economic future, but to a consensus of informed observers there are two far greater threats—schools and housing.

The crisis of the Boston Public Schools, as that of other large urban school systems throughout the country, is well documented. Last March Mayor Flynn called the situation a "dark cloud" hanging over the city. In May Boston University President John Silber described the Boston schools as "a complex system of child abuse." And even more recently Hubie Jones, dean of Boston University's School of Social Work, said sadly, "I am in more despair than I have ever been about the schools. We gave all these kids out there, who are in desperate need of education and human service, support and they're just not getting it."

The figures are fairly well known but nonetheless horrifying. More than 44 percent of students drop out of school before the end of ninth grade, 60 percent of the children are on welfare, 75 percent come from single-parent or foster homes, and 2,500 have to report to court probation officers. The dream of integration has long gone, burned on the crucible of one of Boston's greatest traumas, school busing. The system is now only 25 percent white, almost 50 percent black, 16 percent Hispanic, and 8 percent Asian.

To say that the task facing Boston School Superintendent Laval Wilson is monumental is to put it mildly. Yet a school system that cannot produce young men and women capable of entering the work force is a formula for disaster.

There are approximately 56,000 students in the Boston system. There are, however, 26,000 other school-age children in the city who go to parochial or other private schools or, under a METCO plan for black students, to suburban schools. If almost half of the 56,000 Boston students, taken as a single wave, drop out during the course of their school years, the waste in human lives is incredible because most who drop out are functionally illiterate.

Wilson has put forward an education plan stressing fundamentals, a plan that recognizes that because of difficult home conditions, many students, if they are to learn, will have to do their learning in school, which means extending the school day where necessary.

Wilson's plan—at least twelve of its thirteen parts—has won the support of the school committee but has raised the ire of teachers, as voiced by Edward Doherty, president of the Boston Teachers Union. Wilson advocates a single reading text for each elementary grade; Doherty claims this gives teachers no autonomy. He charges that Wilson's plan is an expensive hierarchical structure. The Citywide Education Coalition's executive director Ellen Guiney questions whether there is enough money to support Wilson's ambitious initiatives. But outside support from Mayor Flynn, the media, and civic organizations has been strong, even though it may be on a "What else can we do?" basis.

A quite separate package of management reforms, however, put together by the mayor and Samuel R. Tyler of the Boston Municipal Research Bureau, successfully won approval of the school committee and the city council. These reforms give the superintendent the right to hire and fire teachers without school committee interference, a right sought unsuccessfully by previous superintendents. The thirteen-member school committee deserves praise for, in effect, voting itself out of the teacher patronage business. But it would look even better if members dropped their insistence on each receiving a $50,000 annual personnel allowance for staff assistants and secretarial help, plus a $7,500 stipend—a total of almost three-quarters of a million dollars a year.

One encouraging sign was a recent improvement in test scores throughout the Boston system, but if these are not maintained and Wilson's plan fails to produce results, more dramatic steps will be necessary.

Mayor Flynn, dissatisfied with the rate of improvement, as well as the cost of operating the school committee, recently proposed that in the future school committee members be appointed rather than elected, a move which sent a few shock waves through city hall.

The fact is the dismal quality and conditions in the Boston school system deprive it of the very children it needs—the children of upwardly mobile young people. In countless cases middle-class families pull their children out after three or four grades of elementary school. Colin and Joan Diver, principals in Anthony Lukas's *Common Ground*, the story of school integration in Boston, did just that. They moved to Newton. But now that their two sons have graduated, they have returned to Boston. They are not alone.

The two in the one-two punch is housing. A city cannot function without affordable housing, especially in a service economy. If those who would normally fill lower-echelon jobs cannot afford to live in the city or afford to commute, how does business recruit? It can move out of the city to cheaper labor pools and cheaper housing—a Fall River or a New Bedford—or it can raise wages, which it congenitally resists.

But it can do something else, although it has taken business a long time to get around to thinking about it. It can become involved in building affordable housing.

And Boston's solution to affordable housing has got to be a public-private partnership. According to BRA Director Stephen Coyle who spent twelve years with HUD in Washington before coming to Boston: "Even though President George Bush and HUD Secretary Jack Kemp outline a new, enlarged, and subsidized national public housing program, it would take six and a half years before anything happened. That's how slow the system is. We can't wait. If we want to get something done, we'll have to do it ourselves."

And Coyle believes, through imaginative financing and cooperation from the private sector and other city departments, that Boston can begin to resolve its affordable housing dilemma. The current goal is to add 3000 to 4000 units of new housing a year, but Coyle predicts that housing square footage will, by the early 1990s, exceed commercial. "In the next eight to 10 years I expect the city to add 15 to 20 million square feet of new housing to 10 million square feet of commercial space." So what does he foresee? "I'm a transitional director," says Coyle, rather humbly, meaning he can't do it all, "but I see Boston, by the year 2000 as a mature, established city." And with maturity, many hope, will come a lessening of racial tensions, an open city, an end to group turf.

Boston's national image still suffers from what is called the "Landsmark incident," when, on April 15, 1976, Ted Landsmark, a 29-year-old black civil rights lawyer walked across City Hall plaza to attend a meeting on affirmative action. Midway across the plaza, he was surrounded by a group of angry whites who had been protesting court-ordered school busing. One, wielding an American flag like a spear, lunged at Landsmark who was struck in the face by the staff.

The incident, caught by a photographer, appeared in every major newspaper in the country—an innocent black being struck by the American flag over court-ordered busing. Boston is still struggling to put that incident behind it. So, too, is Landsmark, currently dean of the Massachusetts College of Art, who declines to discuss the subject any more except to say, forgivingly, "it was something that happened in one moment of time . . . and to keep going back to it is very boring."

Boston, historically Yankee but for almost a century an Irish citadel, has never looked lovingly on minorities and especially, in recent years, on blacks. Professionally, the city offers excellent opportunities for blacks but, according to black professionals, a very limited social life. The result is that even today few blacks are to be seen in the city's prestigious firms, or in restaurants, the Faneuil Hall marketplace, or sports events.

Landsmark, quoted in the *Boston Globe* recently, said, "Say I wanted to meet interesting black women professionals, where would I go? The simple reality is you look at any of the downtown watering holes, the neighborhood watering holes, you never see black professional women. Never."

At the other extreme is the group-turf syndrome—that neighborhoods such as Charlestown and South Boston are off-limits to blacks and Roxbury is off-limits to whites. South Boston, which bloodily fought integrated school busing back in the 1970s, is now fighting the integration of public housing demanded by HUD. Boston's public housing projects are still segregated. Of some 2,000 units in three South Boston projects, none are occupied by blacks. Conversely, in Roxbury the tenants are up to 99.2 percent minority.

It took Kevin White a dozen years in office to admit that Boston is a racist city. "It's a joke," he said in 1980. "There's no access [for blacks] in this town." Five years earlier Boston Celtic basketball star Bill Russell said, "I have never lived in a more segregated city in my life."

A reason for Boston's black/white tensions is one that few outsiders realize. Despite its current glitter, its building boom, and its wealth, Boston down deep is a poor city, one of the poorest in the nation. There are poor whites as well as poor blacks, and they live predominantly in the segregated areas. One in five of Boston's citizens is on some form of welfare. The poverty rate (income under $10,690 for a family of four) in the nation's central cities in 1985 was 19 percent. In Boston it was 21 percent.

Boston, in fact, exemplifies the increasing gap between rich and poor. The city (population 620,000) has an estimated 3,000 homeless (10,000 statewide), offset to some extent by a shelter program. The challenge remains, as in other cities, to provide homes and not just cover.

On Boston's problems of racism and group turf, so embarrassingly documented over countless years, all that can be said is that no greater effort has been made to face them down in decades than the current efforts by Mayor Flynn and Police Commissioner Francis Roche. As Flynn is quoted as saying, "If there is an incident, the police know to call me. I'll be there. Harassment won't be tolerated in this city."

One exciting indicator that the city could become more tolerant lies in the latest demographic data showing population dilution. The surprise is that 45 percent of the current population moved to Boston within the past ten years, suggesting that historic hates could lessen. Poverty may be lessened by the massive multibillion dollar projects about to get under way; housing, despite Mayor Flynn's praiseworthy efforts, must await a more caring national administration.

There is no question that as Boston looks toward the 1990s and the turn of the century, its future seems strong. Huge projects that will on the one hand produce turmoil but, on the other, billions of investment dollars, are all set to go—the third harbor tunnel, depression of the Central Artery, the cleanup of Boston harbor, the Fan Pier project, and more.

This is a city whose bedrock strength lies in its many colleges and universities, its young people, its technology, and its entrepreneurial spirit. Its Achilles heel is its embattled school system, its lack of affordable housing, its traffic congestion, its street crime, group turf, and social-racial tensions.

But what is positive, even among the negatives, is that each is being addressed, even though the outcome is uncertain.

Part 3

Developing a Comprehensive Urban Policy—Maximum Hopes, Minimum Results

8

National Urban Policy: Where Are We Now? Where Are We Going?

Marshall Kaplan

Since 1960 every administration has expressed concern over the health of American cities, particularly older central cities.[1] Both the New Frontier and the Great Society initiated programs such as the War on Poverty, Model Cities, and urban renewal, aimed in part at the urban poor and in part at deteriorating urban neighborhoods. New Federalism, Nixon-style, while generating a shift in the relative flow of aid funds to reflect its nonurban constituencies, increased the absolute volume of federal funds flowing into urban areas. President Carter promised the nation a comprehensive urban policy. His administration delivered something less—a set of federal programs and a cluster of activities tilted toward responding to the assumed ills of distressed central cities. President Reagan linked his perception of city problems to the failure of the broader economy to provide cities with taxes and jobs. According to Reagan, improved economic performance would benefit most, if not all, cities. As a result, his administration downplayed urban policy and program-development initiatives.

Federal urban policy at this juncture in our nation's history is up for grabs. We can help define an efficient and equitable response to cities, particularly distressed cities, if we reflect on where the nation has come from in the development of national urban policies and if we provide a snapshot view of where the nation is now with respect to urban policies and commitments.

Where We Have Come From

Arguably, urban historians pointing to the pre- and postwar public housing and planning initiatives could make a case that national concern for urban policies began more than forty years ago. But depression era urban agendas were related more to pump priming—getting the national economy working again—than they were to specific strategies to help cities in trouble. Similarly, postwar housing and renewal efforts were limited concerning focus and/or geographic coverage, while efforts to generate comprehensive land use planning were not directed at any type of city or town—small or large, distressed or healthy.

By and large, America's efforts to define comprehensive or strategic policy initiatives that addressed the problems or ills of cities, particularly distressed cities, were an outgrowth of the civil rights and antipoverty movements of the early and mid-sixties. They were reflected in the numerous speeches, agency reports, public-interest-group statements, executive orders, prescriptive mandates, and categorical and block grant programs that were generated by Kennedy's New Frontier, Johnson's Great Society, Nixon's New Federalism, and Carter's New Partnership. While they granted visible, sustained attention to cities and their residents, they never added up to a cohesive set of policy initiatives. Put another way, the whole appeared always less than the sum of the parts.

Over time, certain changes have occurred in the themes and principles that seemed to guide federal policymakers concerned with cities. Clearly, we have moved away from viewing the problems of cities as caused primarily by physical decay to being caused by multiple factors—physical, social, economic, etc. Urban renewal, housing, and transportation were the centerpieces of early efforts to help cities. They were capital investment programs aimed at responding to the physical problems of cities. This fact is understandable. Historically, "housers," businessmen concerned with downtown decay, and the media, whose headquarters were often located in deteriorating parts of cities, composed the initial coalitions that generated urban concerns in Washington. Furthermore, HUD and its predecessor HHFA, the agencies most concerned with cities, were driven by their most amply funded programs—housing and urban renewal.

Only after data indicated renewal often destroyed more housing than it created, and only after it became clear that good housing units did not necessarily mean good lives for the people living in them, did the nation come to view the physical transformation of cities as only part of a comprehensive, or indeed strategic, set of urban policy objectives. The advent of the war on poverty and programs like Model Cities broadened the focus of urban initiatives to include concern for the health and well-being of people, as well as the health and well-being of the structures they lived and worked in. While it is an advance perhaps in terms of sophistication, increased national awareness of the number of variables that affected the vitality of cities and the choices open to their residents did not lead to increased knowledge with respect to how best to develop urban initiatives that would produce lasting, positive impacts. The nation's ability to define strategies of city revitalization that offer more than just the possibility of success remains marginal.

We have moved away from viewing city problems as those related to too many people requiring homes in cities to those related to too few people or to too many of the "wrong" kinds of people requiring residence in cities. Most individuals and groups concerned with cities during the sixties were not overly concerned with the loss of city population, or "white flight." The literature related to the period defines the increased concentraton of the poor, often in areas hidden from the white majority, as a policy problem. Concentration generated fiscal problems related to increased needs for cities to provide welfare and social services. It also led to housing difficulties related to the absence of household income sufficient to foster rehabilitation efforts among the poor. And it fostered increased educational difficulties because of the concentration of minorities in local schools.

Surprisingly, in retrospect, the reports and books about cities in the pre-birth-control period also talked of a population explosion. Most asked where the nation was going to put the millions of people likely to want to live in cities and their environs before the year 2000. Many mayors of central cities, through their national organizations, authored a report calling for America to build several score new towns to house the nation's anticipated population growth. Congress responded and in the early 1970s enacted a new-town bill to assist private developers in building new towns outside of central cities — supposedly to provide residences for a population that would soon overflow city boundaries.

How quickly times and thinking change. By the mid-seventies growth projections had been toned down. The birth-control pill and related changing life-styles lowered the number of births. No longer were we worried about overpopulation and the need to provide new communities for increasing numbers of people who would or could not find homes in cities or their suburbs. Instead, we began to look at census data that reflected a tremendous loss of population in many older, sometimes distressed central cities. Our cities were decanting their more affluent white population. Left behind were a disproportionate number of poor and minority households. Left behind also were bottom-line social, economic, and environmental problems that could not be remedied easily, given the fiscal difficulties faced by cities without federal help.

By the late seventies and early eighties city demography again seemed to change and again seemed to cause policymakers some difficulties. The popular media called attention to the gentrification of older neighborhoods. Statistics from the census pointed to increasing numbers of minorities moving out of central cities. There were some signs that some cities had stabilized in terms of population.

The seemingly good news about cities was not easy to decipher from a policy perspective. On studied reflection the revitalization of older areas of cities appeared to be stimulated from within; from the movement of households from one area within a city to another and from the breakup of one household into two or more households. In some areas it generated social difficulties as old neighborhoods, generally of low-income minorities, were pushed out by higher-income whites. The movement of minorities from central cities seemed to be limited and seemed to be focused on older suburban areas. Put another way, one ghetto was being substituted for another. Finally, aggregate population figures continue to suggest that central cities particularly are losing population. Stability and/or gains in numbers are restricted to a relatively few cities.

American cities, by and large, remain the home to disproportionately large numbers of poor and minority households. In most areas central cities, when compared to their surrounding suburbs, provide the primary place of residence to low-income Hispanic and black families and individuals. This fact continues to translate into fiscal disparities between city and suburb and limited education, housing, and job opportunities for large numbers of urban residents. Urban policy advocates now appear more concerned with who is living in cities than with broad population trends.

We have moved from urban policies that had to be discovered from the implicit program commitments of presidents and Congress to the explicit commitment of President Carter to define a comprehensive approach to urban ills. We now have come full circle. The Reagan administration's urban approach relied more on the assumed positive impact of national economic growth on cities than on either direct federal urban policies or program assistance.

In the sixties and seventies over 400 categorical programs, or programs for every category of urban problem that seemed politically popular, were enacted by Congress, most often at the request of the White House. Most were directed at responding to one or more city-related problems. They were bred of the optimism of the era that federal funds combined with intelligently defined programs could remedy urban ills.[2]

The categorical program era created a hodgepodge of federal initiatives, agencies, guidelines, mandates, and federal-local relationships that affected cities and that, when pieced together, added up to sometimes consistent and sometimes inconsistent urban policies. Some efforts were aimed at expanding the economic opportunities and mobility of the urban poor; some at providing them with base-level services and income. Some programs were directed at expanding the housing supply available to low-income families and individuals; some led to reducing the housing options open to these same households. Some federal strategies were directed at improving residential neighborhoods; some federal aid programs generated the weakening of city neighborhoods.

Although analyses related to impact suggest at times contrary results, some people and some areas seemed to benefit. The poor were provided with better access to health, housing, and select social services in many areas. Civil rights legislation secured increased opportunities for many minorities to gain access to improved education and jobs. Distressed central cities were granted more resources to respond to the needs of their low-income residents.

But despite the anecdotes and statistics relating the positive effect of federal efforts, most scholars and political figures looking at the diverse and multiple federal programs flowing into or used by cities and groups related to cities suggested that we could do better. They noted the absence of coordination, the varied inconsistencies between and among federal initiatives, and the limited impacts caused by bureaucratic complexities. The federal system, according to many, had become overly congested. Neither city hall nor any federal agency often understood the totality of available federal initiatives. Unpredictable events unrelated to federal policies and programs and nonurban federal policies and programs often swamped federal urban initiatives and, in so doing, negated sought-after results.

In the early seventies Congress began to convert categorical programs to block grants in key functional areas. Simultaneously, it asked the administration through the Department of Housing and Urban Development to prepare a biennial urban policy report. Ostensibly, the former would provide cities with more flexibility to respond to their own perceptions of their problems than did categorical programs, while the latter would extend the ability of the Feds to define cohesive and more comprehensive policies.[3]

Neither worked as well as the rhetoric. Block grants increased the general support for urban areas while decreasing the targeting of federal funds into the worse-off cities and parts of cities. Block grants also did not eliminate categorical programs; they primarily added a new type of federal aid or a new mode of the delivery of federal aid.

HUD's biennial urban policy report to Congress, at least during the Nixon and Ford years, was long on data and trend analysis and short on policies.

Most submittals failed to stimulate the adrenalin or the action of Congress or the federal bureaucracy. The urban policies of the early and mid-seventies still had to be defined from an examination of the collective actions of the two administrations and not from any written, cohesive urban policy statement.

President Carter promised that his administration would be the first to develop a comprehensive urban policy. The commitment and the effort were admirable. But the product was flawed. Clearly, an operational definition of the term "comprehensive" and, indeed, "urban" escaped most of the Carter staff granted responsibility to prepare the comprehensive urban policy. Did the term "comprehensive" mean that everything affecting the health of American cities was to be covered? Did the term "urban" mean that all areas of the county classified as urban by the census were candidates for inclusion in the urban policy? Was the urban policy sought by the president to be directed at helping cities abort or adapt to change? Could anything the Feds do impede or significantly affect broad economic or market trends having an impact on cities? What was the policy relationship between national and regional shifts in economic activity and the limited opportunities open to low-income households in some cities?[4]

Methodological, political, institutional, and resource problems were severe, particularly at the outset, when the president's charge seemingly provided little in the way of substantive boundaries. Over time the president's commitment was translated into relatively limited terms. Distressed central cities became the focus of the Carter policymakers, and their economic and physical revitalization became the primary thrust of the urban policy effort. Targeting of existing and whatever new federal programs could be squeezed from the Congress became the focus of most White House and agency initiatives. What emerged as the Carter urban policy was primarily "place-oriented;" that is, it dealt with cities as geographic entities and jurisdictions rather than as the home of specific populations or groups that needed different kinds of direct federal help, including help to leave the city. Strategies were directed at buttressing local economies, at improving local neighborhoods, at providing increased jobs within cities, at improving local services—at creating a better economic, social, and physical environment in the assisted cities.

The Reagan presidency granted short shrift to specifically urban concerns. To the president and his colleagues, most federal efforts aimed at assisting cities in the past had been a waste of money. Cities had become overly dependent on federal aid and in effect functioned as grant-in-aid junkies. The best urban policy to the administration would be in effect a nonurban, national economic policy.[5] According to administration spokespersons, a rising economic tide would float all ships, including city ships.

Regrettably, increased GNP performance has not reduced the severity of the problems faced by needy central cities or their poorer residents. Indeed, despite national economic growth, many central cities remain the home of relatively large numbers of poor people and minorities. Unemployment and underemployment among the urban poor continue to be high. Access to health care, adequate housing, and solid education programs appears to have narrowed considerably for the low-income inhabitants of many of our older distressed communities. Increased fiscal needs in many central cities and growing fiscal disparities between cities and suburbs have been documented by administration and congressional reports.

We have moved away from federal support of citizen involvement in the planning and allocation of federal funds directed at cities and have moved toward reliance, once again, on established local government institutions. Citizen-participation prerequisites governed the flow of a large share of the federal money going to cities in the sixties and seventies. They reflected the ideological biases of the academic community and the legacy of the poverty and civil rights battles of the sixties. People were poor and/or entrapped in deteriorating neighborhoods because they lacked power to influence their lives and the lives of their community. The way to help the poor was to empower them with authority to participate if not control the use of federal resources aimed at responding to city problems.

Federal support for citizen involvement waxed and waned during the Nixon, Ford, and Carter years. By and large it was ended during the Reagan years. Part of the evolution away from formal recognition and support of citizen groups in the distribution of federal funds stems from a political and institutional reaction to the ostensible excesses of the sixties; part comes from the feeling among many in Washington that, given limited resources, efficiency should command more priority than equity and psychological parity at the local policy table. And part results from the assumption of power through the electoral and appointive process of many of the resident activists of the sixties and seventies. They, in effect, became part of the formal process of governance and in the process lost their enthusiasm for participation in governance by former allies in the neighborhoods.

The federal government fostered the growth and development of resident involvement in local government decisionmaking. Despite the absence of federal support, at the present time, the participation genie likely will never be put back in the bottle. Neither will it likely be granted sustained federal commitments in the future. As a substitute, the Feds may join groups, like the Ford Foundation, and provide assistance to locally administered community development corporations. But contrary to the resident groups of the sixties and seventies, such community development corporations will have an agenda narrowly prescribed by specific development projects, and they will function as partners with the local public and private sector.

We have moved away from "marble cake" back toward dual federalism with respect to the delivery of federal aid to cities and their residents. The New Frontier and the Great Society fostered numerous direct and complicated relationships between varied federal agencies, local and regional governments, and citizen and nonprofit groups. State government during this period often seemed like the orphan of the federal system.

The diverse relationships between and among the Feds and others resembled what one author called "marble cake federalism." Lines of authority were blurred. Nothing was neat. Roles were constantly in flux. Despite the absence of predictability concerning responsibility, however, the system, or nonsystem, prevailed by and large until the Reagan era.

The Reagan administration has moved to change the balance of power among federal, state, and local governments regarding urban policy concerns. While its ill-conceived efforts to shift welfare programs to the states went nowhere, it has allocated to the states a significant role in administering its new block grant programs, and it has devolved upon the states many additional regulatory functions. It has also transformed many programmatic links from federal-city relationships to federal-state-city relationships. While the Washington shuttle remains a fact of transportation life for many mayors, the airplane or bus route to their state capitals has become equally, if not more, important.

We appear to have moved away from local leadership by fiat to local leadership by consensus building. Citizen participation may no longer carry with it the moral and legislative clout of the federal government. But in many respects citizen groups have more influence on key decisions in many cities now than they had during the heyday of the war on poverty. Put another way, citizen groups may have lost the battle for formal recognition, but in many communities they have won the war for informal places at the table of local decisionmaking on key resource allocation issues. Significantly, what the residents gave up with the diminution of federal legitimacy was involvement in the use of federal funds; what they have won is involvement and, in many instances, veto power over the distribution of all funds. The behavior patterns generated by federal prescriptions, combined with the changing demography of many cities, have granted residents the power to make or break resource allocation patterns. The new mayors are not cast in the mold of Mayor Daley. They are not lawgivers or prescription makers. They are facilitators and mediators between and among groups competing for limited resources. Group concurrence is often a key prerequisite preceding public sector action.

We appear to have moved away from a federal focus on city-specific economic development programs to a focus on broader economic policies that might benefit cities. Urban development action grants and community development block grants still exist. The Economic Development Administration still maintains marginal activity in cities. But neither the present administration nor any likely future administration will place their city bet on place-specific economic development initiatives. The costs are too high and the results too limited. Further, the programs are subject to being swamped by unpredictable, unanticipated, and uncontrollable national and international economic variables.

Although broadcast economic policies premised on a rising economic tide helping cities have not won the hearts and minds of many advocates of cities, concern for developing strategic national economic and/or industrial policies that do benefit cities has won the support of many urban scholars, political figures, and urban practitioners. Indeed, of late, dialogue concerning the impact of tax reform, of industrial shifts, of trade initiatives, of interest rates, and of the relation between fiscal and monetary policies on cities has become more visible and attracted more attention than discussions about specific new economic development program initiatives. Even presidential candidates, once prone to articulating the need for new grant or loan programs for particular urban places, have been noticeably shy about calling for major new economic development assistance to cities. Rather, their speeches call for new trade strategies that will help certain areas of the nation, including assumedly distressed cities, and new tax policies that will enhance the winners and buttress the losers among industrial firms, many of which are located in cities.

We have moved away from a federal focus on city-specific community-and/ or neighborhood-based policies to aid the poor to a focus on broad adjustment or reform of social welfare policies to help low-income households. Federal initiatives to help residents of older declining neighborhoods revitalize those neighborhoods have not escaped critical review. Most initiatives have been too small to make a real dent on the city landscape. Some have led to benefits for newcomers to neighborhoods instead of to existing, often poorer, residents. Many initiatives aimed at revitalization have been swamped by unanticipated economic and social changes in cities. Very few policies have consciously linked physical improvement objectives to social policy objectives. As a result, federal initiatives have worked at cross-purposes. For example, in some cities, neighborhood improvements have generated higher housing costs and reduced housing opportunities for neighborhood residents. Consistency regarding neighborhood efforts has been rare. Most federal assistance has not been directed at the worst areas. This fact has raised equity questions concerning the allocation of scarce federal resources.

Formula and criteria changes have spread benefits from formerly neighborhood-based federal programs that remain on the books to the nonpoor and to nonpoverty areas of the cities. No strong consensus exists about developing new targeted neighborhood development or revitalization initiatives. Instead, the apparent failure of neighborhood-based programs to help low-income households has shifted attention to broader social welfare policy. Welfare reform, job training and placement, expanded educational opportunities, and mobility have become the favored policy options to expand the choices of the poor. Put succinctly, we have moved from place- to nonplace-oriented urban policies.

We have moved from a predominantly public sector approach to urban problem-solving to a willingness to define and foster broader partnerships between and among public, nonprofit, private sector, and community groups in responding to urban ills. Budget deficits, combined with a recognition that despite often noble attempts past public-sector-driven urban policies have generated uneven results, has opened up new options concerning collaboration between public and private sector as well as among public, private sector, nonprofit, and community groups. While success stories of partnerships remain anecdotal and often related predominantly to downtown revitalization, they do exist. Development activities and service provision involving more than the public sector have and will continue to secure increased attention from individuals and groups concerned with the health and well-being of cities. Whether the faith in partnerships expressed in some areas, however, goes beyond limited projects and lunchtime speeches will depend on the ability of their advocates to define fair ground rules concerning the public interest and reasonable incentives concerning the interests of the assumed partners.

Where We Are Now

Cities remain popular in the nation's literature, its drama, and its poetry. They continue to receive high marks as places to live on the part of relatively large numbers of Americans. They command our respect as the home for multicultural activities and facilities. They win our attention as places where continued waves of new immigrants find their initial homes and jobs. They generate guilt because they serve to remind us of how far we have come and how far we still have to go in building an integrated society. They secure our frequent analyses, given their importance to our nation's economic health and its future. Despite the warm, sometimes affectionate view many Americans have of their cities, and despite the almost thirty-year effort to define consensus policies and programs, the federal role regarding cities remains uneven and unclear.

At the present time it is clear that the federal government does not have anything resembling a comprehensive urban policy. As noted above, the Reagan administration abandoned any effort to forge comprehensive or strategic urban policies in favor of reliance on macroeconomic policy. Perhaps the administration's skepticism concerning the wisdom of urban policies was justified given the experience of the Carter and previous administrations. It was easier for Kennedy, Johnson, Nixon, and Ford to sustain interest in their respective urban programs because they appealed to narrow and limited constituencies and specific objectives. Carter's effort at comprehension won few supporters because it initially lacked definition and preciseness. Only when distressed cities became the focus did the activity really win even modest political support. Clearly, the cities that stood to gain admired the president's courage; just as clearly, however, the areas of the country that stood to lose and the agencies that supported them were not enthusiastic.

The Carter initiative to forge a comprehensive policy would have left a more interesting intellectual legacy had it been able to resolve at least some of the knowledge gaps concerning the relationship of key economic, social, and environmental factors to one another and to the health of cities. But methodological difficulties, combined with time and budget constraints, denied it the opportunity. The question of whether or not this nation can ever define a comprehensive urban policy is still up for grabs. Certainly the Carter experience suggests that political, institutional, economic, and research obstacles make success at best difficult and at worst impossible.

The federal government does not have a theory of city development and city decay. Urban policy efforts to date have not been grounded on any consistent set of theories relative to the behavior of cities. Indeed, policies and programs have reflected several often inconsistent premises relative to city growth and decline. For example, some scholars and practitioners suggest that the national economy sets the temperature of American cities: if it grows, the cities will reflect good health; if it declines, the cities will suffer. Others contend that the national economy does not affect all cities in the same way. Some cities appear immune to national growth and decline. Regional economies and local variables are more important to the well-being of cities. In a similar vein, some observers contend that urban poverty is caused by the absence of good education, the absence of jobs, the absence of political power in poverty communities, the concentration of poor people in ghettos, or by individual weaknesses of character.

None of the models put forth to explain urban problems and/or city trends stand up well under sustained scrutiny. Very few offer us real help in explaining diverse social and economic occurrences in cities or offer us real assistance in anticipating future patterns. Much of what the federal government has to work with regarding theoretical constructs stems from the non-strategic work of an earlier generation of geographers or the now outdated base-service models of urban economists. The Feds have yet to create appropriate models to test the relevance or irrelevance of governmental policies aimed at slowing down or aborting decentralization trends, at increasing the incomes of the urban poor, and at developing the fiscal base to sustain urban services. Strikingly, although the importance of international economic trends on the viability of America's urban areas is increasingly evident, we have yet to define and measure hypotheses concerning their specific impact on cities.[6]

The federal government has not developed an appropriate administrative mechanism to develop an urban policy or policies. HUD has not lived up to its role and mission.[7] Irrespective of administration, the agency has not been able to develop a comprehensive or even a strategic set of urban policies. The agency has been rowing rudderless in attempting to secure agreement concerning urban policy. As noted earlier, no solid theoretical underpinnings exist upon which to base urban policy initiatives and no firm political consensus exists concerning the wisdom of varied policy alternatives or varied policy priorities. Recent biennial urban policy reports prepared by the agency have been little more than a summary of demographic, social, and economic trends facing cities. They have been filled with numbers and self-serving analysis and short on policy.

HUD, as the youngest, smallest, and weakest of the federal cabinet agencies, has been in no position to force or drive an interagency urban policy effort. Many federal agencies can claim with some justification that their policies and programs affect the health and well-being of cities more than HUD's. And, internal to HUD, housing policies have often conflicted with urban policy options and weakened HUD's advocacy among and between agencies and interest groups. Put another way, the past efforts of HUD's urban policy staff, right or wrong, to ration housing production in the suburbs has raised the hackles of HUD's housing staff. It has been perceived as inconsistent with their effort to increase or enhance housing development in the suburbs and beyond. The housing part of HUD clearly has been in the driver's seat. It has more history, a more precise mission, and more bucks to dispense to relatively visible and powerful client groups.

The Feds have yet to reach consensus on urban problems and the causes of such problems. Put two urban analysts in a room and, even if they are of the same political persuasion, you will likely get three definitions of urban problems and four solutions. Despite the expenditure of millions of dollars on research since the early sixties, the nation does not yet agree on the problems faced by cities, or whether or not city problems, if they exist, deserve a national response.

At the present time the debate over how well or how sick cities are remains subject more to opinion than fact, or to ideology than analysis. Indices assumedly recording the distress of cities rarely receive the universal consensus of competent researchers. Population decentralization, declining housing values, annexation, racial concentration, racial dispersion, income concentration, income dispersion, varied economic growth trends, the decline of American values, management or the lack thereof, patriotism, God, and so forth, have been defined both as problems and as the salvation of urban areas. Absolute wisdom is absent; the definition of urban problems is subject more to possibilities than probabilities. Few seem to come at urban problem analysis wearing the hat of a positivist.

The federal government lacks an understanding of the impact of its policies and programs. Debates still frequent the pages of our best journals over the effect of America's social and urban policies. Regrettably, much of the analysis about the Great Society and its aftermath uses partial data to support the preformed or preanalysis hypothesis of the analyst. Charles Murray's[8] recent damning critique of welfare and social service programs and John Schwarz's[9] recent positive look at the same programs serve to reaffirm the nation's inability to easily trace cause-and-effect relationships regarding federal initiatives.

The government's marginal capacity to evaluate the direct effect of its urban actions is compounded by its failure most times to look at second- and third-level impacts and by its utter lack of ability or interest in discerning the urban impact of nonurban initiatives.

Federal evaluation activities have been and remain partial and episodic. Questions are rarely asked in advance of implementation concerning the likely impact of new programs—programs that many times resemble previous federal initiatives. In this context urban policy-related arguments often resemble William James's theological argument about God. That is, policy-makers, like theologians who accept James's propositions, often accept the wisdom of their proposals based on faith and initiate them with great leaps forward based on little empirical evidence concerning anticipated success or failure. Examples abound of urban and nonurban actions that were carried out with little advance study concerning urban impact. Some ended up hurting a number of cities and their residents. The dishonor role includes urban renewal, beltways around but outside of cities, and the interstate highway system. More disheartening, examples abound of programs that were initiated after analysis suggested negative impact of similar earlier efforts. The results could have been predicted. They were not. Cities suffered when they need not have. Policymaking by inference when direct data are lacking is not a long suit of the federal government or indeed of any level of government.

The advocates of a specific urban policy have lost a good deal of their political clout. Despite the romance about cities, the hard numbers are against urban supporters in Congress and the administration. When cities were expanding, a case could be made that visible support of urban initiatives made for good and successful politics. Many central cities have lost and continue to lose population. The aggregate reduction in urban population since the mid-sixties is significant. More relevant perhaps, the population left behind in cities contains a proportionately large share of the poor and powerless. Becoming an urban advocate in this milieu is risky for many politicians.

The Next Steps

National urban policies in the Bush administration may rely more on retaining what exists that works well than on creating new initiatives. Budget and political constraints combined with a lack of certainty concerning the link between untried options and desired impacts suggest difficulty for any elected official tempted to make urban policy a major concern.

Perhaps the most innovative approach for those who care about cities would be to figure out how nonurban policies that are likely to win favor in the Congress—welfare reform, infrastructure assistance, education help —could best benefit cities. Put another way, the best urban policy could well be to help ensure that provisions of popular nonurban policies either guarantee cities a fair shake or grant cities a favored position.

9

Chasing Urban Policy: A Critical Retrospect

Charles J. Orlebeke

". . . I believe he has a great deal to answer for." (general laughter)

The target of this quip was David B. Walker, assistant director of the Advisory Commission on Intergovernmental Relations, and the marksman was James L. Sundquist, senior fellow at the Brookings Institution.[1] Walker was sitting on Sundquist's left at a 1975 hearing before the House Subcommittee on Housing and Community Development, and Sundquist had learned from Congressman Thomas "Lud" Ashley that Walker "had a rather considerable amount to do"[2] with the drafting of "Part A—Development of a National Urban Growth Policy" of the Urban Growth and New Community Development Act of 1970. The subcommittee—after five years of congressionally mandated national urban policymaking, including two presidential reports in 1972 and 1974—was assessing what had been learned in the course of chasing this thing called national urban policy. Published after the hearings, the committee's report ran on, inconclusively, for 673 pages; thirteen years later we are still at it, asking what we have to show for, and perhaps answer for, our efforts.

"Where have we come from?" It is clear that the idea of a national urban policy now is off the national political agenda. In 1970 Congress decided that the nation urgently needed an urban policy and that presidents should take a lead in defining one. In the summer of 1988 the ninth biennial President's Urban Policy Report was again months overdue, and neither its traditional tardiness nor its eventual appearance will get much notice. Although urban policymaking and report-writing should not be equated, the irrelevance of the President's Report is a fitting metaphor for the state of explicit urban policy.

If the 1970 congressional urban policy mandate has become a dead letter —and Jim Sundquist declared it so already in 1975[3]—how did this happen? To find out, we need to look at the world as Congress saw it in the late 1960s and discover what prompted Congress to make the development of urban policy the law of the land. Then we need to examine what happened in the executive branch of the federal government, as presidents from Richard Nixon to Ronald Reagan, White House staff members, cabinet officers, and federal bureaucrats disputed the meaning of urban policy and its implications for program turf. And as they were contending, of course, the world around them was changing, prompting further redefinitions of what urban policy might be. Finally, having seen the eclipse of urban policy in the 1980s, we need to ask whether it really matters; has anything important been gained or lost, or has a bad idea simply been replaced by better ones? If the idea of national urban policy is to be revived in the 1990s, what shape should it take?

Urban Policy + Growth Policy = Urban Growth Policy, or Whatever

Congress's call in 1970 was for the development of a "national urban growth policy," and in picking that particular formulation Congress was in typical fashion stirring together two quite different, if overlapping, perspectives and political constituencies.

For the proponents of "national *urban* policy" the backdrop for national policy development was, first, the outbreak of civil disorders in cities and the stifling of opportunities for racial minorities; second, the economic, social, and fiscal disparities between cities and suburbs; and third, the lack of institutional capacity at the state or metropolitan level to address such disparities. When Daniel Patrick Moynihan, early in his relatively brief stint as Nixon's assistant for urban affairs, circulated his memorandum outlining ten "fundaments of urban policy,"[4] these ideas were at the top of his list—the federal government's assertion of "a specific interest in the movement of people"[5] was only sixth on a list "scaled roughly to a combined measure of urgency and importance."[6]

The institutional vehicle for "the formulation and implementation of a national urban policy"[7] was the Council for Urban Affairs, created by Richard Nixon on the third day of his administration, and composed of eight cabinet officers from the domestic agencies. The appointment of Moynihan as executive secretary of the Council for Urban Affairs was a signal that the central cities would be the focus of urban policy. Moynihan was considered to be "the mayors' man" in the White House. It was he who spoke of urban politics becoming "the art of the impossible" and of mayors throwing up their hands and quitting the troubled cities—"It is not to be wondered [given city problems] that they flee."[8]

If the central cities were the spur for national urban policy, the advocates of "national *growth* policy" fixed on the nation's population growth and distribution—particularly the loss of urban-rural "balance" and the rise of "megalopolis"— as the malignant threats to man and nature. The color-coded maps of the U.S. census told the story: the young and the strong of rural America were steadily moving to only a handful of sprawling metro-politan regions. As demographers looked to the future, the trend was evi-dently relentless. According to Nixon's National Goals Research Staff, the "discouraging vision" of the future was of "gargantuan megalopolis and rural desolation," and it was a vision which had "become widely accepted among experts studying the problem."[9]

The numbers used by the experts were big and round: 100 million per-sons would be added to the national population by the year 2000, a 50 percent increase. Over half of the total population would be piling in to just three "metropolitan belts" stretching from Chicago to Pittsburgh, Boston to Washington, and San Francisco to San Diego; most of the rest would be drawn to only nine other rural regions.[10] Seventy percent of the nation's people would occupy only 10 percent of its land. The image was of people mindlessly attaching themselves to a dozen megalopolises as nine-tenths of the nation's area languished and withered.

It was an image that registered vividly on the popular consciousness and "led to a prevalent sense of gloom for both urban and rural America."[11] A public opinion survey sponsored by the Commission on Population Growth and the American Future found: "54 percent of Americans think that the distribution of population is a 'serious problem'; half believe that, over the next 30 years, it will be at least as great a problem as population growth."[12] In 1969 both the mayors and the governors declared support for national policies that would address the population distribution problem. The Na-tional League of Cities called for "a specific policy for the settlement of people throughout the nation to balance the concentration of population among and within metropolitan and non-metropolitan areas. . . ."[13] And the National Governors' Conference also called for "a national policy . . . for a more even distribution of population residence in our states" and pleaded for "a sense of direction in Federal planning and Federal programs which would seek to alleviate the growing frustration that is occurring in overpopulated areas and in areas which are losing population."[14] Responding to this broad support, Nixon in January 1970 said in his State of the Union Message:

> I propose that before these problems [of population distribution and "decayed central cities"] become insoluble, the nation develop a national growth policy.
>
> In the future, decisions as where to build highways, locate airports, acquire land or sell land should be made with a clear objective of aiding a balanced growth.[15]

The mingling of "urban policy" and "growth policy" yielded "national urban growth policy," the term adopted by Congress in December 1970. Congress took the term from the National Committee on Urban Growth Policy, a sixteen-member committee cosponsored by the National League of Cities, the U.S. Conference of Mayors, the National Association of Counties, and Urban America, Inc. The committee included seven key congressmen and senators, as well as a group of local and state elected officials. After organizing in 1968 and securing a major grant from the Ford Foundation, the committee toured the clean and comely new towns of England and Scandinavia. In early 1969 the committee sponsored a series of conferences which included civil rights leaders, environmentalists, homebuilders and developers, bankers, and federal officials. National urban growth policy was a tent under which many could gather.

Later in 1969 the committee issued its handsome and influential report, *The New City*,[16] a broadside against the evils of megalopolis and a call for a national urban growth policy with a new communities program as its centerpiece. The analysis laid out in *The New City* contained elements of both "urban" policy and "growth" policy themes: "The American metropolis is monumentally ugly"; spreading suburbia "cannot capture the breadth of experiences, the excitement, the intensity of the core"; "spontaneous urbanization . . . is both wasteful and destructive of natural resources"; metropolis is ungovernable because of "a crazy quilt of political jurisdictions"; "the great core cities . . . are steadily going broke"; and finally, the one flaw "that could prove fatal"—confinement in the ghetto of the urban poor and minorities.[17] The report also joined in the chorus of warning that population growth would by the end of the century add 100 million persons, most of whom would merely extend the spreading blot and blight of existing metropolitan regions.

Urban Policy, New Communities, and the National Capacity to Act

Whether one chose to stress the "urban" or the "growth" elements of national policy, a common thread running through all the discussions was that the national leadership possessed the capacity to analyze the problems identified, to develop a coherent body of policies, and to implement them. Despite the humbling frustration of Vietnam and the scars of riots in twenty cities across the land, confidence in the national capacity to understand and act was very much alive. Hence, Richard Nixon, in establishing his National Goals Research Staff in July 1969, spoke of

> an extraordinary array of tools and techniques . . . by which it becomes increasingly possible to project future trends—and thus to make the kind of informed choices which are necessary if we are to establish mastery over the process of change.
>
> These tools and techniques are gaining widespread use in business, and in the social and physical sciences, but they have not been applied comprehensively to the science of government. . . .[18]

And he could conclude with a hubris typical of new administrations: "We have reached a state of technological and social development at which the future nature of our society can increasingly be shaped by our own conscious choices."[19] In addition, as a positive metaphor of national capacity, there was the space program with its technological dazzle, its mastery of complex management systems, and its successful march toward a distant goal. The moon shots signaled that the national will could be done on earth as it was being done in the heavens.

If a persistent faith in the efficacy of concerted national action was a common theme in urban policymaking, the new communities movement was the unifying programmatic concept. A national program of new city-building would capture a good share of population growth and would also have strong symbolic value in recasting the image of what cities should be like.

The rough arithmetic of the most enthusiastic new communities proponents went as follows: "If we allocate one-half of the coming 100 million people to existing peripheral growth around existing cities and 10 percent to small towns and farms, the remaining 40 million would require the building of 20 cities of one million people each and 200 new towns of 100,000 each."[20] More modestly, the National Committee on Urban Growth Policy, in making its own recommendations, simply sliced the goal in half to ten big new cities and one hundred smaller ones.[21]

The symbolic import of new communities was also powerful. Against the background of ticky-tacky suburban developments and charred urban ghettos, new communities stood for "a fresh start," an opportunity to do something right for a change. As Vice President Spiro T. Agnew put it in his foreword to *The New City*: "Unlike planning for a single aspect of urban life, the planning for the new city involves fresh examination of nearly every concept we have taken for granted. It promises an intellectual understanding as great as that of the space age itself."[22] William E. Finley of the Rouse Company was more lyrical, speaking of new cities as "better places to live, to work, to invest, to be educated, and to grow old; places of safety, convenience, excitement, and beauty, places free of all the conditions that make Americans anti-city."[23]

The proponents of new communities had no doubts either about the market for their product, or about the national capacity for mounting a large-scale program. Finley's certitude on this point is charming:

> The locational planning, financing, and construction of new cities is a task which our society can handle. We have most of the management tools and an understanding of the economics. Ideas about social programs and financial resources are available. . . .
>
> The most affluent nation in the world has the capacity to create the most wonderful urban places on earth through public power, public financial leadership, and wise use of private enterprise. All it needs is the political framework within which to act.[24]

To fashion "the political framework within which to act" was Congress's intent in the Urban Growth and New Community Development Act of 1970. If one looks at the "Findings and Declaration of Policy" which Congress used to base its call for a national urban growth policy, the key words which dominate Sections 701 and 702 are "balanced," "orderly," "stabilization," and their opposites, "imbalance," "disorderly," and "uneven." "National urban growth policy" were code words for taking charge of a situation which seemed to have spun out of control, and the new communities program would be one important way for getting back on track.

Between the Idea/And the Reality/ . . . Falls the Shadow

Everyone who has been in government or studied it knows there is a big difference between the shapely pronouncement of State of the Union messages, congressional findings, and commission reports and the messier interchange between executive agencies and their constituencies as they seek to convert lofty policies to programs that work on the ground. As an idea, national urban policy had sufficient coherence and force to challenge the executive branch to organize itself around the idea and then deliver an array of federal programs in a helpful way to places that needed them. The Nixon administration, particularly in its first two years, took up the challenge, as did the Ford and Carter administrations. How and why national urban policy failed as an effective organizing idea is a complicated tale, and my capsule history will suggest only a few of the reasons.

The experience of the Nixon administration—the first to make explicit urban policy a White House function—demonstrated how the search for broad policy can be quickly overwhelmed by the pressures of ad hoc decisionmaking, the unavoidable complexity of policymaking machinery, and the competition among executive agencies. Clearly, the frustration associated with these forces was part of the reason the Nixon White House, in effect, gave up on national urban policy at midterm and shifted to advocating a radical restructuring of domestic programs along New Federalism lines.

As noted earlier, the Nixon Council for Urban Affairs was created in the first days of the administration, with one of its mandates being the development of a national urban policy. But the nature of the CUA's activity was signaled on the day of its creation when Moynihan announced the formation of nine subcommittees: the future of the poverty program, the future of the model cities program, minority business enterprise, welfare, crime, internal migration, surplus food and nutrition, mass transit, and voluntary action.[25] Typically, the cabinet officer with the most closely related program responsibility chaired the relevant subcommittee, and several others would sit as members. By June 1969 the number of subcommittees had grown to ten,[26] and to twelve by September.[27] At that point HUD Secretary George Romney, whom I worked for, chaired two CUA subcommittees and was a member of six others.

The CUA had no subcommittee on "urban policy" and no process for defining one. Instead, it was an arena—and a useful one in many respects—for cabinet officers and White House staff to thrash out positions on the legacy of Great Society programs and to test out initiatives for the new administration. The approach was fragmented, ad hoc: policy did not drive decisions; policy was an accretion of decisions.

The "Record of Action" of the July 11, 1969, CUA meeting is instructive in its jumble of agenda items and decisions. Interior Secretary Walter Hickel was directed by the president to "look into" ways to be more responsive to urban Indians; Counselor Arthur Burns was to prepare a message and draft bill on revenue sharing; Moynihan was to arrange for

CUA members "to take a helicopter ride over Los Angeles during the peak hours and observe the effects of automobile pollution and congestion"; the subcommittee on transportation was "to prepare 'something quite precise' for the President to say to the Governors' Conference"; and the attorney general, the budget director, and each department head were to designate staff members who could "be dispatched to cities struck by civil disturbances . . . and assess needs as conflagration is brought under control."[28] There are shards of "urban policy" here, but not much evidence that the president and major domestic appointees were systematically grappling with the future shape of urban America.

In addition, despite the broad mandate of the CUA and its panoply of a dozen subcommittees, it did not come close to monopolizing the urban policymaking machinery of the White House. Operating side-by-side with CUA were several other cabinet-level units, including the Environmental Quality Council, the Cabinet Committee on Economic Policy, and the Cabinet Committee on Construction. Also, competing with Moynihan's CUA staff group in the White House were the National Goals Research Staff and Arthur Burns's Office of Program Development. Then, in November 1969 Nixon created a Cabinet Council on Rural Affairs as a political balance to the Council for Urban Affairs. Finally, in July 1970 the White House implemented an overhaul of its domestic policy machinery: the urban and rural councils were merged into the Domestic Council, and John Ehrlichman was put in charge.

The Domestic Council was designed to advise "the President in an integrated way on total domestic policy,"[29] but its style of operation was to be more flexible. Instead of standing subcommittees, the Domestic Council policymaking process would be set in motion by a task-oriented "study memorandum"; then a committee of cabinet officers would be formed to work on the issue with departmental and White House staff support and would go out of existence when the work was done by a stated deadline. The implementation of the council process was less tidy. The early study memoranda established groups around such topics as federal planning assistance,[30] the national energy situation,[31] rural development,[32] and the blue-collar worker.[33] It was not long before proliferating and overlapping committees, subcommittees, task forces, and working groups began to resemble the previous White House structure.

The most "urban" of the Domestic Council committees was the Committee on National Growth Policy which was chaired by the HUD secretary. This committee had on its agenda a mix of program proposals designed to respond to perceived threats of population maldistribution—the "urban-rural balance" problem. The Economic Development Administration proposed to aim a barrage of federal program grants and development incentives to preidentified lagging rural counties (about 1,400 counties would be eligible) and also to about a hundred designated "growth centers"—medium-sized metropolitan areas located away from "megalopolis."[34] The idea was to encourage some rural dwellers to stay down on the farm and to steer others to smaller urban centers.

The administration's new communities proposals were also on the committee's agenda, although the main action had shifted to dealing with Congress where new communities were being debated. Central city problems as such were not really on the agenda, and a White House staff memorandum drafted for the president was defensive on this point: "To approach the problems of urban areas by dealing with those of rural areas may hardly seem a frontal assault. However, if our analysis of the close relation between the two is correct, the long term effects on the most urban areas will be beneficial, and the net national gain will be considerable."[35] Despite objections by HUD and the Council of Economic Advisers, a "growth center" strategy went forward to the president in December 1970,[36] just weeks before the president signed the national urban growth act into law.

Did this mean that after two years of muddling and maneuvering among the executive departments and the White House, and bargaining with Congress, that some confluence of policy on "urban growth" had finally occurred in late 1970? The irony is that exactly the opposite was true. Congress had enacted an urban policy mandate at the very time Nixon and his key domestic advisers had concluded that such a quest was misguided and probably quixotic. The critical domestic problem, in this view, was not the agony of central cities nor the spread of megalopolis; the real problem was the management chaos of the federal government and its inability to direct resources intelligently at particular places.[37] Partly because the Council for Urban Affairs and the Domestic Council had both been unable to bring coherence to domestic policy, Nixon's domestic policy for the second half of his first term was largely inspired by the President's Advisory Council on Executive Reorganization chaired by Roy Ash.

It was a startled cabinet that learned in late 1970 that Nixon planned to revamp the entire federal domestic structure through a three-pronged approach: reorganization of most federal agencies into four new cabinet departments; merger of most categorical aid programs into six broad-purpose "special revenue sharing programs"; and the shift of most management responsibility and political accountability from the federal government to state and local officials. General revenue sharing was also a part of the package.

One of the new departments proposed in the plan was a Department of Community Development, to be built around HUD and drawing together the major development programs from Transportation, Commerce, and Agriculture, plus the vestiges of the OEO community action program. This superdepartment would administer three "special revenue sharing programs" for transportation, rural development for states, and urban development for cities. If this proposal had succeeded, it is possible to imagine a department in some future administration with sufficient leverage to make an urban and metropolitan development strategy feasible. But it failed, as did the rest of the reorganization package; the proposals were so radical that they were not taken seriously—many of the president's own appointees in the agencies lobbied against them more or less openly. General revenue sharing, however, was enacted; and, shortly after Watergate drove Nixon from office, the Community Development Block Grant program also became law.

Once the Nixon administration made its critical domestic policy turn in early 1971, the urban growth policy mandate of the 1970 act was politically dead almost before the ink was dry as far as the Nixon high command was concerned. Congress, however, had directed the president to prepare a biennial report on progress toward developing a "national urban growth policy," the first being due in February 1972. The charge could not be avoided.

Let the record show that the urban growth policy report assignment was indeed taken seriously by some Domestic Council staff and by HUD. The first meetings on the report were in July 1971,[38] and by October a thirty-eight-page outline was ready to be circulated for comment.[39] Meanwhile, several HUD GS-15s with Ph.Ds were producing monumental draft chapters based on the outline. Comments on the outline by Herbert Stein of the council of Economic Advisers foreshadowed the fate of the HUD draft.

> The comments focus on chapter II [Problems Stemming from Growth Trends]. By ignoring the facts that tastes differ and resources are limited, this chapter leaves the impression that everything that "we" don't like (which seems to be practically everything) is a problem to be solved. It holds out the prospect of mammoth programs. . . . The opposition will use our chapter II as the platform for their programs which we will then be embarrassed to resist.[40]

When the Nixon report was issued, it turned out to be a slim, toned-down discussion of urban and regional trends and problems and a recapitulation of past budget and legislative proposals. On the policy development mandate, the report punted: "It is not feasible for the highest level of government to design policies that can operate successfully in all parts of the Nation."[41]

In addition, the specifically "urban" or central city thrust in urban policymaking was losing force. The reason was straightforward if not very edifying: the cities were not in flames. Nixon could say in his 1974 State of the Union message: "Peace has returned to our cities."[42]

Ford and Carter: The Changing Context of Urban Policy

"Peace" had returned to the cities, but strife engulfed the Nixon White House as the Watergate affair gathered momentum in early 1974. The urban growth policy report, due by statutory requirement in February, had been pushed aside and finally arrived from HUD on the new president's desk in December. In transmitting the draft report to President Gerald R. Ford, HUD Secretary James T. Lynn (a Nixon carryover later named OMB director by Ford) called it

> "a no win" kind of situation. . . . Frankly, except for reporting on popu-
> lation changes and other demographics of growth, the whole concept of
> a bi-annual report of this kind of "growth" — overlapping as it does the
> whole spectrum of matters affecting American life, economics, the envi-
> ronment, welfare, housing, etc. — doesn't make sense. Be that as it may,
> it clearly presents any Administration with a "damned if you do and
> damned if you don't" choice on report content.[43]

Despite Lynn's ambivalence and sense of foreboding, the report got better marks than the Nixon effort. ACIR's David Walker—"the man who has much to answer for"—called it "a substantial improvement over its predecessor,"[44] although faulting it because it did "not yet confront the tough substantive issues questions of national growth and development, especially the locational issue."[45]

Walker's statement to the House subcommittee was correct, but it also ignored the startling testimony of witnesses who had appeared before the subcommittee four days earlier. Richard L. Forstall, a Census Bureau de-mographer, and Calvin L. Beale, a Department of Agriculture economist, had presented a new set of color-coded maps which showed nonmetropoli-tan counties *gaining* in population in relation to metropolitan areas.[46] "So," said Beale, "the push of people out of the rural and small town areas has ended, or essentially ended, in most parts of the country," and the "resi-dential preferences" of many people have shifted to "a rural or small town setting."[47] The turning point was evidently around 1970, the same year that Congress called for national urban growth policy based on an opposite view of population trends. The 1970 mandate had lost one of its key underpinnings.

Although "growth policy" issues were fading fast, "urban policy" bounced back onto the national policy agenda in 1975 with the New York City fiscal crisis. Racial conflict had quieted, but the older central cities were falling apart and some were going broke. The question was: How many New York's? A small industry in urban research quickly developed around urban distress indices and typologies of "declining" and "growing" cities.

President Ford initially took a hard line against any federal assistance for New York, attributing the crisis to profligate spending and fiscal misman-agement. Treasury Secretary William E. Simon warned Ford that if the federal government helped New York

> the incentive for other municipalities to endure the stress of reconciling income with outgo would be reduced. Structural deficits in countless municipalities would be the end result of this process. . . .
>
> [The federal government] would become enmeshed in the politics of thousands of political subdivisions. Direct Federal aid, a guarantee or partial guarantee might avoid default. But it would also begin the Feder-alization of state and local affairs.[48]

However, letting New York City default was not risk-free either. As influ-ential banking lobbyist Charles Walker wrote to Ford, "Bill Simon may be right about the minimal impact of default, but I personally believe that there's simply no way of knowing in advance just what the economic and financial fallout would be."[49] Walker was worried that Congress might pass "a bad bill" and that Ford would be politically damaged if he "vetoed it in the public interest, NYC defaulted, and the roof fell in."[50] The pragmatic and conciliatory counsel of Walker and others eventually prevailed, and Ford agreed on a compromise plan to provide New York with an emergency federal loan in exchange for pledges of future fiscal austerity.

The predictions of widespread municipal bankruptcies of course turned out to be wrong—cities generally learned from New York's mistakes and tightened control of their finances—but New York's crisis did help to define a new category of cities as a target for urban policy formulation. These were the "cities in distress," primarily older cities with declining popula-tions, a shrinking industrial base and fiscal capacity, and crumbling hous-ing and infrastructure. Problems of decline replaced problems of growth as a national priority.

The human side of cities in distress was that the young and the talented were deserting the cities, leaving behind the old and infirm, the poor and the unemployed, and the embattled defenders of declining middle-class residential neighborhoods. The latter group organized into what came to be called the "neighborhood movement," ably led by Gale Cincotta of National People's Action and Father Geno Baroni, director of the National Center for Urban Ethnic Affairs (and later a HUD assistant secretary in the Carter administration).

In March 1976 an informal staff group was formed in the Ford White House "to review where we are and where we are headed in regard to the cities."[51] Later, after Ford had met with a group of neighborhood movement leaders, the urban policy action shifted to the cabinet with the creation of the Cabinet Committee on Urban Development and Neighborhood Revitalization, chaired by HUD Secretary Carla A. Hills. The Hills committee had a broad mandate—to develop an urban policy to guide the hoped-for Ford second term—and a short deadline.

In the scant four months of its existence before the 1976 elections, the Hills committee charted a policy in its report which might be termed "targeted New Federalism."[52] The policy called for targeting more federal money to distressed areas by revising the distribution formulas for general revenue sharing and other block grant programs. Tax revision was also proposed which would encourage housing rehabilitation and central city redevelopment. Although the policy statement did not promise any new spending, it did advocate a countercyclical "kicker" to the Community Development Block Grant program, which, if enacted, would have sent an additional $900 million to cities with high rates of unemployment.

Ford helped to put the "urban" back into urban policy, and Carter made it official by getting Congress in 1977 to drop the word "growth" from its 1970 urban policy mandate. Carter also came into office with a determination to be the first president to grapple successfully with the development of national urban policy. The organizational method he chose was virtually identical to Ford's: creation of a cabinet-level group chaired by the HUD secretary (Patricia R. Harris) and staffed at HUD.[53]

As the urban policy group began the inevitable rounds of interagency meetings and the generating of staff policy papers, Carter was pushing through Congress an aggressive antirecession economic stimulus package of programs which were in fact quite effective and responsive urban policy initiatives. Grants for antirecession fiscal assistance—an add-on to revenue sharing, public service jobs, and public works—were a big help to struggling central cities in the 1977–79 period.

The official urban policy process had a less happy outcome. After a

year-long delay marked by interdepartmental bickering and presidential ambivalence, the "comprehensive national urban policy" emerged in March
1978. The 132-page report outlining the policy included an elaborate edifice
of seven governing principles, four broad goals, ten major policies, and
about fifty strategies for implementation.[54] Backing up the policy report
was a separately issued $8.3-billion package of budget proposals, most of
which were grants, loans, and incentives aimed at shoring up central city
economies and providing job opportunities for the urban poor.

The Carter urban policy and the accompanying budget proposals added
up to an impressive rhetorical commitment to address the economic and
fiscal problems of older central cities—the so-called targeting principle.
But Carter had also telegraphed his ambivalence when at the last moment
before the policy's public release, he nearly withdrew large parts of the
budget proposals. Not surprisingly, the proposals went nowhere in Congress, and most were later pulled back by Carter himself as Proposition 13
sentiment moved east to the Potomac.

The Carter administration's last major statement on urban policy was the
1980 *President's National Urban Policy Report*, the fifth such document to
be issued under the 1970 statutory directive. Recommendations outlined in
the final chapter, "An Urban Policy for the 1980s," were heavy on administrative tinkering—interagency agreements, guideline revisions, improved
criteria for measuring urban impact, and the like—and light on actions that
cost money.[55] Ironically, the development of an explicit urban policy in
1978 turned out to be a harbinger of leaner times for cities.

Furthermore, the Carter urban policy record had to endure a painful
footnote when the president's own Commission for a National Agenda for
the Eighties flatly opposed the targeting principle, contending instead that
economic forces affecting older central cities were essentially irreversible.[56]
In the oversimplified terms of the "people vs. places" debate, it was people
who mattered.

The Reagan Era: Urban Policy in Eclipse

The central idea of Carter's Commission for the Eighties has in effect been
adopted by the administration of President Ronald Reagan. In the 1960s
and 1970s the question was how the federal government should use its
considerable financial and programmatic leverage intelligently to achieve
outcomes which would improve the quality of new development, preserve
the value of stable areas, and revitalize those that are blighted. The question in the 1980s has not been the *use* of financial and programmatic lever-

age, but whether the federal government should possess such leverage at all.

Under the Reagan doctrine, the federal government's role is to promote general prosperity by holding taxes and government spending down and letting private market forces work their will with a minimum of governmental interference. Economic growth, it is assumed, will generate sufficient revenues at all levels of government; however, the main policy decisions regarding the mix and quality of public services should be made by officials at the state and local levels, not the federal. Similarly, the individual citizen should seek opportunity wherever it may beckon; if his inclinations are for a better job, warmer winters, or a smaller town, he should, as President Reagan has said, "vote with his feet."

By 1984 the *Reagan National Urban Policy Report* could claim that its policies had laid the "foundation for a new era of prosperity and stability in our nation's cities. . . . There is increasing evidence that this strategy is sound and is working."[57] The photogenic evidence of urban revival is indeed impressive: the Sunday magazine of almost any major newspaper will include features on the latest riverfront boutiques or the next neighborhood about to undergo restoration. The urban crisis rhetoric of the 1960s has been nearly displaced by a kind of urban happy talk of the 1980s, to which the Reagan administration contributes on the rare occasions it speaks of city issues at all.

Conclusion

Chasing urban policy in the 1970s gave way to nonurban policy of the 1980s. Whether cities and their citizens are better off is a complex question. The Urban Institute looked at "Reagan and the Cities" and concluded that "cities appeared to fare better in the first Reagan term than might have been expected, certainly better than most advocates of city interests had predicted."[58] According to the Urban Institute's George Peterson, the urban targeting strategies of the Ford and Carter administrations were based on a theory that the large older cities suffer the most from national economic cycles, a theory that "now appears to have been wrong."[59] City budgets took the double blow of recession and federal cuts in the early 1980s and ended up "in better shape" than in the glory days of federal aid in the 1970s.[60]

But Richard Nathan and Paul Dommel presented another view in testimony before the U.S. Senate Committee on Governmental Affairs. "All we have today . . . is *bad news*," they said. "The problems of community distress are getting worse; the federal government is doing less about them; and to top it all off, the programs that we do have that are targeted on the most needy communities are deteriorating before our very eyes."[61] Nathan and Dommel pointed to the widening socioeconomic disparities between central cities and their suburbs, and the growing number of cities which are crossing the boundary into severe hardship, as measured by the city hardship index developed by Nathan and Charles Adams in the 1970s.[62] More ominously, Nathan and Dommel cite 1980 census data showing a sharp rise in the number and concentration of black poor crowded into poverty areas of the nation's fifty largest cities—"the hard and unpleasant reality of a second America in the ghettos of our cities."[63] They also present evidence that the Community Development Block Grant (CDBG) program, enacted in 1974 as a flexible and quite well-targeted urban assistance program, is steadily losing its targeting feature; not only is CDBG as a whole being whittled away, but distressed cities are tending to get smaller grants and better-off cities are getting more.[64] In response, Nathan and Dommel revive a concept advanced during the Ford administration—a CDBG add-on which would be tied to an index of urban hardship.

Post-Reagan presidents should assess the lessons learned in the pursuit of explicit urban policy and decide whether to resume the chase. This analysis suggests at least a couple of obvious lessons. First, the 1970-vintage "growth policy" mandate surely deserves to be discarded: the idea that "we" could in any sense "allocate" the next 100 million people to new communities or anywhere else should only be recalled as a lesson in humility. Second, the various efforts in the 1960s and 1970s to design a White House or interagency mechanism to "coordinate" the "delivery" of federal programs to particular places proved to be failures. In an imperfect world the block grant seems to be the best way to dispense federal money.

A third lesson, perhaps more debatable, concerns the role of the state. State governments—scorned by the federal government in the 1960s and given mixed encouragement in the 1970s—have in the Reagan period become the chosen instruments for managing much of what remains of federal domestic assistance.[65] On balance, states have done a good job of taking on additional responsibilities, and some have shown remarkable resourcefulness in shaping economic and social policy within their borders. The idea of "state urban policy" seems far less implausible than it did twenty years ago.

The fundamental question confronting President George Bush will be whether to address again the challenge of place-oriented national policy. If Bush fails to look beyond the cities' fiscal resilience, their continuing capacity to deliver basic urban services, and their shimmering downtown architecture, urban policy will remain as a postponable low-level chore in the HUD bureaucracy. We should hope for better: a president whose vision penetrates into the shadows of the urban condition—the decay of vital infrastructure, the sickness of city school systems, the desperation of a growing underclass. When that happens, urban policymaking will again be a lively quest.

10

Policy Liberalism, National Community Liberalism, and the Prospects for National Urban Policy

William A. Schambra

No one would be shocked, I suspect, by the assertion that the United States is not likely to see again, anytime soon, a comprehensive, national urban policy resembling the one unveiled by President Jimmy Carter on March 27, 1978. The reason seems clear: we are currently in the grip of a conservative reaction against the very notion of comprehensive federal policies. Many believe, however, that once the political pendulum swings back, we will turn again to the business of drafting another such urban policy.

If in fact we do ever return to that endeavor, however, I would suggest that it will still be a profoundly problematic undertaking—not because of conservative interference, but because of an unresolved tension within liberalism. This tension—between two liberal views of governance—came to light during, and was left unresolved by, the Carter administration. One view, the policy approach or "policy liberalism," gave birth to the nation's first comprehensive urban policy. It was also politically disastrous for Carter. The other view—"national community liberalism," with which Carter experimented briefly—promised to solve the political problems faced by liberalism, but only by jettisoning key elements of the policy approach. Until liberalism sets its house in order with respect to these competing views of governance, it is not likely to produce again soon a national urban policy—or any other kind of comprehensive policy, for that matter.

One can begin to appreciate the problems policy liberalism caused for Carter by examining his urban policy a bit more closely. The policy was, in a sense, a microcosm of his general approach to governance throughout the first years of his administration.

The Carter Urban Policy

Perhaps the central characteristic of that policy, as critics and friends alike pointed out, was complexity. It proposed to tackle the problems of cities — *all* cities, declining, stable, and growing — by dealing with, and in some cases trying to deflect, a number of the most complicated economic, social, and demographic trends affecting the nation. All this would be accomplished through, as one skeptic put it, "an elaborate edifice" of seven governing principles, four goals, ten policies, and thirty-eight strategies for implementation.[1] Carter's urban policy promised not only that the "Federal Government will administer existing and new programs in a coordinated, efficient and fair manner" — a bold enough claim, given the experience with Model Cities[2] — it also vowed that all new, major government actions would be "evaluated ahead of time with respect to possible urban impacts and, to the extent possible be shaped and carried out in a manner consistent with our overall urban policy."[3] But far more was promised: the policy proposed to include, and to coordinate the activities of, states and local governments as full members of a "new partnership" to address urban ills. As "The New Partnership" put it, "we must carefully plan the total range of Federal, State, and local actions" in urban areas.[4] Finally, the policy went so far as to enlist the new neighborhood movement and other, primarily business, elements of the private sector in the "partnership."

Critics of this new policy quickly pointed out the problems associated with such a complex plan. It was, for instance, difficult to discern a clear set of priorities in the welter of goals, principles, and policies. As one critical evaluation put it, "the final urban policy message . . . gave no indication of the relative priority or importance of various parts of the Urban Policy."[5] Furthermore — because the plan seemed to acknowledge and include some benefit for virtually every interest associated with urban life — it was open to the charge of being merely a creature of the "special interests"; thus Anthony Downs's comment that the Carter policy "promised to do just about everything good conceivable for just about everyone in all urban areas."[6] Finally, given the profusion of goals to be reached, trends to be harnessed, and political actors to be coordinated, the policy seemed to critics to be almost ludicrously ambitious. Charles Orlebeke noted that the Carter administration "intends to work with, encourage, support, and stimulate every other level of government plus the private sector and neighborhood groups — all at the same time with equal fervor."[7] Given the scope of the policy, the administration — and the government — had inevitably set itself up for a fall, it appeared.

Friends of the new urban policy, on the other hand, were not daunted by the complexity of the scheme. Indeed, they seemed to wear it as a badge of honor, because it was precisely the complexity of the plan that substantiated its claim to being the first genuine, comprehensive national urban *policy*, as opposed to the mélange of often conflicting *programs* that had theretofore characterized federal intervention in the cities.

Policy vs. Program

This distinction between policy and program goes to the heart of Carter's urban plan and of his approach to governance in general. The essence of the policy approach, as Daniel Moynihan pointed out, is the sophisticated understanding that "everything relates to everything" and that "social problems arise out of complex systems." The policy approach therefore seeks to "encompass the largest possible range of phenomena and concerns. . . . Knowing what we do about the nature of society and of social intervention, we have no choice but to seek to deal in terms of the entire society, and all the consequences of intervention."

Earlier liberal administrations, Carter and Moynihan knew, had relied on a program approach to social problems, with unfortunate results. The essence of that approach, Moynihan points out, is "that it is directed to a specific situation." Given the interrelatedness of reality, however, it is impossible to confine interventions in this way. Unforeseen, uncontrollable, and usually undesirable vibrations are thus set up throughout the complex web of society. Because programs do not "adequately reflect a large enough part of reality," they "usually end by distorting" it. Ultimately, the program approach is "self-defeating."

This had been particularly true, Moynihan argued, of past programs directed at urban problems. Because cities are "complex systems, . . . interventions that affect one component of the system almost invariably affect second, third, and fourth components as well, and these, in turn affect the first component, often in ways quite opposite to the direction of the initial intervention." The policy approach, however, now permitted us to avoid shooting ourselves in the foot; government could "seek out its hidden policies, raising them to a level of consciousness and acceptance—or rejection."[8]

President Carter's plans for the cities reflected an understanding of the difference between "policy" and "program"—and a wholehearted embrace of the policy approach. The documents describing the program bespeak, for instance, an acute awareness of past failures to appreciate the urban consequences of seemingly nonurban programs. As "The New Partnership" suggested, "at times, Federal urban assistance efforts have not achieved their objectives, because nonurban Federal activities pulled in another direction or made urban problems worse."[9] The Carter program, by contrast, promised to "raise to consciousness," through the urban impact statement and other measures, all the consequences of existing and proposed federal programs. His plans thus evidenced a sophisticated awareness of the complex nature of society and a conviction that only a complex policy approach could deal with it. "The complexity of urban problems makes a meaningful response possible only through a number of different, but related policies. No simplistic 'centerpiece' policy will achieve our urban commitments. Instead, a comprehensive policy approach is necessary."[10]

To supporters of the Carter policy, then, complexity could be taken as a measure of accomplishment, not failure. If one could not discern in the policy one or two priority projects, it was because the drafters proudly refused to compromise the comprehensiveness of the program with "simplistic centerpiece policies." If the policy included some provision for virtually every urban "special interest," that was simply an effort to "encompass the largest possible range of . . . concerns" — a realistic acknowledgment of the vast number of actors within the urban system that would have to be coordinated and so accommodated. If the program seemed too ambitious, that was just a recognition of the futility of a more modest program approach and an affirmation of the need to tackle all parts of the complex urban system at once in order to avoid the "self-defeating" consequences of partial interventions. The urban program's complexity and its attendant characteristics, in other words, were simply the inevitable by-products of a sophisticated, "state-of-the-art" policy approach to urban problems.

The Policy Approach and Carter's Political Problems

As many have pointed out, the policy approach to social problems was perhaps *the* trademark of the Carter administration. In addition to an urban policy, Carter's agenda included a major jobs and incomes policy and an energy policy; he had plans for major family and neighborhood policies; and countless "minor" policies virtually blanketed the public affairs agenda. James Ceaser notes that "Carter seemed to view the task of governing in terms of the management of complex and interrelated policies."[11] Or, in James Fallows's words, Carter "thinks he 'leads' by choosing the correct policy," and so he came to hold "explicit, thorough positions on every issue under the sun."[12]

This view of governance was, in the final analysis, Carter's political undoing. The specific criticisms of his urban policy, suitably amplified, soon came to be applied to his administration as a whole. Commentators across the political spectrum complained that Carter was failing to lead the nation because no clear, simple set of priorities, purposes, or goals had emerged from his complicated policy agenda. Hamilton Jordan would subsequently comment, as he left the White House, that "my most basic regret is that in doing so many things, we never clearly fixed in the public mind a sense of our priorities."[13] Furthermore, Carter's administration seemed to be swamped and its measures stalemated by a vast swarm of "special interests"—a fact that President Carter himself would eventually acknowledge in his "malaise" speech of 1979. Finally, in spite of, or rather, because of, its incredibly ambitious policy agenda, the administration in the end seemed utterly incapable of accomplishing anything at all. Great expectations—generated by the promise of comprehensive policies for every major social ill—inevitably turned into bitter disappointment once the normal political processes yielded only partial policies and those much-despised noncomprehensive "programs."

Just as the policy approach was responsible for the perceived defects of Carter's urban policy, in other words, so it surely compounded, if it did not actually give rise to, the perceived defects of the administration in general. Given that approach, however, things could hardly have been otherwise. After all, if the social system is an interrelated whole, how can one say that certain policy interventions should take priority over others? If virtually all actors in the system will need to be involved in any given policy, how can one avoid the impression (and the reality) of accommodating a vast number of special interests? And if the entire range of policies must be pursued simultaneously—partial interventions being inevitably "self-defeating" —how does one avoid the image of failure and impotence once the political system gives us, as it inevitably does, nothing *but* partial interventions?

The Program Approach and
National Community Liberalism

If Carter's "policy liberalism" contributed so substantially to his political undoing, however, we must then ask: how did the great liberal presidents of the past handle the problem of policy? After all, they somehow managed to project a clear set of priorities or goals, to avoid the impression of being mere playthings of the special interests, and to convey a sense of accomplishment and governmental efficacy. We can discern the secret of their success in this trenchant critique of Carter's approach by a "Capital Hill Democrat," quoted by Haynes Johnson:

> I remember when Carl Albert had a wall with sixty pens on it that Lyndon Johnson had given him after signing bills. LBJ didn't say "I have a comprehensive Great Society program—pass it all in one bill." He'd send up a cancer bill today, an aid-to-education bill tomorrow, and an arts-and-humanities bill the next day, and a poverty program the next. Some got passed immediately, some got watered down, some got defeated. But at the end, the mosaic of those pens was the Great Society. It was the same with Franklin Roosevelt and the New Deal. They were masters at sending up those bills. They weren't neat and comprehensive, which is what Carter wants.[14]

The successful liberal presidents of the past, in other words, simply did not fret about a comprehensive policy approach to problems; they relied, rather, on the program approach so despised by policy liberals. But something stood behind those seemingly unrelated programs, creating a reasonably coherent Great Society and New Deal out of "mosaics of pens." Johnson's and Roosevelt's particular legislative initiatives ultimately emanated from, and so finally added up to, a coherent, general public philosophy. This was, of course, precisely the element missing from Carter's policy liberalism, as James Fallows and others have noted.[15]

The public philosophy shared by Roosevelt and Johnson was a commitment to what Samuel Beer calls "the national idea," or the national community. Both presidents believed it their duty to draw Americans together, to forge a sense of national oneness by summoning the people to common endeavor. America was to become as much as possible like a tightly knit family or small town. As Johnson put it in 1964, "I see America as a family . . . with its people bound together by common ties of confidence and affection, and common aspirations toward duty and purpose."[16]

This strikingly simple, coherent vision of America, inspiring and weaving together specific legislative programs, enabled Johnson and Roosevelt to avoid the profound political problems that bedeviled Carter. Both presidents were able to project a clear sense of priorities or goals, pointing toward the single end of national community. Moreover, because their programs flowed from a forcefully stated commitment to the national interest, both administrations escaped the charge of being mere playthings of the special interests. (Indeed, one of the primary goals of the national community idea was to make a unified whole out of diverse and discordant special interests.) And finally, because the success or failure of the legislative program did not turn on the passage of comprehensive policies—that is, because it was a modest program approach—great expectations were not built up and subsequently dashed, leaving an impression of governmental impotence. As the "Capital Hill Democrat" noted, some bills were watered down and others defeated, but enough survived—propelled through the political process by the moral force of the national community vision—to give a general impression of effective government, measured by the standards of the program approach.

The Carter Administration's Unresolved Tensions

President Carter himself seemed ultimately to acknowledge the superiority of national community liberalism to his own policy liberalism. In his famous malaise speech of July 16, 1979, he confessed that he had failed to communicate a coherent set of goals for America (he quotes a southern governor's remark to him that "you are not leading this Nation—you're just managing the Government"); that the government appeared to be "twisted and pulled in every direction by hundreds of well-financed and powerful special interests"; and that "what you see too often in Washington . . . is a system of government that seems incapable of action." The answer to this "loss of unity of purpose for our Nation," he maintained, was a "moral equivalent of war"—a familiar technique borrowed from the arsenal of national community liberalism, and used so effectively by Roosevelt and Johnson to bring the nation together on earlier occasions. In this case, the war would be fought on the "battlefield of energy." Here, Carter claimed, we could "rekindle our sense of unity . . . and give our Nation and all of us individually a new sense of purpose."[17]

When Carter thus finally turned to the techniques of national community liberalism, he saw the wisdom of focusing his efforts on a single "priority" area of legislation—energy. And here, the presentation of his program took the form of a clear, concise (for Carter) six-point program. He was compelled to abandon the bewildering laundry lists of complex, comprehensive policy proposals that had previously characterized his approach. (A bit earlier Carter had found it expedient to reduce his agenda in general and had cut the number of "priority" presidential initiatives from sixty to a mere thirty.)[18] Given the departures from the policy approach that national community liberalism seemed to demand, the experience of the Carter administration suggests a deep tension between the two approaches to governance.

The Carter administration itself never came to grips with this tension; it may, in fact, be unresolvable. The policy approach insists that only a truly comprehensive plan can solve a given social problem. Partial, programmatic interventions inevitably trigger unforeseen reactions within the social system, often making the problem only worse. The policy approach, however, has certain intrinsic political vulnerabilities, as became apparent through the experiences of the Carter administration: it complicates the setting of clear priorities; it exposes government to the charge of special interest influence; and it leads to dashed expectations and the appearance of ineffectiveness.

National community liberalism, on the other hand, resolves the political dilemma so frustrating to policy liberalism through the enunciation of a coherent public philosophy—but only by simultaneously resorting to a program approach to social problems. Government can now act against urban difficulties, but only in the fragmentary, "ultimately self-defeating" way that, according to policy analysis, inevitably characterizes such an approach. Policy liberalism can properly object that incoherence in the realm of policy is an unacceptable price for coherence in the realm of public philosophy.

Is it possible to reconcile policy liberalism and national community liberalism? In other words, is there some way simultaneously to meet the rigorous requirements of public policy *and* public philosophy? This is, of course, the question faced in *Politics and the Professors* by Henry Aaron, who was one of the first to discuss the tension between social science research and the "simple faiths" of liberalism. He concluded that it might, in fact, be possible to combine "sober attempts rationally to solve increasingly complex problems" with the "sense of mutual obligation and community."[19] His optimism was quite guarded, however, for good reason. The essence of policy is complexity; the essence of public philosophy is simplicity. Public policy would like to believe that it falls into the realm of science; public philosophy points us toward the realm of faith. The two approaches would inevitably tend to pull any liberal presidential administration in diametrically opposed directions.

At any rate, this is the tension that must be addressed before we, as a nation, seriously consider another "comprehensive" approach to urban problems, or social problems in general. As things stand now in this area, liberalism seems to confront, and to present the nation with, a choice between a politically effective but unsophisticated and ultimately "self-defeating" program approach to social problems and a sophisticated, comprehensive, but politically unpalatable policy approach. Until liberalism sets its own house in order, it will not do to blame lack of action in the cities or within society simply on the "conservative reaction."

11

American Neighborhood Policies: Mixed Results and Uneven Evaluations

Marshall Kaplan

Since early in the 1960s America's urban policy, or what purports to be its urban policy, has focused, in part, on neighborhood revitalization. While the names of the initiatives have changed over time, the conventional wisdom did not. The federal government had a responsibility to and, perhaps more relevant, could help improve the physical condition of older deteriorating or already deteriorated urban neighborhoods. Most often, neighborhood revitalization policies have been viewed as synonymous with efforts to reduce or ameliorate poverty—a linkage that seemed obvious to most federal policymakers in light of the concentration of low-income households in poorer-quality neighborhoods and a linkage, sometimes, required to secure resources politically. Only recently have we begun to seriously critique the role and impact of the federal government in neighborhood revitalization. Similarly, only recently have we begun to question the assumed relationship between neighborhood improvement and poverty reduction.

American Neighborhood Revitalization: Mythologies and Policies

Americans have had a romance with their neighborhoods almost since the country's birth. Neighborhoods have been symbolized in the nation's mythology and have illustrated in fact the "American way of life . . . the safety of familiar space . . . a cluster of like-minded families and kids . . . service provision by government at a human scale." Neighborhoods have been the building blocks of our community planning and education programs. They have been used to foster civic concern for amenities, for the protection of property values, and for the expansion of group and household life-style choices.

Table 11.1   Place and People Neighborhood-Related Program Initiatives

Place
Urban Renewal and Redevelopment
Federal Housing Programs (support for production)
Model Cities
War on Poverty
Neighborhood Housing Services
Urban Homesteading
Neighborhood Strategy Areas
UDAG
Community Development Block Grants
Tax Incentives (e.g., historical preservation)

People
Welfare Assistance
Provision of or access to Services
Social Security/Income Enhancement Programs
Federal Housing Programs (subsidies for rent/lease; Vouchers)
Tax Incentives (e.g., tax deductions and tax exemptions, rate structure)

Our continued attraction to neighborhoods has troubled some and mystified others. Some scholars have questioned whether, given our mobility, many of us really live in neighborhoods. They claim that most middle- and upper-class households no longer are bounded by the spatial limits of neighborhoods in choosing friends and in fulfilling household, community, and economic roles. The spatial map they would use to describe how we live is much larger and is bounded mainly by transportation and telecommunication variables.

To some analysts, the neighborhood has become an obstacle to social progress. For example, they would argue that protection of the neighborhood school has become a code word for resistance to school desegregation. Similarly, protection or maintenance of neighborhood values and integrity has become coincident with resistance to the development of housing for low-income households in neighborhoods.

By and large, the support for national neighborhood policies has reflected the positive attributes most Americans associate with neighborhoods. But the actual content of these policies has reflected many of the ambiguities raised by scholars and practitioners. In this context, neighborhood policies have focused either on places or on people who live in places (see table 11.1). Put another way and perhaps more relevant, they have focused on neighborhoods as physical environments or on the "disadvantaged" people who live in neighborhoods. But even here distinctions are not always clear.

Place Policies

Since 1949 Congress has indicated that every American is entitled to a decent home in a suitable living environment. Congressional intent, while laudable, has never really been backed up by sustained and predictable initiatives or resources. Generally, however, Congress has provided an envelope for a variety of sometimes consistent and sometimes inconsistent neighborhood redevelopment, revitalization, and service provision programs. Among the more important:

— Redevelopment. The federal government has supported the wholesale clearance of relatively large blighted areas of cities and their redevelopment for public use and/or purpose. In many instances neighborhoods — whole or part — were demolished and replaced by varied uses, including but not limited to housing.

— Revitalization and/or rehabilitation. The federal government has supported local efforts to engage in strategic clearance and/or development of blighted neighborhood areas. Through varied means, they also have aided efforts of local communities, nonprofit groups, profit-making companies, and households to rehabilitate deteriorated housing units.

— Service provision and delivery. The federal government has aided local government, nonprofit groups, and citizen organizations in providing or delivering increased or, assumedly, better services in deteriorated or deteriorating neighborhoods.

People Policies

The federal government, through a variety of initiatives, has provided money (e.g., welfare) and/or surrogates for money (e.g., entitlements to health care services, housing, food stamps, etc.) to low-income households. Expenditures by the poor are not limited to neighborhoods. But the implicit, if not explicit, assumption of many of the programs is that through increased income (and/or access to the goods that income will buy) will come more stable neighborhoods and improved neighborhood quality.

Additionally, the federal government has helped fund "empowerment" efforts; that is, efforts by the poor or representatives of the poor to establish neighborhood organizations to advocate and/or deliver programs, ostensibly favored by low-income inhabitants of neighborhoods. Assumedly, permitting the poor to influence, if not control, the flow of resources into and the planning of their own neighborhoods will help them secure a better fit between expenditures and need. More importantly, allowing the poor to gain access to power will reduce one of the key variables identified by some as resulting in poverty and poor neighborhoods—that is, powerlessness.

American Neighborhood Revitalizing Policies: Effectiveness

A vigorous debate exists concerning the effectiveness of federal policies and programs initiated to help neighborhoods and their residents. Indeed, there are data on all sides of the impact question.

It is fair to say that the broad purposes of many federal neighborhood policies have not been achieved. Most of the neighborhoods receiving "place" type assistance remain prone to the kinds of problems that initially qualified them to receive assistance. Many of the neighborhoods that appear to be in better physical shape seem to have improved their lot in part because of changing economic, market, and social conditions. Clearly, it is difficult to establish causal linkages between federal aid and improved neighborhood status.

Importantly, the relationship between neighborhood physical improvement fostered by the federal government and changes in the income and/or job, education, health choices, etc., of the residents of older neighborhoods is still to be determined in a definitive manner. While national policies, initiated during the late sixties and early seventies, aimed at adding to or complementing household income were successful in ameliorating the conditions associated with poverty and in reducing poverty among certain cohorts of the American population (e.g., the aged), significant questions remain as to how effective they were in stimulating qualitative changes in neighborhood status. Similarly, while anecdotes and case studies point to some successes in resident upgrading of the physical condition of certain neighborhoods, it is not clear what impact such successes had on the income of residents. Physical improvement in many neighborhoods appears to have occurred almost simultaneously with or subsequent to demographic changes in household class or income. The net effect, in these instances, on poorer residents who were forced to leave or who left voluntarily is still subject more to anecdote and evaluations of limited numbers or cases.[1]

Regrettably, despite more than two decades of uneven but sometimes vigorous federal intervention, poverty in urban America remains at relatively high levels. National economic growth has not floated all ships or areas equally. The relationship between increased urban poverty and race reflected in expanding neighborhood ghettos in many cities seems clear. Low-income and minority households continue to reflect relatively poor housing conditions. Substandard housing conditions, while statistically relatively minor by historical and perhaps world standards, appear on the increase in many cities, particularly among rental units occupied by poorer households.

Neighborhood Revitalization Policies: Why Mixed Results?

Analyses of American neighborhood policies suggest several, sometimes competing, reasons why they have failed to secure more than mixed results.

Neighborhood Policies Often Failed to Reflect Consistent Neighborhood Definitions

Federal neighborhood initiatives illustrated varied views of neighborhoods and their characteristics. Most federal efforts relied at least in part on local governments to describe the boundaries of their neighborhoods assumed eligible for federal assistance. Several local governments, however, set relatively arbitrary, and often different, limits concerning population and/or area size. Similarly, several required relatively arbitrary, and often different, income, job, and housing-related characteristics. Finally, a few seemed to predicate the identification of a neighborhood on the presence of political representation or the availability of an active group to speak for residents in the area.

Differences in federal views of neighborhoods implicit, if not always explicit, in diverse federal initiatives were important. Lack of consistency and certainty concerning criteria to define neighborhoods helped foster uncertainty and inconsistencies concerning revitalization approaches. Paraphrasing one former assistant secretary responsible for a number of neighborhood programs, "if we don't have a clear idea of what a neighborhood is . . . if we don't know whether to define a neighborhood in economic, social, or physical terms or any combination thereof . . . if we are not certain that neighborhoods make sense as a viable way to describe a discrete urban place, with distinguishable characteristics . . . then how can we develop effective policy approaches?" Use of neighborhoods as a focus of federal aid often seemed related more to the need for a convenient political ledger or fiscal accounting sheet than to any clear set of ideas concerning their residents' future.

Neighborhood Revitalization Policies Have Failed to Be Guided by an Overall Consistent Theory

Consistent theories rarely have driven neighborhood policies. To secure an understanding of assumed theoretical underpinnings, one often has to journey back in time to legislative testimony and/or the speeches of program or policy advocates. For example, urban renewal seemed directed at aborting and redirecting market trends through dramatically changing the physical conditions of an area and its historical land use and related social patterns. Model Cities appeared focused on helping people in neighborhoods adjust to or accommodate local market and social trends. Implicit in its approach was the stabilization of neighborhoods for people who lived in them through improved and expanded service delivery and through neighborhood involvement in the planning and allocation of public monies. The War on Poverty, through funding services and through granting residents power to plan, aimed at assisting people find the means to break out of dependence and, conceivably, their neighborhoods. Welfare programs provided cash to help poor people secure threshold levels of service (see table 11.2).

Only recently have American academics paid much attention to the definition of hypotheses that lend understanding to the dynamics of neighborhood change and to the relationship between public intervention, neighborhood revitalization, and household income. Put another way, our policies until recently have been guided by a varied, often disparate, set of ideologies and theologies. Theories offering possible explanations of observed neighborhood trends and their relationship to neighborhood residents generally have been tested only by anecdote and by limited evaluations of specific cases over short periods.

We have been told that neighborhood change is natural; that it relates to broader metropolitan area population and income trends; that it will lead to neighborhood segmentation along class and caste lines; that such segmentation in certain kinds of markets may either open up and/or limit housing choices. For example, according to Katharine Bradbury, Anthony Downs, and Kenneth Small: "United States urban development is dominated by the 'trickle down' or filtering process. No one person or group consciously designed that process: it evolved from separate decisions and actions taken by millions of households, developers, local governments, federal agencies, homebuilders, lenders and politicians. . . ." Speaking of new hous-

Table 11.2 Neighborhood Revitalization Strategy—Key Federal Initiatives[a]

Ameliorate Effects of Decline
Welfare
In-Kind Services
War on Poverty

Change Physical Character
Urban Renewal

Stabilization
Model Cities
Urban Homesteading
Select Housing Assistance Programs
Community Development Block Grants

Upgrading
Select housing assistance programs—assisted and nonassisted
Neighborhood Housing Service
Neighborhood Strategy Areas
Community Development Block Grants

Gentrification
Economic Development Assistance
UDAG
Nonassisted Housing Programs
Tax Incentives

[a]The above attempt to classify federal initiatives around key neighborhood strategies or initiatives is relatively subjective. Federal program initiatives often reflected multiple, sometimes inconsistent strategies and were used by and in communities to secure multiple and sometimes inconsistent objectives. The typology, at a minimum, helps focus attention on the relationship between diverse federal efforts and neighborhood strategies. Stabilization refers to activities aimed at halting or impeding neighborhood change—physical or demographic; upgrading refers to activities aimed at improving the physical character and delivery of services in a neighborhood by existing residents; gentrification refers to the in-migration of and a simultaneous or subsequent effort to improve the physical character and delivery of services in a neighborhood by the in-migrants or newcomers.

ing once built for middle- or upper-income households, the same authors indicate:

> But as they got older, and new growth moved out beyond them, they gradually trickled down through the income distribution. They were successively occupied by groups with relatively lower incomes. During most of their history, these housing units provided good quality dwelling for their occupants. But in many cases, they eventually became occupied by households too poor to maintain them or to pay rents sufficient to induce

landlords to maintain them. In U.S. metropolitan areas, most of the lowest ranking neighborhoods are close to the older cores of the area; most
—but usually not all—of the highest ranking neighborhoods are close
to the outer periphery; and most middle ranked neighborhoods are some-
where in between. . . . The socio-economic and ethnic segregation deeply
embedded in U.S. urban development strongly contribute to physical decay
and population losses in many older big city neighborhoods."[2]

Conversely, we have been told that neighborhood differentiation both in
terms of condition and occupancy is related primarily to transportation costs
or the linkages between job commutation costs and household housing desires. Succinctly, higher-density neighborhoods will be found in central
cities because land costs are high and lower-income people who live in
them sacrifice housing for minimal journey-to-work costs. Apparently, higher-
income people are willing to bear the costs of commuting to gain larger,
more amply endowed housing units on the fringes of urban areas where
land costs are cheaper. The highest-income household, ostensibly, can secure the benefits of inner city living including good housing and low transportation costs. As portrayed by Michael Schill and Richard P. Nathan:

> employment is concentrated in the urban core . . . the journey to work
> constitutes the major transportation cost for most households. In the core
> of the city, commercial, industrial and residential users compete for scarce
> space, so land values are highest closest to the center and decrease with
> distance from the center. A particular household decides how it wants to
> make the trade-off between relatively cheap land in the suburbs and easy
> access to downtown in the center city. . . . higher income households
> will locate at the periphery, thereby consuming more space than they
> could near the core while spending additional time and money commut-
> ing to their jobs in the center. The poor will locate in the center at high
> densities so as to minimize the costs of land and transportation. . . .[3]

In explaining why wealthy families or households sometimes move into
older neighborhoods, Schill and Nathan indicate that "well-to-do people
who move into revitalizing neighborhoods value both land and accessibility, and can afford to pay for them both. They thus outbid all other groups
for land close to the urban core."[4]

Analyses and related theories linking income and race to neighborhood
change still are of relatively recent vintage. David Varady, in his book *Neighborhood Upgrading: A Realistic Assessment,* suggests that, "although there
is a relatively large body of research on neighborhood racial change and on

ghetto expansion patterns, there has been minimal linkage between those subjects and theoretical works on neighborhood physical and social decline."[5]

Generally, all other things being equal, households with higher incomes will outcompete households with lower incomes and over time likely lead to neighborhoods that look alike in terms of class lines. Racism and its offspring, various forms of publicly sanctioned and/or induced discrimination, limit minority choices in urban and metropolitan housing markets. Indeed, racism combined with poverty appear to be key variables leading to ghettos or the compaction of minority households in single or contiguous impoverished neighborhoods—neighborhoods that illustrate relatively high degrees of social pathology. Taken together, they also seem to be obstacles to the upgrading of nearby neighborhoods by their existing residents and the gentrification or revitalization of a neighborhood area by the in-migration of higher-income people.

Neighborhood Revitalization Policies Are Premised on Insufficient Knowledge and Analysis of Cause-and-Effect Relationships

Our knowledge of the causes of neighborhood change and the relationship of changes to the health and well-being of different kinds of households, while improving, remains uneven. For example, we still do not know the link between urban growth patterns and neighborhood transition. Similarly, we still remain at the stage of preliminary hypotheses when we try to explain why some neighborhoods with similar physical and/or demographic characteristics reflect vastly different development trends. The role of historical variables in causing neighborhood evolution, the role of different cultural and ethnic characteristics in affecting neighborhood renewal or decline, the role of public and private sector investment in hastening or inhibiting change, and the role of different household decisions on neighborhood dynamics and change are all yet to be definitively determined.

The relationship between household well-being and place-specific revitalization efforts has never been clear. Policies aimed at building better neighborhoods and improved social services, if linked to subsidies that permit low-income families to remain in such neighborhoods, could slow down mobility and possibly sustain long-term household income improvements. Conversely, policies aimed at providing people with supportive services to gain access to the job market, if not related to housing and neighborhood initiatives, could, at least in the short term, leave them facing difficult living conditions. Finally, policies aimed at the physical revitalization of low-income neighborhoods, if not matched with income enhancement programs, could encourage in-migration of higher-income households and either force existing residents out or require them to pay a higher percentage of their already meager income for housing.

Independent Neighborhood Policies Often Fail to Reflect
Explicit Doable Objectives and/or Objectives Which Are
Consistent with Other Neighborhood Policies

Measurable objectives have rarely been the long suit of American neighborhood revitalization efforts. More often than not they are generalized to avoid offending different constituencies or, more positively, to build support among different constituencies. Frequently, they read like a menu of all that is good under the sun in order to gain public and congressional acquiescence. Model Cities provides a good example of the norm. Its mandate was to cure slum conditions existing in selected neighborhoods and to provide extended jobs, education, health services, etc., to residents of such neighborhoods. It also aimed to encourage neighborhood involvement in the development of revitalization plans. All objectives were to occur within a relatively short period—less than a decade. Similarly, the War on Poverty initiatives contained multiple, often nonquantifiable, objectives. Its programs were to ameliorate poverty, permit the poor to control their own lives and the future of the areas in which they lived, reform the delivery and affect the content of public services, make the poor self-sufficient, coordinate public delivery systems, and reform those delivery systems.

Neighborhood initiatives sometimes either joined place and people objectives in a confusing and potentially inconsistent manner or granted priority to one initiative without acknowledging its likely effect on the other. For example, Model Cities in mixing objectives concerning physical revitalization and amelioration of poverty sometimes made it tougher to achieve either objective. Successful revitalization often required deep subsidies that frustrated the start-up of service-related programs. Successful revitalization in some areas generated household migration and encouraged new household in-migration; both resulted in unplanned benefits to some and costs to others. Minimal funding only exacerbated difficulties concerning multiple goal achievement.

The goal of the War on Poverty to empower neighborhood residents helped frustrate another proposed goal—the coordination of federal, state, and city programs. It proved difficult for neighborhood groups to secure cooperation from public entities concerning program delivery and reform while they were attacking or criticizing them for incompetence or worse. ''Power to the people'' had a ringing sound and it made for nice speeches. But if and when converted into adversarial relationships between the newly empowered and the historically powerful, it rarely generated resources for the former and help from the latter.

The Urban Homestead and Neighborhood Service programs were premised on the hope that public initiatives would generate multiple neighborhood spillover effects. Both programs often let their supporters down and their evaluators short of positive stories to tell. Public investments and actions were not able to achieve the desired private investment objectives or related private household actions.

Neighborhood Policies Rarely Have Consistent or Precise Strategies

Without guiding theories and clear-cut objectives, neighborhood policies in the United States have rarely reflected definitive strategies. As indicated above, some programs attempted to provide people with opportunities to secure threshold or improved services and make their lives better; some attempted to allow people to break out of poverty and gain income and neighborhood mobility. Only recently have we focused on the kinds of discrete spatial strategies that could be related to different kinds of neighborhood characteristics. Only recently has the literature on neighborhoods attempted to distinguish efforts to stabilize areas from efforts to upgrade areas. Only recently have analysts focused on linking the objectives of varied federally assisted neighborhood redevelopment strategies to the impact associated with the possible range of initiators of such strategies — investors, developers, community groups, newcomers, existing residents, etc. Only recently have we begun to place a time and resource dimension on diverse neighborhood improvement efforts. Finally, only recently have policymakers begun to raise questions concerning the effect of regional and local housing markets on neighborhood revitalization efforts. In this context, and without sustained and successful federal housing initiatives, filtering and trickle-down processes—processes that lead to a decline in housing conditions and prices—may be the most effective way to improve the housing conditions of relatively large numbers of poor households. In tight housing markets particularly, federal intervention to abort the decline of neighborhoods or to stabilize neighborhoods, without compensating strategies, may negatively affect the quality of life and housing conditions of those least able to fend for themselves.

*Neighborhood Policies and Programs Have Rarely Been Subject to Sustained
and Useful (Read "Policy-Relevant") Evaluation Concerning Their Impact*

It has been and remains tough to subject American neighborhood policies
and programs to evaluation. While the literature is growing, the techniques
of evaluation often remain quite subjective, the choice of neighborhoods
for study relatively few, the factors or variables reviewed in distinguishing
neighborhood development patterns narrow, the time spans associated with
analyses restricted, and the use of surrogate measures for signs of neighborhood improvements relatively conventional (e.g., housing, household satisfaction, etc.).

Measurements of performance often focus more on input (dollars spent,
units rehabilitated) than output measures (effects on people's lives and long-
term effects on neighborhoods). Perhaps as relevant as the lack of measurement criteria in inhibiting effective evaluation efforts has been the short and
often chaotic life of neighborhood policies and programs. Both have been
governed more by the policy or political fad of the moment than by a long-
term commitment to defined objectives. In a similar vein, and directly related to their episodic character, they have often been significantly underfunded and/or—a variation on a theme—limited in scale.

The small size of many programs, their uneven support, and their short
life spans have made it difficult to separate non-project-related from program-
related variables and impacts. Put another way, factors affecting the national or even local economy and factors associated with other federal or
local policies often swamp the sought-after effect of specific neighborhood
initiatives. Sometimes it is next to impossible to define and evaluate cause-
and-effect relationships with any degree of confidence.

Sustained evaluation of neighborhood programs has faced other obstacles. We have yet to establish an "evaluation culture"—one that supports
the possibility of critical data and conclusions resulting from federally funded
studies. Federal and local administrators rarely like to be told they are
wrong or that they are administering a flawed or failed program. Evaluation
as a function is often placed in or has a strong relation to political officers
who have strong stakes in "success" stories. Further, longitudinal studies
generally require the certainty of appropriations and the commitment of
agencies for many years—both difficult to achieve when election cycles are
relatively brief and/or the probability of leadership changes frequent. Finally, at least during the last few years federal initiatives to secure neighborhood improvements were reduced to the barest minimum by the Reagan
administration. The president and his colleagues viewed most federal neigh-

borhood initiatives as following a Gresham's law! To them, to allocate federal dollars to distressed cities or areas was like throwing good and limited resources into bad situations. It was inefficient or worse. In this environment, evaluation efforts funded by the feds were at best marginal and episodic.

Neighborhood Policies Often Have Not Been Linked to Other Urban and Nonurban Policies in America

Ideally, neighborhood policies would fit within a comprehensive set of urban policies and would be related to nonurban policies, where and when relevant. But our nation has not been able to develop a comprehensive urban policy or a set of reasonably refined and coordinated objectives from which resources flow and programs are designed.

As a result of the failure to link urban policies together and to relate neighborhood policies to other kinds of urban and indeed nonurban policies, we often face the situation of the right hand not knowing or caring what the left hand is doing. More perversely, perhaps, we often have programs initiated by good and decent people that negatively affect other programs initiated by good and decent people. Without some sense of the strategic, anticipated or hoped-for impacts are muted and/or positive objectives are turned into negative happenings (see table 11.3). For example, urban renewal, particularly in its early days, cleared a lot of land and resulted in the relocation of many disadvantaged people. It did this often during periods of housing shortages and in areas with housing shortages. The effect in some parts of the nation was to force people or households to seek shelter in already deteriorating or deteriorated areas—areas frequently subject to federal initiatives to either expand the housing choices of their residents and/or to improve the physical and social conditions of the area. The net result was overcrowding and further compaction of poverty problems and related neighborhood difficulties. Similarly, America's love affair with federally supported highways and freeways began in the mid-fifties. Many analysts view the interstate highway system and the advent of beltways around cities as heightening decentralization trends and weakening the fabric of downtowns and older neighborhoods; yet this occurred simultaneously with other federal initiatives aimed at encouraging the return to downtown and older neighborhoods by the middle class.

Inside HUD, the federal agency most responsible for urban policy initiatives and formation, tension has existed between the "housers" and the neighborhood revitalization folk. Both have laudable objectives, but sometimes they compete. Federally insured housing production, by and large,

Table 11.3 Examples—Inadvertent Negative Neighborhood Effects of Select Federal Initiatives

Initiative	Effect
Fostering Housing Production in Suburbs	Weakening of Older Neighborhoods
Urban Renewal	Displacement of Low-Income Households, Concentration of Low-Income Households in Declining Neighborhoods
Highway and Beltway Construction	Facilitate Decentralization of Population, Weakening of Older Neighborhoods

Tax Reform
  Lowering of Marginal Rates
  Changes in Depreciation
	Minimize Investor Interest in Municipal Bond Market, Rental Units

Restricted or Tight Monetary Policy	Higher Costs for Mortgage Money
Development of Subsidized Housing	Concentration of Low-Income Households in Select Neighborhoods
Welfare Assistance	Rules Sometimes Impede Household Mobility

takes place in the suburbs where it is cheaper to build. Building large numbers of units in the suburbs, particularly in markets with high vacancy rates, weakens the housing market in older neighborhoods. Federally assisted or subsidized housing units, if located in neighborhood areas struggling to remain viable sometimes negatively affect federal initiatives aimed at securing neighborhood stabilization and improvement. Concentration of public housing in certain urban neighborhoods has limited the ability of such neighborhoods to retain an integrated population and income mix and has often limited household as well as commercial investment incentives.

Conclusion: Starting Over, Demonstration and Evaluation

A new administration has taken over in Washington. Budget deficits combined with an uncertain national economy make it difficult to mount any new large-scale neighborhood revitalization policies in the near future. It is a good time, therefore, to take stock of where we have come from and to initiate careful analyses of what has worked and what has not. It is also a good time to attempt to reconcile social welfare and neighborhood revitalization strategies. It is to be hoped that the federal government, along with state and local governments, will initiate demonstrations that test and reflect the degree of coincidence between both. Both the demonstrations and their evaluations should be structured to help generate efficient and equitable neighborhood revitalization efforts by all levels of government in the United States and by public/private sector as well as by community groups. Paraphrasing that old but wise neighborhood policymaker, Socrates: "An unexamined neighborhood policy is not worth having."

12

The Rise and Fall of National Urban Policy: The Fiscal Dimension

Robert D. Reischauer

Before the Great Depression the federal government provided little in the way of financial assistance to local governments either directly or through the states. Then in the mid- and late 1930s Washington responded to the erosion of urban tax bases and the widespread hardship of the era with a surge of support for local public works, unemployment relief, and public housing programs. Federal aid to local governments rose from $10 million in 1932 to $278 million in 1940.[1] World War II brought a sharp reduction in this aid, but after the war a modest level of federal assistance was reestablished as the federal government acted to support airport construction (1946), urban renewal (1949), urban planning (1954), and education in areas affected by military installations (1950). From 1960 to 1978 a veritable explosion occurred in federal urban policy. The number of federal grants directed at cities and their problems increased dramatically, and, as a result, federal aid became an important source of money for many urban budgets for the first time. The period since 1978 has been characterized by a steady retrenchment, which, if continued, could return federal-local fiscal relations to the levels existing before the Great Society buildup.

This essay reviews the dynamics of the 1960–78 expansion in federal urban aid and its subsequent contraction. The objective of this review is to determine whether national urban policy is currently experiencing a temporary setback that, like the World War II contraction, will be followed by a renewed expansion, or whether the 1960 to 1978 period was an historical aberration that will not be repeated.

The views in this chapter are those of the author and should not be attributed to the staff, trustees, or supporters of the Brookings Institution.

Table 12.1 Total Number of Federal Grants and Grants Available to
Local Governments

	1960	1967	1975	1981	1987
Total	132	379	448	539	422
Localities Only	n.a.	n.a.	20	23	15
Localities and Other Recipients	n.a.	n.a.	260	317	243

Source: U.S. Advisory Commission on Intergovernmental Relations (unpublished tabulations).

Some Magnitudes

It is impossible to measure precisely the amount of federal aid received by urban areas or how this aid has changed over time. One reason for this is that few federal grant programs are directed exclusively at local governments. In 1987, only fifteen of the federal government's 422 grants were reserved solely for localities; the remaining 407 were available only to states or to combinations of states, localities, and nonprofit organizations (see table 12.1). Of the money directed at local governments, only a small portion is received by large cities and could, therefore, properly be classified as part of the nation's urban policy. Suburban and rural counties, school districts, and municipalities all obtain a share. A second reason why estimates of federal aid to urban areas are imprecise is that much of federal urban aid money is received initially by state governments which then pass it through to local governments. But in such cases the aid may lose its federal identity because it is mixed with state funds. Similar difficulties arise with grants provided to nonprofit organizations that may provide services and programs in urban areas. These difficulties should be kept in mind when interpreting table 12.2, which provides a picture of the recent pattern of direct federal aid to cities.

Through the mid-1960s direct federal aid for cities was relatively inconsequential, especially when compared to the own-source revenues of these governments. But this began to change when the number of grant instruments through which cities could receive direct or indirect federal assistance expanded tremendously during the mid- and late 1960s. New initiatives were begun in many areas, including community action programs (1964), mass transportation (1964), manpower development and training (1964), neighborhood youth programs (1964), elementary and secondary education assistance (1965), basic water and sewer facilities (1965), com-

Table 12.2 Federal Intergovernmental Aid to Municipalities, 1950–1986

Fiscal Year	Federal Aid		
	Millions of Dollars	Millions of 1984 Dollars[a]	As a Percentage of Own-Source Revenue
1955	121	760	1.9
1960	256	1,138	2.8
1965	557	2,149	4.5
1970	1,337	3,748	7.1
1975	5,844	11,066	19.3
1978	10,234	15,654	25.8
1980	10,872	13,778	22.8
1982	10,990	12,210	18.4
1984	10,440	10,440	14.5
1986	9,813	9,039	11.6

Source: ACIR, *Significant Features of Fiscal Federalism, 1985–86 Edition.* (February 1986), M-146, and U.S. Bureau of the Census, *Governmental Finance in 1986*, November 1987.
[a]Deflated by the implicit GNP price deflator for state and local purchases of goods and services.

munity health services (1965), and law enforcement assistance (1968). However, the funding for these efforts remained relatively constrained during the 1960s.

It was not until the 1970s that the budgetary impact of these programs and other new initiatives became significant. Between 1970 and 1978 there was a fourfold real increase in direct federal aid. Such aid peaked in importance at over one-quarter of the own-source resources of city governments in 1978. For some large distressed cities, which Richard Nathan once characterized as "federal aid junkies," dependence on Washington reached much higher levels. For example, federal aid to Phoenix, Cleveland, and Detroit amounted to over half of their local tax revenues in 1978.[2]

The explosion of federal aid not only reflected increased funding for categorical programs but also for two new federal policy thrusts. The first was general revenue sharing which was an intergovernmental income redistribution scheme. The second was the effort made by the Carter administration to enlist states and localities as agents of federal stabilization policy. The countercyclical revenue-sharing program (the Anti Recession Fiscal Assistance Act of 1977), the local public works program (the Public Works Employment Act of 1976), and the expansion of Titles II and VI of CETA (the Comprehensive Employment and Training Act) all poured money into local government budgets in an effort to reduce unemployment and maintain basic public services in areas hit hard by the recession.

While the number of grant instruments available to local governments continued to expand at a healthy clip between 1978 and 1981, federal aid did not keep pace with inflation. The major reason for this was the phase-down of the antirecession effort. A second, less important reason was that most (thirty-nine of forty-two) of the new programs enacted during this period were project grants with fixed budgets rather than formula programs and entitlements with their open-ended funding.[3]

The 1981 initiatives of the Reagan administration reduced the number of grant programs by one quarter.[4] A few small programs were terminated, and many more were consolidated into a dozen block grants. Funding levels for both the consolidated grants and many of the remaining categorical grants were cut sharply, leading to the first nominal dollar reduction in federal aid in decades. Since 1981 the specter of the federal budget deficit has precluded any expansion of aid to cities.

The Forces Behind the Expansion

The reasons why federal aid to urban areas soared from 1960 to 1978 are no mystery. First, federal policymakers thought that they had the financial resources to take on a number of long-neglected domestic problems. These resources were to come from the "fiscal dividend" that would be generated by the interaction of a growing economy and a progressive federal tax system. At that time the federal budget was not dominated by mandatory programs or entitlements, the spending for which increases automatically. Medicare, Medicaid, Supplemental Security Income (SSI), food stamps, Guaranteed Student Loans (GSLS), and the Earned Income Tax Credit (EITC) did not exist in the early 1960s.

Second, federal policymakers felt that they had the intellectual ability and political will to take on the complex set of problems facing America's cities. This spark was embodied in the social scientists and policy activists who were drawn to Washington by Presidents Kennedy and Johnson. This cadre was anxious to test out the theories and proposals they had developed during the 1950s.

Third, federal aid to cities expanded over this period because the American people and their representatives in Congress were willing to accept the propositions that there were serious unmet needs in the cities and that these problems could be effectively addressed through public sector actions.

The fourth reason why urban aid exploded was that these domestic problems became identified with the geographic areas in which they were most apparent. Inadequate housing, poor public transportation, deteriorating

neighborhoods, crime, failing schools, and limited job opportunities became identified as big-city problems, not as general domestic problems or
as problems of the low-income population. The riots of the mid-1960s
only reinforced the view that a preponderance of the nation's unmet needs
were located in cities.

A fifth factor underlying the surge of federal assistance to cities was the
feeling in Washington that the solutions to these problems were city, not
state, responsibilities. Cities were portrayed as a worthy or deserving level
of government. States were held in relatively low esteem. They were viewed
as backward and uninterested in the plight of the underprivileged. Many
states, it was felt, had systematically shortchanged their large urban areas
while benefiting rural, and, to a lesser extent, suburban jurisdictions. States
could not be trusted to do what was right for their big cities even if they
were given federal resources. Therefore, direct federal intervention offered
the best hope for addressing urban problems.

A contradictory subcurrent of thinking, one critical of cities, also existed. This view held that political and business forces within the large
cities had not come to grips with core urban problems. Sometimes jurisdictions lacked the capacity or resources, but more often indifference, incompetence, or even corruption were to blame. Rather than leading to a policy
of federal restraint, this line of reasoning convinced some Washington activists that more radical change was necessary, that improvements would
occur only if the federal government intervened to change existing power
structures in cities. In other words, some federal officials saw themselves
compelled to reform local institutions and political structures if they were
to successfully tackle the most pressing domestic problems of the day.

Finally, federal assistance to cities grew because it was good politics.
Direct aid to cities and indirect assistance through states provided congressmen with tangible benefits. There was the opening of the health clinic
to attend, the new city buses to deliver, and ribbons to cut at the economic
development project. It is doubtful that a federal strategy of providing aid
directly to individuals or to states in the form of true block grants could
have provided as much political payoff.

In addition, the proliferation of grants generated a system of support
that kept the grants strategy alive and well long after serious questions
had risen concerning its ability to deal with the underlying causes of urban
problems. New congressional subcommittees were created to oversee some
grants, and the importance of many existing subcommittees was enhanced.
New agencies and offices were created both in the federal government
and in individual city governments to administer the new programs. And

special interest lobbies developed to defend and expand each new grant program.

The Seeds of Destruction

The expansion of federal assistance to local jurisdictions carried within it the seeds of its own destruction. By choosing to deal directly with localities, the federal government became entangled in the complexity that characterizes local government in America. Different governments have different functional responsibilities and different taxing authority. Problems which might be dealt with effectively by the municipal government in New York might require a coordinated response from the county, the municipality, and several independent school districts in Dallas. In some areas the urban problems that concerned federal policymakers were exacerbated, if not caused, by various restraints state laws placed on cities. Examples of this include the limited annexation authority that most large cities had and their inability to tax workers in the city who commuted from the suburbs. In addition, few urban problems respected local jurisdictional boundaries. Thus, the recipient of a federal grant often had only a piece of the problem within its area of responsibility.

By choosing to deal with hundreds of localities, the federal government was confronted with jurisdictions of vastly different capacities, internal structures, and politics. Faced with this complexity, Washington had two options. One was to admit that no central government had the capacity to design and monitor programs that could accommodate even a majority of the different circumstances which would arise. Such an admission would have led to a block grant strategy. Under such a strategy, resources would have been given to jurisdictions for use in solving certain basic types of problems. But the recipient jurisdictions would have been allowed to choose which specific approaches would best address the problem in their particular area.

The second option, which was the one taken, was to design programs in excruciating detail to try to anticipate every circumstance that might arise. This created a system characterized by red tape and regulation under which recipients were forced to submit plans, pre-proposals, proposals, and progress reports. Federal bureaucrats were charged with reviewing these submissions at every stage, thus maximizing the opportunity for conflict and contention. This approach reflected not only the confidence Washington's politicians and policy planners had in their own abilities, but also a political imperative. Loosely directed federal funds were more likely to end up misdirected, sometimes in scandalous ways. This might come back to visit political damage on the sponsoring agency, committee, or individual congressman.

The chosen strategy produced a reaction from both the grant givers and the recipients. The latter chafed under the red tape, excessive regulations, and delays imposed by Washington. The former were overwhelmed by the work load and stung by the criticism they received from what were supposed to be grateful beneficiaries.

The congestion created by the proliferation of grants spawned an intellectual backlash as well. Soon policy analysts were arguing that the intergovernmental fiscal system needed to be rationalized. Many experts came to question whether the needs being addressed by federal-local grants were truly of national importance. Calls for simplification and a sorting out of functions became more frequent.

The inherent inability of Congress to target local grants represented another destructive seed. Severe urban problems were not present in every, or even most, large cities. And yet, for a new grant program to be enacted or an existing one to receive a larger appropriation, the program had to spread its largess widely across as many congressional districts as possible. The incongruity between concentrated needs and dispersed federal aid helped to generate perceptions of inefficiency and waste.

The growing importance of federal-local fiscal relations caused strains with the state governments. Some cities were accused of being more attuned to the wishes and priorities of Washington than to those of the state capital. Some states, witnessing Washington's active interest in urban problems, slacked off their own efforts to deal with the problems of their large urban centers.

The Era of Retrenchment

In the past decade the conditions that contributed to the 1960–78 expansion of federal aid to cities disappeared and a new era of retrenchment began. The retrenchment drew strength from the turbulence that afflicted the economy in the late 1970s and early 1980s and from the growing perception that federal domestic programs were not working. The Reagan administration forcefully articulated these perceptions.

The most significant factor contributing to this retrenchment was the budgetary squeeze that the federal government found itself in starting in the late 1970s. With the tax cuts of 1981, the Reagan administration's defense buildup, and the 1981–82 recession, the squeeze was transformed into the crushing force of $200 billion annual deficits. The battle to reduce these deficits revealed that discretionary domestic spending, of which nonentitlement grants to state and local governments make up a significant portion, was not high on the nation's list of budgetary priorities. Over the 1978–88 decade nonentitlement federal grants were cut by 41 percent in real terms. General revenue sharing and Urban Development Action Grants were eliminated entirely. CETA was replaced by the Jobs Training Partnership Act at one-half the CETA funding level. On an inflation-adjusted basis grants for community and regional development were cut by two-thirds, and those for education, training, and social services fell by 45 percent.[5] Under the strictures of the Gramm-Rudman-Hollings deficit reduction targets, continued pressure to reduce aid to cities should be expected.

While the extreme fiscal restraint of the current period should ease somewhat if the Bush administration deals effectively with the deficit, the long-run outlook for increased urban aid does not look bright. Relative to a decade or two ago, a much larger fraction of the federal budget is now devoted to relatively uncontrollable commitments such as Social Security, Medicare, debt service, farm price supports, veterans' benefits, and military and civilian pay. With the income tax indexed and reformed, there is no possibility that bracket creep or economic growth will generate a significant "fiscal dividend" that could be devoted to expanded domestic programs. Therefore, any significant expansion of domestic programs will require a tax increase, something that is not likely after the deficit issue is resolved.

In addition, the optimism about the effectiveness of government programs that existed in the 1960s has given way to an equally exaggerated feeling that little that the federal government tries works very well. As a mechanism for achieving federal objectives, categorical grants have fallen out of favor. Many programs are regarded as ineffectual; a few are accused of being positively harmful. For example, many analysts argue that federal mass transit aid has built uneconomical subway systems, led to excessive pay for transit workers, and distorted local transportation decisions. Others think that federal economic development efforts have heavily subsidized downtown development that would have occurred without this assistance. Even advocates of federal intervention are hard-pressed to document the programs that have generated dramatic, measurable results. The best they can do is to point to such programs as Job Corps, Chapter 1 (Compensatory Education for the Disadvantaged), Head Start, and WIC (the Supplemental Food Program for Women, Infants and Children), for which there is some evidence of modest positive impacts.

Unlike during the earlier period, cities are no longer perceived as the most worthy or deserving level of government. Their relative status began to fade with the New York City fiscal crisis in the mid-1970s. The wave of municipal corruption, which was covered by the media in excruciating detail, accelerated this fall from grace. States have emerged as the new darlings of Washington policymakers. In large measure the rising status of state government reflects the genuine strengthening of this level of government since the early 1960s. State revenue structures have been strengthened considerably, and there has been a significant improvement in the quality of elected and appointed state officials as well as their staffs. Moreover, when the federal government began to relinquish its role as a policy innovator during the Reagan administration, the states stepped in. In the areas of health cost containment, education, work-welfare, the environment, economic development, housing, and tax reform, states have exhibited a good deal of leadership and innovation.

But Washington's renewed fascination with states also has a practical dimension. As long as retrenchment is required, the federal government will want to distance itself from the ultimate beneficiary of the programs it is cutting back. By channeling grants through the states and by transforming categorical programs into block grants, the political repercussions of federal cutbacks can be diffused. States may compensate for federal cuts by allocating more of their own money to the affected programs. If states choose to validate the federal cuts, some of the criticisms of the cutbacks may be directed at them rather than at Washington. But this is only the case when the aid is channeled through the state.

Not only have states replaced local governments as the focus of federal intergovernmental attention, but "people" have replaced "place" as the primary locus of policy concern in the 1980s. The limited success of the place-oriented strategies of the past and the mobility of the population have led policymakers to look more toward people-oriented approaches to solving the nation's domestic problems. New initiatives are more frequently shaped around individual entitlements, vouchers, or tax expenditures to individuals and businesses than around grants to governments. Housing vouchers, training and retraining payments, tuition tax credits, and tax incentives for economic development and historic preservation are some examples of this trend.

In addition, new actors have appeared on the local scene, actors that compete with and complement local governments. There are the nonprofit organizations and quasi-governmental organizations that often serve as the delivery agents of federal policy. Twenty years ago there were fewer such organizations, and cities had this niche almost entirely to themselves. Furthermore, public-private partnerships, a form of policy intervention which is not conducive to an active federal role, are playing an ever greater part at the local level.

Finally, demographic and economic trends are working against a resurgence of federal fiscal assistance to large cities. The fraction of the population living in large cities continues to decline. Congressional redistricting has taken seats away from the areas of the country which contain the most distressed urban environments. A further reduction, based on the results of the 1990 census, will occur for the 1992 congressional elections. The relative economic position of the large urban centers also has continued to slip. As a result of these trends, the political clout of urban areas has eroded considerably since the mid-1960s, leaving them without the capacity to mount a successful legislative effort to expand federal aid to cities.

Conclusion

The conclusion that arises from this brief review of the past twenty-five years of fiscal federalism is that the 1960 to 1978 era was an aberration, one that is not likely to be repeated. There never existed a neatly defined or coherent national urban policy—a clear notion of what the federal government was attempting to achieve through its interventions to local governments. At first, federal involvement was portrayed as an effort to redevelop blighted neighborhoods. This was replaced by an emphasis on empowering underprivileged city residents and providing them with opportunities to better themselves. The next focus of federal policy was on ensuring that poor urban residents were provided with essential city services. Federal programs then focused on enhancing the fiscal health of cities and on the pursuit of federal antirecession objectives. The final federal thrust emphasized city economic development in partnership with the private sector. The inability to sustain a coherent focus for federal urban policy has not been the fault of the nation's policymakers but rather was inevitable given the inherent complexity and diversity of the federal system and the economic turmoil that characterized the past fifteen years.

Considering the resurgent role of the states, the long-term fiscal constraints that face the federal government, and the diminished political clout of the big cities, renewed efforts to establish a national urban policy that channels significant federal resources to the nation's distressed cities are likely to be futile.

13

A Nonurban Policy: Recent Public Policy Shifts Affecting Cities

Peggy L. Cuciti

There are two ways to approach an assessment of urban policy. One is to ask whether an administration has a clear view of the problems confronting cities as a class, and whether based on that view it has developed a conscious strategy for solving or ameliorating those problems. The second approach ignores the issue of intent and proceeds from the premise that a wide range of policies have impacts on cities. Indeed, it has sometimes been concluded that "nonurban federal policies" may have bigger impacts on cities than urban policies. From the first perspective, not every administration has an urban policy. From the second, all administrations have one.

Interest in the development of a comprehensive and conscious urban policy is relatively recent. During the sixties the cities became a more visible element in the federal system, and there was a shift in the allocation of federal funds toward metropolitan areas.[1] But the primary focus of Great Society programs was not on cities, but rather on enhancing opportunity for disadvantaged persons and on strengthening the communities in which they lived. Cities benefited from many of the Great Society initiatives, but that was primarily because they were inhabited by poor people.

Cities themselves came to be viewed as a problem in the 1970s. Many cities that had been centers of economic activity in the industrial era were losing their vitality. A sectoral shift was occurring; many cities were dependent on declining industries. The advantages of concentration that had once spawned the growth of new firms had given way to technological changes in transportation and communication. It now made economic sense to decentralize many activities—to the suburbs, to newer metropolitan areas, to nonmetropolitan areas, and indeed in some instances to overseas locations.

With the overall economic decline and the shift in the structure of the economy toward services, there are fewer jobs available for people with few skills. Furthermore, there seems to be an increasing bifurcation between lower- and higher-level jobs so that the opportunity for upward mobility is limited even for those who do manage to find jobs.[2]

As their economic base shifted, so did cities' population composition. They were faced with population out-migration of a selective nature. Younger, better-educated people were more likely to move. Older workers, the poor, and minorities had fewer options and came to make up an increasing share of the city's population base. City governments began to realize the fiscal consequences of these economic and demographic shifts. The changes served to weaken the tax base. Expenditures were harder to limit given an aging infrastructure and a relatively dependent population.

During the seventies consensus developed regarding the direction of economic change.[3] There is little consensus, however, on the desirability or feasibility of fashioning a policy to influence market-driven trends or ameliorate their consequences. Advocates of an urban policy argue that public intervention is desirable to alter the speed with which the economic transition is occurring and reduce hardships for those left behind. Under the best of circumstances, they argue, it is possible to reshape economic contours and help cities develop new functions consistent with the future shape of the economy. The strongest advocates of an urban policy are committed to "place-oriented" assistance as well as programs designed to help individuals. Effectively this was the position taken by the Carter administration.

An alternative position advocates development of an urban policy but would shift the emphasis to programs aiding individuals to adjust to new economic realities. Place-oriented programs would be deemphasized. Essentially it is argued that market forces and nonurban policies exert too strong an influence to be countered. "The fates and fortunes of specific places" should "be allowed to fluctuate. . . . People—more so than places —should be insulated from the multiple hardships that accompany the transformation of the nation."[4] The President's Commission for a National Agenda for the Eighties argued that the government should focus on policies that foster economic growth; that it "should aim principally to remove barriers between people and economic opportunity. . . . A people-to-jobs strategy based on vigorous government programs of assisted migration and skill acquisition should receive the emphasis. . . ."[5]

The Reagan administration picked up a number of themes articulated by the President's Commission but projected a much lower profile for government.[6] It reiterated the strength of the forces driving the transition of the economy and affecting the well-being of cities. It argued that the best hope for the nation's cities lies in the strong performance of the national economy. This confidence in market forces was combined with a willingness to accept its distributional consequences. In the administration's view, places, industries, and people have to adjust to economic realities. If places and industries lose their competitive edge, they have to be replaced by others better suited to current conditions. Individuals must adapt by retraining and voting with their feet, shifting jobs and residences in pursuit of opportunity. Leave the market alone, they said, and adjustments will be made. The administration quite explicitly argued that federal support of local economic development programs (the core of place-oriented urban policy) was inappropriate. "Nor should the federal government fund state and local governments in activities that assist only specific geographic areas or allow areas simply to compete with each other at the expense of the taxpayers as a whole."[7] It was the administration's position not to have an "urban policy," and in the following pages we will argue that its "nonurban policy" has had a deleterious effect on cities and their residents.

The Reagan Administration's Nonurban Urban Policy

President Reagan sought the presidency in 1980 committed to two basic goals: building up national defense and decreasing the federal government's role in all other aspects of American life. He believed that federal government programs themselves were a problem rather than a solution to other pressing problems within American society. High federal taxes, extensive regulation, and dependence on federal handouts had interfered with market dynamics and sapped individual initiative necessary for maximum economic growth, productivity, and community problem solving. Immediately upon taking office, the Reagan administration sought to implement its philosophy by proposing sweeping changes in public policy. By historical standards the administration was remarkably successful in obtaining congressional approval for its initiatives—the two most significant of which were the Omnibus Budget Reconciliation Act and the Economic Recovery Tax Act of 1981. But as in the past, the window of opportunity for major change was relatively short-lived. In the remaining years of the Reagan presidency, budgets were proposed that were consistent with the president's ideology, but more often than not they were judged dead on arrival at Capitol Hill; the political system was characterized by stalemate, and policy changes were generally incremental in nature.

There were several components or themes to the Reagan program:

Reduction of federal taxes. Based in part on the supply-side theory of economics, the administration argued that taxes could be cut without reducing revenues because existing tax rates negatively affected savings and investment. Aptly dubbed voodoo economics by candidate George Bush during the 1980 presidential campaign, supply-side theories have since been largely discredited. Nevertheless, the tax cuts were effective in two respects. They stimulated the economy by putting more dollars in the hands of consumers. More important, the tax cuts were effective in furthering the president's long-term goal of limiting the growth of the federal government. In the continuing atmosphere of budget crisis that resulted from the large deficits created by the budget cuts, it has been difficult to enact any legislation with a price tag even if a problem is serious and the proposed program offers reasonable promise of a solution.

A shift in spending from domestic programs to defense. The Reagan administration did little to actually reduce the overall size of government. At the same time as it sought substantial cuts in domestic programs, it proposed massive increases in defense spending. The cuts in domestic programs were concentrated in other state and local government grant programs, direct federal operations, and in means-tested programs.

Reorientation of the federal system. The administration sought to sort out the roles played by various levels of government. It proposed that states and localities assume responsibility in areas where the federal government had previously exercised leadership. State governments were identified as the key partner in those areas where the federal government would continue to play a role. Direct federal-local government relations were minimized, forcing cities to deal instead with state governments. The administration's megaproposals for reassigning responsibilities fell far short of adoption, but a number of block grants were enacted and the terms of debate regarding intergovernmental relations shifted over the period.

Reliance on private sector initiatives. The president lauded such initiatives at the local level and called for the development of public-private sector partnerships to solve problems.

In tracing the impacts of these policy changes on cities, several questions are of interest. Have resources been directed toward the programs that traditionally have assisted distressed cities and their impoverished residents, or have new initiatives directed at city problems been enacted? Within programs, have resources been targeted on distressed cities? Have other changes been made to the structure of programs that are particularly beneficial or harmful to cities? Taking all forms of federal spending into account, what share enters urban economies, particularly those of distressed cities?

We hypothesize that cities did not fare well under the Reagan administration. Programs of importance to cities bore a disproportionate share of the cuts; within programs there has been a shift in resources away from the most distressed cities; structural changes in programs put cities at a disadvantage; and, overall, distressed cities have lost out in the competition for federal spending.

Overview of Budgetary Changes

A review of budgetary trends is the starting point for an analysis of economic and domestic policy changes. While the president would have liked to lower spending overall, he was unable to do so given his commitment to increased defense spending. Instead, spending has continued to increase but at a lower rate than it would have under prior policies, and there has been a significant shift in budgetary priorities toward defense. Tax laws have been changed substantially, greatly reducing revenues below what they would have been. The tax structure has also become substantially less progressive with increasing reliance on the payroll tax and shifts in the personal income tax rate structure.[8] With tax cuts outdistancing budget cuts, a deficit of major proportions developed. These trends in the budget are analyzed in table 13.1. A striking change is in the size of the deficit. It increased from $73.8 billion in FY80 to $150.4 billion in FY87, having peaked at $221 billion in 1986. The deficits incurred over the period are a relatively new phenomenon inasmuch as they are structural in nature. In the past, while there were often current account deficits, in future years one could always project a surplus as the nation approached full employment.

In response to the size of the deficit and forecasts of continuing red ink, Congress adopted the Gramm-Rudman-Hollings Act and then the Balanced Budget Reaffirmation Act. These acts set targets for deficit reduction over a period of several years and put in place automatic across-the-board (with exceptions) budget-cutting mechanisms designed to pressure the Congress and president into reaching an agreement on budget-balancing actions.

Shifting Budgetary Priorities

As shown in table 13.1, total budget outlays increased by 77 percent between 1980 and 1987. The biggest percentage increase, 164 percent, occurred in the net interest category—a direct result of high deficits and high interest rates. The other category showing significant growth (111 percent) was defense spending—a direct result of the administration's push for major expansions in weapons systems.

Table 13.1   U.S. Budget Totals, 1980–1989 (in Billions of Dollars)

	1980	1987	Percentage Change 1980–87	1989 President's Budget
Total Outlays	590.9	1044.6	76.7	1094.2
National Defense	134.0	282.0	110.5	294.0
Direct Payments to Individuals	245.6	413.1	68.2	467.6
Payments to Individuals via Grants to State and Local Governments	31.9	56.4	76.5	63.8
All Other Grants to State and Local Governments	59.4	51.8	(12.8)	54.9
All Other Federal Operations	87.4	99.2	13.4	102.9
Net Interest	52.5	138.6	163.9	151.8
Undistributed Offsetting Receipts	(19.9)	(36.5)	82.8	(41.0)
Total Revenue	517.1	854.1	65.2	964.7
Deficit	(73.8)	(150.4)	103.8	(129.5)[a]

[a]CBO's re-estimate of the president's budget suggests a deficit of $165 billion, not $129.5

Benefit payments to individuals rose at rates slightly below total outlays. Other grants to state and local governments decreased over the period—by 13 percent in current dollars and 37 percent in inflation-adjusted dollars. All other federal spending showed a small increase in current dollars (13 percent), but declined if inflation is taken into account. For this analysis, changes in means-tested entitlement programs and other grants to state and local governments are most important. Means-tested entitlement program outlays increased by 59 percent between 1980 and 1987, while non-means-tested programs increased by 73 percent.[9]

Outlays for grants to state and local governments are shown in table 13.2. Three categories of grants are distinguished. Those programs that support payments to low-income individuals rose over the last seven years but at a lesser rate than in past periods. The lower rate is in part attributable to changes in rules limiting program eligibility and benefit levels. Grants for capital investment decreased from 1980 through 1982 but after that increased through 1986. Other grants supporting a range of state-local

		(Constant 1982 Dollars in Billions)	
1980	1987	Percentage Change 1980–87	1989 President's Budget
699.1	859.3	22.9	868.4
164.0	249.8	52.3	241.6
287.3	347.5	20.9	365.4
37.4	47.4	26.7	49.9
68.4	43.0	(37.1)	42.2
103.8	84.7	(18.4)	119.5
62.0	117.5	89.5	82.0
(23.8)	(30.5)	28.1	(32.2)
611.7	730.6	19.4	765.6
(87.3)	(128.7)	47.4	(102.8)

billion.

social programs totaled $28 billion in 1987, approximately $9 billion less than in 1980. In constant (inflation-adjusted) dollars, capital investment programs suffered an 18 percent decrease, while the "other" category decreased by 56 percent between 1978 and 1987. Overall, state and local government dependence on federal funding has decreased from a high of 26.8 percent in 1978 to 18.2 percent in 1987.

Unfortunately, data on grant flows by city are limited. This is in part a function of program reporting, of complicated intergovernmental financing relationships, and of varying structures of governance within states. Hence, we present several different types of analysis to substantiate the view that state and local governments in general and cities in particular have borne a disproportionate share of the cuts.

Within the budget accounts listing, several programs have been especially important to urban local governments. These include the municipal wastewater treatment construction grant program, urban mass transportation assistance, the urban and secondary roads component of the highway

Table 13.2   Grants to State and Local Governments (in Millions of Dollars)

Year	Total Grants	Grants for Capital Investment	Grants Payments to Individuals	All Other
1975	49,717	10,880	16,445	22,392
1976	59,005	13,517	19,540	25,848
1977	68,318	16,164	22,177	29,977
1978	77,830	18,328	24,175	35,327
1979	82,765	20,061	26,854	35,850
1980	91,358	22,484	31,927	36,947
1981	94,687	22,149	36,931	35,607
1982	88,127	20,151	37,875	30,101
1983	92,409	20,510	41,636	30,263
1984	97,482	22,686	44,284	30,512
1985	105,710	24,875	48,090	32,745
1986	112,357	26,220	52,836	33,302
1987	108,392	23,792	56,352	28,249
1988[a]	116,666	24,993	60,995	30,678
1989[a]	119,015	24,777	63,848	30,390

Source: Office of Management and Budget, *Historical Tables: Budget of the United States Government*, FY 1989.
[a]Estimates from the president's FY89 budget.

trust fund, the community development block grant program, the urban development action grant program, training and employment services, compensatory education, and general revenue sharing. These programs were selected since urban local governments are the primary recipients and because they are helpful in relieving fiscal stress and in buttressing local development efforts.

As shown in table 13.3, grant programs of special importance to cities have been (or are proposed to be) cut by 47 percent. This cut is substantially larger than the cut imposed in other grant programs. General Revenue Sharing, a program of benefit to all local governments, but which has been shown to be targeted somewhat to needy cities, has been zeroed out. The president has proposed ending the Urban Development Action Grant Program which has allowed cities to work with private sector partners in development projects, but Congress has rejected the proposal. Employment and training programs were cut back substantially with the shift from CETA to JTPA. Urban-oriented infrastructure programs have been cut, even though the total of infrastructure programs has managed to hold its own over the period.

To get a general view of the flow of grant funds to more distressed cities

Table 13.3 Programs of Importance to Urban Local Governments

	Budget Authority[a]			
	1980	1987	President's Budget 1989	Percentage Change 1980–87
Wastewater Treatment Construction	3,400	2,304	1,500	−32.2
Urban Mass Transportation	2,430	3,097	1,394	−27.4
Urban and Secondary Roads[a]	932	722	500	−22.5
Community Development Block Grants	3,752	3,000	2,480	−20.0
Urban Development Action Grant	675	225	216	−66.7
Housing Subsidy Programs	18,141	7,851	8,272	−56.7
Training and Employment	5,532	2,986	2,659	−46.0
Compensatory Education	3,570	3,938	4,554	10.3
General Revenue Sharing	6,855	0	0	−100.0
Grant Programs of Special Importance to Urban Governments	45,287	24,123	21,575	−46.7
All Other Grants	59,700	87,614	93,330	46.8
All Other Grants Except AFDC and Medicaid	37,591	49,542	49,874	31.8

Source: Office of Management and Budget, *Special Analysis H: Federal Aid to State and Local Governments*, Fiscal Years 1988 and 1982.
[a]All figures are budget authority except in the case of urban and secondary roads, where in recognition of the trust fund mechanism, obligations are reported.

versus healthier cities, we drew upon the Consolidated Federal Funds Report.[10] The classification of distress was developed by Franklin James for the National Urban Policy Advisory Committee.[11] It focuses primarily on the overall level of economic opportunity available to urban dwellers. The classification is based on an index built on the following economic indicators:

1. Percentage of city population with incomes below the poverty level in 1979 (Index weight: 40 percent)
2. Percentage change in real per capita income between 1969 and 1979 (Index weight: 40 percent)
3. Unemployment rate in 1980 (Index weight: 20 percent)

In addition to a high score on the above index a city had to have lost 10 percent or more of its population between 1970 and 1980 to be classified as distressed. The healthiest cities had low resident need and an increase in population size of 10 percent or more.

Even though the classification of distress is based on cities, the data shown in table 13.4 are actually for the counties which comprise or overlie

Table 13.4 Grant Funding to Counties that Overlay or Comprise Distressed and
Healthy Cities, 1980 and 1986

	1980	1986	Percentage Change
Distressed Areas			
Atlanta	$985,830	$914,887	−7.2
Baltimore	$1,358,786	$885,832	−34.8
Boston	$1,488,442	$1,189,881	−20.1
Buffalo	$609,960	$466,331	−23.5
Chicago	$2,501,755	$2,173,133	−13.1
Cincinnati	$305,290	$368,921	+20.8
Cleveland	$675,008	$735,936	+9.0
Detroit	$1,338,901	$1,354,163	+1.1
Louisville	$338,065	$206,662	−38.9
New York City	$6,060,063	$6,510,121	+7.4
Newark	$581,564	$582,191	0
Norfolk	$141,419	$92,235	−34.8
Philadelphia	$1,655,007	$1,371,627	−17.1
St. Louis	$1,973,192	$359,479	−81.8
Total	$20,013,282	$17,211,399	−14.0
Healthy Areas			
Albuquerque	$180,513	$174,536	−3.3
Austin	$927,925	$1,179,452	+27.1
Charlotte	$111,564	$126,820	+13.7
Honolulu	$433,296	$362,800	−16.2
Houston	$646,097	$850,004	+31.6
Phoenix	$510,044	$663,721	+30.1
San Jose	$478,793	$588,008	+22.8
Virginia Beach	$61,236	$33,067	−46.0
Total	$3,349,468	$3,978,408	+18.8
Total, United States	$104,792,467	$119,012,044	+13.6

Source: Executive Office of the President, Geographic Distribution of Federal Funds, FY1980
and U.S. Bureau of the Census, Consolidated Federal Funds Report, FY1986.

the cities of interest. Grant funding for the distressed (city) counties declined 14.0 percent between 1980 and 1986, while it increased 18.8 percent for the healthy (city) counties. The comparable figure for the nation as
a whole was 13.6 percent. Part of the difference between the distressed and
healthy area figures is attributable to population shifts. Between 1980 and
1984 the distressed counties in the aggregate lost .4 percent of their population, while the healthy counties increased their population by 12.1 percent.

Shifting Responsibility: Block Grants and
Re-Sorting Responsibilities

Budget cuts are only part of the New Federalism story. The administration sought to decentralize responsibility within the federal system by establishing block grants (collapsing seventy-seven categorical programs) and easing regulations. The effects of these structural shifts on cities are assessed below.

Local governments have benefited little from the New Federalism. They have had to deal with budget cuts but gained little in the way of flexibility. The administration focused its attention on state governments, more or less ignoring cities and counties. This is obviously true with respect to the block grants. But the implications go further. In the design of the New Federalism swap-turnback reform (which never got off the ground) the administration's primary negotiations were with the National Conference of State Legislatures.

The implications for cities of a devolution of authority to states will vary. There are fifty states, and their legal, political, and financial environments differ. Critics have contended that cities and their low-income residents have fared poorly—that federal involvement was necessary to meet urgent needs. Mayor William Schaefer of Baltimore told the Joint Economic Committee, for example, that "states were either unable to pay for the programs or have no interest in providing the service. They will not accept the responsibility. When we are able to work directly with the Federal government we are much more effective in being able to provide essential services."[12] Supporters of the New Federalism counter that states have changed. Prompted partly by court action and federal law, states have reformed their political procedures and governing structures. They may *now* be more responsive to the needs of distressed cities and low-income residents.[13]

Several concerns have surfaced regarding process, targeting, and red tape. At this stage, however, it is difficult to assess the number of states in which these concerns are warranted.

Process

Critics have contended that states implemented block grants without adequate consultation with affected groups or localities. This criticism was heard most often in 1981 and 1982 and could be attributable to the confusion accompanying rapid change. In early 1982 the U.S. Conference of Mayors charged that "few states have made efforts to involve local governments in block grant planning and implementation." They complained that it was hard to get information or influence the decision process.[14] This theme was picked up again in 1983 in congressional testimony by the executive director of the National Association of Counties. "While the block grant flexibility has allowed the states to shift their priorities to other areas of need, it has been at the expense of local governments. . . . The states have not brought counties into the decision-making process."[15] On the other hand, the General Accounting Office, which has monitored the implementation of several of the block grants, reports that state officials perceive public participation to be higher now than under the replaced categorical programs.[16] There is greater attention paid to the programs by elected state officials as part of normal planning and budgeting procedures. Interest groups surveyed painted a mixed picture. Since GAO did not specify *who* participated in the decision process, or which interest groups were dissatisfied, it is hard to integrate their findings with the criticisms mentioned above.

There appear to be two issues in regard to participation. The first is whether special procedures (i.e., public hearings, advisory boards, etc.) were established by states to guide them in decisionmaking or whether they relied on normal political processes. Second, and more important, is whether the cities and their poor and minority constituencies have any clout in state capitals either in special or regular decisionmaking procedures. It has been reported that the president's enthusiasm for returning authority to the states was in part motivated by a belief that the clout of minority and poor constituencies would in fact be less in state capitals. In a meeting with Republican members of the House Appropriations Committee the president is reported to have said, "It's far easier for people to come to Washington to get their social programs. It would be a hell of a lot tougher if we diffuse them back to the states. All their friends and connections are in Washington."[17]

Targeting

At recent hearings Senator Paul Sarbanes (D-Md.) expressed grave concern that "targeting is being eliminated . . . the funding itself is being cut back . . . and to the extent the money continues to come, it's coming on a more generalized basis, which means that the amount of it that finally gets down to those cities with pressing need is diminished."[18]

There are a number of instances cited where specific large distressed cities have lost funding because states felt rural areas should get a greater share of funding than they did when programs were administered by the federal government.[19] This shift has been especially commonplace in the Community Services Block Grant. In the state of Washington, for example, the block grant was cut 53 percent, but to avoid eliminating rural-based programs completely, Seattle and other large cities were cut much more than the overall statewide reduction.[20] A case study of the New Federalism's impact in Arizona noted that under state administration of JTPA, additional service delivery areas were established, primarily in rural areas, and as a result a smaller pot of money is being distributed more widely.

In hearings before the Joint Economic Committee, George Latimer, mayor of St. Paul, cited a University of Minnesota study of the state's implementation of three block grant programs. The study concluded that "funding distribution patterns will change substantially with a shift away from cities that had previously received large grants directly from the federal government." Latimer also reported that the Minnesota Department of Health had proposed that the maternal and child health block grant be folded into the state's community health services program. This would have meant an allocation among counties on a per capita basis—a sharp departure from the needs basis on which funds were distributed by the federal government.

Targeting has to do not only with the distribution of funds among places but also with their use on behalf of needy persons. Responsibility for the reduction in targeting is shared by both the federal and state governments. A reduction in targeting can occur either through a shift in budget priorities *among* programs or *within* programs. Both have happened.

As noted earlier, the biggest shift in priorities was from social programs to defense. Among domestic programs the changes made in entitlement programs aiding low-income people were significant. Evaluations of state response show they were less likely to use their own revenues to offset federal cuts in entitlement programs than in operating or capital grant programs, where the beneficiaries were not limited to poor people.[21] This has led numerous observers to conclude that the poor bore the brunt of the negative impacts of recent federal policy changes.

A report prepared for the U.S. Civil Rights Commission by the National Council of La Raza found a significant shift in the use of funds away from services benefiting the poor and minorities. The problem was found to be especially acute for education block grants. "Funds once used for special teaching help for inner city urban children are now being shifted to 'general support' purposes such as buying computers in wealthier districts."[22]

Administration actions reducing Community Development Block Grant program regulations also led to a "spreading" of funds away from low- and moderate-income neighborhoods. Shortly after taking office, the Reagan administration rescinded a number of regulations, including those requiring CDBG recipients to use a specified percentage of funds in low- and moderate-income neighborhoods. Particularly when budgets are tight, there is tremendous pressure to use federal grants to fund regular activities of local governments, including those in more affluent neighborhoods. Congress was sufficiently concerned about urban response to these pressures that it amended the legislation to require that at least 50 percent of funds be spent in low- and moderate-income neighborhoods. This is less money, however, than was previously required under the Carter administration.

An assessment of JTPA concluded that the program's rules would force states to focus resources on people who are relatively easy to place in jobs rather than working with the hard-core unemployed.[23] This tendency was summarized by one program director: "This legislation won't tolerate failure. That means it won't tolerate risk. . . . No government is going to take much risk on tough groups unless that government feels it has lots of support to do so. JTPA doesn't give you much support. You have to exploit its waivers, its exceptions to get at the hard core. . . ." A Private Industry Council chairman reiterated: "JTPA was not designed for the hard core unemployed."[24]

Flexibility and Red Tape

The legislation establishing the block grants is quite brief and dictates only a few aspects of program design. Federal agencies have been equally circumspect about promulgating rules and regulations. States *have* been given a fair amount of flexibility. Still, local governments and service providers contend that these changes have not made the task of administering programs any easier. Matthew Coffy, executive director of the National Association of Counties, testified: "We know the states did not pass on the flexibility they receive to local government, nor did they reduce regulations governing these programs. To the contrary, many of the block grant programs now require more paperwork than previously. . . . States did not streamline the procedures at all."[25] Local JTPA officials say state reporting requirements generally exceed federal reporting requirements under CETA. They complain that states were slow to transmit policies and procedures and that regulations are burdensome in their volume and scope. A California study picked up the same theme. "Flexibility received by the state became strictures imposed on counties. States can apparently pursue 'creeping categorization' as effectively as did the national government."[26]

The Overall Pattern of Federal Spending

A final consideration in this analysis of changes in the administration's nonurban policy is to look at shifting geographic patterns of federal spending. Any spending, regardless of purpose, is likely to have a positive impact on the local economy in which it occurs.

We know that urban-oriented programs have been cut differentially, so we would expect some diminution in the flow of funds toward city locations. But at this point we don't know the spatial implications of other shifts in the federal budget. One study has found that "the Reagan era has involved a dynamic reallocation of federal spending among the regions, and this reallocation has led to a sharp decline in spatial disparity in the allocations among the regions." It found that the advantage traditionally enjoyed by the West and the South had diminished as the Northeast and North Central states increased their allocation in per capita terms.[27] This report of a regional shift in spending patterns was promising since a relatively high percentage of distressed cities are located in the regions which had realized increasing shares of the federal spending pie.

However, the distressed cities tracked in this chapter did not share in the gain accruing to their regions. Earlier we reported that the flow of grant funds to distressed cities declined while increasing marginally in the nation as a whole. If we look at *total* federal spending, we find an increase between 1980 and 1986 of 15 percent in the amount spent in the thirteen cities identified as distressed. This corresponds to a 57 percent increase in spending nationwide and a 66 percent increase in the group of healthy cities. Once again, distressed cities appear to be disadvantaged by shifts in federal policy. Interestingly, if we focus exclusively on defense spending, the distressed cities appear disadvantaged but only by a small amount. Defense spending in distressed cities increased by 70 percent. Nationwide the increase was 81 percent. In the healthier cities the percentage increase was 75 percent. This increase in defense spending, however, is more than offset by the decrease in other kinds of spending. Federal spending in distressed cities increased by just 6 percent, while in healthy cities it increased by 60.4 percent.

Conclusion

The term "national urban policy" generally connotes a set of programs or policies designed to assist cities with declining economies or to increase opportunities for residents, especially poor residents, of those cities. As-

Table 13.5 Percentage Change in Federal Spending 1980–86

	Total Spending	All Other Federal Spending	Defense Spending
Nationwide	57.0	49.5	80.8
Distressed Cities	15.3	6.0	70.1
Healthy Cities	65.7	60.4	75.4

suming that is the definition of urban policy, the Reagan administration can be said not to have had one. Indeed, in pursuit of its other goals — reducing the role of government in domestic affairs while increasing defense spending — it did much to dismantle existing programs that were of special benefit to cities. Grant programs, especially those important to urban governments, bore a disproportionate share of budget cuts.

The administration eschewed "place-oriented" economic development programs and urban fiscal assistance. It sought to shift power and authority to state governments and minimize direct access by cities to the federal government. Federal policy was unresponsive not only to the needs of city governments, but also to poor urban residents. Means-tested entitlements were cut substantially in the early 1980s despite rhetoric concerning the importance of a "safety net." There were no attempts to develop programs to assist the residents of distressed areas to move in pursuit of economic activity. Enforcement of civil rights and fair housing laws slackened, further limiting opportunities for mobility. And despite the opportunities presented by a smaller youth population, there was no emphasis placed on human capital development programs.

The conclusion that Reagan administration policies were deleterious to distressed cities is further supported by an examination of federal funding flows. Relative to the nation as a whole and relative to a set of economically healthy cities, distressed cities found their share of federal spending decreased between 1980 and 1986.

Part
4

**Institutions and
Institutional Capacity**

14

HUD in the Nineties: Doubt-ability and Do-ability

Robert Wood and
Beverly M. Klimkowsky

The Heritage: Establishing the Department

A properly credentialed historian undertaking to establish the origins of the U.S. Department of Housing and Urban Development (HUD) will find a torturous and poorly marked trail. It is dotted by obscure references to unrecorded conversations; occasional papers of policy instigators with disparate motives; poorly drafted memoranda of imperfectly fashioned conceptualizations; purportedly learned treatises reflecting clashing theories of public organizations; divergent programmatic philosophies; intemperate congressional debates; excessively enthusiastic presidential rhetoric. At least eight years in the making, HUD came neither easily nor naturally upon the Washington scene. More than most cabinet departments, it was contrived, then compromised.

The initial impulse for HUD's creation was both outside the executive branch establishment and contrary to it. One source was academic: in the late 1950s, when the social sciences "discovered" cities as a legitimate field of inquiry, analysis led to policy, policy to organizational considerations. The call for a cabinet department appeared and reappeared in professional associations' panel discussions across the country — most prominently at the American Political Science Association annual meeting in 1959. Simultaneously, an increasingly vigorous lobby of big-city mayors and urban renewal directors through the U.S. Conference of Mayors demanded a place at the cabinet table, a symbolic (not organizational) recognition that urban issues belonged on the national agenda.

The two forces found common cause in the Democratic policy groups that Paul Butler established at Adlai Stevenson's behest, and that the Democratic congressional leadership boycotted. The alliance became explicit in the 1960 presidential campaign as first the Kennedy brain trust and then the Pre-Inauguration Task Force called for departmental status, in lieu, some cynics observed, of new program initiatives.

Washington organizational purists were unimpressed. That keeper of the administrative flame, the Bureau of the Budget, now the Office of Management and Budget, was largely satisfied with its previous handiwork: the Housing and Home Finance Agency. Its staff could conceive of an executive office coordinating arrangement, perhaps a White House adviser, but not a department. It argued with considerable logic that organizations directed toward place constituencies rather than people constituencies ran contrary to the conventional wisdom of public administration.

The unsuccessful struggle of Kennedy and the successful battle of Johnson to gain departmental status did not resolve the issue. Although Senator Abraham Ribicoff's government organization committee prevailed over Senator John Sparkman's Banking and Finance, the coordination school of organization thought persisted at Ribicoff's insistence in the legislation. So, too, did the assurance that housing interests and programs would not be subsumed in the new urban rubric. HUD appeared with a secretary overseeing from a somewhat strengthened position the same constituent units of HHFA—plus two new programs, rent supplements to be assigned to the Federal Housing Administration (FHA), and Model Cities with separate organizational status within the department. It also had a legal mandate to orchestrate urban programs then existing in other departments and agencies. Yet Ribicoff's office of coordination was never staffed, and at BOB's initiative an executive order "convener" authority was substituted.

What HUD did *not* get or lost in the first three years, despite the recommendations of two Task Force reports, were the emerging programs in closely associated fields which might have provided a coherent portfolio. The poverty and environmental programs that could counterbalance the bricks-and-mortar tradition of HHFA and strengthen the neighborhood and metropolitan components stayed outside HUD. The establishment of the Department of Transportation (DOT) in 1967 meant the loss of mass transportation. Finally, HUD did not manage to absorb existing housing guarantee programs in the Department of Agriculture and the Veterans' Administration (VA). More effective program control was achieved by the authority vested in assistant secretaries (which effectively eliminated the traditional independence of bureau chiefs), but it was at best an incomplete array of authorizations and appropriations that HUD's first administration assumed.

Moreover, the programs were bifurcated by housing and urban concerns, frequently competitive in nature and giving rise to intradepartmental policy competition. To address the perceived threat of FHA's rent supplements, for example, the public housing division countered with Turnkey. Threatened by Model Cities, urban renewal responded with the Neighborhood Development Program.

The scale of strategy differed as the tumultuous events of the late sixties proceeded. Model Cities projects, however modified from original estimates, remained small in number compared to renewal and public housing. Less than a third of the congressional districts participated, and, given time, a prototypal, spillover approach might have prevailed. Time was not provided. Nor, as the Vietnam War drained resources, were there sufficient appropriations. The riots of 1967 begat the Housing Act of 1968, and the incoming administration mandated full-scale production. So originally modest and prototypal dimensions became full-scale, massive assembly lines.

In its Great Society years, then, HUD scored legislative victories, achieved considerable internal integration of staffs and programs, but it never had a honeymoon, never a comprehensive mandate, never sufficient resources even if program objectives were feasible. Wrenched by successive tragic events — assassinations, riots, wars, elections — it did not have a shakedown cruise.[1]

The Heritage: Life After the Great Society

The two decades that followed HUD's establishment offered no breathing spell. The years continued turbulent, as administrations at least ideologically hostile to the Kennedy-Johnson aspirations for attention to the poor and concern for the inner city entered office.

Nixon's and Ford's stewardships were rhetorically antagonistic. Nixon declared "victory" over the urban crisis and turned to environmental concerns partly, at least, to anticipate Edmund Muskie's presidential challenge. Both administrations were sometimes operationally hostile to the continued execution of earlier laws such as fair housing. In reality, however, the project pipeline was substantial and the program increasingly popular in Congress, and so it became easier to change the names of HUD programs in the 1974 and subsequent housing acts to reflect new themes of urban growth than to shut the activities down. Appropriations continued to increase, and new approaches such as revenue sharing appeared, even as the department's programs dropped from public view.

The Carter administration returned an ideologically compatible urban philosophy to Washington, but, plagued by inflation and paranoia so far as national politics was concerned, it lacked both the resources and the skills to expand urban programs. Carter did return HUD's focus to distressed urban centers in a domestic version of Woodrow Wilson's Fourteen Points, and the Urban Development Action Grants the department initiated as a third generation renewal program were to compile an impressive record of accomplishments as they came on line in the eighties. But inflation and the energy crisis drove mortgage rates to unprecedented highs and plunged the housing industry into severe recession. Nonetheless, by the 1980s HUD was still more or less intact, a going concern with a sometimes cohesive network of housing interests, mayors, and neighborhood groups for support.[2]

It remained for the Reagan administration to savage the department both ideologically and programmatically. Ideologically, the administration's "New Federalism" left no room for a national role in urban affairs except for a small number of sharply restricted block grants and a vague concept of "enterprise zones." And these were to funnel through the states, with mayors increasingly cut out of the process. Programmatically, HUD program after HUD program was dismantled. Between 1980 and 1987 HUD's budget fell 57 percent, the largest cut of any federal department. The authorization for federally assisted housing dropped from $27 billion to $1.5 billion. Community Development Block Grants were cut from $3.7 to $2.6 billion and UDAGS from $675 million to $20 million.[3]

These reductions took place in an era when the proportion of American homeownership declined, the number of homeless increased, the quantity and quality of rental stock decreased, and the long-standing shortage of public housing intensified. For the 1990s, then, one can reasonably expect a resurgence of the urban crisis, driven by an expanding underclass, a continuing housing shortfall, and a persuasive, almost uncontrollable, urban drug culture. For our purposes, the issue is, of course: how willing, ready, and able as an organization is HUD to respond?

Contemporary Organizational Status

We can gauge HUD's or any department's organizational capabilities by reference to some seven reasonably conventional measures of quality public management. Thomas Cronin has summarized some of the most salient from a presidential perspective;[4] others derive from textbook orthodoxy, i.e., the National Academy of Public Administration.[5] They are, with no particular weighting: (1) the presence or absence of prestige and leadership acknowledged by the Washington community; (2) the extent of intradepartmental competitive and/or complementary behavior—read "feuding fiefdoms;" (3) the comparative power of clienteles; (4) the relative complexity of programs, i.e., implementation issues; (5) the clarity of legal jurisdic-

tion over program areas of departmental concern; (6) the degree of expertise required and, more importantly, acknowledged in the department's work;
(7) the relative frequency of presidential and congressional intervention in
program management, or the obverse, presidential and congressional support or respect.

By nearly all of these standards, HUD fares badly. The department's cu-
mulative ration shows a weak organization with competing and inconsistent
goals, as it faces an increasingly complex and explosive challenge. It is
important to appreciate these limiting characteristics if we are to choose
options for the department's evolution in the next ten years.

Low Prestige and Phlegmatic Leadership

Department secretaries come to the cabinet table with unequal amounts of
power and prestige—ranked in Cronin's terms in several ways, including
seniority, expenditures, personnel, and political power and impact.[6] As an
overall impression, a former public official who served in local government
prior to working at HUD noted:

> I used to think the Secretary of HUD was equivalent to a Cardinal, guar-
> anteeing an invitation to the Pope. Big deal! When you get over to Wash-
> ington, you realize that the Secretary of HUD is the low person on the
> totem pole. It's the least important Cabinet position and no one really
> cares what they think about anything. They don't participate in any of the
> inner Cabinet Committees.[7]

More specifically, by date of establishment HUD ranks tenth out of thirteen,
since departments overseeing traditional functions of government (e.g., di-
plomacy, treasury, defense, and the administration of justice) preceded the
establishment of departments representing more particularistic interests or
specific policy concerns. More intuitively, relying on senses of "political
clout," one Washington insider, ranking executive departments in terms of
"real" political power and impact, placed HUD tenth out of the eleven
departments at the time of its supposed zenith of power.[8] Factors which
enhance power status include access to the president, the presidential priority assigned to a given area, the public's perception of the broadness or
narrowness of the interests represented, and access to the media.

So the president's cabinet is customarily divided into an "inner" and
"outer" cabinet. Inner cabinet departments have secretaries who act as
counselors to the president rather than advocates for particularistic interests, and their departments are perceived as having broad-ranging multiple

interests rather than narrow interests. Accordingly, top leaders in business or the professions can be lured to government by these influential positions. Members of the inner cabinet often are close friends of the president prior to their appointment.

In sharp contrast, presidents often select outer cabinet secretaries who are strangers, aiming to achieve political, geographical, ethnic, or racial balance. In these circumstances they start out without the trust of the president and do not have much opportunity to gain it.

Since HUD is almost the outermost department, its secretaries have been typically selected to achieve political representation. Four of the seven department secretaries are women and/or minority group members, and few entered or left office with high levels of recognition or national political reputations. A senior White House official in the Reagan administration candidly admitted that the current secretary of HUD, Samuel R. Pierce, Jr., "is just not a factor here. Politically he has not been an asset with any group, including blacks or mayors. . . . Right now his biggest contribution is staying in place as a black face in the Administration. No one can say we don't have a black Cabinet officer."[9]

Political representativeness comes before professional expertise in the job description for the secretary of HUD. Prior to their tenure at HUD, only three of its eight secretaries had any expertise in housing or urban development. Furthermore, close departmental observers single out Secretaries Lynn and Pierce as lacking either the interest or will to enthusiastically pursue the mission of HUD. Indeed, the most severe critics categorize them as executive saboteurs, whose agenda was to quietly wind down the department's programs.[10]

Feuding Fiefdoms

When new departments have been formed recently, their missions have overlapped with preexisting agencies. Most commonly, the new department absorbed the old agencies. Although start-up problems associated with entirely new agency formation are many, there are advantages to de novo operations which reshuffling and remaining present organizations do not have. Newly formed agencies attract competent people into government who wish to make their mark where it will have a lasting result. Despite initial chaos, a high level of enthusiasm and sense of mission often enable a department to get on its feet and launch programs with energy and impact.

In contrast, combining preexisting agencies can accentuate bureaucratic rivalries and diminish the power of the parts. The little "new blood" which is brought in faces the resistance of old-timers who wish to assume positions of greater importance. Further, a new department so constructed absorbs agencies with cross-purposes. A previously autonomous agency suddenly finds itself vying with other agencies for the ear of a department secretary. Throughout the years HUD has come to exemplify this pattern of organizational behavior with great fidelity. Intradepartmental rivalries simmer from the outset. FHA with its semi-independent statutory authority competed with public housing over the administration of rent subsidies. Urban renewal and Model Cities rivaled each other from the first days of the department. A fresh sense of mission, a commitment to "new days," waxed only briefly in HUD and quickly waned.

Impotent Clienteles

Although departments with specific clienteles generally have less prestige than broadly based inner-cabinet ones, if one is clientele-oriented, it is best to have large, cohesive, well-organized, articulate, and well-financed parties-in-interest. HUD suffers because it has numerous clienteles, none of whom is especially strong, and the strongest are narrowly focused in their objectives. Building coalitions among them has always been an arduous undertaking, ever since the 1966 Model Cities legislation. It is no accident that the department's principal statutes are known as "omnibus" laws, for almost every interest group could claim a specific section or subsection as its own.

HUD's most potent clientele is the building industry—home builders, mortgage financiers, realtors, building goods manufacturers, and unions. These well-organized groups share a common goal: the production of new housing with as substantial a subsidy as possible and a minimum of regulation. The pressure they exert tilts HUD toward housing policy, away from urban development.

Other HUD clienteles include mayors, minority groups, and housing consumers. As a coherent pressure group, mayors suffer from both turnover and the conflicting perspectives of big-city and small-city officials. The Conference of Mayors and the National League of Cities reflect these differences, well summed up by Suzanne Farkas over a decade ago and persisting down to today: "Conference members tend to factionalize along the lines of North-South on civil rights issues, liberal-conservative on issues bearing on 'federal participation,' and small city–large city on issues such as mass transit, rent supplements, and civilian review boards."[11] The influence of other intergovernmental lobby groups in Washington waxes and wanes as they struggle to maintain a common front.

The political position of the poor is, today, even weak. The Great Society held out high hopes for citizen participation. A generation later an assortment of community-based organizations descended from the Community Action Program and Model Cities remains. They leave a legacy of varied track records, volatile leadership patterns, staffs of uncertain professional standing, shaky financial foundations, and a grab bag of missions and programs that almost defy consistent ordering. Their local influence steadily declined throughout the seventies and eighties in most cities, diminishing their already small capacity to influence national policymaking. As a former congressman noted: "The interest of the poor got short-changed as it usually does. And, there never was a very across-the-board view taken of the needs of the poor. It was always done in terms of housing programs. It should have been done in terms of family background, income—all of the problems of poverty."[12] In short, it is the sheer number of interest groups and their widely different objectives that make necessary a coalition to support HUD's programs and simultaneously guarantee that it is a weak one. Unable to fashion a genuinely common cause, but forced to support one another, the urban/housing coalition perforce adopts the "omnibus" strategy of something for everyone that has been its legislative keystone since its inception.

Program Feasibility

A generation of experience in carrying out programs that presume to alter human behavior suggests some basic conditions for successful program implementation. Clear, consistent policy directives are an obvious requirement. So are an adequate supply of scarce resources like trained staff, information, authority, and time. The staff must have an incentive to carry out policy directives as intended by decisionmakers; effective follow-up must be done.[13]

HUD's ability to meet these conditions, even minimally, remain dubious. Policy conflicts aside, three characteristics of its implementation efforts stand out.

First, it has undertaken a sizable number of genuinely new, untested programs of extraordinary complexity: Model Cities, new communities, metropolitan planning, housing assistance experiments such as vouchers, Urban Development Action Grants (UDAGS), private-public partnership, and neighborhood assistance. Many of them undertake to modify human behav-

ior or alter local political relationships. It is fair to say that in some instances program requirements exceed the stockpile of reliable professional
knowledge.

Second, even when programs appear substantively feasible, the stop-
start characteristics of changing administrations and economic circumstances
preclude a sustained and steady course of development. The initiatives that
the 1966 and 1968 Housing and Urban Development Acts authorized were
mothballed by 1972. Congress first criticized and then modified the emphasis on public housing in the 1974 Housing and Urban Developments
Acts. A contrary-minded philosophy after 1980 confronted the new approaches put forth by the Carter administration.

Finally, and most important, Congress never appropriated resources
sufficient to the tasks at hand. Shortfalls induced by the Vietnam War began
with the inception of the department. Impoundments and moratoriums characterized the early 1970s; recession and inflation were the hallmarks of the
latter years of the decade. Reagan's budget cutting characterizes the 1980s.

By 1987 HUD's appropriations had dropped from 7 percent of the total
federal budget in 1978 to less than 1 percent. Departmental personnel fell
from 17,000 in 1975 to a little over 12,000 in 1985—a decrease of 29
percent. What is less familiar are the statistics on housing, after the Reagan
administration savaged HUD program after HUD program—cutting the department budget by 50 percent from $36 billion to $18 billion between
1980 and 1987; reducing authorization for assisted housing from $27 bil-
lion to $7.5 billion; the units of rental housing from 129,000 to 19,000
annually; reducing public housing reservations 93 percent from 205,000
to 14,000 units; and shifting to a voucher program in which 62 percent of
the applicants reported no housing was available to them.[14]

Limited Jurisdiction

Congress did not attempt to place all major programs affecting urban development into one department when it established HUD. On the contrary, it
considered and explicitly excluded housing and community facilities programs then assigned to Agriculture, Interior, and Health, Education, and
Welfare. Despite the pretentious preambles of legislative intents in HUD
statutes that prescribe departmental oversight of urban development, other
agencies have major programs which affect urban growth and development.
The Department of Transportation spectacularly alters the face of cities and
suburbs in its national highway programs. The Department of Labor over-
sees job training programs which focus principally on unemployed urban

residents. The Department of Commerce carries out substantial urban economic development programs. The Department of the Treasury administers revenue-sharing plans and powerfully shapes fiscal policies, sometimes to the detriment of the home building industry. Even the newest Department of Education in its principal grant programs supports school activities in bilingual, special needs, and poor neighborhood programs that are concentrated in urban areas.

HUD's limited jurisdiction over programs affecting urban development has three major consequences. First, the prestige of the department suffers, since several departments spend more on urban problems than HUD does and have greater impact on local government decisions. Second, HUD continues to be thrust into the role of coordinator of urban programs—a gargantuan task considering that HUD's only power is persuasion. How gargantuan—and how infeasible—was made clear in HUD's first year when the so-called "convenor" order proved a failure in an effort to establish multipurpose neighborhood centers. Subsequent efforts in new communities and CDBGs have not recorded substantial improvement.

Third, limited jurisdiction restricts and divides the energy of HUD's clienteles. Urban interests must court and support several departments which have programs affecting them. Therefore, their attention and support of HUD is less than it would be if the department had a commanding jurisdiction over policies affecting them.

Doubtable Expertise

Expertise—the assertion of authoritative knowledge of problems and a monopoly on prescriptions for their solution—is a major source of bureaucratic power. The Corps of Engineers, the National Institutes of Health, the National Bureau of Standards are prime examples. Actuality and perception of scarce skills and technical sophistication combine to constitute a special source of administrative power, not possessed in the same measure by the legislative and judicial branches.

In general, expertise renders a department more powerful when it scores highly on both a real and perceived monopoly of a particular area of knowledge. The more arcane a body of knowledge, the more someone who has mastered it will be recognized as an expert. The more monopolistic the control over knowledge and information, the harder it will be for laypersons to dispute the experts. The more widely recognized an agency's expertise, the more prestige it will be accorded.

Expertise in housing and urban development is neither esoteric nor concentrated solely in HUD. At best, it rests in the discipline of economics, typically in public finance, and land economics. In these fields there is no pretense of governmental monopoly in theory or practice. Builders and developers know the physical and financial requirements of building housing as well as administrators overseeing housing projects. Officials in local governments are more knowledgeable about the problems of their particular areas. What expertise which exists in HUD is found mostly in the technical areas of mortgage finance, and its practitioners are far removed from the real policymaking center in Treasury.

Even in the mundane area of statistical data assembly, HUD often does not exhibit expertise in gathering facts. Its 1983 study on homelessness yielded an estimate of 250,000–350,000 homeless people on any given night.[15] This estimate seems a patchwork of other studies of the time which produced estimates of 1–3 million (Department of Health and Human Services), 2.5 million (National Housing Law Project), 2.5 million (National Housing Conference), and 2–3 million (Center for Creative Non-Violence).[16] The 1983 HUD study on homelessness seriously discredited the agency's expertise.

Excessive Vulnerability to Presidential and Congressional Oversight

Two other characteristics separating HUD from other departments are the extent to which its programs' success depends on a typically volatile disposition of the White House toward the department and the fragile character of congressional support. Perhaps Philip Brownstein's comment best summarizes HUD's current state: "The tragedy of HUD is its lack of governmental advocates at every level."[17]

Conventional wisdom has it that presidents usually find the federal bureaucracy, whether cabinet-level or not, to be intractable. They meet with frustration and failure when they try to place their imprint on it. Either the bureaucracy is inert when the president tries to fire it up with his agenda, or else its momentum for its own programs or a prior administration prevents him from superimposing his own agenda. HUD is a notable exception to these trends. Presidents frequently succeed in forcing HUD to adhere to their urban agendas.

The disjointedness of HUD's policy throughout the years reflects the fact that its history coincides with a period of rapid turnover in the presidency. Since HUD's founding, only President Reagan has served two full terms. In addition, the ideology of the incumbent president has often shifted.

Not surprisingly, HUD's period of greatest support came during the presidency of Lyndon Johnson. His 1965 *Message on the Cities* was the first of any American president. Thereafter, the White House maintained a sustained interest and intervened frequently and in detail in the shaping of urban legislation and assuring its enactment.

The administration which followed continued an interventionist posture —although in the Nixon years it was essentially negative in character. From the Moynihan Task Force through the evasive responses to the 1970 congressional requirement for a biennial urban report, Nixon sought to constrain the department's activities and to reduce its role. When it became apparent that George Romney was successfully implementing the Democratic program contained in the Housing and Urban Development Act of 1978, Nixon replaced him with James Lynn, whose job was reputed to be to shut down HUD. Nixon also impounded $12.9 billion, much of which was earmarked for HUD's public housing and Model Cities programs.

Although not as antiurban as Nixon, Gerald Ford did not place a high priority on HUD during his tenure as president. Jimmy Carter enlarged the role of HUD by pumping up the Section 8 housing program and stressing urban development through the UDAG program. He was the first president whose report to Congress in 1978 came close to responding to the original congressional mandate for an urban policy report as further specified in the 1977 amendments to the National Urban Policy and New Communities Development Act. Nevertheless, White House oversight continued to be vigorous, active to the point of evoking formal secretarial protests.[18]

One institutional constant encouraging presidential intervention is the key role that interest rates play in housing production. Since most of the national housing programs subsidize the financial costs, not construction or land values, they are especially sensitive to changes in interest rates. Inevitably, this sensitivity—and HUD preference for low rates—sets the department against contemporary monetary policy of the Treasury, the Council of Economic Advisers, and the Federal Reserve Board. When presidents wrestle with issues of inflation and recession, the second-order consequences on HUD are likely to be unpalatable. Still, the "broader view" of the other institutions usually prevails.

Moving down Pennsylvania Avenue to Congress, the level of support for HUD does not improve dramatically. HUD has never had a committee all its own, cautiously rejecting the opportunity in 1966 when it was embroiled in one legislative battle after another and preferred to deal with the "known devils" of the existing committees. The House Committee on Banking, Finance, and Urban Affairs and the Senate Committee on Banking, Housing, and Urban Affairs still oversee HUD's concerns. However, these committees have broader agendas and have not protected HUD as other committees shield "their" departments from outside attacks and are often lackluster or outright hostile in departmental matters.

The most dramatic example of Congress's antagonism toward HUD was its passage of a floor amendment to the Housing and Community Development Act of 1978 establishing a one-house legislative veto over all rulemaking of HUD. Garry Brown, a member of the House Housing and Community Development Subcommittee, proposed the amendment. On its introduction he stated: "The Executive Branch has used its regulation writing authority not to flesh out the law but to undermine the law. It has used its authority to thwart the will of Congress. . . . Of all the Executive Branch Departments, I believe HUD is one of the worst offenders."[19] The evaluation of the HUD legislative veto has been mixed. Some officials complain about increased work loads, confusion, uncertainty, and delays. However, others claim that the salutary effects have been a more organized approach to the regulatory process and a reining in of the "overaggressive pursuit of [HUD's] mandates."[20]

One outside researcher who evaluated the effects of HUD's legislative veto wrote:

> The HUD congressional review procedure appears, then, to allow members of Congress and congressional sub-committees to evaluate individual regulations on an ad hoc basis. This kind of review fails to take into account that HUD must reconcile legislative mandates that are often at odds with one another when it acts through its rulemaking process. Alteration and rejection of isolated rules may jeopardize the department's ability to coordinate its legislative mandates, thereby preventing the department from carrying out the intent of the laws for which it is responsible.[21]

In sum, the general absence of governmental advocates leaves HUD comparatively vulnerable among executive branch departments. Presidents have been able to impose their special agendas on it, while Congress has rarely been disposed to rally decisively to its defense, as the successive deep Reagan budget cuts have made clear.

Inconsistent and Competing Goals

Over and beyond the organizational deficiencies of HUD, a primary source of departmental frailty is the persistence of conflicting and inconsistent program goals. Given the fact that most public policies are the product of reconciling conflicting goals, an inescapable management obligation is to transform ambiguous and contrary legislative mandates into workable, reasonably straightforward programs arranged in some order of priorities. HUD has not succeeded in this "transformer" task, for it has temporized in making clear with any specificity who is to be served and where. It has been inconsistently clumsy in juggling its priorities between people and places and among people, i.e., the poor and the not-poor. Where HUD's programs are located is an extension of who is to be served. Mortgage assistance, housing insurance, and water and sewer grants principally serve suburbia. Public housing, directly subsidized private housing grant programs aimed at downtown and neighborhood renewal, and Section 8 housing programs are geared to fulfill city needs. UDAGs and Community Development Block Grants (CDBGs) most immediately affect private development interests, in league with urban politicians. As these benefits can filter down to lower-income constituencies, the clash between neighborhood and downtown interests is often intense.

In an effort to serve all, in the "omnibus" strategy which has been its legislative trademark, HUD serves none well. In Anthony Downs's words, a kind of "iron law of political dispersion"[22] prevails, and many programs receive money in such small allocations as to insure that national program goals cannot be met. Frequently, in one area after another, HUD's efforts are tantamount to trying to put out a forest fire with a garden hose. While the effort may be valiant, the impact too often inconsequentially affects the course of urban development.

Accordingly, Anthony Downs argues that HUD is "an ineffective symbolic gesture of concern."[23] He contends that it was never meant to succeed —instead, it was intended to show concern, alleviate some problems, but not to change the tide of urban problems or alter the direction of underlying economic and social forces. So, in its apparently ineffective pursuit of incompatible goals, HUD tilts toward the middle class with its urban and suburban development programs (urban renewal, UDAGs, CDBGs, new communities, sewer and water grants), housing insurance, and secondary mortgages. It has targeted the poor in Model Cities, some CDBG plans, low-income and moderate-income assisted housing, as in Sections 235 and 236, and public housing, most recently in Section 8 subsidies. These differences so permeate the daily operations of the department and set its staff at such cross-purposes that as one HUD official observed, the different units of HUD literally do not speak to one another.

The Lost Ark of National Urban Policy

To the confusion of reconciling short-run goals of diverse constituencies must be added the intellectual—and historical—quest for a grand framework. If one had been consistently fashioned, conceivably it might have imposed some order on constituency aspirations. But from the beginning, and repeatedly thereafter, HUD's formulation of its goals took on the appearance of a seed catalog: expensive items reflecting diverse tastes and assorted priorities. Underneath the expansive 1949 commitment of "a decent home in a decent environment," below the 1966 congressional declaration "to provide for full and appropriate consideration of the needs and interests of the nation's communities," down under the present ideological position that the marketplace—with some assistance by state and local government—can build the shining "entrepreneurial city," the omnibus tradition of a laundry list of programs prevails.

Even worse perhaps has been the confusion of HUD's goals and objectives with those of civil rights. The department and the civil rights movement are products of the same decade, found legislative sanction in the same three years of Great Society programs, and endured the 1967 riots together. It is not surprising that the two phenomena—the call for minority rights and the drive to renew our cities—should be mistaken to rise from one and the same need. Urban needs and black needs were often taken to be interchangeable. Helping cities was interpreted as helping minorities.

Yet this confusion has twisted, distorted, and thwarted urban programs since their inception. Analytically treating urban and minority problems as one—as "people" problems not "place" problems—obscures the racism and injustice of nonurban areas and delimits the statement of the urban problem by ignoring issues of design, culture, variety of neighborhood, and potential for rebuilding. The failure to treat the consequences of high densities and compact space requiring multiple uses in rigorous and consistent analytical terms has meant that our urban programs come one by one, without reference to an overall concept, always susceptible to being thrown aside as another new "issue" becomes fashionable. So the urban crisis of the sixties was transformed into growth policy, then environmental policy, then back to urban policy, and finally to a denial that any policy about our cities was required at all.[24] The seed catalog expands and contracts, the list of unreconciled priorities continues, but they are never supported by a persuasive, comprehensive statement of what the real urban needs are, why they come about, and how they might be met. The city remains a stage, across which issues of race, income distribution, jobs, health, and education parade, but it never emerges as a thing in itself, except in the vernacular "sense of place" that nags at one's intuitive senses.

Options for the Future

Twenty-three years of operations is long enough not only to strike an organizational and policy reckoning but also as HUD comes of age to sketch some scenarios for needed changes in our housing policy. The most adversely affected groups are the 2 million to 3 million homeless who are without permanent shelter, the 10 million families in inadequate or overcrowded dwelling units, the 24 million families in units classified as having a "household problem," and the more than 1.6 million young families who could have afforded a house at 1980 rates but could not afford one at 1986 rates. America undoubtedly needs more housing in the 1990s — 1.7 million new households will be formed by our still growing population, and 1.7 million units will be required for frail and elderly households.[25]

Several options stand out as possibilities for HUD and will determine whether it plays a part in meeting the nation's urban needs or whether it sits on the sidelines. HUD could:

1. Maintain the status quo.
2. Resolve the public housing dilemma.
3. Concentrate support for a housing program for middle-class homeowners.
4. Develop prototypes to demonstrate new strategies for urban development for local officials.
5. Abolish the department.

While some of these options can be combined, at least the last stands alone.

Maintain the Status Quo

Continuing the status quo for HUD would mean two basic things: successful programs like UDAG and Block Grants would continue, but so would their inherent structural weaknesses and programmatic conflicts. Funding levels need not remain at current Reagan lows, since they have varied tremendously over time. Yet policy would continue to be subjected to presidential directives because the departmental structure would be neither strong nor cohesive enough to provide traditional bureaucratic resistance.

Whether maintaining the current posture for HUD is a desirable policy goal presents another question entirely. It is clear that HUD consistently falls short of achieving its stated objectives. The department has not been able to coordinate "the various Federal activities which have a major effect upon urban community, suburban, or metropolitan development,"[26] nor has it been able "to encourage the solution of problems of housing, urban development, and mass transportation." Recessions in the seventies and eighties hampered HUD's ability "to encourage the maximum contributions that may be made by vigorous private homebuilding and mortgage lending industries to housing, urban development and the national economy." The inherent conflicts among HUD's constituencies and the lack of consensus over its role have prevented HUD from providing "full and appropriate consideration, at the national level, of the needs and interests of the nation's communities and of the people who work and live in them." In short, by any measure customary in the evaluation literature, HUD has fallen far short of meeting its statutory objectives.

Would matters have been worse or better without HUD? Organizationally, in terms of serving as a coordinator of federal activities affecting cities, HUD's coequal status with other departments having major urban programs clearly prevents it from being recognized as a lead agency for urban policy. If HUD did not exist, federal urban activities probably would not be any less coordinated than they are now. The logic of the Bureau of the Budget of the sixties was probably correct—real coordination can occur in the Executive Office, but it would need strong presidential backing or some other superordinate position. The convenor order experience is ample demonstration of this organizational axiom.

Again, by output measures, cities are not in an appreciably better position than they were in when HUD was founded. Central cities have higher concentrations of impoverished and often unemployed minorities as the tendency of out-migration continues. Infrastructures deteriorate faster than they are being replaced and repaired. Urban poverty continues, more affected by economic and education policies than by urban and housing ones.

Whether or not housing policy would have been better without HUD is a tantalizing question. Most of HUD's identifiable success falls in the area of homebuilding in urban and suburban areas. However, a sharp difference exists between private and public construction success rates. A congressional report noted:

> in 1968 the Congress attempted to recognize total social needs by calling for the construction or rehabilitation of 26 million housing units over 10 years, including 6 million specifically for low- and moderate-income families. . . . The private sector performed very well, with 18.8 million

units being produced or rehabilitated from 1969 through 1978. Thus, 94 percent of the unassisted sector target was achieved. Subsidized production for lower income families, however, fell well short of the target: 2.7 million units were produced or 45 percent of the goal.[27]

Overall success in housing construction goals is not surprising for two reasons. First, the housing components of HUD predate the establishment of the department and were strong units which had succeeded in achieving their goals. Second, the constituencies supporting homebuilding, financing, and insurance are politically powerful and have concrete, cohesive goals. The constituencies have a financial stake in the continuation or expansion of HUD's housing programs. Since these programs operated well before HUD, it can be assumed that they would have been able to continue that success if HUD had not been formed.

At rock bottom, however, HUD's failure to achieve its stated objectives does not mean that the status quo might not continue. As Herbert Kaufman showed a decade ago, bureaucracies tend to be immortal, even if they fail to achieve their stated purposes or if their purposes have been fully accomplished.[28] Maintaining the status quo is simply equivalent to not rocking the boat. The cabinet position and its symbolism remain, incremental changes in policy will probably occur, but seismic shifts are not likely.

Resolve the Public Housing Dilemma

Most Americans still regard decent housing as a right. Historically, middle-class America strives for homeownership and receives support from the government in the form of mortgage tax deductions, mortgages, and insurance. Most of us do not question the desirability of policies which benefit us greatly. We are not concerned by the fact that the Treasury loses $4.50 in tax receipts for upper- and middle-income housing tax deductions for every $1 spent on HUD programs to house the poor.[29] When policy turns to providing decent housing to those who cannot afford to pay market rates, however, there is trouble in River City. The perennial questions rise: how much should be spent on public housing and what form should the assistance take? When asked about the disappointments in HUD, a former congressman named the failure to develop a low-income housing program. He stated, "We never could figure out how to do it."[30]

Part of the problem stems from the stigma of public housing in this nation. Too many Americans perceive public housing to be "parasite palaces," which house welfare mothers, drug pushers, and addicts. The United

States never established a firm tradition of public housing for the working class which is integrated into a community. Public housing in this nation today by and large serves the most impoverished households—families on welfare, the elderly, and female-headed households. The projects are most often located in cities because other areas resist their construction more effectively.

HUD continues to vacillate as to whether or not public housing should be in the form of assistance payments (vouchers), or new housing construction and rehabilitation, or both. HUD currently combines both forms in its Section 8 programs, although new construction has been almost completely halted. The Rand and ABT reports, while favoring direct payment assistance, remain largely inconclusive, except for casting doubts on the elasticity of housing demand.[31] That conclusion, in effect, undermines HUD's basic justification for existence.

The rationale for providing each form of assistance varies. Vouchers permit lower-income persons to choose their housing and to be dispersed among the middle class. The absence of the stigma of living in "public housing" and a better environment contribute to the opportunity to improve one's lot in life.

The primary disadvantages of the current allowance approach are its inability to deal with the shortage of rental property and the rent collusion which occurs between tenant and landlord. Most frequently, persons eligible for Section 8 allowances are locked out when the availability of rental units falls short of demand. Since the current Section 8 program permits increases in operating costs to be passed through to the government, neither landlord not tenant has any incentive to keep rents low; the tenant knows that his rent will remain fixed at 25 percent of his income. During the 1970s expenditures for the Section 8 program expanded rapidly because of this collusion and the rapid rise in energy costs. However reformed and expanded, a shift to transfer payments suggests consolidation with other benefit programs, not their continuation under HUD's auspices. Certainly, the department is not a vital vehicle.

New housing construction alleviates the problem of an inadequate housing supply—and sustains HUD's organizational position. Yet new construction occurs only when favorable economic conditions prevail—and new construction for low- and moderate-income housing is possible only when the federal government provides strong incentives. As *The Report of the President's Commission on Housing* notes: "The 1968 legislation that followed the Kaiser Report created conditions of government subsidy and tax incentive that made it virtually impossible for anyone not to make money by promoting or building homes."[32] Ralph Taylor confirmed that the "failure [to make money] here is due to total incompetence."[33] The costliness of new housing construction combined with the added costs of inefficiency make public housing construction very expensive. That expense is part of its political liability.

Although it is hard to imagine any administration committing the funds necessary to make a sizable dent in the public housing shortfall, housing for the homeless probably will be addressed by the next administration. Surveys indicate a public willingness to pay higher taxes for shelter for the homeless. But whether or not additional temporary shelters are built merely to get people off the street or substantial quality public housing will be authorized remains an open question. Whatever the response, new housing construction will still be subjected to resistance stemming from state and local politics. There is little reason to be optimistic that funds would not be diverted from the area of greatest economic need (i.e., public housing), to the area of greatest political need (i.e., moderate-income housing). In addition, given the lack of guarantees that block grants will be carried through over time, state and local governments are still likely to be reluctant partners in the enterprise.

Provide "Affordable" Housing

If HUD were to concentrate on problems that were more tractable, its programs would be more successful and it would enjoy more political support. The fashionable, doable problem today appears to be "affordable housing." Although concentrating on middle-class needs can be seen as forgetting the poor, meeting middle-class needs of first-time homebuyers and moderate-income professional workers, often in local government, is likely to be politically attractive.

The problems of "starter" homeownership are well documented. The rise in mortgage rates during the past fifteen years, the escalation in the median value of a home, the difficulty in saving for a down payment, and the lack of growth in housing supply relative to the number of new households being formed are the principal obstacles. During the past decade homeownership declined from 65.4 percent of households in 1981 to 63.8 percent in 1987. Among young households, the declines have been higher, from 41.7 percent to 35.5 percent for 25–29 year olds and from 59.3 percent to 53.3 percent for 30–34 year olds.[34]

The shaky economy and demographic changes over the past decade are the principal factors boosting demand. Inflation has driven up the price of moderate homes, without providing a concomitant increase in wages and salaries. The rise in mortgage rates exacerbates the rise in housing value since one is paying a higher price for both house and credit. The difficulties that the savings and loan associations have been experiencing have led to stricter credit requirements (often in the form of higher down payments) and higher interest rates.

In addition, the demographics of the baby boomers entering their initial housebuying years and many older couples seeking smaller houses compound the problem. Because of the economy, new home construction slowed considerably and nearly halted at several junctures in the last decade, reducing the supply of new housing. Although the current economic recovery has brought interest rates down from historic highs, the rates still are relatively high and the housing supply needs to grow dramatically.

HUD could do several things to facilitate homebuying. First, it could serve as a source of information about creative home financing. If the conventional thirty-year fixed rate mortgage has become a dinosaur, HUD can help homebuyers realize that alternatives do exist.

Second, HUD could attack the rise in the price of homes by emphasizing measures that bring down the price of housing: prefabricated units, trailers, condominiums, rehabilitations, smaller units, and attached homes—even at risk of opposition from traditional supporters.

Third, HUD could support means which would help first-time homebuyers save for the all-important down payment. One device already extensively discussed is an Individual Housing Account which would be similar to the Individual Retirement Account. Essentially, new homebuyers would be able to set aside a certain amount of money each year in a tax-free account until they had enough for a down payment. Although such an account would not solve the problem of high mortgage rates or high housing costs, it would reduce the total taxes paid, as well as not taxing the interest the money earned while it was being saved for the purchase of a home.

HUD could also try to help local governments plan areas within their jurisdiction set aside as moderately priced housing for county employees. An expensive way to do this would be to have counties buy properties which would be rented back to employees at below-market rates. Another option would be to have subsidies to help buy a property. A possible source of funding for these proposals would be a tax on new construction. Impact fees, which are used to fund new roads, sewers, and schools, could be expanded to include housing for county employees.

Develop Urban Prototypes

Many cities throughout the country have developed creative means to alleviate their own problems; most have also sponsored programs which have been abysmal failures. Unfortunately, the wealth of experience about which programs and approaches work well and at what cost is widely dispersed; local public officials who need this information the most cannot easily attain it.

Although some of the best mayors in the country scout out ideas from other cities, most mayors do not. Returning to an early venture of urban observatories, HUD could serve a vital role by collecting and disseminating information about urban projects in a far more systematic and effective way than it now does. Since the potential range of projects is great, HUD could provide either information referral, prototypes, or both. For example, if a city were interested in developing a harbor area, it could be referred to local officials in Baltimore and Norfolk. Or, if it were interested in gun control or antismoking legislation, it could be referred to cities which have passed such ordinances. A more recent problem facing cities is the provision of housing and health care for AIDS patients, many of whom exhaust private resources.

Helping cities to learn from each other would be a relatively inexpensive program for HUD and would enhance its image among local officials if it were done well. A former local government official notes: "When working at the local level, we viewed HUD as the enemy. It was never trying to help out, second-guessing decisions made, and never showing what was working elsewhere."[35] Development of urban prototypes and an information referral system would do a lot to erase HUD's negative image. Casting HUD as a teacher and source of information would also balance its role of dispersing funds, or "dispensing the bribe" as Anthony Downs notes less gallantly.[36]

Abolish HUD

Although the mind of man runneth back not to such a circumstance, policymakers can abolish an agency or a department which is not accomplishing its goals or which is no longer necessary. Terminating unneeded or dysfunctional units saves taxpayers money and simplifies the web of bureaucracy.

The case for terminating HUD is strong. It began as an eclectic collection of agencies and continues to operate as such. It has not been able to develop a consensus on its priorities or has it been a very effective voice for cities at the cabinet table. Since the era of Richard Daley, from Johnson at least until Carter, mayors of large cities have the president's ear more often and more effectively than does the secretary of HUD. Moreover, HUD has failed in its "convenor" role. It has little influence over the urban programs of other departments and has not been able to coordinate them.

Nor has HUD succeeded in clarifying what urban policy is and which goals of urban development are most desirable since its establishment. Indeed, it has not even made clear that its programs involve long lead times and continued capital expenditures—thus preparing public and public official alike for the hard truth that there are no quick political payoffs in urban affairs.

If HUD were abolished, its programs could be dispersed among smaller organizational entities. These agencies could devote their full attention to missions which, lacking a grand design, are carried out separately and with focus.

The symbolic implications of the abolition of HUD probably would be stronger than the functional implications. Critics of the move would cry that the voice of cities has been removed from the cabinet table. The fact is that the voice has not been heard for at least eight years, and when it has been heard the counsel has often been disparate and divisive.

The option of abolition has at heart the virtue of honesty. The hypocrisy of the other options is that they require substantial appropriations. HUD has been chronically underfunded since its inception. In these deficit-ridden days, when the financial outlook is even bleaker, simply "shucking" the cities might be the most forthright strategy.

The Critical Event: The 1988 Election

The first few months of the Bush administration are too short a time to permit a prediction about HUD's future. Nonetheless, there are at least three important clues about the course of coming events: Jack Kemp's appointment as secretary, the savings and loan crisis, and the continually unfolding scandals of HUD in the Reagan years. These suggest a new administration which in fact may be more responsive to housing issues in particular and urban problems in general than the last one.

Bush's choice of Kemp signals at the minimum a sharp departure from the largely invisible line of secretaries which Republican administrations have chosen in the past and that Samuel Pierce exemplified so well in the 1980's. Kemp, a national figure even before the 1988 Presidential primaries, retains a power base of conservative supporters, which no previous secretary since George Romney has possessed. Paradoxically, in his confirmation testimony, he advanced at least quasi-liberal views in the emphasis he placed on resolving the problem of the homeless and on his favorite policy strategy of enterprise zones. On the evidence to date, Kemp will be an activist secretary, constrained by the budget deficit, but certainly disposed to develop urban prototypes, information referral systems, and supportive efforts for not-for-private housing enterprises. Imaginative financial schemes and new patterns of state and local programs are likely to follow. In short, Kemp will not play the role of "a friendly undertaker," which Republican HUD secretaries have done in the past.

As for the savings and loan debacle, Bush's first package of new bonds, new fees, and new regulations, however they come to fare, is a refreshing change from the studied indifference of the Reagan administration. The crisis Bush inherited is an action-forcing event of major proportions. Now that an effective policy is in place, the entire foundation of housing finance in America may be radically altered.

As for the scandals now tumbling one after another in a seemingly unceasing stream, this outrageous betrayal of the public trust offends and outrages all who were present at HUD's creation and were the advocates of its first programs designed to help and house the urban poor. The sheer greed that rich and politically powerful developers and consultants, former cabinet officers, and former senators showed is unforgivable as they pursued for eight years a reverse Robin Hood strategy. Indeed, the revelations may make the option of abolishing the department a reality.

More hopefully, the revelations of mismanagement, nonfeasance, misfeasance, and malfeasance may set off a sea change of reorganization and reform. Finally, after a generation, a president and a congress may be prodded into giving HUD a clear mandate, a firm set of priorities, a consistent philosophy, and sufficient resources to provide this urban nation, at long last, with an urban consciousness and conscience to build cities in which we can take honest pride.

15 Who Gets the Jobs in the New Downtown?

Bernard J. Frieden

One of the longest and most tenacious campaigns of local government has been the effort to rebuild the downtown areas of American cities. It began in the early 1950s when the rise of suburbia led big-city mayors to join with business leaders to save what was left of downtown. Its first phase was one of desperation when the new coalitions threw their support behind highway construction that devastated city neighborhoods and urban renewal projects that evicted families and business firms by the thousands. The protests against highways and renewal brought this strategy to a halt in the late 1960s and forced the coalitions to find less disruptive ways to proceed. By the 1970s they were concentrating on filling the holes left over from earlier clearance and operating within new political and financial limits. And by the 1970s and 1980s their thirty-year campaign began to pay off with impressive new construction.

The long-awaited revitalization of downtown is now a reality in many large cities, but it has done less for city residents than its supporters had hoped. Critics, as a result, are questioning whether the long campaign that produced new downtowns in the 1980s is a triumph of public policy or a sellout of city interests. A review of the results so far suggests that it is neither a triumph nor a sellout. It is, however, a tribute to the ability of both city governments and their business allies to make the most of the limited options open to them and to come up with new strategies when old ones were no longer working. The downtowns that they built have not fully resolved the economic problems of central cities, but they have generated a wide variety of jobs that can improve the lives of city residents.

Changes in the Workplace

After thirty years of rebuilding, the downtowns of the 1980s are very different from what they were not long ago. Gone are the manufacturing districts of the 1950s, the working harborside warehouses, the freight terminals, some of the once-thriving department stores and specialty shops, and most working-class neighborhoods. Gone, too, are the rubble fields that littered downtown areas during the 1960s when the wrecking crews were finished but the builders were nowhere in sight. The new city centers feature clusters of office towers mixed with new hotels and civic buildings, freeways pumping heavy traffic in and out, modern housing complexes, one or more shopping malls, renovated office buildings and warehouses, many new restaurants, and at least one restored Victorian neighborhood.

These changes are visible enough to have an impact on the public. Despite the widespread image of big cities in crisis, most people recognize that they have at least a few advantages over small cities, suburbs, and rural areas. By 1978 half the people polled in a national survey considered large cities best for job opportunities, health care, colleges and universities, culture, public transportation, and restaurants and movies.[1]

Less visible but equally important to city residents are changes in the work people do. Far fewer people have production jobs, and many more are in service, professional, or government occupations. In metropolitan Cleveland, where two of every three workers used to have manufacturing jobs, the current figure is down to one of three. In industrial Pittsburgh, where the last of the blast furnaces closed in 1980, manufacturing jobs dropped from half the area's total to less than one-fifth, while downtown acquired the nation's third-largest concentration of *Fortune* 500 corporate headquarters. Core cities that used to rumble with industry turned into silent office canyons. In 1953 half the workers in Philadelphia had production jobs, while only one of ten were in information-processing and other high-skilled services; by 1980 half were in these services and only one of four in production. White-collar cities of the 1950s kept breeding more office jobs. Boston, with one-fifth of its jobs in information and high-skilled services as early as 1953, had more than half in these lines of work by 1980. Even the skyscraper citadel of New York still had four of every ten workers in manufacturing or construction in 1953, but less than one of four by 1980.[2]

But the prospering office economy was not enough by itself to reduce poverty and unemployment for city residents. Most large cities of the Northeast and Midwest lost manufacturing jobs faster than they gained white-collar work, so that they had fewer jobs overall. At the end of the 1970s the central cities of metropolitan areas, as a group, continued to have higher unemployment rates than the rest of the nation, and as of 1979 they were worse off relative to the suburbs than they had been in 1970. City families earned lower incomes, with the median down by 4 percent in constant dollars from 1969 to 1978, in contrast to a 5 percent increase for suburban families. Meanwhile, the number of people living in poverty remained unchanged in the central cities, while it went down in the rest of the country.[3]

Even in those cities where the office boom was strongest, resident unemployment and poverty grew worse after 1970. The ten cities that led the nation in downtown office development from 1950 through 1984 all had higher unemployment in 1982 than in 1970. Nine of these ten also had higher proportions of people with poverty-level incomes in 1979 than in 1969. From 1979 through 1985 the poverty population in the nation's central cities grew from 16 percent to 19 percent of the total. New York and Chicago, the top two office producers, are among the few individual cities for which we have 1985 information: they had as many as one person out of four living in poverty.[4]

Researchers who make comparisons among cities usually use a composite index to rate economic well-being. An index that takes into account unemployment, the proportion of people in poverty, and changes in real income between 1970 and 1980 reveals that Atlanta, Baltimore, New York, and Philadelphia—all among the heavy hitters in downtown development —slipped from better conditions in 1970 to join the ten worst-off cities in the country by 1980. If downtown revitalization was a renaissance, it was still no protector of city people.[5]

One reason why downtown growth made only a small dent in resident poverty and unemployment was that commuters filled many of the white-collar jobs. In 1980 suburbanites held more than half the professional, technical, and managerial jobs in Boston, Detroit, and San Francisco, and more than one-third in many other big cities. In the new downtown office buildings commuters held about 60 percent of the jobs in San Francisco and 70 percent in Boston. While Boston and San Francisco are not typical, they do illustrate why downtown expansion disappoints some city residents. A flourishing office district turned Boston into more of a commuter city during the 1970s, with the resident share of city-wide jobs dropping from 36 percent to 33 percent, then climbing back a notch to 34 percent by 1986. In San Francisco office growth created some 166,000 new jobs between 1965 and 1980. Yet during that same period the total number of employed San Francisco residents dropped by almost 18,000, leading Chester Hartman to conclude: "it is indisputable that office growth has not provided net employment benefits for the city's residents."[6]

There is no simple explanation for who works where in an urban area, but a few trends are worth noting. While downtown jobs were changing, so were city populations. They were changing in opposite directions. The jobs were increasingly for people skilled in speaking, writing, and managing, with the right appearance and manner for the executive suite; and for experts in law, finance, computers, and other fields needed to run businesses. Even as the work became more demanding, the best-educated and most skilled people continued to leave the cities, while less-educated minority groups and foreign immigrants expanded their numbers. As a result, the central city was more and more the home of people with limited educations and job skills, and particularly of minority groups struggling against many handicaps. Most had neither the education nor the work experience for high-skilled service jobs. The new offices also included jobs requiring less education and experience: jobs for people to run the copy machines, answer the phones, and operate the word processors. City people had better prospects for getting this work, but some companies did most of their white-collar recruiting in the suburbs.

Yet the rebuilding of downtown also brought other kinds of businesses with more jobs for city residents. Hotels, restaurants, and retail stores all had a greater share of entry-level jobs and generally hired a higher proportion of people from the city. Retail centers, in particular, created hundreds of jobs for residents with limited education and experience. In Boston city residents landed 40 percent of the jobs in newly built retail stores and half the jobs in new hotels. In Baltimore 40 percent of the permanent jobs at Harborplace went to minority workers.[7]

Blaming City Government

With new downtowns rising while low incomes and unemployment continued for city residents, it was easy to blame city hall for promoting the wrong kind of development. Academic researchers, slow to discover the extent of downtown development and grudging in their recognition of any merit in it, saw little social value in the growth of corporate headquarters and business services. They accused cities of selling out resident interests in order to do what was good for business.

Norman Krumholz of Cleveland State University, formerly the city's planning director, argued that the alleged successes in city development "have for the past thirty years, worked to enhance and expand the institutional, cultural, and downtown areas of many cities. Sometimes these projects

added new taxes to the dwindling coffers of their cities. But these projects
have done little or nothing for the poverty, joblessness, and declining neighborhoods of poor and working-class central-city residents."[8]

Or Desmond Smith, writing about the information-based economy of
New York, saw it leading mainly to "the rise of a super-rich mercantile
class at the expense of the disadvantaged. New York, after a hundred or so
years as the melting pot, has entered the age of the Uncommon Man. The
common man has virtually no future in the brave new city. White-collar,
high-technology jobs are no help to the unskilled poor."[9]

The critics were right when they accused city officials of deliberately
fostering the growth of white-collar and corporate jobs. But once city governments focused their attention on downtown development, promoting office
growth was the most practical thing for them to do. Chasing after manufacturing while production jobs were in nationwide decline would have been a
prescription for failure. Cleveland's attempt to follow this strategy is instructive. In the late 1970s the city spent more than $1.2 million to assist
an inner-city industrial park that promised jobs for hundreds of people living in nearby public housing projects. Two new firms—a mattress factory
and a bakery—and two existing plants that expanded with city help eventually hired a grand total of eight people from the neighborhood, three of
them for short-term openings.[10]

Manufacturing Myths

Suppose a production-center strategy could somehow succeed: how many
more jobs would it create for the poor? A close look at workers and jobs in
New York City reveals that manufacturing has no sure-fire solution to the
problems of unskilled city dwellers. When it comes to hiring, manufacturers and office managers are not as different as the critics assume. True to
the stereotype, 37 percent of the workers in New York's manufacturing
firms had less than a high school education in 1980, compared with 14
percent of workers in finance, insurance, real estate, and business and professional services. But contrary to the stereotype, manufacturers also hire a
large number of suburban workers: commuters held 23 percent of all manufacturing jobs, as against 20 percent of office jobs, and at every education
level their share of jobs was higher in manufacturing than in office and
service firms.

Analyzing the distribution of jobs by education level, moreover, explains
how New York's increasing concentration of office work has actually been
able to *expand* opportunities for people who never finished high school.

Between 1970 and 1980 New York lost about 100,000 manufacturing jobs but added about 300,000 office and service jobs. At 1980 educational levels for each group, the manufacturing decline eliminated some 37,000 jobs for high school dropouts, while office growth produced 42,000 jobs for dropouts. These same changes did much more for college graduates, producing a net increase of about 100,000 jobs for them, but for dropouts at least the supply of jobs more than held steady. At the same time, since office firms are more likely than manufacturers to hire city residents, the change from production to office work gave residents at all education levels an edge over commuters.

Nothing short of massive growth in manufacturing would resolve the job and income problems of high school dropouts, and massive manufacturing growth in the heart of the city is simply unrealistic. Calculations for New York, where 16 percent of 1980 jobs were in manufacturing, show that even a doubling of this share (with proportional cuts in all other lines of work) would raise the proportion of jobs for dropouts only from 22 percent to 25 percent.

Further, the allegedly one-sided economy of New York, where two out of every three jobs are concentrated in the office stronghold of Manhattan, employed as high a proportion of dropouts in 1980 as the national economy. So the argument that the corporate-center job mix is responsible for city unemployment and poverty rests on shaky ground. Since this prototypical city of advanced services hires as many dropouts, proportionally, as the country at large, city development policies can hardly be faulted for shortchanging the unskilled. New York's high poverty and unemployment rates in 1980 did not result from an exceptionally small share of jobs for dropouts but from an exceptionally large proportion of dropouts in the population—40 percent, compared with 33 percent nationally. Other big cities troubled by economic distress in spite of their downtown revival also lagged behind national education levels, with the proportion of dropouts in Baltimore, Cleveland, Philadelphia, and St. Louis even higher than in New York.[11]

Critics of downtown development fail to recognize how many jobs are still open to people with little education. In reality, office establishments hire a combination of unskilled, semi-skilled, and highly skilled employees. Fully half the jobs in Manhattan financial firms, for example, go to some 250,000 secretaries, stenographers, and clerks. In an analysis of labor requirements in nine of the largest cities sociologist John Kasarda classified industries as "entry-level" when their mean employee education level was less than twelve years, and "knowledge-intensive" when their mean education level was more than fourteen years. Since every one of these cities has had major downtown office development in recent years, it is not surprising that jobs in entry-level industries declined in seven of the nine between 1970 and 1980. What is surprising is that even after this decline the nine cities in 1980 still had a total of three times as many jobs in entry-level industries as in knowledge-intensive ones.[12]

Recent experience in Pittsburgh also raises doubts about the general handwringing over alleged problems of the service economy. Between 1977 and 1982 the Pittsburgh area had heavy losses in manufacturing that wiped out close to 15 percent of the jobs in this field. While manufacturing was in decline, however, professional and personal services were growing almost enough to make up for the losses. On balance, the total number of employed workers dropped by a little less than 4 percent. The job decline was concentrated in a field with high earnings—durable manufacturing—and the growth was concentrated in a field where average 1977 earnings were little more than half as high—professional services. If relative wage levels had remained the same after 1977, the people of Pittsburgh would have been in for heavy income losses.

What happened instead is that as the service sector grew, its wage levels and working hours both increased substantially. As a result, the average Pittsburgh area worker earned 6 percent more in real dollars in 1982 than in 1977. At worst, the transformation of the Pittsburgh economy may have slowed the rate of increase in earnings, but the total payroll increased. There were unquestionably income losses for laid-off manufacturing workers; but at the same time enough people were leaving production jobs voluntarily to create nearly three times as many vacancies as there were layoffs. Economist Louis Jacobson, who conducted the study, concluded that it is possible for communities to maintain high pay levels even as they shift from manufacturing to services. In addition, even at a time of exceptional decline, normal turnover made it possible for displaced manufacturing workers to find jobs similar to the ones they lost. The record in Pittsburgh as in New York shows the service economy to be troublesome enough to make its critics believable but not so troublesome as to make them right.[13]

In New York and Boston typical office jobs pay about as much as manufacturing work. Comparisons have to be inexact because wage and salary data usually ignore fringe benefits and fail to report the number of weeks people actually work in a year. Still, evidence at hand for New York and Boston shows a rough parity in wages between service and manufacturing jobs at comparable skill levels. Administrative support staff in New York, consisting mainly of clerical workers, earned an average of $10,700 in

1980, while semiskilled factory and transportation operatives, fabricators, and laborers earned $10,200. In Boston in 1985–86, general office clerks earned as much as assemblers and fabricators, and typists in service firms earned as much as stock clerks in industry. In moderate-skill occupations, word-processing typists made as much as precision textile, apparel, and furniture workers, legal secretaries did as well as precision printing workers, and sales agents for service firms had higher earnings than sheet-metal workers or drafters.[14]

In the country at large, wage differences favored manufacturing over service jobs, but not for all occupations and not by wide margins. The bedrock blue-collar occupations of operatives, assemblers, and inspectors, for example, had median weekly earnings of $287 in 1985 in comparison with $286 for administrative support and clerical workers. Yet as many as 30 percent of the administrative support and clerical workers earned less than $7,400 a year (in 1986 dollars) compared with 26 percent of operatives and 23 percent of transport workers and material movers. And at the upper end, only 5 percent of administrative support workers earned more than $29,600 compared with 10 percent of operatives and 15 percent of transport workers and material movers. The large blue-collar occupation of laborers, however, lagged far behind administrative support workers, with 51 percent earning less than $7,400 a year and only 3 percent more than $29,600.[15]

The advantages of blue-collar work are probably greater than wage differences indicate, since fringe benefits tend to be more generous and employees tend to work more hours per year in manufacturing than in service firms. If cities had been able to capture a greater share of manufacturing, they would be better off in several respects. Diversification would make them less vulnerable to future downturns in finance and other cyclical fields; a wider variety of jobs would help those residents who have a hard time fitting into offices; and even marginally higher earnings in manufacturing would improve opportunities for low-income workers. Yet the differences between blue-collar and white-collar work are not great enough to explain the persistence and recent increase of urban poverty. Those critics who lay heavy blame on the job mix created by corporate-center development have based their case more on stereotypes than on data.

Because offices hire a wide variety of employees with different levels of education and experience, low-income groups and average workers both benefited from the main downtown growth industries. One of the highest-growth fields, finance and business services, added some 154,000 jobs to New York City between 1977 and 1984: only one-third of these new jobs were in high-status professional, technical, and managerial categories, while half were clerical and one-sixth were blue collar and service. Because of this diverse mix of occupations, most groups in the city had a stake in expansion of the downtown office economy. When New York's economic recovery got under way in the late 1970s, blacks and other racial minorities increased their job totals even faster than the rest of the city. From 1977 through 1982 their employment was up by 20 percent, with nearly six of every ten new jobs in white-collar fields. Hispanic workers increased their employment by 15 percent during these years, with virtually all the gains in white-collar jobs.[16]

Blacks are about as well represented as other New Yorkers in the leading growth sectors of business and professional services, finance, insurance, and real estate: 25 percent of all employed blacks and 26 percent of all employed New Yorkers worked in these fields in 1980. Hispanics are nearly as well represented, with 20 percent in the same lines of work. In Chicago, Cleveland, Detroit, Philadelphia, and Washington, the proportion of blacks working in finance, insurance, and real estate in 1985 was within two percentage points of the proportion of whites. None of this is to say that blacks and Hispanics do as well as whites in getting the top office jobs; but it does place them squarely among the people who work in the heart of the new downtown economy. Their incomes depend on the prosperity of corporate offices: in New York nearly three times as many blacks work in the corporate headquarters/corporate service complex as in manufacturing.[17]

Where Development Falls Short

Why, then, have strong downtown economies not done more to eliminate poverty and joblessness among city residents? There are at least three explanations. One is that low-income people fail to learn about office job openings for which they are qualified or could be qualified with minimal training. If they have no friends or relatives working downtown, they miss the informal contacts that most people use to find work; and company recruiters have a habit of avoiding inner-city neighborhoods. Acting on this theory, a number of cities have tried to change the job recruitment and training practices of downtown firms along lines described later in this article.

Another explanation is that many city people lack the education to function well in either a factory or an office. The exceptionally high proportion of high school dropouts among city residents lends support to this explanation. So, too, does the experience of many companies with city recruits who cannot handle basic reading and arithmetic. A New York bank, for example, tried to recruit tellers without requiring a high school diploma but found that barely half the applicants were able to pass an examination geared to the eighth-grade level. Similarly, the New York Telephone Company discovered in 1987 that only 16 percent of city applicants could pass its entry-level examinations for jobs ranging from telephone operator to service representative.[18]

Still another explanation is that many of the poor in central cities are not in the job market at all. In New York almost four out of five women who headed poverty families in 1980, and nearly half of the men, were neither working nor looking for work. Of these people who were not in the labor force, three-fourths of the women and 60 percent of the men had either never worked or had last worked more than five years ago. If the downtown economy expanded enough to create a severe labor shortage, rising wages for ordinary jobs might pull some people off the streets or off welfare. Driving up wages through extra-full employment, however, is probably beyond the power of even the most ambitious mayors, and city officials usually look to the states and the federal government to help the long-term unemployed.[19]

Negotiating for Downtown Jobs

Some city governments, having invested so heavily in the new downtowns, tried to do more for their residents than wish them luck at landing a job. In order to get projects built city officials learned to negotiate complicated deals with developers. Managing downtown development through face-to-face negotiation opened a way for the city to bargain over resident jobs and business opportunities in the new projects. City negotiators had learned through experience that developers would cut deals many different ways in order to make projects work. There was no right or wrong way to do a project: almost any way that promised a reasonable return could be acceptable, and developers were even willing to share that return with the city as part of a deal.

The negotiating agenda proved to be open to new items. Many cities insisted on provisions for hiring minority contractors for construction work on downtown projects, and a few bargained over permanent jobs and business options for city residents. Mayor Coleman Young of Detroit stood out in this respect. Presiding over a mostly black city plagued by problems of deindustrialization, Young followed a typical strategy of cutting city services while promoting the growth of the private economy—but he did it with a difference. He and his business allies worked openly to develop a black professional and managerial class and to encourage black entrepreneurs.

Young increased the proportion of city jobs going to blacks, particularly in administrative and professional slots. The Detroit purchasing department invited black entrepreneurs to review city needs for products and services. An official preference system gave bidding advantages to small businesses owned by "disadvantaged persons" and to local firms over outside ones. And all companies that bid on city contracts, applied for tax abatements, or took part in city economic development projects had to meet strict affirmative action hiring standards.[20]

Oakland is another industrial city that gave local residents a direct stake in downtown development. With several new office buildings and a twenty-one-story Hyatt Regency Hotel, the city acquired an "urban renaissance" image. Mayor Lionel Wilson used public-private negotiations to manage the process, including putting together a consortium of thirty local corporations to acquire majority ownership of the new hotel. The city council set a series of contracting and hiring targets for all publicly assisted projects, including 26 percent of all construction expenditures to go to minority firms and 50 percent of the construction work force to be minorities. The city also arranged for neighborhood-based development corporations to acquire equity shares in publicly assisted projects, including the hotel and a downtown office building. Kansas City, Missouri, also required set-asides for minority contractors and equity shares for minority-owned corporations in several development projects.[21]

These strategies are reminiscent of the way political machines eighty years ago used the city payroll and contracts to get jobs for immigrants. Patronage possibilities for city work are more restricted now, with civil service laws and competitive bidding requirements on the books, although there is some latitude to favor minority and low-income residents. In an era of public-private deal-making, however, city governments have greater opportunities than ever to influence private business decisions on jobs and contracts.

Although resident hiring is often lost in the shuffle while negotiators focus on financing and design, pressure from city officials or residents themselves can give it high priority. In Baltimore a coalition of black contractors and religious leaders made an issue of economic benefits during the campaign for a bond issue to finance the Harborplace retail project. The Rouse Company, eager for voter support in the black community, made a series of public commitments to affirmative action in construction contracts, construction jobs, permanent jobs, and tenant selection. "We had to win a referendum," explained James Rouse. "If the black community had not supported Harborplace, it would have been defeated in the referendum. . . . That meant we had to talk about . . . the employment of black people and . . . bringing black businesses into Harborplace."[22]

The Rouse Company set targets of 10 percent of total contract value for minority contractors, 25 percent minority participation in construction jobs, 50 percent minority participation in Harborplace jobs under the control of the Rouse Company, assistance to minorities in finding jobs with businesses in the project, and a special effort to find and help minority merchants for Harborplace. The company exceeded its targets for minority contractors, construction workers, and permanent jobs, and twenty-two of the original 128 businesses in the project were minority-owned. Rouse conceded readily, however, that his goodwill alone would not have produced these results. Asked whether he thought outside pressure was important in promoting minority economic development, he answered that "it takes pressure; it takes endless, endless, endless pressure." As for whether business is willing to make the commitment without pressure, he had this to say: "I think business may be willing to but I think it won't. Business is busy. It is occupied by all kinds of deadlines and demands and budgets, and all kinds of things that are occupying you enormously in the completion of a task."[23]

In Baltimore the pressure came from an unusual requirement for voter approval of the Harborplace bond issue. In Boston public-private negotiations over the Copley Place project produced similar results. When the Urban Investment and Development Company (UIDC) proposed to develop a retail-hotel-office complex over a Massachusetts Turnpike interchange, state officials responsible for the site decided to set up a citizen committee to review the plans and try to negotiate an acceptable project. To reduce the risk of public controversy, Governor Michael Dukakis wanted to involve resident groups early enough to work out whatever changes might be necessary to deal with their concerns.

The Copley Place site is on the edge of downtown, near low-income and minority neighborhoods. The new project was going to be a large workplace with an estimated 6,300 permanent employees, of whom 3,300 would be newly hired and 3,000 would be office staff transferred from other locations. Citizen negotiators were quick to focus attention on who would be hired to fill these jobs. A resident task force proposed hiring goals of 50 percent of the permanent jobs for Boston residents, 50 percent for women, and 30 percent for minorities. Since a defined "impact area" of neighborhoods close to the project contained 17.2 percent of the city's labor force, they proposed a target of 17.2 percent of the permanent jobs for people living within that area. In addition, they proposed that UIDC set aside retail space for minority- and community-owned businesses at below-market rents.

This was a tall order. It would have a direct impact on the developer's ability to find hotels and retail tenants for the project, since they would be subject to special hiring commitments. Nevertheless, UIDC accepted these terms among others as part of a package deal written into its lease agreement with the Turnpike Authority. UIDC agreed to provide 15,000–20,000 square feet of community-oriented retail space at reduced rents, to set up a recruitment and referral office for affirmative action hiring, and to work with a city-state-resident committee at helping project businesses meet the goals. To make relations with its tenants more manageable, UIDC insisted on applying the hiring goals to the entire work force rather than to each individual business, and agreed to encourage rather than require tenants to give advance notice of future job vacancies.

There was still more to come. When UIDC and the city decided to apply for UDAG funds for the project, the federal Department of Housing and Urban Development added further targets specifying percentages of low- and moderate-income workers. Then, later agreements with the city required UIDC to sponsor job fairs and meetings, produce tenant handbooks describing the hiring commitments, fund programs for preemployment and skill training, and give the city advance notice of those job vacancies for which UIDC management had direct hiring responsibility. Eventually, UIDC laid out more than $700,000 for special recruitment and training programs.

With these elaborate agreements in place, city government and neighborhood residents acted on James Rouse's point that pressure is necessary to get the development company's attention. The city set up a new agency to enforce hiring agreements on government-funded projects. This agency as well as the state-city-citizen liaison committee kept close watch on hiring procedures and results. Governor Dukakis and Mayor Kevin White maintained contact with UIDC executives, and White met personally with the managers of the Marriott and Westin hotels to impress on them that good relations with the city would depend heavily on their hiring performance. A group of community organizations filed a complaint with the Department of Housing and Urban Development charging faulty administration of the hiring agreement, and then led protest marches outside Copley Place. Mayor White held back a UDAG payment to UIDC until he got more specific commitments to job action. And the liaison committee insisted on holding face-to-face meetings with retail tenants to browbeat them into meeting hiring goals.

By late 1984 Copley Place employers had hired 3,100 new permanent employees for hotel, retail, or property management positions: 62 percent of these were Boston residents, 35 percent were minority, 50 percent were women, 26 percent lived in the impact area, and 83 percent fell within the low-to-moderate-income category. Although individual employers did not meet all the goals, collectively the project met or exceeded them. Employment figures for other hotels and department stores in Boston show that the two Copley Place hotels and the Neiman-Marcus department store were in line with industry-wide staffing practices in most categories, but hired significantly higher proportions of minority employees, particularly in better-paying managerial and professional hotel jobs.[24]

Just as local officials in other cities used their places at the negotiating table to increase their control over the makeup and design of downtown projects, so Massachusetts officials used their bargaining power to get far more control of job hiring than they could have through ordinary procedures. That Copley Place netted more than 1,900 new jobs for city residents, of whom nearly 1,100 were minority workers, was no small accomplishment.

In San Diego city officials made similar use of their position as investors in the Horton Plaza retail center to get jobs for city residents. Mayor Roger Hedgecock turned to the Private Industry Council of San Diego County, a training and placement organization, to find jobs for low-income and unemployed San Diegans in Horton Plaza and other city-assisted development projects. The council then served as the main employment office for Horton Plaza. By March 1986 store openings created nearly a thousand new jobs, and the council filled just over half of them. Of the people placed by the council seven out of ten were minority workers, and six out of ten came from high-unemployment, low-income neighborhoods targeted for recruitment.[25]

Connecting Schools to Jobs

Several cities also took steps to give their high school students better preparation for office jobs and help in finding them. A program in Boston illustrates how cities tried to link high school education to downtown work opportunities. In the early 1980s up to 40 percent of the freshmen entering Boston high schools were two or more grades behind in reading skills, half never finished high school, and of those who graduated school authorities estimated that perhaps only half were going on to college or full-time jobs. In 1982 school officials and business leaders signed a formal agreement known as the Boston Compact committing the schools to specific improvements and committing the business firms to offering first hiring priority to Boston high school graduates for specified job openings. As part of the plan, the Boston Private Industry Council hired a full-time career specialist to work in each high school, sharing the cost with the city. Participating firms offer summer and part-time jobs as well as permanent employment for students who meet attendance and performance standards.

By 1985 students scored higher on math and reading tests and improved their attendance record. More than five hundred firms, mostly downtown offices, hired high school students for summer jobs as secretaries, receptionists, word processor operators, and maintenance workers at pay that averaged more than a dollar above the minimum wage. In the fall of 1985 1,300 students were continuing to work part-time while they finished school, and 1,700 graduates—80 percent of them blacks or Hispanics—had found full-time jobs under the plan.

A survey of the class of 1985 six months after graduation found 93 percent either working full-time or continuing their education; of those who were working, 87 percent got their jobs through the Boston Compact. The companies that hired them are almost entirely downtown firms in service fields, led by the Liberty Mutual and John Hancock insurance companies, the Bank of Boston, and the State Street Bank. Two-thirds of the full-time jobs were in banking, insurance, retail and food services, and health and hospitals. Two of every three jobs were clerical, in such functions as accounting, data entry, filing, library work, mail service, secretarial work, and word processing. The average starting salary was five dollars an hour, and only two graduates began at the minimum wage of $3.35.[26]

These results supply further evidence that the corporate-service economy has put a wide variety of jobs within reach of average city people. Many other cities have organized similar programs, and in 1987 the National Alliance for Business awarded funds to Indianapolis, San Diego, Seattle, and four other communities to apply elements of the Boston Compact to their own school systems. Negotiated agreements over public education and private hiring are one more illustration that a new blending of public and private functions can have social value.[27]

The problems of raising education levels of city residents remain formidable, however, and so far programs like the Boston Compact have been more successful at job placement than at keeping young people in school. Of Boston's potential graduating class of 1985, 43 percent never finished, and in 1986 the proportion of dropouts increased to 46 percent. These figures are comparable to New York dropout rates of 43 percent in 1984 and 50 percent in 1986. They are a clear sign that many city workers will continue to have educational handicaps even while the schools help their graduates to a larger share of downtown jobs.[28]

Many cities are not taking full advantage of the potential benefits from their new downtowns. By promoting development projects, they are creating a basis for economic recovery; but development alone will not eliminate poverty and joblessness among city people. Now that downtown is once again a viable place for doing business, the next challenge for city government is to help their own residents land the new office and service jobs. Several public-private agreements on targeted hiring, job training, and placement of high school graduates have shown promising results. With downtown work diverse and expanding, and with public-private negotiations widely accepted as a way to get things done, cities are now in a strong position to spread the benefits of downtown development more equitably.

16

The Shifting Focus of Neighborhood Groups: The Massachusetts Experience

Langley Keyes

As the Reagan era draws to a close, urban policy issues that have been on hold or submerged for the past eight years are reentering the domain of serious public dialogue. For example, the federal role in housing and community development, pushed to the back of the stage by the ideological convictions and budgetary curtailments of the Reagan administration, is once more up for debate. The President's Commission on Housing focused in 1982 on the view that "Americans today are the best-housed people in history."[1] That lens has shifted in "A Decent Place to Live," the recently issued report of the National Housing Task Force (Rouse-Maxwell), which argues that for many Americans "housing is unavailable, unaffordable, or unfit" and that the time has come to "raise these conditions to a compelling level of concern."[2]

At the heart of the Rouse-Maxwell report lies the conviction that a new housing delivery system "has taken root and has grown over the last decade. It has emerged from the community level in response to local needs and dwindling federal support. It is marked by vigorous new efforts by state and local governments and non-profit developers and has enlisted the strength and experience of private, for profit developers."[3]

With its emphasis on public-private partnerships and the "new wave" of community sponsors, the report sets a framework that will structure the policy debates in the months ahead about the future of federal housing and community development.

Community-based housing sponsors are but one manifestation of neighborhood groups "whose sensibility is focused on the physical, social and economic aspects of community building."[4] This chapter is concerned with how that range of groups in one state, Massachusetts, has been transformed in the decades since the Great Society and how the paradigm of neighborhood-based organizations, their goals, ideology, and strategy has shifted in the state since the 1960s when community control and maximum feasible participation were the rallying cries of neighborhood organizations.

Through its funding of community-based sponsors in urban and rural settings, the Commonwealth of Massachusetts, operating primarily through the Executive Office of Communities and Development (EOCD), is "working to advance the competence and capacity of those organizations whose scale is local, whose clientele is disadvantaged, and whose sensibility is focused on the physical, social and economic aspects of community building."[5]

In Massachusetts over the past decade a system of public and quasi-public organizations has developed which represents a broad-ranged effort to carry out such community building. EOCD provides state financial resources or passes through federal funds for support staff and technical assistance to three types of institutions: Community Development Corporations, Neighborhood Housing Services, and Community Action Agencies. While not coordinated in any systematic way, the goals and objectives of these three are mutually reinforcing and their constituencies often the same. This chapter looks at these three institutional forms: what they do and the ways in which they differ from neighborhood-focused organizations of the past.

The "neighborhood movement" in the United States has undergone a steady transformation since the turf-focused protests generated by urban renewal and highway dislocation, the power and process concerns of the War on Poverty, and the synthesis of neighborhood control represented by the Model Cities program in the late 1960s. Each of these efforts—urban renewal, the poverty program, and Model Cities—marked an evolution in thinking as to how neighborhood people could influence the decisions, both public and private, made for their community.

While varying from situation to situation, there were, in general, five elements in the "model" of neighborhood organization in Massachusetts that emerged at the end of the 1960s.

1. *Area focus and concern for turf.* The experience with urban renewal, particularly in Boston, focused local groups on their physical environment and the need to define organizational concern in terms of a bounded physical area. These boundaries might represent a historic definition of physical community or the mechanical imposition of urban renewal planners. In either case the lines determined who was "in" and who was "out" of the neighborhood.

2. *Control of area-impacting decisions.* A central goal of the Model Cities program in Boston and other Massachusetts cities was the formal involvement by the citizens' board in decisions involving the use of public

and private funds for projects in the neighborhood. The range of projects over which such control was to be exercised and the definition of control itself were hotly debated issues, fueled by deeply held convictions of both the neighborhood and city hall as to the operational meaning of the term.

3. *Resident participation.* "Maximum feasible participation" was the rallying cry of the War on Poverty, and variations on the theme were found in the Model Cities program and the community development corporations that sprang up in Massachusetts during the early 1970s. The underlying premise of the participation focus was that the legitimacy of an organization's role in decisionmaking was a function of broadly based neighborhood involvement in those decisions.

4. *Access to resources.* Through control and participation, local groups would have a significant impact on the level of resources allocated to the area by city hall and on other actors, both public and private, wanting to do business in the neighborhood. Model Cities was concerned with all aspects of community well-being and the coordination of public resources needed if one were to truly better the social, economic, and physical life of the area. That comprehensive ideal was short-lived, but it exercised a powerful hold over the evolving neighborhood paradigm while it lasted.

5. *Communication and confrontation.* The neighborhood-based organization was seen as a means of advocating local needs and desires at city hall. Communication could lead to conflict or confrontation as neighborhood and downtown interests clashed. The "us" in the neighborhood and "them" in city hall made for an almost inevitable environment of confrontational politics as the neighborhood strove to make its presence felt at the bargaining table.

In Massachusetts in the 1980s the five points outlined above have been transformed in a number of ways. At the risk of oversimplification I argue that three of the elements—turf, control, and participation—have dropped into the background as attention has focused on resources and communication.

The holistic model of community control of all major resource allocation decisions, of neat area boundaries within which the "community" participates in the decisionmaking process about the social, economic, and physical development issues which affect the future of the area, has given way to a more pragmatic approach. In the current model professionals working for nonprofit organizations focus on specific deals which allocate public and private resources for services, jobs, housing, and economic development to the low-income residents of the target area. The concepts of "deal-making" and "entrepreneurship" seem more relevant to the activities of these local professionals than "participation" and "confrontation." The holistic construct of community control, with its concern for process and inclusion, has given way to result-focused incrementalism. Leveraging public and private funds in complex packages has replaced applying for inclusive federal grant-in-aid programs.

So far I have talked in general terms about the shifting characteristics of "the neighborhood system." To ground the discussion, we need to look at the specific characteristics of those organizations that see low-income neighborhoods as their constituents. In what ways do these groups carry out deal-making involving resources and communication? What are the results of such efforts?

The passage quoted earlier talks about a local scale, a disadvantaged clientele, and a "sensibility focused on the physical, social, and economic aspects of community building." In expressing the range of community-based activities with which the agency is involved, EOCD does not emphasize control of turf or local participation but rather focuses on specific economic, social, and physical means of advancing the situations of low-income residents of the commonwealth.

The organizations included under the EOCD definition of "community-based" are both smaller and larger in service area and narrower in function than those envisioned in the five-point paradigm of "neighborhood organization" that reached its high-water mark in the Model Cities program.

EOCD works with and/or funds three kinds of community-based organizations which meet the agency's criteria of being local in scale and serving a disadvantaged clientele with a sensibility focused on the physical, social, and economic aspects of community. Those are (1) a network of over fifty community development corporations (CDCs); (2) six Neighborhood Housing Service Organizations (NHSs); (3) and twenty-five Community Action Agencies (CAAs).

Each of these organizations represents a set of institutions with a unique history, clientele, agency focus, and its own view of power, resources, and communication. The three are not coordinated into the area-focused model of local control and participation envisaged in the days of Model Cities and maximum feasible participation. But collectively they do carry out many of the model's explicit service and development tasks. In the following sections the three types of organization are described and their use of power, resources, and communication analyzed.

Community Development Corporations

In Massachusetts the statewide network of community development corporations is a direct heir of the community control model of the sixties. That network is made up of more than fifty organizations involved in aspects of community development in both urban and rural areas. Through EOCD the commonwealth provides annual funding of over $1,250,000 for staff support for thirty-five of the fifty organizations through the competitively bid Community Economic Enterprise Development Program (CEED).[6]

Two quasi-public organizations, the Community Development Finance Corporation (CDFC) and the Community Economic Development Assistance Corporation (CEDAC), were set up in the late 1970s to provide technical assistance to the CDCs through CEDAC and long-term capital equity or debt for housing and economic development through CDFC.

The CEED, CEDAC, CDFC "system" makes available funding for staff, project feasibility, and long-term financing to the commonwealth's extensive network of CDCs. In the aggregate this system has in the past five years leveraged $150 million in public and private funds for community and housing development; held onto or created over 5,000 jobs; developed an annual average of 500 units of new or rehabilitated housing a year since 1983; and, on average, leveraged $50 of project development for every $1 of CEED funding spent.[7]

CDCs range in size from those in Boston or Lowell which deal with a few city blocks to the Franklin County CDC which serves a vast rural area. While minimum levels of participation and community involvement are required for utilization of CDFC and funding through the CEED program, I argue that the control and participatory aspects of the CDCs are of less significance than development of projects: a technical, political, and production competence that through physical and economic results has a positive impact on the lives of the low-income residents of the neighborhoods the CDCs represent.

Many of the CDCs deal exclusively with housing. Housing production has increasingly moved to the center of the CDC agenda, a logical response to the saliency of the issue in the lives of the commonwealth's low-income residents. Other organizations focus solely on economic development. Within the economic development area CDCs exercise a variety of approaches. Some are concerned with holding on to and reinvigorating the "mature industries" that have constituted the traditional economic base of the local community. Others target cottage industries, small crafts, and new service industries as an alternative to a manufacturing base.

The fifty CDCs represent a range of local nonprofit entrepreneurs concerned with job opportunities, housing, and services for low-income people. At their best the professional staff of the organizations are both articulate advocates for local interests and effective producers of concrete results in housing and jobs. They know how to work with city hall, private developers, state agencies, and nonprofit funding sources. Cooperation with public officials has for the most part replaced the confrontation of the sixties. But as effective political maneuverers, the most experienced of the CDEC directors know when and how to mobilize their constituencies. At their most creative the professionals running these organizations, joined by a handful of board members, have become strikingly adept at attracting resources to their neighborhoods.

Neighborhood Housing Services Corporations

The Massachusetts Neighborhood Housing Service Program was established within EOCD in 1980 to supplement federal and private support to Neighborhood Housing Services Corporations and thereby to assist homeowners unable to meet private lending criteria for home improvement loans. A Neighborhood Housing Service Corporation (NHSC) is a community-based organization providing housing rehabilitation services to a designated neighborhood within a city or town. The directors of the organization are made up of neighborhood residents, municipal officials, and representatives of local financial institutions. The organization operates a revolving loan fund which makes financing available at flexible rates to community residents.

While NHSCs are a small element in the overall picture of the commonwealth's neighborhoods—they exist in only six communities—they play an important role in those municipalities in which they do function. Pragmatic, focused on specific results, very much a top-down organizational form, NHSC has successfully demonstrated its capacity to fill in an important source of residential financing and technical assistance for older neighborhoods in Massachusetts.

Community Action Agencies

In 1986 EOCD distributed roughly $7 million in federal funds to twenty-five CAAs throughout the commonwealth. The agency also provides the organizations with administrative support and program guidelines.

Most CAAs have been in existence for over twenty years. With one exception, they have evolved dramatically from their initial focus on advocacy.

They are currently major providers of social services for the elderly, youth, and children while being deeply involved in issues of housing for the homeless. In some rural areas CAAs are the sole providers of social services to widely scattered small towns.

Some CAAs have spun off community development corporations to focus on issues of neighborhood development and the specialized housing needs of low-income people. PACE, for example, the New Bedford-based CAA, is currently negotiating to develop housing for the mentally handicapped. TRI-CAP, another agency, has focused its three-town housing network on the complex set of issues producing homelessness in those communities.

With the emergence of homelessness as a major issue in Massachusetts, the CAAs have established an additional niche for themselves in helping to carry out the policy mandates of the commonwealth's extensive effort to deal with the homeless phenomenon. Many of these poverty agencies have become major actors in the complex system which the state has developed to deal with homeless prevention, emergency shelter, and rehousing of individuals and families from temporary quarters.

Working cooperatively with the establishment, i.e., city hall and local business leaders, the directors of the CAAs have become politically adept at the local as well as the state level. While much of the ideology of the CAAs of an earlier era remains verbally present—maximum feasible participation, local control—in reality the effective CAAs, like the CDCs, have become nonprofit entrepreneurs—focusing on the pragmatics of resources and communication, able to play political hardball if necessary but more likely to be working in tandem with others.

Even in the heyday of the War on Poverty, the Community Action Agencies did not focus as much on "turf" as on constituencies—the low-income, the politically disadvantaged. What they did share of the "sixties' model" of neighborhood organization was the thrust for local participation and control. In many ways the agenda and goals of the CDCs and the CAAs have converged during the past decade. Political sophistication and joint agendas have emerged from years of hard struggle. At its best this convergence means that the two organizations complement each other at the local level and reinforce entrepreneurial competence focused on the needs of low-income residents.

The CDCs and the CAAs are dealing with the tough local issues of community development and service in rural and urban neighborhoods in the commonwealth. Often filling in where there is no other public or private agency, the organizations in the two systems provide entrepreneurship on behalf of constituencies sorely in need of that professional competence.

While the goals of participation and control seem to have faded, the capacity to articulate the social, physical, and economic needs of low-income citizens has not—at least in those areas of the commonwealth serviced by aggressive, entrepreneur-led CDCs and CAAs.

What are the consequences in Massachusetts of the transformation of the neighborhood model from one focused on turf, control, and participation to the more pragmatic approach described above? On the positive side, confrontation has been replaced by partnership and cooperation—a sense that city hall and neighborhood groups can do more in physical, social, and economic terms for an area by working together than they can by arguing over who is in control and who speaks for the community. Particularly in an era of diminished federal resources, the need for cooperative leverage, public-private partnership, and other concepts involving joint resolving of issues has found fertile ground in the commonwealth.

The CDCs are seen by many city halls as taking on the tough jobs of trying to make low-income housing work at a time when the private sector cannot be troubled to master the complex range of programmatic pieces necessary to build or rehabilitate housing for low-income people.

The CAAs have become central providers of services for low-income households. As such, they are a critical link in the service network. In some rural areas of the state the CAAs and CDCs go beyond the role of carrying out the public agenda and have become in fact the initiators of that agenda. In the absence of local community development and social service capacity the CDCs and CAAs have filled the void.

In addition to their local development and service roles, the two networks have become effective advocates at the state legislature. As federal dollars for housing, community development, and social services have been cut back, the state has moved in to fill the slack where possible. The CDCs and the CAAs have articulated where and how those resources should be used. Massachusetts has been fortunate over the past several years to have had the funds with which to respond to many of these service and development needs. An expanding financial pie, at least until this year, has meant that such advocacy met with a string of successes. Federal cuts in the CAA budget have been made up for by the state, and state funding for CDC staff has expanded as have the capital resources for housing production.

Over the past decade Massachusetts has built up a formidable array of institutions to help promote and support neighborhood-based development corporations. Some of the most significant have been in existence even longer. Greater Boston Community Development, Inc., for example, a nonprofit group providing technical assistance to community-based housing sponsors, has been helping local organizations since the late sixties. Its track record is probably the most extensive in the nation.

But even with this impressive array of institutional supports, there are significant limits to the CDC network's capacity to produce housing. In an era of scarce federal deep subsidies, the CDCs' capacity to produce large numbers of units is limited. The Boston Housing Partnership, one of the most sophisticated and elegantly orchestrated of the "new wave," produced 700 units of "deep subsidy" rehabilitated housing for low-income people in its first phase of development. Depending on one's point of view and level of optimism, one can see 700 as a large number with more large numbers to follow, or one can see it as an indication of how much effort and work is required in the "post federal deep subsidy world" to produce shelter for low-income people.

Massachusetts has been fortunate in having a number of factors converge to make possible the neighborhood-based network which currently exists: a tradition of state support for neighborhood-based organizations; strong technical assistance organizations; a governor committed to the neighborhood partnership idea; and during the first six years of his current administration expanding state funds which have been creatively directed to various aspects of the neighborhood system.

The Massachusetts system has its resident skeptics who argue that the advocate organizations have been co-opted by the establishment; the scale of their operations is not sufficiently large; the fundamental inequities of society are smoothed over but not frontally addressed; community control has given way to a willingness to go along with city hall and the statehouse to insure that the neighborhood and the organization gets its piece of the pie. While these concerns are worth noting and perhaps relevant in some situations, the level of political sophistication of the CAAs and most of the CDCs is such that the organizations are able to occupy the tenuous space between cooperation and co-optation with a high degree of success.

When one looks beyond the state's boundaries and asks how many other states either have or could have a "neighborhood network" to do the kind of community development and service jobs described in this chapter, the plot thickens. The neighborhood advocates see a "new wave" of organizations that have risen in the early eighties made tough and lean by the austerity of the Reagan years. The argument is that the group is ready to take off if given any encouragement and support by a reengaged federal government. The skeptics, some veterans of the War on Poverty, Model Cities, and other neighborhood efforts of the past, are more cautious. They ask about staying power, volume, and depth.

These are legitimate questions, and this short essay makes no effort to answer them in depth. It is worth remarking, however, that there are other states not unlike Massachusetts: New York, Connecticut, New Jersey, California, for example, that have a variation of the neighborhood network in place. Others like Maryland, Virginia, Michigan, and Pennsylvania are working to put such a system together. The great challenge for the Bush administration is to craft legislation and urban policy that energizes neighborhood-based networks where they exist or have the potential for developing out of genuine local roots. The models of neighborhood networks cannot be laid on from the top; but the federal government can go a long way toward establishing supportive policy that leverages local creativity.

17 Building a New Low-Income Housing Industry: A Growing Role for the Nonprofit Sector

Benson F. Roberts and Fern C. Portnoy

Over the past decade the fundamental balance between housing supply and demand in most local housing markets—and especially in the low-income/low-cost end of these markets—has shifted dramatically. Homelessness is, of course, the most visible sign of this imbalance. But homelessness is indicative of a much larger, less apparent, and more damaging problem. Mortgage interest rates have risen sharply, especially in real (i.e., inflation-adjusted) terms. The existing low-income housing stock is aging and deteriorating, especially in distressed neighborhoods.

Higher energy and liability insurance costs have driven up operating expenses, causing some landlords to abandon properties. The number of households has risen, driving up the number of housing units needed. With demand exceeding supply at the top end and mid-range of the housing markets, fewer units are filtering down to the lower end. The result is that housing costs have been rising substantially faster than incomes, causing affordability problems even for middle-income households, to say nothing of low- and moderate-income people. Homeownership, perhaps the central image of the American dream, has faded out of sight for many. Among the poor, even rental housing is hard to find, as the number of low-income renters steadily rises while the number of affordable rental units drops. Many low-income neighborhoods are losing affordable housing to either gentrification or decay in a process that often spirals out of control. And a surprisingly large number of people cannot afford any homes at all, or are only a missed paycheck away from homelessness.

To compound the problem, federal support for low-income housing has dropped precipitously since 1981. HUD spending is down 75 percent; the number of new federally assisted housing units has fallen by 89 percent; and more than 500,000 low-income units receiving federal subsidies are in jeopardy as subsidy contacts and use restrictions near expiration. Large profit-motivated developers and syndicators have turned their energies from low-income housing to luxury residential and commercial projects in hot suburban (and some downtown) markets. In short, an entire system for producing low-income housing has been dismantled.

This chapter examines a new wave of local efforts to build systems for providing low-income housing and describes a growing role for nonprofit community-based development corporations (CDCs).

The old low-income housing delivery system was federally driven, principally by Section 8 rental subsidies and other programs, and consequently was relatively uniform around the country. In contrast, the new wave of low-income housing efforts is locally driven and depends on a custom blend of scarce public resources with private funds to address particular local housing needs. These new programs are still uneven in their coverage, but their surprising number, variety, and inventiveness suggest that they are not merely interesting oddities, but rather the vanguard of a more effective and efficient housing system.

This new wave of low-income housing efforts is poorly understood and just beginning to be documented. It is a fragmented system that developed as a result of several forces, including the perception during the early eighties that grass-roots, locally driven activities could be an effective counterpart to big government solutions.

Profit-motivated developers have not been totally absent from the new wave, but it has mostly been small-scale and mid-sized local developers rather than large national developers that have participated, usually in response to programs initiated by other public-purpose partners. And, while profit-motivated developers will doubtless continue to be important in any rejuvenated low-income housing industry, what is new about the new wave is the increased centrality of state and local governments and nonprofit organizations.

The second part of this chapter describes the key players in the emerging new low-income housing industry — local CDCs, the intermediary organizations that support them, the investors, and the role of state and local governments.

A future agenda for expanding the low-income housing production system is described in the third part of the chapter. This section also examines the strengths and weaknesses of CDCs, the elements of the system that need to be strengthened, and an expanded role for intermediaries. The third section also describes a proposed expanded role for the federal government built on the experiences of the past eight years and an important role for CDCs. We want to stress that no developer — whether nonprofit or profit-

motivated—can be expected to produce low-income housing on a substantial scale without significantly more public subsidies. Low-income housing
problems are national in scope, and the federal government must play a
greater role if they are to be seriously addressed.

The Players in the New Low-Income Housing Industry

The production of low-income housing is increasingly being undertaken by
partnerships among CDCs and other nonprofit developers, state and local
governments, private financial institutions, foundations, nonprofit financial
and technical assistance intermediaries, and socially motivated investors.
Small- and medium-scale profit-motivated developers also participate in
these programs, often in partnership with nonprofit sponsors. In addition,
the federal government is still playing a critical, albeit a diminished, role
—primarily through the Community Development Block Grant program,
tax incentives (primarily the low-income housing tax credits), and a handful of other small programs.

The Emergence of CDCs

CDCs are the frontline players in this new wave of low-income housing
efforts. CDCs are nonprofit organizations, are accountable in some way to
the low-income communities they serve, and are development corporations.
A recent national survey by the National Congress for Community Economic Development[1] estimates that 1,500 to 2,000 CDCs have at least
some housing or economic development experience under their belts. About
87 percent of CDCs undertake housing activities: primarily new construction or rehabilitation. A sample of 631 CDCs responding to the NCCED
survey reported having completed the development of 125,000 housing
units. Low-income households occupy 90 percent of the units that CDCs
have produced. And CDCs undertake other community development activities: 30 percent develop retail, office, or industrial facilities; 35 percent
assist business enterprise development; 65 percent conduct community organizing or advocacy; and substantial proportions also undertake tenant or
homeowner counseling, child care, and other services.

The active involvement of CDCs and other nonprofit developers is not a
recent phenomenon, but only recently have they become widespread housing producers. The first CDCs drew attention in the late 1960s and early
1970s as attractive development vehicles because of their commitment and

sensitivity to community needs in selecting, structuring, and implementing projects. In very real terms CDCs enabled low-income community residents to take direct control over whether and how development takes place in their neighborhoods. Without CDC involvement, many low-income neighborhoods saw no development activity at all. CDCs enabled low-income community residents to define the scope, design, and location of proposed ventures, as well as to participate in the political process through which many development decisions are made.

The late 1970s saw the first major expansion of CDCs with support from the Ford Foundation and the Community Economic Development program operated by the Community Services Administration (CSA). Ford and CSA gave substantial assistance to only a limited number of CDCs, primarily for venture capital and other economic development programs. But the leadership of Ford and CSA added both visibility and legitimacy to the CDC approach and was catalytic in involving other foundations and governmental agencies in assisting a larger number of CDCs. CDCs began to obtain federal government funding through various programs, most of which were designed for profit-motivated developers or for tangential purposes, such as energy conservation or employment training. With additional experience, community groups were able to attract even more support from a small number of foundations; private below-market lenders, including major insurance companies; and some market-rate private investors. In response to community priorities, funding availability, and technical capacity, housing rehabilitation quickly became the primary activity for a new generation of CDCs.

Federal funding cutbacks in the 1980s have focused more attention on CDCs, and their role in producing low-income housing has grown more prominent. Part of this prominence is attributable to the withdrawal of profit-motivated developers; in other words, nonprofit developers are in many cities the only low-income housing developers still active. But nonprofits have not simply been good survivors of federal subsidy cutbacks; their number and sophistication have actually multiplied in the 1980s.

At least three factors explain this phenomenon. First, many communities realized they could no longer depend on profit-motivated developers to produce low-income housing, and with housing needs rising, they decided to take on the responsibility for developing housing themselves. Second, as CDCs and other nonprofits have become more widespread and successful, they have become far more visible. So as churches, social service agencies, neighborhood activists, city and state governments, local foundations, and others committed to providing housing have searched for new solutions, the CDC model has been much easier to identify and has been perceived more often as legitimate. Third, the technical and financial support available to CDCs and other nonprofits has grown substantially over the past several years, enabling more CDCs/nonprofits to get started and undertake more complex projects. The advent of nonprofit "intermediaries," such as the Local Initiatives Support Corporation, has dramatically helped to expand CDC activities (as we discuss in depth later).

The interest CDCs have sparked rises not solely from their increasing number and skills in a period of federal retrenchment. Indeed, the CDCs are still too uneven in terms of their coverage and capacity to be the primary instrument of national low-income housing policy. But a wide range of policymakers in both the public and private sectors are deciding that CDCs/nonprofits are worth encouraging because of:

— Their knowledge of community housing needs, markets, and opportunities and their ability to draft flexible and effective programs that respond to these circumstances.
— Their commitment to serving low-income households on a long-term basis. This commitment feature is becoming increasingly important as existing HUD-assisted low-income housing projects become threatened with defaults and conversions to upper-income use.
— Their ability to produce housing within the context of an overall neighborhood preservation strategy. Section 8 and some other traditional housing programs were operated with little regard for their impact on housing in the surrounding community; after all, Section 8 virtually guaranteed owners a rent roll without requiring them to compete for tenants within the local housing market. Yet most existing low-income housing is unsubsidized and is concentrated within distressed communities. Stabilization of this existing stock should be an important element in an overall housing strategy. CDCs use new investments in housing to bolster neighborhood housing markets.
— Their willingness to undertake projects that profit-motivated developers consider too small, too risky, insufficiently profitable, and located in neighborhoods that are too distressed.
— Their political and technical skills, as well as tenacity, in assembling multiple public, private, and charitable resources to make projects feasible and in marshaling community support.

Here are a few examples of what CDCs have accomplished.

— In New York City the Mid-Bronx Desperadoes have developed over 1,100 low-income units.

—In Boston, Inquilinos Boricuas en Accion (IBA) has built or rehabilitated over 800 units to preserve low-income housing opportunities in a neighborhood experiencing rapid gentrification.

—In Cleveland the eight CDCs that make up the Cleveland Housing Network have rehabilitated more than 400 housing units, most of them single-family homes for eventual ownership by poverty-level families. The homes are provided on a lease-purchase basis to families that could not qualify for bank financing.

While there are patterns common to the development of these organizations and initiatives, little work has been done so far to document the history, achievements, and limitations of these groups. The NCCED survey and research currently under way at the New School for Social Research in New York are beginning to document what CDCs have achieved. These studies are apparently corroborating the anecdotal evidence contained in Peirce and Steinbach's *Corrective Capitalism: The Rise of America's Community Development Corporations*. Though CDCs have not come close to meeting low-income housing needs and have been plagued by difficulties assembling adequate project financing and general operating support, they are growing in capacity, effectiveness, and scale of production.

The Parallel Emergence of Nonprofit Intermediaries

The proliferation of CDCs over the past several years has been paralleled by a new kind of entity: the community development intermediary. In this context the term "intermediary" means an entity that marshals financial and technical resources and coordinates their distribution to the CDCs. Intermediaries are the investment bankers of community development, in that they assemble the resources—including charitable grants and loans, and technical assistance—that CDCs need to make their projects happen. Intermediaries package the financing and then select the projects, assist in their development, and monitor them after development is complete.

By acting as intermediaries, these organizations make participation in community revitalization activities easier for financing sources by relieving them of the time-consuming, costly, and difficult responsibilities of selecting and packaging projects and administering grants and investments. Moreover, intermediaries insulate the contributors from project failure.

These private intermediaries have addressed the particular needs of CDCs in the following ways.

—Providing grants to CDCs for core administrative operations and as seed capital to initiate projects.

—Providing financial support (or financing commitments) early in the development process, giving credibility to CDC projects, and facilitating the process of securing necessary public and private market-rate commitments.

—Making below-market-rate loans and equity investments to projects for which anticipated revenues are too limited to support borrowing large amounts of private capital at market rates.

—Accepting a greater degree of risk than other lenders, or sharing risk with other lenders to attract their participation.

—Providing technical assistance resources along with financial resources. This support enables CDCs to plan complex transactions, such as those that involve equity syndication, and encourages further private investment by assuring that CDCs will have the capability to solve problems over the long term. In fact, without such predevelopment support, many projects would never reach the point at which financing can be sought.

Intermediaries operate on both the national and local levels. On the national level intermediaries have raised private charitable funds and equity investments for local community-based development efforts. The commitments national intermediaries receive from corporate and foundation contributors most often take the form of grants, low-interest loans with relatively limited terms, and equity investments for projects qualifying for low-income housing tax credits. Intermediaries, in turn, channel these funds to CDCs. Often funding commitments to CDCs from national intermediaries are contingent on the receipt of matching funds from other, principally local, sources.

There are three major intermediaries that operate nationally.

The Local Initiatives Support Corporation (LISC) was established in 1980 with initial capitalization from the Ford Foundation and others. LISC has raised about $230 million, primarily from corporations and foundations, and has provided financial and technical support to about a thousand ventures sponsored by about five hundred CDCs. LISC operates twenty-two local, regional, and statewide programs. Approximately 17,000 units of low- and moderate-income housing as well as 4,000 jobs have been generated. Through its subsidiary, the National Equity Fund, equity investments are made in projects qualifying for low-income housing tax credits.

The Enterprise Foundation, founded by real estate developer James W.

Rouse, was created to serve and actively involve poor people with annual incomes below about $10,000. Building upon community institutions such as churches, the Enterprise Foundation concentrates its efforts on projects that involve residents directly in the development process. To date, seventy CDCS in twenty-seven cities across the country have developed 6,000 units of low-income housing with technical and financial support from Enterprise.

The Neighborhood Reinvestment Corporation, a national quasi-public organization, is best known for its Neighborhood Housing Services programs. Some 243 NHS programs rehabilitate housing in 138 cities around the country. NHS programs are locally initiated and focus on the rehabilitation of single-family, owner-occupied homes. Through a related program, large apartment buildings exerting a blighting influence on their neighborhoods are upgraded.

Intermediaries are also being created on the local level. Like national intermediaries, local versions raise grants and socially motivated funds for CDCS. But it is often difficult for organizations that operate solely on a national basis to perform many of the day-to-day functions of operating a CDC program on the local level. For example, arranging the participation of various local financing sources and nurturing new and less sophisticated CDCS to the point where they are ready to undertake projects are activities that require an intensive local presence. There is an increasing recognition that the presence of such a local coordinating vehicle, or intermediary, is important, and the number of these entities is now growing. Consequently, LISC and the Enterprise Foundation are increasingly decentralizing their operations through satellite offices in several cities. Moreover, independent local intermediaries are forming in several cities.

In Denver the Piton Foundation has established several joint initiatives with local and national funding sources to provide a wide range of assistance for community development, including operating support for CDCS, loans for site acquisition and construction, and limited partnership syndications involving socially motivated individual investors. Through its Community Development Project, Piton is acting as the intermediary through which over $4 million in grants and loans from the Ford Foundation and others are being channeled to CDCS in Denver.

The Boston Housing Partnership (BHP) is a coalition of Boston's large financial institutions, state and local government, CDCS, and community leaders. Since 1983 BHP has financed the rehabilitation of more than 1,800 units of housing in over 150 buildings. Eleven CDCS developed the projects.

The Investors

Low-income housing projects involve both traditional and nontraditional investors. Among traditional investors, financial institutions provide loans to the extent possible within underwriting constraints, and limited partnership syndications attract equity investors seeking tax benefits at or near market levels of return. On the nontraditional side are below-market lenders, including foundations and some major insurance companies. Nationally, LISC and Enterprise are tapping corporations for equity investments based on the low-income housing tax credit, the only new federal tax incentive created under the Tax Reform Act of 1986. Since 1986 the National Equity Fund, a subsidiary of LISC, has raised $65 million from corporate investors. LISC has also created the Local Initiatives Managed Assets Corporation to operate a secondary market program through which LISC and others will sell loans they have made.

State and Local Governments

Although they are not the focus of this chapter, state and local governments increasingly play key roles in low-income housing projects. Localities and states provide land, gap financing, and in some cases CDC operating support. Until very recently, localities and states have not used much of their own money for community development projects and instead have used federal funds they administer or issued tax-exempt bonds for which they assume no repayment obligations. However, there are clear signs that this is beginning to change.

New sources are now being tapped both on the national and local levels to address the need for more subsidy. On the public side states and localities are starting to employ a variety of techniques to obtain subsidies by carefully structuring tax-exempt housing bond issues, tapping strong real estate markets, generating new sources of revenue, and dedicating existing revenue streams. In addition, states and localities are beginning to appropriate general fund revenues to establish new programs. Since 1985 fifteen states have created housing trust funds that have already generated $275 million.[2]

One example of a local revenue source that many communities could tap is a small tax (or surtax) on transfers of real property. Dade County, Florida, is generating about $12 million annually for lower-income housing from such a surtax, enough to assist well over five hundred lower-income households each year. Maine and New Jersey have similar taxes.

New York state and New York City have tapped a variety of resources, including surplus revenues from the city's Municipal Assistance Corporation and certain revenues from two major publicly assisted real estate development projects—Battery Park City and the World Trade Center—to provide housing subsidies. State general fund appropriations have also been used to fund several new low-income housing programs. California has devoted tidelands oil lease revenues to a housing trust fund that will support a variety of housing assistance programs. Seattle is using its general revenues to retire general obligation bonds issued to develop about 1,200 units of affordable housing for senior citizens. In Atlantic City gambling casino revenues are being tapped through the Casino Reinvestment Tax to generate a source of low-cost, long-term debt for housing and other revitalization projects.

The Future of the Industry

Numerous new financing techniques are evolving in response to federal funding cuts. These techniques are complicated and usually involve several different types of financing from several different sources, including private investment attracted through federal income tax incentives. Lacking a source of deep and ongoing federal subsidy, the typical low-income housing project has become smaller and more complex and tends to serve more of a working-poor or moderate-income clientele than a very poor one. Sponsors have designed creative and sophisticated financial packages that assemble available public, charitable, tax-exempt, and conventional financing resources to undertake development projects. The complexity of financing low-income housing in this new fashion has spawned a sizable and growing cadre of developers skilled in devising and implementing innovative financing packages. However, the transactions they undertake tend to be extremely time-consuming, expensive to establish, and difficult to replicate. Moreover, limited access to large capital markets as well as insufficient subsidy resources have restricted the amount of low-income housing, and tax reform has forced developers to seek out new kinds of investors (i.e., corporations and small-scale individual investors) who are subject to fewer tax shelter restrictions.

Given this context, it should not be surprising that definitive solutions have not been found and that the volume of production has been relatively low. Indeed, it is remarkable that any low-income housing is being produced under these circumstances. Moreover, the new wave of local initiatives suggests that the expectation of any single "silver bullet" solution to the low-income housing "problem" is almost certainly mistaken. Instead, a range of flexible approaches is needed to meet a variety of needs with the resources that can be assembled.

In order for these promising experiments to grow into production systems that can operate on a meaningful scale in communities nationwide, several important limitations must be addressed. In particular (i) the federal government must renew its commitment to low-income housing; (ii) states and localities must continue to step up their support and become more flexible, creative, and proactive; (iii) the capacity of local development organizations must be greatly expanded; (iv) access to private market investment—especially long-term debt and equity—must be expanded; and (v) the high fixed costs of establishing complex financing structures must be spread over a greater volume of activity.

Elements of the New Production Systems

Although the process of establishing new systems for undertaking low-income housing has only just begun, some broad elements of such systems are starting to emerge. These elements are likely to take very different shapes in different communities, depending largely on local needs and resources.

1. A Renewed Federal Commitment

A wide range of partners—state and local governments, profit-motivated and nonprofit developers, financial institutions, foundations, and nonprofit intermediaries—are all demonstrating their willingness to participate in new systems for producing low-income housing. The missing partner is the federal government.

The federal government must renew its fifty-year commitment to low-income housing if the new wave of housing initiatives is to attain substantial scale and reach truly low-income people. But we do not advocate a return to the programs the federal government used to operate.

We believe that the following principles should guide new federal low-income housing programs:

Federal policy should encourage partnerships among the federal, state, and local governments; CDCs and other nonprofit sponsors; and the private sector.

—Federal policy should support the new wave of low-income housing production systems already emerging on the local and state levels.

—New programs should be workable for all kinds of developers—including nonprofit and small for-profit developers, not just larger profit-motivated developers.

—Federal policy should leverage new sources of housing investment by both the public and private sectors, not replace existing sources.

—The use of nonprofit financing and technical assistance intermediaries should be encouraged.

Housing should be closely linked with community development.

—The effect of housing development on distressed communities is substantial, especially when undertaken as part of a comprehensive community development strategy.

—Neighborhood stability is important to the preservation of low-income housing—whether the housing is federally assisted or not. As already noted, most low-income housing is (and will be) privately provided with no public subsidy and tends to be concentrated in low-income neighborhoods. Housing policies must give substantial weight to stabilizing local and sub-local housing markets in order to preserve the low-income housing that already exists.

—Involvement of community residents—especially through CDCs and other nonprofit housing developers—is essential to achieving this linkage.

—Programs should be workable for projects of varying sizes, including scattered-site and small-scale projects, to accommodate community needs.

—Homeownership increases residents' control and stake in their neighborhoods. Federal policies should foster homeownership opportunities.

Federal policy should recognize and respond to the different housing needs of various communities.

—Low-income housing needs differ from city to city. For example, in cities like New York and Boston housing supply shortages and affordability are critical problems even for moderate-income households; in cities like Cleveland and Baltimore deterioration of existing single-family houses is a greater concern.

—Different neighborhoods within a given city vary. For example, federal programs should give communities the tools they need to retain and attract a stable mix of low- and moderate-income people.

—Federal policies should not impose a single rigid view of local housing needs. Rather, programs should offer flexible tools that can work under different market conditions to meet the needs of low-income people and communities. Subject to certain basic federal standards, local communities should decide for themselves on the strategies (e.g., new construction vs. rehabilitation, ownership vs. rental housing, single-family vs. multifamily structures), the tools (e.g., second mortgages, loan guarantees) and the projects to be pursued.

Federal policy should encourage a range of local initiatives.

—There is no single solution to low-income housing problems; instead, there are literally hundreds of solutions.
—Local initiatives have been the source of numerous successful housing efforts over the past several years, especially since relatively inflexible federal programs, such as Section 8, have been curtailed.
—Local initiatives have important research and development value; they are cost-effective experiments for testing new program ideas.
—It would be wasteful not to harness local creativity, energy, and financial resources.

Low-income housing opportunities created under federal programs should be sustainable over the long term. Low-income use of federally assisted, privately owned housing is now threatened because previous federal policies failed to look far enough into the future. New housing policies must not make the same mistake.

—Federal programs should encourage quality construction, sound management, and long-term low-income use.
—Housing production subsidies should be regarded as an investment, not as a payment for providing housing services for a finite period of fifteen to twenty years. Production subsidies (as distinguished from *rental* subsidies) should be repayable upon termination of low-income use, perhaps with deferred interest at some modest rate.
—CDCs and other nonprofit sponsors, limited equity cooperatives, mutual housing associations, and other public purpose organizations committed to providing long-term low-income housing opportunities should be used to the greatest extent possible.
—Residents should participate and have a long-term interest in the housing they occupy.
—Profit-motivated sponsors should be encouraged to transfer ownership of housing to public purpose ownership.

Federal programs should both target resources to low-income households and be made as cost-efficient as possible in terms of the cost per low-income unit.

—It should be acknowledged that some earlier federal housing programs were too costly and that this inefficiency undermined public support for these programs.
—Federal assistance should be tied to low-income units; assistance amounts should be based on the number of low-income households served.
—Deeper subsidies should be available for units targeted to very low-income households.
—To the extent feasible, subsidies should be repayable when low-income use is discontinued.

Accordingly, we heartily support the approach of the National Housing Task Force convened by Senators Alan Cranston of California and Alfonse D'Amato of New York. The Task Force recognized and strongly encouraged the new wave of local housing initiatives, including the role of nonprofit developers and intermediaries within this system. The centerpiece of the Task Force's recommendations is the establishment of a new Housing Opportunity Program (HOP). HOP would provide new federal funding of $3 billion annually to support state and local housing initiatives. The federal funds would be targeted primarily to housing very low-income people, but states and localities would otherwise have broad discretion in using HOP money. Funds could be used for acquisition, rehabilitation, and construction of housing; homeownership and rental use; single-family and multifamily buildings; and expanding the capacity of CDCs. Ten percent of the funds would be reserved for CDC activities. To encourage states and localities to contribute their own funds to the effort, one-half of the $3 billion would be contingent on state/local matching funds.

In addition to establishing a flexible capital subsidy program like HOP, the federal government should stimulate private equity and debt investments in low-income housing. The Low-Income Housing Tax Credit should be continued and improved to attract equity investors since they cannot be expected to invest in low-income housing on the basis of cash flow and capital appreciation. FHA mortgage insurance and co-insurance should be made much more flexible to be compatible with the way low-income housing will be financed in the 1990s.

2. State and Local Sources of Subsidy

It is clear that substantial subsidies will be needed on the state and local levels to bridge the gap between the costs of the project and the rents and sales prices that can be supported in economically distressed neighborhoods. No realistic level of new federal funding will be nearly sufficient to meet low-income housing needs, and it would be unfortunate if new federal funding were to replace the modest level of state and local support instead of encouraging additional commitments. Moreover, the case for federal funding would be far more persuasive if states and localities were prepared to offer matching funds of their own. In the National Housing Task Force's proposed Housing Opportunity Program, one-half of the relatively modest $3 billion in federal funds would be contingent on matching funds from states and localities.

3. Building CDC Production Capacity

While CDCs and other nonprofit developers are attractive vehicles for producing low-income housing, more groups with greater capacity are needed if the nonprofit approach is to fulfill its potential. In order to grow, CDCs need grants to cover core administrative operations which are among the scarcest and most important forms of support. Without a stable source of operating funds, many young CDCs struggle to attract and keep experienced staffs, staff directors must divert much of their time and energy from project development to basic fund-raising, and it is difficult for CDCs to develop the organizational depth they need to be truly effective.

The housing projects CDCs undertake are inherently risky and unprofitable, and many prospective projects never get off the ground. It is for precisely these reasons that profit-motivated developers shun these projects and CDCs are needed. Moreover, CDCs often find it essential to undertake community planning and advocacy work that is not directly allocable to the development of specific projects. For all these reasons it is simply unrealistic to expect many CDCs to fulfill their potential without core administrative grant support.

In addition to operating grants CDCs should also be allowed to receive reasonable fees for developing projects, much as profit-motivated developers do. Some funders suggest that CDCs should not receive development fees because they do not operate for profit. But we strongly disagree: development fees serve as a form of performance-based operating support; CDCs need the fees to cover overhead costs, establish liquid reserves, and launch new projects. Fortunately, development fees are increasingly regarded as legitimate for nonprofits.

Given the complexity of development in economically distressed communities in today's environment, the successful CDC requires a sophisticated staff and access to technical assistance in structuring and then obtaining project financing as well as in carrying out many project implementation tasks, starting with project planning and continuing through construction, marketing, rentals, and project operation. Despite these clear needs, it is not feasible for each CDC to attract and support the capacity it requires in-house.

It appears to be more cost-efficient to establish and support a continuing local technical assistance organization that could be available to several project sponsors, as now exist in several cities. These organizations provide technical assistance to local development organizations on a continuing basis, thereby reducing the need for each group to keep technical development experts on its own staff. The technical assistance provider could also help CDCs to get organized and to build community leadership. Nonprofit intermediaries like LISC can help by establishing local technical assistance organizations or by serving in that capacity directly with on-site staffs.

Joint ventures between CDCs and more experienced development partners should also be encouraged to build CDC capacity while developing projects consistent with community needs. Some critics of CDCs express concern that it can take five years or longer for a CDC to be able to produce on a substantial scale. But more and more CDCs are showing that properly structured joint ventures can accelerate their productivity without sacrificing community concerns or managerial prudence.

4. Increasing Access to Private Market Sources of Long-term Financing

Because the availability of subsidy funds will always be limited, in order to achieve even minimal levels of production it will be essential to maximize the use of private market-rate financing. In many areas few private financial institutions are willing to make loans for lower-income housing, especially now that Section 8 rental assistance contracts are no longer available to guarantee a dependable long-term source of project revenues. Many lenders lack the specialized expertise and are otherwise reluctant to underwrite loans on projects that are small, located in distressed neighborhoods, involve subordinate public loans, and are sponsored by a nonprofit or small for-profit organization with limited experience or capitalization.

Where lenders are willing to participate, they may require some form of mortgage insurance or third-party guarantee to insulate them at least partially against the risk of default. Even if risks can be reduced to acceptable levels, however, lenders are unwilling to make long-term, fixed-rate loans that they must retain in their portfolios. While loans may be originated locally, many lending institutions seek to make only adjustable-rates loans or loans that they can sell on the secondary market. In order for these secondary markets to function efficiently in very large volumes, the loans must conform to standardized structures and meet stringent underwriting criteria. In addition, such institutional lenders as insurance companies and pension funds often will consider investing only in projects that are much larger than most CDCs can develop.

Although these obstacles can be difficult to overcome, attracting private market sources of long-term debt financing is broadly recognized on the state and local levels as critical to producing lower-income housing, and several approaches are showing that it can be done. A relatively long-standing approach has been to issue tax-exempt bonds backed by FHA insurance. In Chicago the South Shore Bank has made community development lending its primary business. In Cleveland, Ameritrust has set up a development bank subsidiary to make community development loans. In some areas, consortia of lenders have been formed to act as centralized vehicles for making lower-income housing loans. In other cases innovative credit enhancement mechanisms are being used to reduce risks to lenders and attract their participation. The establishment of similar efforts will be critical.

5. Programs That Combine Multiple Financing Sources

One of the most frustrating aspects of low-income development today is that so much effort is required to produce a single (and often small) project. In the wake of substantial cutbacks in federal program funding, many states, localities, and CDCs have devoted considerable energies to establishing innovative financing structures for their projects. These financing structures must often be very complex to effectively use the unique blend of financing resources that are available at a given time. Reconciling the different—and sometimes conflicting—needs of various financing sources with the needs of the project requires considerable sophistication, and it is often very time-consuming and expensive. For example, loans from different sources involve different underwriting criteria, interest rates, and terms of repayment. Public and charitable sources of gap financing are often either unavailable, available only in inadequate amounts, or difficult to secure on a timely basis. Attempting to obtain the last piece of funding can be frustrating —especially if previously committed sources drop out along the way. Finally, technically demanding financing vehicles such as equity syndications entail substantial up-front legal and accounting work. The resulting high costs of structuring financing in this manner are often prohibitive for a single small project. However, these costs are much more acceptable if spread over a larger volume of activity by either increasing the scale of individual projects or by applying a given financing vehicle to multiple projects. In general, these economies of scale have not been realized.

More recently, however, as sophistication with regard to project financing has increased on the local level and as low-income housing development capacity within some localities has grown, it is becoming both possible and worthwhile to assemble an array of financing resources into a coherent program that can be used for multiple projects. In terms of housing, this approach has been reflected in the formation of several innovative public/ private partnership programs, several of which were discussed earlier because they involve local intermediaries. The partnership programs help finance multifamily rental housing by combining equity syndications, low-rate permanent financing, and public and charitable funds. They assist homeownership by blending first mortgage financing with low-rate second mortgages from public and charitable sources. As a group, such partnerships are among the most sophisticated and comprehensive efforts to finance lower-income housing.

The Chicago Housing Partnership is a good example. Through the Partnership, Cook County provides tax-foreclosed buildings, corporations make equity investments based on the low-income housing tax credit, LISC provides bridge financing, three banks provide first mortgage financing at slightly below-market rates, the city provides deferred payment second mortgages, and CDCs select and rehabilitate the buildings. This system produces about 500 units per year.

Conclusion

Over the past ten years low-income housing problems have worsened in many markets, and a new wave of local initiatives has sprung up to address these problems with little federal support. Clearly, low-income housing is a national issue that requires a national commitment. From budgetary, political, and programmatic perspectives, it is neither likely nor appropriate for the federal government to bear the entire responsibility for funding and carrying out new housing programs. But over the last decade a broad range of other institutions—states and localities, CDCs and profit-motivated developers, lenders, nonprofit intermediaries, and foundations—have joined to form creative and productive partnerships. These local initiatives are the basis for a new housing production system that is more effective, efficient, and responsive to local needs than previous federally driven efforts, but their growth will be stunted without the level of public subsidy that only the federal government can provide.

The open question is whether the federal government's commitment to housing, which except for this decade has been strong since the depression, will rise again soon. Given budgetary constraints, housing would have to become a much higher domestic priority than it has been—perhaps ranking with AIDS, drug abuse, and education. Two recent trends have the potential to galvanize public opinion in this direction: homelessness and the affordability gap facing young, middle-class homebuyers. These developments could make housing a central social policy issue in the post-Reagan era.

Part

5

**Looking to the Future: A Set of Nonurban
Urban Policy Initiatives**

18

Has America Lost Its Social Conscience— And Can It Get It Back?

James L. Sundquist

A little more than twenty years ago, in a burst of national euphoria and confidence, President Lyndon Johnson and Congress completed the enactment of the Great Society—the greatest outpouring of domestic legislation in thirty years, and the most concerted attack in history on the deep social problems that beset the nation's urban centers and rural areas alike. In an effort that was at the same time systematic and chaotic, the country mobilized its resources for a War on Poverty and concurrent assaults on a host of associated evils: racial discrimination, decay of educational systems, flight of job opportunities, rising crime rates, and all the other factors that combined to rob so many Americans, most tragically the children of the urban ghettos and rural backwaters, of their share of the promise of American life.

The Great Society was one of the most exuberant expressions of social conscience in our history, a surge of national compassion for the disadvantaged unmatched—except by the moral crusade of an earlier century that brought an end to slavery in America. And the country felt good about it. The Congress that created the Great Society had a popular approval rating certainly exceeding that of any Congress since, and probably higher than that of any Congress since the 1930s—71 percent approval late in 1965, by a Louis Harris poll.[1] And President Johnson was riding nearly as high; his approval rating in the Gallup poll was in the high 60s and 70s throughout most of that climactic year. Books about America's underclass, such as Michael Harrington's *The Other America*, got through to presidents in those days, presidents acted on what they learned, and their political popularity soared in consequence.

That may come as a surprise today, for politicians act now as though political rewards come not from facing the problems of the poor and disadvantaged but from looking the other way. Supporters of governmental activ-

Table 18.1   Total Annual Giving, 1955–84, and Giving for Social Services, 1970–84

Year	Total Giving (Billions of Dollars)	Total Giving as Percent of GNP
1955–59 (avg.)	9.03	2.05
1960–64 (avg.)	12.21	2.15
1965–69 (avg.)	17.47	2.15
1970	21.02	2.12
1971	23.44	2.17
1972	24.48	2.06
1973	25.70	1.94
1974	26.98	1.88
1975	28.61	1.85
1976	32.06	1.87
1977	36.34	1.89
1978	38.95	1.80
1979	43.69	1.81
1980	49.08	1.86
1981	55.88	1.89
1982	60.07	1.96
1983	66.82	2.02
1984	74.25	2.03

Sources: Figures on giving from American Association of Fund-Raising Counsel, Inc., *Giving USA*, annual report 1985, pp. 41, 76. Gross National Product data used in computation

ism have been in retreat for almost two decades, outgunned and outnumbered in a defensive battle, and much of the time they have been losing. The term "liberal" has become almost an epithet in political debate, and even "compassion" something of a dirty word. Many agree with the bitter summation of Sargent Shriver, the man whom Lyndon Johnson made his commanding general of the War on Poverty. "A sense of caring has been lost," Shriver told a gathering of onetime poverty warriors at the LBJ Library in Texas. "Nobody cares about anybody else any more. Especially nobody cares about anybody who's a loser."[2]

Is that really true? Has America indeed ceased to care? Has it lost its social conscience? No questions are more important for those who remain undaunted in struggling with the concentrated social problems of today's cities. Fortunately, we have some solid public opinion data bearing on these questions. And even more fortunately, the data bring not gloom but cheer.

We may begin with the report entitled *Giving USA*, published by the American Association of Fund-Raising Counsel. That report shows a steady

Giving for Social Services (Billions of Dollars)	Social Giving as Percent of GNP	Social Giving as Percent of Total Giving
2.88	.29	13.7
2.92	.27	12.5
2.99	.25	12.2
3.06	.23	11.9
3.12	.22	11.6
3.04	.20	10.6
3.06	.18	9.5
3.52	.18	9.7
3.97	.18	10.2
4.45	.18	10.2
4.83	.18	9.8
5.42	.18	9.7
6.33	.21	10.5
6.94	.21	10.4
8.01	.22	10.8

are from *Economic Report of the President*, 1985, p. 232. The 1985 report does not show social service giving for the years prior to 1970.

rise in total giving year after year (see table 18.1), as well as in giving for social services—to the United Way and kindred charitable organizations. As a percentage of the gross national product—a more significant indicator —giving declined during the 1970s but rose rather briskly in the 1980s, reaching a level in 1984 about the same as a quarter of a century earlier in the late 1950s. The fluctuations between those dates appear to reflect the state of the national economy rather than any change in public attitudes. Total giving in proportion to national resources rose during the prosperous 1960s, declined during the years of high inflation during the 1970s, and turned up again in the 1980s when inflation was brought gradually under control. Indeed, there is a remarkable correlation between the rate of inflation and the rate of giving. In every year since 1956 that the inflation rate was less than 6 percent, giving was more than 2 percent of gross national product. In every year that the consumer price index rose by more than 6 percent —that is, the years 1973 to 1982, inclusive—the giving rate fell below 2 percent. What happened, it seems clear, is that during the decade of high inflation givers simply did not apply a full automatic cost-of-living increase to their charitable contributions. But after the low point in 1978, they raised their giving at a rate faster than the rate of inflation. In the last three or four years the cut in tax rates and the increased confidence in the economic outlook also probably contributed to the upturn.

When total giving turned down, contributions to social service organizations declined more than gifts to other organizations—educational, religious, health, and so on—in the aggregate. From nearly 14 percent of total giving in 1970, the share of the social services fell to 10 percent or below during the years of highest inflation; but in the 1980s the social services have recovered at a faster rate than their competitors, approaching 11 percent in 1984. Giving to charitable organizations is an easy and natural place to skimp when people feel pinched, but it also displays an ability to recover when people feel more flush and confident in their economic prospects.

In addition to money, Americans contribute an enormous number of hours of volunteer work to charitable organizations. Trend figures on these contributions are not published in *Giving USA*, but at least one set of data is worth notice. The Gallup poll has asked on three occasions, in identical language, whether its respondents are personally "involved in any charity or social service activities, such as helping the poor, the sick or the elderly?" The proportion answering yes was 27 percent in 1977, 29 in 1981, and 31 in December 1984, which suggests a healthy warming trend in the national social conscience—or, at the very least, allowing for a margin of error, no cooling.[3]

Examined in the light of changing economic circumstances, the data show essentially stable habits of charitable giving. Certainly, there is nothing to suggest a drastic change in America's social conscience, in its sense of caring.

But if Americans as individuals have not suffered a loss of social conscience, why did they choose, and support for eight years, a national government that had? Surely that was what was bothering Sargent Shriver when he lamented that nobody cares about anybody any more. He did not mean the United Way and the charitable religious bodies and all the people who continue to contribute generously to them. He meant Ronald Reagan and the then Republican Senate and the Democratic House of Representatives. The anomaly is that the same people who support the United Way and other private charities placed in office—and sustained there—a leadership more bitterly hostile to the government's whole structure of social legislation than the country has known since the foundations of that structure were laid half a century ago.

To explore this paradox, we have to dip into the store of data on public attitudes toward the poor and toward government and politics, as collected by the many public opinion polling organizations that have flourished in recent decades. When these data are mined, four distinct patterns can be discerned.

Public Opinion Pattern 1: The People Maintain a
Deep Sympathy and Concern for the Poor

Surveys that probe directly into public attitudes toward poor people confirm what the healthy figures on private giving suggest. Most Americans look on the poor with feelings of sympathy, concern, charity, and generosity. They do not blame the poor people themselves for their plight.

One of the most comprehensive national surveys of this cluster of attitudes, conducted by the *Los Angeles Times* in April 1985, found that by margins of two-to-one or better Americans believed that the poor are hardworking rather than lazy, that most poor people would rather earn their own livings than stay on welfare, and that the inferior status of poor people is not mainly due to any lack of inborn ability to get ahead. The analysts who interpreted this poll for the *Times* and for *Public Opinion* magazine concluded from the entire range of data (about a hundred questions were asked) that "the American public has an enormous reserve of sympathy for the poor and their plight" and that there is "precious little evidence of 'a new selfishness' in American culture."[4]

The regular preelection poll conducted in 1984 by the University of Michigan's Center for Political Studies (CPS) produced findings that may appear somewhat more ambiguous. Yet even the slight margin of agreement by the CPS respondents with the statement, "Most people who do not get ahead in life probably work as hard as people who do," has to be interpreted as a favorable attitude toward the poor and the unsuccessful, given the wording of the question. The same is true of a Gallup poll response that put about equal blame for poverty on the poor themselves and on "circumstances beyond their control." By better than five-to-one the CPS respondents recognized that failure often is due to other causes than failure to work hard, even though by seven-to-one they believe that anybody who works hard has "a good chance" of succeeding. By substantial margins, the sample endorsed equal treatment of people and an equal "chance in life" for everybody but also agreed with the proposition that the country "would be better off if we worried less about how equal people are." Answers to the pertinent questions from these samples are presented in table 18.2.

Table 18.2 Public Attitudes toward the Poor

Question	Response of National Sample (Percentage)			
1 Do you think most poor people are lazy, or are most hard-working?	Lazy 26	Hard-working 51	Don't know 23	
2 Do you think most poor people prefer to stay on welfare, or most would rather earn their own living?	Prefer welfare 25	Earn their own living 63	Don't know 12	
3 Poor people have less education, more difficulty holding jobs, and live in worse conditions. . . . Do you think these differences are mainly because poor people have less in-born ability to get ahead?	Yes 29	No 62	Don't know 8	
Do you agree . . . neither agree nor disagree . . . or disagree that:	Agree	Neither agree nor disagree	Disagree	Don't know
4 This country would be better off if we worried less about how equal people are?	52	11	35	2
5 If people were treated more equally in this country we would have fewer problems?	63	12	23	2
6 It is not really that big a problem if some people have more of a chance in life than others?	35	16	46	3
7 Any person who is willing to work hard has a good chance of succeeding?	83	5	11	1
8 Even if people try hard, they often cannot reach their goals?	78	5	15	2
9 Most people who do not get ahead in life probably work as hard as people who do?	45	9	43	2

Table 18.2   (continued)

Question	Response of National Sample (Percentage)		
10 Which is more often to blame if a person is poor—lack of effort on his own part, or circumstances beyond his control?	Lack of effort	Both equally	Circumstances beyond control
Answers in 1984 (December)	34	32	35
1967	43	37	20
1964	35	34	31

Sources: Questions 1–3, *Los Angeles Times* survey, April 1985, reported in *Public Opinion*, June/July 1985, pp. 6, 7, 26. Questions 4–9, Center for Political Studies, University of Michigan, preelection survey, September–November 1984. Question 10, Gallup Poll, *Public Opinion*, June/July 1985, p. 28.

The final question listed in table 18.2 was asked in identical wording in earlier years, which sheds light on the question of whether attitudes have changed. The answer in this case is they have not changed much—but, if anything, they have changed for the better. In the Great Society days of 1964, 35 percent of the public blamed the poor for their own plight. This rose to 43 percent in 1967—at the point where the poor were being associated in the public mind with two years of race riots in the cities—but by 1984 the attitudes were slightly more favorable toward the poor than they were during Lyndon Johnson's honeymoon year two decades earlier.

Opinion Pattern 2: The People Are Cynical about Governmental Programs for the Poor—Especially Welfare

The deep sympathy that the public continues to feel toward the poor is not matched by confidence in the ability of government—particularly the federal government—to design and administer effective programs to assist them. The opinion data on this point, some of which are assembled in table 18.3, reveal preponderantly negative attitudes about the federal government, no matter how the questions are worded. By three-to-one margins the public believes that the government does not know enough about how to eliminate poverty, that tax money for human services is not well spent, and that the federal government cannot be described as efficient and well run. About twice as many people believe that antipoverty programs have generally not worked as those who believe they have, although by about the same two-to-one plurality they concede that the War on Poverty of the 1960s did make things at least somewhat better for the poor. Compared to state and

Table 18.3 Public Attitudes toward Past and Current Governmental Programs to Help the Poor

Question	Response of National Sample (Percentage)		
1 Even if the government were willing to spend whatever is necessary to eliminate poverty in the United States, do you think the government knows enough about how to do that, or not?	Knows enough 22	Does not 70	No opinion 7
2 Have anti-poverty programs almost always, often, seldom, or almost never worked?	Almost always or often 32	Almost never or seldom 58	No opinion 10
3 The "War on Poverty" . . . made things much better for the poor, somewhat better, had no impact, or made things worse for the poor?	Better 55	No impact or worse 28	No opinion 17
4 In general, do you think tax money spent for human services is used well or not?	Used well 21	Not used well 70	No opinion 8
5 Does the phrase "efficient and well run" describe	Yes	No	No opinion
Private voluntary organizations?	60	23	17
Small business corporations?	70	20	10
Large business corporations?	56	33	10
Your local government?	43	49	7
The federal government?	20	74	6

6 [Is] the present balance of responsibility between the federal government . . . and the state and local government . . . is about right, tipped too far toward the federal government, or, . . . too far toward the state and local governments?	Tipped too far toward			
	federal government 55	state and local government 9	About right 24	No opinion 12

local government, the federal government fares badly. More than half the respondents to an ABC News/*Washington Post* poll expressed the view that their respective states would run social programs more efficiently than does the federal government, and local governments received twice as much credit

Table 18.3   (continued)

Question	Response of National Sample (Percentage)		
7 [If] states took over some social programs now run by the federal government. . . . Thinking of your state, would [they] be run more efficiently . . . less efficiently, or what?	More efficiently	Less efficiently	About same
	55	30	15

Sources: Questions 1–3, *Los Angeles Times* survey, April 1985, *Public Opinion*, June/July 1985, pp. 6, 7, 59; questions 4–6, Roper Organization survey, November 1981, ibid., February/March 1982, pp. 27–29; question 7, ABC News/*Washington Post* survey, January 1982, ibid., June/July 1985, p. 30.

as did the federal government for being efficient and well run. Corporations and private voluntary organizations did about three times as well as the federal government in that measurement of public images.

The public's view is especially negative when attention is focused specifically on welfare programs, as in the questions in table 18.4. By a three-to-one margin, according to the *Los Angeles Times* survey, people believe that welfare programs make poor people dependent and encourage them to stay poor rather than give them a chance to "get started again." They believe that welfare programs are sullied with fraud, that the food stamp program is abused, and that families getting too much assistance are a more serious problem than families getting too little. The question on welfare fraud, asked by the Gallup poll in 1982, had been asked in identical form eighteen years earlier—and the trend is disheartening. The proportion of people who think that most welfare recipients are on relief for dishonest reasons has doubled—from 8 to 17 percent—while the number believing that none or hardly any are cheats has declined by half, from 22 to 11 percent.

Opinion Pattern 3: The People Think
the Government Should be Doing More for the Poor
Despite Its Past Failures

The average American, then, feels warm toward poor people in general but cold toward the federal government as the instrument for assisting them. How, then, do Americans reconcile the conflict—by supporting more governmental effort or less? Perhaps with faith in the learning ability of legislators and administrators, they wind up by giving the government the benefit of the doubt and asking it to spend more of the money that, in their view,

Table 18.4 Public Attitudes toward Welfare Programs

Question	Response of National Sample (Percentage)			
1 Do welfare programs give poor people the chance to . . . get started again, or . . . , encourage them to stay poor?	Get started again	Stay poor		No opinion or neither
	19	59		22
2 What proportion of persons do you think are on relief for dishonest reasons—most, some, hardly any, none?	Most	Some	Hardly any	None
Responses in 1982 (March)	17	72	9	2
Responses in 1964	8	69	19	3
3 What do you consider a more serious problem . . . families not getting enough welfare benefits to get by, or families getting more welfare benefits than they need?	Not getting enough	More than they need		Neither or both
	32	54		14
4 Have you ever seen someone use food stamps to buy something that you think should not be bought with food stamps?	Yes			No
	57			42

Sources: Question 1, *Los Angeles Times* survey, April 1985. Question 2, Gallup poll. Question 3, CBS News/*New York Times* survey, September 1984. Question 4, ABC News/*Washington Post* survey, January 1982. All published in *Public Opinion*, June/July 1985, pp. 6, 29. On last three questions, respondents with no opinions are excluded.

has in the past been unwisely spent for programs that seldom worked.

Table 18.5 presents the responses to survey questions asking directly about whether governmental activities, and spending, on behalf of the poor should be expanded or contracted. By overwhelming majorities the people believe that the government should be active on behalf of the poor, that it should be doing more than it is now doing, that it is not coddling the poor, and that it should increase spending for poverty programs in general. In one poll, only 7 percent of those with opinions thought that the government "should not get involved" in helping the poor. In another, only 2 percent thought that "doing nothing" was the best approach to the problem of poverty. Perhaps most impressive of all, three Americans would be willing to pay an additional 1 percent sales tax to help the poor for every two who would be opposed.

The public does, of course, believe that government spending in the aggregate should be cut. It has always been easy for the pollsters to get an overwhelming affirmative response to the question, "Should the government spend less money," when the question has been worded in general

Table 18.5   Public Attitudes toward the Future of Governmental Programs for the Poor

Question	Response of National Sample (Percentage)		
1 In principle, are you in favor of govern- mental actions in behalf of the poor, or . . . opposed . . . ?	Favor 73	Oppose 18	No opinion 9
2 Should [the government] do more than it now does, or . . . should not get involved, or . . . the government is doing just about enough . . .	Should do more	Is doing enough	Should not get involved
for the poor? (1982)	59	34	7
for the poor? (1968)	61	33	6
for people on welfare? (1982)	25	56	18
for people on welfare? (1968)	32	57	11
3 Do you think we're coddling the poor . . . or . . . poor people can hardly get by on what the government gives them?	Coddling 23	Can hardly get by 68	No opinion 8
4 Do you think the federal government should spend . . . more money on poverty programs, or . . . less . . . ?	More 59	Less 29	Not sure 12
5 In principle, would you be in favor of a one-cent-a-dollar sales tax to be used to help the poor, or would you be opposed to that?	In favor 57	Opposed 39	No opinion 4
6 Which one of the following alternatives is the best thing to do about the poverty problem?	Best thing to do		
Give . . . education and training for private jobs	71		
Create government jobs for poor people	20		
Provide services like food, clothing, and health care	5		
Make poor people less poor by giving them money	1		
Do nothing and wait for a strong economy to lift poor people out of poverty	2		
Don't know	1		
7 Should federal spending . . . be increased, decreased or kept about the	About		Don't

Table 18.5   (continued)

Question	Response of National Sample (Percentage)			
7 Should federal spending . . . be increased, decreased or kept about the same . . . on	Increased	About same	Decreased	Don't know
Social Security	44	37	3	16
Food stamps	17	37	26	20
Medicare	41	38	4	17
Government jobs for the unemployed	44	26	12	18

Sources: Questions 1 and 3–6, *Los Angeles Times* survey, *Public Opinion*, June/July 1985, pp. 3, 7, 26, 27. Question 2, surveys by Yankelovich, Skelly, and White, ibid., p. 28. Question 7, Center for Political Studies, 1984 postelection survey.

terms. In 1980 President Reagan won his landslide on his promise, among others, to cut spending and thereby reduce inflation. But when the question is put, "Should the government cut services," the response is likely to be quite different. While spending should be cut, services—with a few exceptions like food stamps, welfare and foreign aid—should not. How does the public reconcile that seeming contradiction? The answer is simple: Eliminate waste. When the CPS asked in 1984 whether the government wasted "some" or "a lot" or "not very much" of its tax money, two-thirds answered "a lot." Fewer than 4 percent said "not very much." When the Gallup poll in 1979 asked its sample to put a figure on waste, the median response was 52 cents of every dollar. A year earlier the estimate was 48 cents.[5]

In supporting increased spending for the poor, the public distinguishes sharply among particular programs. It likes programs that give the poor opportunity to earn their livings, and it dislikes "handouts." For every respondent who believes that giving money to the poor is the best solution to the problem of poverty (question 6 in table 18.5), seventy-one specify giving the poor education and training as the best approach and another twenty choose creating government jobs.[6] Asked whether spending on particular programs should be increased, decreased, or kept about the same, more than three times as many respondents in the CPS poll would boost spending for government jobs for the unemployed than would cut it. More than half of all those with opinions favored increased spending for jobs. Social Security and Medicare, which give money to the nonpoor as well as the poor, had overwhelming support. The ratios of budget expanders to budget cutters in those two programs were 15-to-1 and 10-to-1, respectively. But food stamps received more negative than positive votes; those who favored cutting the program outnumbered those who would expand it by a three-to-two majority.

Clearly, the public is making the familiar distinction between the "deserving" and the "undeserving" poor. Training and jobs are perceived as going to the hardworking and the ambitious who are in poverty through no fault of their own, who are the victims of circumstances, and who are willing to help themselves. Welfare and food stamps go to the shiftless and dishonest as well as the industrious; they seem actually to reward laziness, and they hold no promise that those whose poverty is their own fault will be encouraged, or helped, to mend their ways. This distinction comes through sharply in the responses to the second question in table 18.5. A substantial majority believes the government should do more for the poor, but an equally substantial majority believes the government is doing enough already for people on welfare. Indeed, a rather startling 18 percent believes that the government should not be involved in welfare at all. Compared to 1968, the public's support of programs for the poor is essentially unchanged; the 1968 poll found 61 percent believing the government should do more for the poor, compared to 59 percent fourteen years later. But attitudes toward people on welfare have changed markedly for the worse. Only 25 percent in 1982 were in favor of the government's doing more for people on welfare compared to 32 percent in 1968, and the 18 percent who believed the government should not get involved with welfare was up from 11 percent.

Opinion Pattern 4: The Reagan Administration
Is Out of Step with the People on Policies
Toward the Poor—But So Are the Democrats

If the people believe the government should be doing more—and spending more—for the poor, then why, one may ask, are they supporting Ronald Reagan as he cuts, trims, and dismantles the programs the government is now engaged in? The answer is, they don't. They approve of Ronald Reagan for many reasons, but his treatment of the poor is not one of those reasons. On that issue the public has consistently parted company with him. Indeed, if what the Democrats called the "fairness" issue had been the only consideration on the voters' minds in November 1984, Walter Mondale would have won the election.

The fairness issue came into being as soon as the Reagan program was announced in 1981. A Harris poll taken in August of that year—the year of the great dismantlement—found the public already branding it unfair. Asked whether they felt that the Reagan budget and tax cuts would be fair and equitable to various groups or would be unfair and cause hardship, the respondents singled out the poor and the elderly as being unjustly treated.

Table 18.6 Public Response to Service Cuts to Balance the Budget

Services to Be Cut	For the Cuts (Percent)	For Not Balancing the Budget (Percent)
Federal Aid to the Elderly, Poor, and Handicapped	17	83
Social Security	22	78
Federal Health Programs	38	62
Federal Aid to Education	44	56
Defense Spending	49	51
Food Stamp Program	63	37

Source: *Public Opinion*, December/January 1982, p. 28.

Only 43 percent of the respondents with opinions considered the Reagan programs as unfair to people like themselves, but 59 percent thought it unfair to the poor and 63 percent believed it unfair to the elderly and those on pensions.[7]

Throughout 1981 the ABC News/*Washington Post* poll asked its respondents whether they thought President Reagan cared more about serving poor and lower-income people, middle-income people, or upper-income people, or all people equally. In the early months—before the Reagan program had been put forward—he was given the benefit of the doubt; a majority thought he sought to serve all people equally. But by September 54 percent of the respondents with opinions thought he cared more about serving upper-income people, and two months later this figure had risen to 56 percent.[8]

After Reagan demanded an additional $75 billion in spending cuts, Harris asked his sample in September "if the only way to have a chance to balance the federal budget by 1984 were to make sharp cuts in" a series of six items, "would you favor such cuts, or would you favor not balancing the budget?" Of the six items, only food stamps should get the ax, in the public view. The responses are given in table 18.6.

In November the ABC News/*Washington Post* poll found the public realistic, or cynical, about the Reagan administration's ability to eliminate waste in government. The survey asked whether, if Reagan's proposed spending cuts—put in terms of an additional 12 percent reduction—took effect, "will that mainly reduce waste in domestic programs, or will that mainly damage programs the country needs?" By a margin of 54 to 29 percent, the people thought it would mainly damage programs the country needs.[9]

The polls of 1982 and 1983 showed no improvement in the public judgment of the Reagan policies. In both May and August 1982 the ABC/*Washington Post* survey found that the proportion regarding Reagan as caring more about upper-income people had risen to 59 percent of those with opinions. The same poll in February–March 1983 found 67 percent agreeing that Reagan "is a rich man's president" and 63 percent considering him "unfair to the poor."

In 1984, of course, the people reelected him overwhelmingly. But that was not because the country had become as conservative as Ronald Reagan and his Republican party. Those voters who identified "fairness to the poor" as the most important issue in the election cast their ballots four-to-one in favor of Mondale, according to the CBS News/*New York Times* exit poll. The trouble, for him, was just that there were not enough of them. More people said that keeping America prosperous and militarily strong were more important issues, and those voters went heavily for Reagan. He won other votes as a strong leader, as in favor of religion, as a foe of abortion, and so on.

Moreover, while the majority of voters regarded Reagan as too far to the right on domestic social policy, that did not hurt him much, on balance — because the majority saw the Democratic party and its candidate, Walter Mondale, as also far out of line with public opinion — even a little further, actually, than the Reagan Republicans. The 1984 CPS survey asked its respondents to classify themselves as liberal, moderate, or conservative and then characterize parties and candidates. As shown in table 18.7, the average voter perceived Ronald Reagan and the Republicans as far to the right of center and Walter Mondale and the Democrats as almost as far to the left. But because the average of the voters' self-placement came out slightly to the right of center, the electorate was a little closer to the Reagan Republicans than to the Mondale Democrats. The terms liberal and conservative have many meanings, of course, and when the respondents were asked what they had in mind when they used the terms, not many replied with specific references to attitudes toward the poor. But much the same result was found in responses to two other questions that are directly relevant to the topic of this chapter. In regard to whether government spending for services such as health and education should be cut or much expanded, the CPS sample saw Reagan and Mondale as far apart and placed themselves in the middle — but somewhat closer to the perceived Reagan position. The result was similar when the sample was asked whether "the government in Washington should see to it that every person has a job and a

Table 18.7 Comparison of Public Attitudes with Perceived Positions of Parties and Candidates

Question	Response of National Sample (Percent of those with opinions)			
1 In general, when it comes to politics, do you usually think of yourself as a liberal, a con-servative, a moderate, or what?	Liberal	Moderate	Conservative	Placement on 7-point scale
	24	39	38	4.24
. . . of the Republican party . . . ?	18	21	61	4.89
. . . of Ronald Reagan . . . ?	17	20	62	4.96
. . . of the Democratic party . . . ?	54	25	21	3.37
. . . of Walter Mon-dale . . . ?	49	31	20	3.45
2 Some people think the govern-ment should provide fewer services, even in areas such as health and education, in order to reduce spending. Suppose these people are at one end of the scale at point 1. Other people feel it is important for the government to provide many more services even if it means an increase in spend-ing. Suppose these people are at point 7; where would you place yourself on this scale?	Fewer (Pts. 1–3)	Mid-point (Pt. 4)	More (Pts. 5–7)	Placement on scale
	33	36	30	3.94
Where would you place Ronald Reagan?	62	20	18	3.20
Where would you place Walter Mondale?	10	16	74	5.19

good standard of living" or "should just let each person get ahead on his own." The people lean, with Reagan, toward the latter answer, but not nearly as far as they think he does.

The *Los Angeles Times* survey shows that the adverse public reaction to the Reagan policies affecting the poor carry over into 1985. Although 62 percent of the electorate in April approved of the way Reagan was handling his job as president with 31 percent disapproving, only 34 percent ap-proved of the way he was "handling poverty" while 58 percent disapproved.

Table 18.7   (continued)

3 Some people feel the government in Washington should see to it that every person has a job and a good standard of living. Others think the government should just let each person get ahead on his own. Where would you place yourself on this scale? [Government responsibility at point 1, leaving each person on his own at point 7.]	29	23	48	4.29
Where would you place Ronald Reagan?	14	20	66	5.05
Where would you place Walter Mondale?	58	25	17	3.19

Source: Center for Political Studies (CPS), question 1 from pre-election survey, questions 2 and 3 from post-election survey, 1984.
Note: Figures in the placement on scale column are the mean of the placements on the 7-point scale. In the case of question 1 the first three columns of figures are taken from initial responses to the question shown. The final figure is computed from responses to a subsequent question in which respondents were asked to place themselves on a scale ranging from "extremely liberal" (point 1) through "moderate, middle of the road" (point 4) to "extremely conservative" (point 7).

Asked whether they thought the Reagan budget cuts had "left the truly needy unprotected" or whether "the 'safety net' is still in place for these people," 50 percent believed the needy were unprotected compared to 40 percent who thought the safety net remained intact. Those who felt that President Reagan cared more about upper-income and rich people outnumbered by almost two-to-one those who believed he cared equally about every group. And an ABC News/*Washington Post* survey in February found 72 percent of its sample thought the Democratic party would do a better job of protecting the poor, with only 19 percent favoring the Republicans.[10]

In sum, the public opinion data tell us that the answer to the first question asked in the title of this chapter is no. The American people have not lost their social conscience. Their sympathy toward the poor still runs deep. Despite their disillusionment about governmental programs, they still believe that government should be doing more for the poor, not less — and are even willing to pay higher taxes for that purpose. They feel that the Reagan program has been unfair to the poor and that the safety net that Reagan promised would be left in place has in fact been riddled. In the 1984 election the "fairness" issue was one of the few that pulled voters in the direction of Walter Mondale.

Opinion Cycles and Political Cycles

That leads, then, to the second question: When and how will the American people redirect their national government to again express their social conscience—by doing more, and spending more, for the poor, as they want it to? Sooner or later, we can be sure they will. What the people want they ultimately get, because candidates for office and their advisers pore end- lessly over polling data and know that they defy public opinion at their peril.

The public mood, after all, swings back and forth like a pendulum—not with the same regularity but with the same inevitability. The people are no more fixed in conservative attitudes now than they were locked into liberal attitudes twenty years ago at the height of the Great Society. Liberals then thought those days would never end—as the song goes—but they did. And so will these, as surely as those did. Public moods have always followed pendulum swings.

Such a prediction has a solid theoretical base. Relatively few people consider themselves either strong conservatives or strong liberals; only about 20 percent accept either adjective in describing their positions, and barely 3 percent take the extreme positions when asked to place themselves on the seven-point liberal-to-conservative scale. The typical voter, rather, holds a mixture of liberal and conservative attitudes at the same time—liberal on one issue and conservative on another, or, often, both liberal and conserva- tive on the same issue, which is why pollsters can get sharply different results by slightly altering the wording of a question. A voter's views are apt to be not only contradictory but also vague, muddled, uncertain, and changeable, responding to current events and fragments of information. The voters wind up bunched near the center of the liberal-to-conservative scale not because they are fixed and convinced centrists—any more than they are rigid conservatives or liberals—but because they are torn by conflicting impulses. They are ambivalent—a word Everett Ladd constantly returns to in his analyses of political attitudes. "Contemporary political conflict," says Ladd, "is not so much between social groups . . . as it is within individuals."[11] A less charitable way of putting it is that the people, as measured by the majorities of those expressing opinions, want things both ways.

This is evident over the whole range of public issues, as revealed in the polling data:

The majority thinks the government is too powerful and too intrusive. Yet when asked whether the government should guarantee a job to everyone who wants to work and should act to reduce the income gap between rich and poor—all of which means further governmental intrusion into the private economy—a majority says yes.

In regard to poverty, as we have already seen, the majority wants the government to do more for the poor but not for people on welfare—even though those are the poorest of the poor. They want to keep the safety net for the truly needy but stop "giveaways" to the undeserving.

They want taxes cut but not government services—with a few exceptions, such as food stamps—and they also want the budget balanced. (Even so draconian a measure as Proposition 13 in California was sold with the claim that government services would not have to be cut; there was enough waste to be eliminated. When services were indeed cut, the voters felt betrayed—not by the authors of the proposition but by their governmental officials.)

They want the United States to "stand up to the Russians" and prevent the spread of communism. But they do not want to get involved in "another Vietnam," with U.S. troops.

They want to protect and enhance the environment, but not at the expense of economic growth. Or, conversely, they want economic growth, but expect it to be accomplished with no environmental damages. They refuse to accept the notion that tradeoffs are even necessary.

They want an arms control agreement with the Soviet Union but want the United States to insist on superiority in military strength.

They want the government to be tough on criminals, and deny their civil liberties if necessary, but protect the civil liberties of the innocent.

A big majority thinks that decisions on abortion should be left to individual women and their physicians, but almost as large a majority believes abortion should be prohibited except in specified circumstances. In a recent poll a majority of voters agreed with the statement that abortion is murder, but a majority also opposed a constitutional amendment to prohibit it.

They want minorities and women to be given the chance to get ahead, but not at the expense of white males.

And so it goes. The fact that the people want it both ways on most issues gives an advantage to the political candidate who is willing and able to promise it both ways, while the one who feels bound to choose—like Walter Mondale with his promise of a tax increase—gets clobbered. But the loser may have his satisfaction later. When it turns out that in fact the conflicting promises cannot be reconciled, the party and the administration in office have to break some of them, and then they have disgruntled voters on their hands. That is what starts the pendulum on its return swing; when there are enough disappointed electors, they express themselves in the only way they can, by turning the incumbent party out of office and putting the other party in. That is the reason the parties alternate in power.

To put it another way: We noted in table 18.7 that the public is out of sync with both parties; the Republican party is to the right and the Democratic party to the left of the centrist, or ambivalent, electorate. When the Democrats are in power, the voters become more and more aware that the government is too liberal for them. Eventually, they remedy the situation by turning to the conservatives. When the conservatives take over, the people sooner or later come to realize that the new government is too conservative. Meanwhile, they gradually forget why they threw the liberals out in some previous election, so when they are sufficiently fed up they give the liberals another chance.

Over the past century the pendulum swing from the liberal to the conservative end and back again has required about thirty years—which, by coincidence or not, happens to be about the time needed for replacement of one generation by another. The conservatives peaked in the 1890s, the 1920s, the 1950s, and now the 1980s, with Republicans in power. The liberals dominated the 1900s and 1910s, the 1930s, and the 1960s, with Democrats (and the liberal Republican Theodore Roosevelt) holding the White House. If the past rhythms hold, the nation will be in a liberal mood again at least by the 1990s and receptive to Democratic leadership.

But even the Republican party is likely to be at least somewhat more responsive to those who plead for renewed vigorous governmental leadership in attending to the social problems that plague the cities (and rural areas) of America. To repeat, politicians—whether as individuals or as organized in parties—are obsessed with images. They have to be, for political survival depends on their ability to reflect the views of their constituencies. And the weakest element in the Republican image is the one that dates back to Herbert Hoover and the Great Depression, an image of callousness in the face of widespread suffering.

On the like-dislike scale of the 1984 Survey Research Center election poll, the Republican party actually fared worse than the Democrats. The voters liked the GOP for being economical and prudent, for spending and taxing less (the mirror image, of course, of their dislike for the perceived

Democratic waste and profligacy in managing the public purse). But they disliked the Republicans for being, as they saw them, the party of the rich and the powerful, that does not care about the little people, the old and the poor. Well over one quarter of all the people with opinions about the Republican party expressed this complaint in one version or another. That was somewhat more than the number who had objections to the Democrats as liberal overspenders.

There are many reasons that either party always finds it difficult to move toward the center, even when it is clear that that is where the bulk of the electorate resides. Both parties, as the 1988 election approached, witnessed the usual struggle for control between their ideologies—conservative and liberal, respectively—and the pragmatists who would move the party stance toward the center on the whole range of social policy. Both appeared to be moving. The Republicans sounded less extreme in their conservatism, the Democrats more sensible in their liberalism.

Those who are participating in the debate over national urban policy can reasonably anticipate that their concerns and anxieties will find in their new leaders a more receptive audience. The nadir of governmental passivity has passed. A new zenith like that of twenty years ago may be yet a considerable distance in the future. But those who believe that the American social conscience—so happily undiminished through the long period of inaction —should again be effectively expressed through the instrument of government have good reason at this juncture of history to take heart.

19 Eliciting an Effective and Necessary Urban Policy Response

Paul Ylvisaker

Few American mayors have made it into national office—a melancholy prospect that a former boss of mine, Joseph Clark (then mayor of Philadelphia and later U.S. senator from Pennsylvania) early contemplated but managed stubbornly to overcome. He had read Lincoln Steffens's warning that mayors lived too close to the grimy and divisive issues of garbage, potholes, and neighborhood squabbles ever to be seen as potential statesmen of national stature. And Clark made certain that he wouldn't stay as mayor past a single term. He escaped, and from the exalted sanctuary of the U.S. Senate grieved for his mayoral colleagues who had tarried too long.

I've thought of that often when struggling with the difficulty of converting urban problems into national policy. The inescapable reality of urban problems is that they don't easily lend or commend themselves to the political attractions of national action. Presidents have long known that reality and whenever possible have distanced themselves. John Kennedy tried just that, but was finally cornered in the campaign of 1960 by the powerful big-city mayors (so reminiscent of King John and the barons of old) who exacted a reluctant promise of involvement. And one need only scan the history of the presidential obligation to provide biennial statements of "national urban policy" to appreciate how chronic and intense that reluctance is.

And it's become much easier to indulge that reluctance. With voters slipping away into the suburbs, big-city mayors have lost the power they once had in the Democratic party and in national politics. And with business joining the exodus, mayors have lost the anchor of economic alliances they formerly had with downtown. The crisis atmosphere of the sixties for a while gave mayors renewed prominence and leverage, until riots subsided and the nation no longer felt under siege. Nor has it escaped the notice of political vote-counters that participation rates of minority and immigrant electorates are not that impressive.

The essential truth is that not only are urban issues exasperatingly sticky; the agenda that constitutes an urban policy is inherently unpopular. Whereas majority America can rest assured that the system will listen and respond to its needs, the problems of American central cities (historically what have been identified with "urban policy") are a minority concern. Central cities are still losing their more affluent and influential citizens, still accumulating their concentrations of the poor and less influential.

How then does one elicit a national and effective response? So far, the effort has relied on a number of approaches. First, the courts have come to the rescue, committed as they are to human rights and equity irrespective of majoritarian votes and preferences. And the courts have been impressively effective in matters such as education, housing, employment, etc. But now even that urban refuge is being slivered away with the conservative knifing of judicial activism.

Coalition-building has been another device for increasing the leverage of central city leaders. Bringing other interests into the urban tent is an obvious ploy and as American as apple pie; it also helps account for the pervasive use of the phrase "comprehensive urban policy." But even with the recent popularity of "partnerships," the tactic has its limitations. The core concerns of the central city are diluted and often set aside in the course of the alliance; my own experience as commissioner of community affairs in New Jersey was that any urban-aid bill introduced into the legislature quickly became suburban-aid legislation.

Another variant of coalition-building has been a form of jiujitsu—redirecting greater forces to minority advantage. An example is social and tax legislation in which classes of people rather than categories of urban place become the beneficiaries—and in the process, urban concentrations of the aged and the poor find their burdens relieved (as was recently the case when low-income tax relief was enacted as part of federal tax reform). This becomes, in effect, the "nonurban urban policy" advanced by Marshall Kaplan and others.

Still another tactic is that of advocacy, which explicitly and aggressively accepts the condition of a minority cause and borrows on the ancient history of the prophetic role to chide the majority and appeal to the society's instinct for fairness and equity. This last generation's use of that approach represents, I think, one of the noble chapters in American history; but it, too, shows its limitations. Litigiousness has become the corruption of a virtue; and the American conscience seems to be growing calloused, conspicuously so among the leaders of the Reagan administration.

Which returns full circle to the strategy of avoidance. There are several ways of expressing this alternative. One is to define the problems out of existence: we've seen that in the denials of hunger and homelessness in America. One can also downplay and discredit: lower the estimates of urban hardship, blame the victims. Delegation is another attractive device: step aside from the responsibility and leave it to others such as lower levels of government and the private sector to work out and pay for the solutions. That also localizes the problem, cutting it up into less visible, less challenging pieces.

But if there is this one reality, that urban issues are unpopular, there is a matching and equally stubborn reality: what we call urban problems are nationally pervasive, threatening, and consequential. Against all the lessons of history and the cautions of those who founded America, we are encouraging the dividing of this society into two cultures: the suburban culture of the more affluent, and the central city culture of growing poverty and an emerging underclass. Take two examples. One is Boston. The happy news is employment growth, with 75,000 new private sector jobs added in the past decade. But note the contrasts: average family income in constant dollars has fallen by 9 percent in the central city, against a rise of 3 percent in the surrounding metropolitan area. In 1970, 90,000 of Boston's adults were defined as poor; by 1980, even with population loss, that number had risen to 107,000. Forty-two percent of the central city's families now fall below the poverty line; 33 percent lack basic literacy.

The same depressing trends are evident in the New York metropolitan region. According to a recent study conducted jointly by the Regional Plan Association and the Tri-State United Way,[1] 42 percent of the region's households had incomes below $15,000 and together accounted for only 14 percent of the region's total income. The top 17 percent, with incomes over $35,000, garnered over 40 percent of the region's aggregate income.

That haunting and growing disparity has to rank as one of the nation's most urgent problems; it cannot be localized, discounted, or otherwise avoided as just a problem for mayors. The question is not so much whether we have a national urban policy (the kind we've conventionally gone searching for, with all the unreachables of the Holy Grail); it's basically the challenge whether as a nation we're going to struggle explicitly with the problems the urban agenda represents. As we argued in our final publication as the National Research Council's first Committee on National Urban Policy,[2] what is needed is a national commitment and a readiness to consider all sorts of national policies (tax, employment, industrial development, education, training, etc.) in terms of their impact on the special problems of central cities.

Each of us has our own priority list among those problems. Apart from the question of growing social disparities, there are two national-urban linked concerns that have increasingly occupied my own thinking. The first is the turnaround capacity of our individual cities and metropolitan areas, a capacity intimately tied to, and in a major part determining of, our national capacity to adapt to the competitive circumstances of the world's economy. Our NRC study documented how vulnerable individual urban communities are to the change from a manufacturing to a service/knowledge economy. It also showed how much these same communities depended for their adaptation on the local availability of resources ranging from education and research to assistance in training, retraining, and labor mobility. Our nation relies heavily on those local initiatives and adjustments; but they cannot be sustained without national assistance and a national resolve.

I mention that issue first; but my even higher priority goes to our national indifference to the young, particularly those concentrated in our central cities. *This is a generation too precious to waste.* Demographic changes have made it so: we have 25 percent fewer teenagers; the young are no longer, as they were during the baby bulge, a resource in surplus. For the first time since 1972 there are fewer Americans under eighteen than there are citizens over sixty-five—and simply counting the votes demonstrates the likelihood that the concerns of and for the young will take second place. That shortsightedness can and already is costing this nation and its healthy development dearly.

Urbanists, face it! Ours is an uphill fight. Our agenda is undeniably vital, but it will not be attended to simply by verbal discourse on national urban policy. It will take a lot of bashing against the political rocks even to keep the agenda alive. And undoubtedly it will take even more. For in critical respects urban solutions lie outside the dimensions of conventional urban and national policy. Not that money and analysis don't count; they do, and heavily. But urban policy is first and foremost a spiritual challenge. As we discovered in the National Commission on the Secondary Schooling of Hispanics, the critical ingredient in success is the element of caring: a demonstrated belief in those youngsters, a nurturing of their spirit and talents, a pervading sense that they count.

That spiritual dimension of national urban policy is what it will take to convert essentially unpopular (i.e., nonmajoritarian) concerns into an effective national response. And clearly that is what is painfully lacking in the recent presidential leadership, comforting as it has been, of isolating affluence and political passivity.

But this, too, can—and probably will—pass. There's a cyclical nature to urgent national concerns and political response. And without taking recourse to some future crisis, I sense some underlying trends and consensus that might again return the more vital urban concerns to the national agenda. The renewing popularity of Jesse Jackson, the signs of appeal across class and color lines, and the slow but accelerating emergence of political rhetoric about "urban problems," all are harbingers of another time to come. Neal Pierce has recently taken heart from a Gallup poll showing massive support (67–82 percent) for subsidies for low-income housing, mass transit, and other components of national urban policy.[3] James Sundquist, in his chapter in this book, has persuasively documented the continuing nature of that approval over time; it does not seem to be altogether cyclical or episodic. As ever, the art will be to translate this underlying consensus into legislative majorities. And whatever leader sets about doing that, he or she will have to remember the rest of that Gallup poll: less than a majority were willing to pay for the subsidies they favored, and 81 percent who might have been sympathetic to the urban poor wouldn't go to live in their cities.

But whoever said the job would be easy? Only essential.

20

Urban Policy in the Nineties and Beyond: The Need for New Approaches

Marshall Kaplan and Franklin James

The authors in this book remain committed to cities as special or unique places housing special or unique people. Cities play an important economic and cultural role; they are clearly essential to the nation's well-being. Cities play an important acculturation role; they provide safe harbor and a takeoff point for each generation's immigrants and for each region's in- and out-migrants. Finally, cities play an important "houser of last resort" role; they offer shelter to the nation's increasing numbers of poor and near-poor Americans.

Despite the very real commitments—intellectual and romantic—expressed by the authors, almost all express doubt in their respective papers that cities will benefit from federal leadership or federal largess in the future. Clearly, the era of national largess concerning city problems appears to the writers in this book to be over. Urban initiatives no longer appeal to elected or appointed federal officials.

Why? Americans, as Sundquist suggests, still care about the disadvantaged and the downtrodden, large numbers of whom live in cities. Local public and private sector leaders, as Frieden indicates, are still willing to spend time and money to resurrect core areas in cities, particularly when they will turn a buck for involved developers.

No easy answers exist with respect to the reasons for the unpopularity of cities in the halls of Congress and the halls of the federal bureaucracy. The key ones are presented and documented by many of the book's authors. Politics has passed cities by. That is, white flight and decentralization have vitiated the ability of cities to fight and win key political battles. City populations, as James indicates, are disproportionately poor and disproportionately black.

Similarly, although according to Frieden the downtowns and gentrified neighborhoods of a number of cities show some vigor, as Bahl, Pagano,

Apgar, Newman, Edelman, and James suggest, many cities, even some in
the growing sunbelt, reflect serious economic, fiscal, infrastructure, housing, education, and social problems. To many observers, cities are the legacies of a bygone era. The suburbs and beyond are where the political and
market action is and will be.

A New Look

The increasing political impotence and economic weaknesses of cities help
explain why to be an urbanist no longer wins points at parties; or, more
important, generates excitement at congressional hearings. But both hide
or, at a minimum, blur more fundamental factors generating the demise of
national urban policy commitments.

Post-Vietnam and post-Watergate America views with cynicism the 1960s
vision of public policy. No longer do Americans believe that government
plus money means a solution to America's problems. Put another way, skepticism, born of Vietnam and Watergate, concerning what government can
do, juxtaposed with the mixed results of government intervention in the
1960s and 1970s, has placed limits on what the nation politic will tolerate
in terms of new domestic policies.

The public seems to perceive that a Gresham's law governs federal expenditures for urban policy; that is, that good tax money is wasted on
inefficient government action and/or intractable urban problems. This fact
reduces the desire of even the most courageous politicians to articulate
possible new federal urban policies that require significant dollar commitments. More to the point, perhaps, scholarly evaluations, like many of
those in this book, suggesting that cities are still in bad shape, have taken
their toll among urban policy advocates. If "we knew what would work, I
would be willing to give it another shot. But despite billions of bucks, the
problems still remain, and we really don't know what to do."

The marriage between the academic, the politician, and the citizen has
never been as solid. Everyone doubts; no one believes or believes strongly;
national policy has given way to limited demonstrations. Jane Jacobs provides understandable legitimacy to the comprehensive policy doubters when
she decries the lack of wisdom and theory about economic cause-and-effect
relationships. She articulates what many feel when she indicates that

> when a technological enterprise like the design of a machine or a build-
> ing runs into trouble, the appropriate response can be "Back to the draw-
> ing board," meaning the thing is basically sound in conception but needs

to be worked out more carefully. This has also been the response of economists and governments as their economic expectations have crumbled. They have gone over and over and over what they think they already know, trying to use their tools with greater sophistication, shuffling the same old conceptions into new combinations and permutations to run through the computers or the legislatures. However, in the face of so many nasty surprises, arising in so many different circumstances and under so many differing regimes, we must be suspicious that some basic assumption or other is in error, most likely an assumption so much taken for granted that it escapes identification and skepticism.[1]

William Schambra, in his provocative chapter in this book, casts doubts on the political wisdom of recent comprehensive policymakers.

As many have pointed out, the policy approach to social problems was perhaps *the* trademark of the Carter administration. In addition to an urban policy, Carter's agenda included a major jobs and incomes policy and an energy policy; he had plans for major family and neighborhood policies; and he had countless "minor" policies addressing most social ills. . . . In James Fallows's words, Carter "thinks he 'leads' by choosing the correct policy," and so he came to hold "explicit, thorough positions on every issue under the sun."

This view of governance was, in the final analysis, Carter's political undoing. The specific criticisms of his urban policy, suitably amplified, soon came to be applied to his administration as a whole. Commentators across the political spectrum, for instance, complained that Carter was failing to lead the nation because no clear, simple set of priorities, purposes, or goals had emerged from his complicated policy agenda.[2]

Charles Orlebeke and Marshall Kaplan note the difficulties academics and practitioners have in defining acceptable hypotheses concerning city ills and achieving consensus concerning national urban policies. Without knowledge about what works and what doesn't opens doors for the fad of the moment. Yesterday it was public/private sector partnerships; today, it is privatization. Tomorrow, it will likely be an academically defined or practitioner-defined new style of leadership. In this context, only the consulting industry, the university's grant office, and the speechmakers benefit.

Cities and their residents deserve better. While it is unlikely that theoretical breakthroughs will generate a new consensus about urban problems and urban initiatives, the basic decency of Americans expressed in the Sundquist piece may be enough to secure a renewed dialogue on the health and well-being of cities. If this occurs, and if it secures a debate over recent and current urban programs, so much the better. We will, paraphrasing Arthur Schlesinger, be positioning ourselves for the next cycle of American political history,[3] or, in Paul Ylvisaker's terms, be helping to revive America's sense of responsibility for a valued asset—its cities.

At this juncture advocates of cities should probably operate on dual tracks. Track one would generate a thorough evaluation of current models that are articulated to accommodate or explain urban growth and decay. Track two would define politically salable policies that would benefit cities—policies that could win acceptance by Congress and the American people.

Evaluation of Current Models: Track One

Serious issues remain on the table to be resolved prior to any new wave of "comprehensive" urban policies or programs. For example, scholars should examine whether the best urban policy is to foster overall economic growth as suggested by the Reagan administration. Evidence in this regard is not compelling.

Numerous studies suggest that cities, particularly central cities, did relatively well during recent economic down-cycles.[4] Conversely, they did less well during extended up-cycles. Possible explanations for this counterconventional wisdom rests with the availability of federal aid to cushion economic downtrends during the seventies and early eighties. Further, because many manufacturing industries left central cities for the suburbs before recent down-cycles, central cities had already suffered significant losses and may have reached their lowest point.

Data concerning the 1980–86 period indicate that a rising economic tide has not floated all ships or, in this case, all cities equally, and that a rising economic tide has not benefited all crews or all city residents alike. Clearly, as recent Joint Economic Committee of Congress reports indicate, national growth has not eliminated fiscal problems faced by many cities or lessened fiscal disparities between many central cities and their suburbs.[5] Just as clearly, blacks and Hispanics, as various authors in this book have indicated, remain subject to higher levels of unemployment and underemployment than their counterpart white city dwellers.

National economic growth alone, in theory or fact, will not bring many distressed cities back to health. According to some economists, the normal or historical ebb and flow of regional and local markets will help generate city recovery. In brief, they suggest that distressed cities like Newark and Detroit will be returned to grace, if only they wait long enough. Market trends in growing cities will lead to higher costs of housing, the growth of congestion, increased crime, and the spread of pollution. In combination, these negative externalities will cause people and firms to move from once assumedly healthy urban areas back to now-troubled central cities. Denver's brown cloud, LA's smog, Houston's traffic will get so bad that migration trends will be reversed and distressed cities will benefit.

Market equilibrium, as a guiding urban policy theory, sounds nice—in the classroom—but it rarely plays well at city hall. To ask a city to wait on the possibility that renewal will occur because people or firms will get tired of environmental or economic problems in their present locales and decide to relocate is asking much. While equilibrium may lead to urban salvation, or close to it in the long run, waiting for the long run will hurt many people and risk public and private sector investments. Waiting for market factors, or the like, to substitute for urban policies and programs is unlikely to satisfy people, businesses, and political leaders caught up in urban distress. Perhaps if we had better empirical evidence that market factors work, the theory and strategy would sound better. But theology and ideology provide the primary support for the equilibrium advocates among us.

Many urban policy analysts advocate continued federal intervention to respond to city ills. Some suggest that the federal government, if it had the courage and resources, could take steps to slow down or abort the decentralization trends and/or the concentration of social and economic ills facing cities. Others, less heady perhaps, ask the federal government to help cities and their residents adapt to change. They indicate that Berlin walls and/or bundling boards set up by the federal government will not work. While city economic bases change, national urban policy should provide support to the poor and the infirm and should help cities adjust to changing marketplaces. A report developed by the Joint Economic Committee of Congress calls this set of policy initiatives helping cities "grow old gracefully."[6]

Regrettably, neither the aborters or the adjusters have grounded their requests of the federal government on strong testable theories or facts. Given constitutional prohibitions, resource constraints, and political commitments, nothing the feds could or would be able to do would significantly impede historical trends concerning decentralization. Similarly, while policies aimed at making some people's lives better fits the American liberal tradition, they beg the question concerning the proper federal response to distressed cities.

In sum, we still lack a strong theoretically and empirically based construct to guide development of national urban policies. Despite numerous research efforts, we know very little about the precise impact of previous federal initiatives on the long-term health of cities. Finally, there is no real evidence that either the White House and/or Congress have the commitment to move ahead to fill the knowledge gap and, subsequently, define significant national urban policies.

A Nonurban Urban Policy: Track Two

To admit our lack of understanding of what works in cities and to acknowledge the weak political position that cities are in provides the basic wisdom to generate a sound approach to cities and their problems. Marginal politics and minimal intelligence, combined with budget limitations, suggest that a new wave of explicitly urban initiatives are not on the horizon. Instead, urbanists—those who care about cities—should focus on what may be possible. Indeed, what may be possible could well pay off in more visible benefits to cities than the little understood, often symbolic urban policy political gestures of Congress and/or the White House.

National consensus seems to be emerging concerning long-overdue structural reforms concerning federal education, welfare, and infrastructure policies, to name a few. In a similar vein, although not yet visible on the front pages of the media, ferment about U.S. housing policy, or the lack thereof, seems to be percolating through the halls of ivy as well as the halls of Congress. Finally, although the president's proposals about the shifting and sharing of federal responsibilities with state and local government have not seen the light of day, they have generated a healthy dialogue concerning the appropriate roles of the federal government, states, counties, and cities, and of the appropriate relationships between public, private sector, and community groups.

The best urban policy at this juncture in the nation's history, may well be a nonurban policy. That is, the best way to help cities could well be to encourage those fostering national domestic policy reforms to factor in city concerns. Put another way, and perhaps more succinctly, city advocates should try their best to gain the best possible deal they can from the new nonurban policies and programs likely to evolve through the Bush administration and Congress. In this context the following possibilities seem appropriate to consider:

Structural Reform

Proposals to change the roles of federal, state, and local governments and proposals to amend the missions allocated federal agencies often have met with a quick and troublesome response from urbanists. They fear that alternatives to the current set of structural relationships between levels of government and among federal agencies would generate a reduction in the flow of federal funds to cities and/or a reduction in the already diminished power that cities have to influence national policies and programs. Their collective paranoia is well-grounded in recent history. The reader should note Cuciti's and Reischauer's analysis of the effect of the Reagan administration's efforts to shift many federal programs to the states and to share responsibilities with the states in key domestic areas of concern.

But history need not repeat itself. A Bush administration, combined with the goodwill of the American people (Sundquist, Ylvisaker) and their support for efficient and equitable domestic initiatives, should encourage urban policy advocates to support a reevaluation of the effectiveness of the federal system and several federal agencies. At a minimum, urbanists should support options to increase the role of states and to restructure the role of HUD.

Increasing the Role of the States

Up to now cities have been literally and figuratively orphans of the American Constitution. Their brief fling with Washington, generated by the New Frontier and the Great Society initiatives, may well have been just that, brief, limited, and a fling. The Reagan administration has, however, opened up the door to an innovative and perhaps more permanent sorting out of roles, responsibilities, and revenues among states, counties, and cities.

Until recently, states have been relatively silent with respect to urban problem solving. However, the efforts of select states—like Massachusetts and California, in designing innovative welfare reforms; like Mississippi and Texas, in developing significant educational reforms; like Washington and New York, in initiating important infrastructure strategies—suggest that states may be ready to become visible partners in key areas of concern of vital interest to cities.

Significant new "big buck" federal initiatives aimed at cities are unlikely. Conversely, block grants to states aimed at responding to welfare, education, housing, and infrastructure needs—needs that go beyond city boundaries—appear on the congressional horizon.

What seems politically possible may well be of strategic importance to cities. State involvement, if premised on state matching requirements, would extend or leverage limited federal aid. Federal and state funds, if targeted to income or other related national commitments concerning need, would end up flowing in a disproportionate way into cities, given their population mix and visible problems.

Increasing the role of states may provide the key to helping central cities and older suburbs solve what up to now have been intractable problems caused by the concentration of poor people and minorities within their boundaries. Succinctly, state involvement in administering federal block grants, if linked explicitly to state willingness to require tough fair housing initiatives would provide the means to open up suburban housing opportunities for low-income and minority households. Further, state involvement in managing and distributing federal assistance, if tied to state willingness to administer federal welfare and welfare-related programs, would relieve local jurisdictions of fiscal strain.

Changing HUD

Willingness of urban advocates to consider amendments to the federal system should be matched by an equal willingness to consider possible amendments to the role and mission of individual federal agencies. Policies that reflect macroeconomic concerns, if they are to end up assisting cities, may require reconsideration of the role of HUD and other agencies. As Wood and Kaplan indicate, HUD's impact on cities has been and is, at best, questionable.

Up to now HUD's urban policy activities have by and large been limited to advocating the cause of cities to other more powerful peer agencies and the Congress and to drafting the biennial urban policy report—a report that has of late contained little policy and often less hard analysis of urban problems or broader economic problems facing cities. HUD's inability to define and carry out meaningful urban policies has several related causes. The agency has not been able to define and develop a cogent, politically salable definition of its urban role. As Kaplan and Orlebeke indicate, no consistent philosophy has guided HUD's urban policy efforts. Further, as Schambra, Orlebeke, and Kaplan note, President Carter's effort to forge a comprehensive urban policy fell on essentially deaf political ears.

HUD's inability to marshal support of other agencies stems from its own lack of clarity concerning its policy mission and its being among the weakest of federal agencies. Indeed, even internal to HUD, consistency concerning urban policy or programs at any one point in time has been more the exception than the rule. HUD is, in effect, two agencies, one related to housing and one to cities. The twain rarely meet. The more powerful side of HUD—the housing side—legitimately is concerned primarily with housing production, housing market trends, and housing developments in suburbia; the urban policy side of HUD, generally, is concerned with restraining decentralization trends and its perceived corollary suburban housing production.

The Reagan years have not been kind to HUD. Its key programs have been cut or eliminated. Morale of its permanent staff is low. Its importance is marginal. HUD's present status should permit and, indeed, foster a thorough reevaluation of its role.

Wood, in his chapter for this book, has proposed eliminating HUD. Kaplan and James,[7] in a paper prepared for MIT's National Housing Project, suggest possible elimination of HUD's urban policy role. Preparation of the biennial urban policy report could be transferred to either the Council of Economic Advisors or the White House. HUD, Kaplan and James suggest, if it became a focused housing and community development agency that had direct relationships with states and if it secured legislative criteria granting program priority to the poor, might benefit cities in far more important ways than HUD with its present confused urban policy role. Cities would continue to secure the bulk of HUD monies, given the large share of targeted or low-income people within their boundaries. HUD, working through states, could move far more aggressively than in the past to expand area-wide fair housing opportunities. As suggested earlier, states, as the recipients of HUD funds that required as prerequisites the initiation of fair housing approaches, could provide increased housing opportunities outside cities for low-income and minority households.

Welfare Reform

As Paul Ylvisaker, Frank Newman, Franklin James, and Peter Edelman note, a disproportionate number of poor people live in cities. Many of the urban poor are on welfare—welfare often supported by limited city resources.

Over the past twenty or so years welfare and welfare payments have loomed large in public sector budgets. We have relied too greatly on welfare as a solution to the ills of the poor. While scholars like Charles Murray overstate the case against welfare and are overoptimistic concerning community-based substitutes,[8] they speak for increasing numbers of Americans who question why poverty and welfare programs have increased simultaneously. Current reform efforts aimed at linking welfare to jobs through job training, child care, and health care should be supported by urbanists. Such efforts offer hope that a dent can be made in urban poverty and urban joblessness.

During its last session Congress enacted a sweeping overhaul of the nation's welfare system. HR 1720 requires states to set up coordinated job, education, child care, and transportation programs directed at moving welfare recipients from a dependent status to self-sufficiency. The basic thrusts of the law will help recipients and cities. For the individual on welfare, HR 1720 promises new opportunities to secure employment and a decent quality of life; for cities, HR 1720 promises new ways to reduce the increasing fiscal burdens associated with the cost of services and general assistance programs aimed at helping relatively large numbers of poor urban residents.

The act represents progress in developing a humane and efficient welfare approach. Yet it suffers from numerous flaws which should be corrected by Congress. For example, Congress should require states to initiate uniform AFDC-UP standards. Under the law as passed, all states must operate AFDC-UP programs. But some states need only administer the program for as few as six months. Similarly, Congress should remove some states' requirement that one parent in a two-parent welfare family work at least sixteen hours a week. The bottom line concerning work requirements should be defined by states based on household characteristics, the status of the local job market, and a state-recipient plan tailored to household self-sufficiency objectives. Finally, Congress should mandate and help pay for state provision of relevant education, health care, and job placement services during and after an individual's participation in the Job Opportunities and Basic Skills Program (JOBS), the basic program created by the act to assumedly assure participating welfare recipients the necessary training and related services to gain sustained employment. Cut-off dates for child care and Medicaid-related health services should be premised on flexible income criteria rather than on time. As acknowledged by an increasing number of political leaders, more than the JOBS program defined in HR 1720 is needed. Threshold or base standards for welfare are required in a nation committed to treating the poor, irrespective of location, in an equal or fair manner. Unemployed males should not be denied welfare in Colorado and secure welfare in Massachusetts. Failure to land a job through no fault of an unemployed person should not deny uniform access to similar levels of welfare support in all states. Further, as noted by Ylvisaker, special attention to the needs of female-headed poor households and children may well be the measure of how well American society manages its social and, indeed, spiritual commitments. Special attention on enveloping welfare mothers and their children with reasonable and uniform health care, education, and, where appropriate, job training opportunities should be a prelude to providing increased employment opportunities to the persistently poor. In this context, while the public sector jobs provisions of the old CETA program were abused, current experience with the JTPA (Job Training Partnership Act) suggests the need for a new jobs strategy to reach the chronically unemployed. Right now, the JTPA is not getting at large numbers of them. Clearly, although exceptions exist, the JTPA program in many states is providing job training and placement to the most readily employable among the poor. Targeting of JTPA funds should be mandated by Congress. Finally, if we are to reduce the significance of welfare as a strategy to help the poor, we should rethink the public sector as employer of last resort. As noted by Lester Thurow,

> the principal way to narrow income gaps between groups is to restructure the economy so that it will, in fact, provide jobs for everyone. Since we regard the United States as a *work ethic* society, this restructuring should be a moral duty as well as an economic goal. We consistently preach that work is the only "ethical" way to receive income. We cast aspersions on the "welfare" society. Therefore we have a moral responsibility to guarantee full employment. Not to do so is like locking the church doors and then saying that people are not virtuous if they do not go to church.
>
> Since private enterprise is incapable of guaranteeing jobs for everyone who wants to work, then government, and in particular the federal government, must institute the necessary programs. No one should attempt to deny that a real, open-ended, guaranteed job program would constitute a major restructuring of our economy. Patterns of labor market behavior and the outputs of our economy would be fundamentally altered.[9]

Health Initiatives

Congressional and state legislative concern over the absence of adequate insurance coverage for the medically indigent and over the absence of insurance for long-term health care, particularly for the aged, likely will lead to new national initiatives to forge more comprehensive insurance packages. They will come in the form of aid to and requirements of private insurance carriers and employers to extend health care coverage to the working poor or near-poor and to the elderly. They will end up helping cities respond to the health needs of large numbers of their residents and thus should be encouraged by urbanists.

Efforts to extend the coverage of Medicaid to the working poor—coverage reduced by the Reagan administration—will likely occur in Congress. Such

efforts should be supported by cities and their friends in light of the disproportionate share of the working poor now living in cities. Further, the cluster of services available to welfare recipients must include, at a minimum,
preventative and primary health care if recipients are to sustain job commitments. Increased national and state initiatives to assure the availability of
health care options to the working poor undoubtedly will be developed over
the next few years. Apart from increases in insurance and medicaid coverage — increases extending the demand for health services — federal and state
governments will be required to address the supply of health services. While
the availability of extended insurance and Medicaid coverage will help providers match revenues to costs, a more comprehensive look at provider
costs and revenues will be necessary if state and local governments are to
assure their low-income residents an adequate number of baseline health
care services. Federal action to evaluate current gaps between services and
revenue will likely occur and should command the attention of urban
advocates.

Education Options

Education remains on almost everybody's list concerning national priorities. The President's Commission[10] served us well. Although its rhetoric
concerning the "rising tide of mediocrity" was not matched by the bold-
ness of its policy recommendations, the report did put education on our
intellectual and emotional front burner. Clearly, efforts by the federal government to strengthen urban school districts would benefit cities. Apart
from expanded block grants for education to make up for reduced urban tax
bases, cities will be helped by "nonurban federal policy" initiatives in the
educational area that would:

   1. Help integrate urban school districts. Efforts to significantly improve
urban schools will lead to marginal results unless and until school integration becomes a reality. Strategies that increase integrated housing opportunities and/or the increased use of metropolitan-wide plans to integrate schools
would help make school integration a fact of urban life. Both should become a prerequisite to receipt of any federal funds by state and local
governments.

   School districts should be provided with funds to support desegregation
efforts and to test innovative approaches to desegregation. Regrettably, the
nation has relied on schools as the primary vehicle to integrate itself. Other
institutions, including the federal and state governments, often accept the
role of cheerleader rather than active participant. The schools have done

admirably well—often against long odds. But their continued roles in helping society integrate should be premised on federal as well as state willingness to pick up a larger share of school costs associated with local integration initiatives.

2. Provide youngsters with certainty concerning college and jobs if they stay in school. An increase in college loans and grants to poor youngsters who commit to remaining in school would be a practical way to reduce junior high and high school dropouts. Job vouchers for high school graduates and summer interns would be both a practical and efficient way to provide incentives to students who remain in and graduate from our nation's high schools.

3. Increase the quality of our nation's public universities and community colleges. Higher admission standards, reformed curriculum, and better teaching would expand the educational opportunities for bright urban, suburban, and rural kids. Greater market segmentation between universities, community colleges, and state colleges would enhance choices open to students. Increased loans and grants would make college a real choice for many low-income youngsters.

4. Increase the quality and quantity of preschool education opportunities. Although not always uniform, evaluations of Head Start and other preschool programs generally receive high marks. They have helped children from low-income families or households gain a firmer base upon which to build or take advantage of their subsequent educational experiences. Absence of funding has made their availability often unpredictable and subject to chance. Federal initiatives to assist communities provide uniformly good preschool facilities and activities would extend educational opportunity to the needy and would help urban school districts and cities, in the process, respond to a real need.

Infrastructure

Our nation's potholes and inadequate water supplies know no boundaries. They are reflected in all types of jurisdictions—cities, suburbs, rural areas.

Cities, however, as Pagano indicates, illustrate a major part of the infrastructure problem. Older cities, particularly, face seemingly insurmountable problems. Weak fiscal positions combined with an aging and outmoded physical plant generate a Catch-22 situation. To raise taxes to fund infrastructure needs exacerbates white flight and limits the delivery of needed social services.

Federal resource problems make any new large federal grant program unwise and unlikely. Congress, however, probably would be willing to consider the following:

1. The creation of a national infrastructure bank. The bank would lend states and cities funds for infrastructure construction and maintenance purposes. Loan funds would be secured from the taxable bond market. Loans would be made at low or no interest. Initial capitalization would be recycled as states and cities repaid loans. Grant monies, if and when available, would be targeted to the most distressed cities. They would be premised on city willingness to respond to priority maintenance and development needs.

2. The relaxation of legislative and administrative rules governing federal infrastructure aid. Often, current federal regulations deny states and cities the ability to use existing federal programs in a locally relevant manner. They should be amended to assure an increased "fit" between local needs and federal funds.

3. The linking of federal mandates imposed on states and cities concerning infrastructure development and maintenance to federal aid. The federal government often asks states and cities to meet national standards concerning road design, clean water, waste disposal, etc. Very often federal prescriptions are not matched by federal assistance. This fact often has forced cities to skew expenditure patterns and to face severe fiscal constraints. As recommended by the report "Hard Choices,"[11] prepared by the Joint Economic Committee of Congress, Congress should match its efforts to set national standards with funds.

All of these options will help cities. They should be encouraged by urbanists.

Housing

Federal housing initiatives and programs, by and large, have become a casualty of budget exigencies. The withdrawal of the Feds, most recently symbolized by the Reagan administration's proposal to sell off FHA, permits us to rethink possible new federal housing efforts. Clearly, the economy and the politics of the time will not stand major new large dollar initiatives.

Currently, federal housing costs reflect both tax incentives provided the middle class and the direct expenditures provided the poor. Serious inequities abound. The affluent receive nearly four times as much benefit as the poor. Assuming a willingness of Congress to retain the total amount of federal funds now spent on housing, but to provide a fairer distribution of such funds, more money would be available to help respond to the affordability and substandard housing problems of the poor and near-poor. Placing a cap on or eliminating the deductibility privileges associated with the property tax and mortgage interest would allow a transfer of significant monies for housing vouchers and for revitalization of a rapidly decaying stock of public housing. In a similar way it could generate the support funds for a limited, but strategic, block grant program aimed at increasing housing production in tight markets for low- and moderate-income households.

Bipartisan support, both in Congress and the nation, seems to exist for a toughening of the nation's fair housing laws. Increased reliance on administrative rather than judicial adjudication would be a proper amendment to current laws. It would make enforcement more efficient. Strengthening penalties for discrimination would grant present antidiscrimination approaches more relevance to the nation's rural as well as urban communities.

Public-Private Nonprofit and Community
Group Collaboration

Good ideas often make good dinner speeches. Ideas incapable of being translated to action often put people to sleep. The concept of public-private, community group, and nonprofit sector partnerships is as old as the development of the transcontinental railroad and other public improvements and as new as the many efforts now occurring to revitalize city downtowns. If, however, partnerships are to become more than limited project idiosyncracies, more time will have to be devoted to proper ground rules that protect the public interest. As Frieden notes, ways also will have to be found to extend collaboration beyond downtown to the neighborhood. Similarly, as Roberts and Portnoy suggest, means will have to be explored to leverage limited public sector dollars with private sector and foundation monies.

Despite waving the public/private sector wand over the nation, the administration has done precious little to translate hopes to pervasive reality. Tax reform has reduced incentives for the private sector to engage in development partnerships with the public sector, foundations, and community groups. The Tax Reform Act of 1986 restricted tax exemption for municipal bond issues that assist private businesses. It also set strict limits on the purposes and dollar amounts associated with redevelopment bonds. The UDAG program—a program aimed at using limited federal dollars to leverage private sector investment—has been cut back. No new initiatives have been taken to extend positive experiences concerning community development corporations by the administration.

Congress, in light of its many oversight functions, will likely examine partnership efforts around the country, particularly those involving UDAG assistance and/or tax exemption. Its foci, hopefully, will be both on the definition of clear-cut public sector objectives and on the development of appropriate federal roles. Both are necessary to protect the public's interest in partnership efforts and to foster partnership efforts in community development. Urbanists should feel comfortable in supporting these congressional efforts.

Paying for a Nonurban Urban Policy

Many of the nonurban urban policy initiatives that Congress will consider will cost money. Just how *much* is still open to debate. To ask for favorable treatment from Congress for cities requires urbanists to recognize the need to cut or reduce many nonessential, inefficient, or inequitable programs, some of them heretofore politically sacrosanct. Supporters of cities can't have it both ways.

Urban scholars and practitioners should acknowledge and support the need to significantly reduce the growth of and even cut back on both Medicare and Social Security expenditures as well as other non-means-tested entitlement programs. They should support a focused, budget-cutting review of many programs, such as agricultural subsidies and federal pensions, whose scope and costs raise questions of fairness and effectiveness. They also should encourage national political leaders to consider further tax reforms, particularly reforms that close remaining tax loopholes and restrain related tax expenditures. Finally, they should not avoid the probability that an effective national response to human capital and infrastructure needs will require tax increases, given current and projected budget deficits.

Prologue

The authors in this book have examined America's attempts to forge an urban policy or policies. They have found both the effort and the product wanting. Paraphrasing John Kennedy, the journey toward a successful, fair, and efficient urban policy must begin with an extended national dialogue concerning its likely impact, objective, and priorities. Paraphrasing an unknown urban philosopher, there are many ways to skin a cat. Hopefully, this book will help reaffirm the importance of cities and the need for a national discussion on appropriate urban and nonurban policies that will assist troubled cities return to health.

Notes

Preface

1 Robert C. Weaver, "The First Twenty Years of HUD," *American Planning Association Journal* (Autumn 1985): 470.

**1 City Need and Distress in the United States
1970 to the Mid-1980s**

1 Recent discussions of such trends in U.S. cities include Paul E. Peterson, ed., *The New Urban Reality* (Washington, D.C.: Brookings Institution, 1985); and the National Urban Policy Advisory Committee, *Urban American 1984: A Report Card* (Washington, D.C.: Joint Economic Committee of the U.S. Congress, 1984). See also U.S. Department of Housing and Urban Development (HUD), *The President's National Urban Policy Report: 1986* (Washington, D.C.: U.S. Government Printing Office, 1986); and Royce Hanson, ed., *Rethinking Urban Policy: Urban Development in an Advanced Economy* (Washington, D.C.: National Academy Press, 1983).

2 A good summary of program and analytic indicators of distress is provided in George Steinlieb, et al., "Measuring Urban Distress: A Summary of the Major Urban Hardship Indices and Resource Allocation Systems" (New Brunswick, N.J.: Rutgers University Center for Urban Policy Research, June 1980).

3 HUD, *The President's National Urban Policy Report: 1978* (Washington, D.C.: 1979).

4 To my knowledge, only one previous effort has been made to calculate a single distress index at two or more points in time so as to describe changes in the relative needs of various cities. The distress index used in this earlier study is highly dubious, relying heavily on pre-1940 housing and population changes. These factors are widely criticized as indicators of distress. The study is Richard P. Nathan and Paul R. Dommel, "Targeting Federal Grants on Community Distress" (Washington, D.C.: HUD, February 1979).

5 For a seminal effort to develop such an index, see Richard P. Nathan and Charles Adams, "Understanding Central City Hardship," *Political Science Quarterly* (Spring 1976).

6 Peggy Cuciti, *City Need and the Responsiveness of Federal Grants Programs* (Washington, D.C.: Congressional Budget Office, 1978).

7 Gordon L. Clark, *Interregional Migration, National Policy, and Social Justice* (Totowa, N.J.: Rowman and Allenhold, 1985).

8 See Robert W. Burchell et al., *The New Reality of Municipal Finance* (New Brunswick, N.J.: Rutgers University Center for Urban Policy Research, 1984).

9 George E. Peterson, "Finance," in Nathan Glazer and William Gorham, eds., *The Urban Predicament* (Washington, D.C.: Urban Institute, 1976).

10 Resident need is calculated first by normalizing each of the three indicators to express values in a particular city relative to values in the nation as a whole; then a weighted average of the normalized values is calculated.

11 For purposes of the index of resident need, the change in per capita income term is defined as follows:

$$PCI_i^{t,t+1} = \frac{\dfrac{PCI_i^{t}}{PCI_i^{t+1}}}{\dfrac{PCI_{Nat}^{t}}{PCI_{Nat}^{t+1}}}$$

where i denotes an individual city and Nat denotes national figures.

12 Harold L. Bunce and Sue G. Neal, "Trends in City Conditions During the 1970s" (Washington, D.C.: HUD, August 1983).

13 Ibid.

14 Ibid.

15 Katharine L. Bradbury, Anthony Downs, and Kenneth Small, *Urban Decline and the Future of American Cities* (Washington, D.C.: Brookings Institution, 1982).

16 As before, the data used to measure resident need were normalized as ratios to national values for the variables during the study period. Thus, resident need roughly indicates the economic well-being of residents of the city relative to the well-being of the U.S. population as a whole in 1970.

17 Reflecting this policy linkage, the congressional requirement that the president prepare a biennial urban policy report was made in Title VII of the National Urban Policy and New Community Development Act of 1970.

18 For an analysis of city economic well-being as of the late 1960s and early 1970s, see John F. Kain, "The Distribution and Movement of Jobs and Industry," in James Q. Wilson, *The Metropolitan Enigma* (Garden City, N.Y.: Anchor Books, 1970).

19 The seven cities on the 1970 highest-need list and *not* on the 1980 list are New Orleans, El Paso, Birmingham, Sacramento, Miami, San Antonio, and Oakland. The seven cities in the 1980 highest-need list and *not* on the 1970 list are Detroit, Atlanta, Baltimore, Buffalo, Philadelphia, New York, and Chicago.

20 Nathan and Dommel, "Targeting Federal Grants."

21 Ibid.

22 It should be emphasized that these measures of resident need are not strictly comparable to those estimated earlier. The main reason is that the most recent

poverty data used to compute the measures do not control for family or household size. As a result, the need indexes incorporating recent data cannot be compared with the earlier indexes. Trends in resident need between 1980 and mid-decade can be measured with some confidence because exactly similar data were used in both years.

23 HUD, *The President's National Urban Policy Report: 1978.*

24 For two excellent assessments of the impact of Reagan administration policies, see John L. Palmer and Isabel V. Sawhill, *The Reagan Record* (Washington, D.C.: Urban Institute, 1984); and Richard P. Nathan and Fred C. Doolittle, *The Consequences of Cuts* (Princeton, N.J.: Princeton University Urban and Regional Research Center, 1983).

25 HUD, *National Urban Policy Report: 1986.*

2 The New Anatomy of Urban Fiscal Problems

1 See also Roy Bahl, "The New Urban Fiscal Economics," in Michael E. Bell, ed., *State and Local Finance in an Era of New Federalism* (Greenwich, Conn.: JAI Press, 1987.)

2 See Roy Bahl and William Duncombe, "State and Local Government Finances: Was There a Structural Break in the Reagan Years?," in *Growth and Change*, forthcoming. This change was undoubtedly spurred in part by the tax and expenditure limitations of the late 1970s. It appears that there was a "structural break" in state and local government financial policy around this time.

3 Some of the earlier sections of this chapter draw from Roy Bahl, "Can Urban Governments Cope with the Newest Federalism?" Presidential Address, National Tax Association–Tax Institute of America, Hartford, Conn., November 10, 1986.

4 A more detailed statistical analysis of the surplus issue is in Bahl and Duncombe, "State and Local Government Finances."

5 See David J. Levin, "State and Local Government Fiscal Position in 1987," *Survey of Current Business* (February 1988), pp. 25–27.

6 The BEA work is reported periodically in the *Survey of Current Business.* The most recent analysis is David J. Levin and Donald L. Peters, "Receipts and Expenditures of State Governments and of Local Governments: Revised and Updated Estimates, 1983–86" *Survey of Current Business* (November 1987), pp. 29–35.

7 Steven Gold regularly tracks the financial condition of state governments for the National Conference of State Legislatures. His most recent reporting is "Developments in State Finances, 1983 to 1986," *Public Budgeting and Finance* (Spring 1987), pp. 5–23.

8 Phillip Dearborn has for many years followed the budgetary position of large cities. His earlier work for the Advisory Commission on Intergovernmental Relations, *City Financial Emergencies: The Intergovernmental Dimension* (July 1972) and *Bankruptcies, Default and Other Local Government Financial Emergencies* (March 1985), give a good comparative view of the changing financial condition of cities. His most recent reporting is in "Fiscal Condi-

tions in Large American Cities, 1971–1984," a paper prepared for the National Academy of Sciences, Committee on National Urban Policy, July 1986.

9 Levin and Peters cite decreased use of debt financing, which does not appear in the general surplus measure, as one explanation. However, census data from *Governmental Finances* do not support this explanation. Total debt outstanding (in 1982 dollars) for local governments has grown faster in the 1980s than in the 1970s. See Levin and Peters, "Receipts and Expenditures, 1983–86," p. 30.

10 Based on NIA data, aid to local governments fell from 38.1 percent of state government expenditures in 1970 to 35.7 percent in 1986. See Levin and Peters, "Receipts and Expenditures, 1983–86," p. 30, and David J. Levin and Donald Peters, "Receipts and Expenditures of State Governments and Local Governments: Revised and Updated Estimates, 1959–84," *Survey of Current Business* (May 1986), pp. 26–33.

11 Between FYS 1979–83 Texas and Alaska accounted (on average) for 45 percent of total general fund balances. By FY 1986 both states were in deficit. See Steven Gold, "State Government Fund Balances, Financial Assets, and Measures of Budget Surplus," *Federal-State-Local Fiscal Relation: Technical Papers*, vol. 2, U.S. Department of the Treasury (Washington, D.C.: U.S. Government Printing Office, 1986); and National Conference of State Legislatures, *State Budget Actions in 1987*, Legislative Finance Paper 59 (Denver: National Conference of State Legislatures, 1987).

12 Dearborn, "Fiscal Conditions in Large American Cities, 1971–1984," p. 36.

13 National League of Cities, *City Fiscal Conditions in 1986*, a Research Report of the National League of Cities, July 1986.

14 National League of Cities, *City Fiscal Conditions in 1987*, a Research Report of the National League of Cities, July 1987.

15 For a review of this literature, see Bahl, *Financing State and Local Governments in the 1980s*.

16 Katherine L. Bradbury, "Urban Decline and Distress: An Update," *New England Economic Review* (July–August 1984), pp. 39–55.

17 Helen Ladd, John Yinger, Katherine Bradbury, Ronald Ferguson, and Avis Vidal, *The Changing Economic and Fiscal Conditions of Cities* (Cambridge, Mass.: John F. Kennedy School of Government, Harvard University, 1986).

18 Daniel Garnick, "Local Area Economic Growth Patterns: A Comparison of the 1980s and Previous Decades," paper prepared for the National Academy of Sciences, July 1986.

19 Metropolitan core counties have a population greater than 1 million.

20 Roy Bahl, Bernard Jump, Jr., and Larry Schroeder, "The Outlook for City Fiscal Performance in Declining Regions," in Roy Bahl, ed., *The Fiscal Outlook for Cities: Implications of a National Urban Policy* (Syracuse, N.Y.: Syracuse University Press, 1978).

21 Real per capita state aid was reduced from $425 in 1979 to $401 in 1983 and has since risen to $441 in 1986. This is based on data from the Bureau of the Census, *Governmental Finances*, and is deflated using the implicit GNP deflator for state and local government purchases.

22 John D. Kasarda, "The Regional and Urban Redistribution of People and Jobs in the United States," paper prepared for The National Academy of Sciences, Committee on National Urban Policy, July 1986.

23 See Gold, "Developments in State Finances," pp. 5–23; and Levin, "State and Local Government Fiscal Position in 1987."

24 Since the NIPA surplus includes spending financed by borrowing but excludes proceeds from borrowing, an increase in capital spending financed by borrowing will reduce the general surplus. See Levin, "State and Local Fiscal Positions in 1987," pp. 25–27.

25 The importance of trying to control the cost of fringe benefits is even more obvious when it is recognized that the $5,158 per employee for supplements to basic wages understates the true cost of fringes. That is to say, an employee receives additional fringe benefits in his paycheck in the form of paid vacations, holiday pay, sick leave, and so forth. When the cost of this pay for time not worked is subtracted from wages and added to the cost of supplements to gross wages, the actual cost of fringe benefits for the typical municipal employee is likely to be equivalent to between 40 and 50 percent of pay for time worked.

26 Detail on the reconstitution of the MSAs is available from the authors.

27 The census discontinued reporting data for all counties in an MSA in 1984. We have used the counties which were reported for 1984 and 1985, although these results are not strictly comparable to those for previous years.

3 Reengaging State and Federal Policymakers in the Problems of Urban Education

The authors would like to thank Pat Callan, B. J. Holmes, Rex Brown, and Van Dougherty for their comments on earlier drafts and Sherry Walker for her editorial assistance. The authors are grateful to Lucy Isenhart and Patty Flakus-Mosqueda for their assistance in pulling together various pieces of data presented and to Judi Nicholes for helping to prepare the manuscript. As always, the views presented in this chapter are the authors' alone.

1 National Governors' Association, *Bringing Down the Barriers* (Washington, D.C.: National Governors' Association, 1987); Andrew Hahn and Jacqueline Danzberger with Bernard Lefkowitz, *Dropouts in America: Enough is Known for Action* (Washington, D.C.: Institute for Educational Leadership, March, 1987); William B. Johnston and Arnold E. Packer, *Workforce 2000: Work and Workers for the Twenty-First Century* (Indianapolis, Ind.: the Hudson Institute, June, 1987); Research and Policy Committee of the Committee for Economic Development, *Children in Need—Investment Strategies for the Educationally Disadvantaged* (Washington, D.C.: Committee for Economic Development, 1987); The W. T. Grant Foundation Commission on Work, Family and Citizenship, *The Forgotten Half: Non-College Youth in America* (Washington, D.C.: The W. T. Grant Foundation Commission, January 1988). Other important reports include the following: Council of Chief State School Officers, *Assuring School Success for Students At Risk* (Washington, D.C.: Council of Chief State School Officers, Statement Adopted November 16, 1987); Gordon Berlin and Andrew Sum, *Toward A More Perfect Union: Basic Skills, Poor Families and*

Our Economic Future, Occasional Paper #3, Project on Social Welfare and the American Future, (New York: the Ford Foundation, February, 1988); The Board of Trustees *An Imperiled Generation: Saving Urban Schools* (Princeton, N.J.: The Carnegie Foundation for the Advancement of Teaching, 1988).

2 Lisabeth B. Schorr, with Daniel Schorr, *Within Our Reach: Breaking the Cycle of Disadvantage* (New York: Anchor Press-Doubleday, 1988).

3 U.S. Bureau of the Census, *Statistical Abstract*, 1987, table 35.

4 U.S. Bureau of the Census, *General Social and Economic Characteristics, 1980, U.S. Summary*, tables 74 and 75.

5 U.S. Bureau of the Census,' *Statistical Abstract of the United States*, 1987, table 19.

6 U.S. Bureau of the Census, *General Social and Economic Characteristics, 1980, U.S. Summary*, tables 149, 159.

7 Ibid., tables 141, 151.

8 William Julius Wilson, *The Truly Disadvantaged: The Inner City, the Underclass, and Public Policy* (Chicago: University of Chicago Press, 1987), p. 46.

9 Ibid.

10 Ibid., p. 49.

11 Ibid., p. 55.

12 Phone conversation with Sue Hendricks of the Urban Institute, March 29, 1988.

13 Ibid.

14 William Julius Wilson, *The Truly Disadvantaged*, pp. 25–26.

15 Ibid., pp. 56–68.

16 "In the fall of 1986, 24 percent of black high school graduates—243,000 young men and women—were unemployed. Perhaps countless more were underemployed." Quoted from William E. Cox and Catherine C. Jobe, "Recruiting Wars: Can Higher Education Compete with the Military," *Educational Record*, Fall 1987–Winter 1988, p. 69.

17 U.S. Bureau of the Census, *General Social and Economic Characteristics, 1980, U.S. Summary*, tables 143 and 153.

18 U.S. Department of Education, *Condition of Education,* 1987, table 1:27-2.

19 Allan Ornstein, "Urban Demographics for the 1980s: Educational Implications," *Education and Urban Society* 16:477–96, cited in Jeannie Oakes, "Improving Urban Schools: Possibilities and Problems in Current District Reforms" (Santa Monica, Calif.: CPRE and the Rand Corporation, October 1987).

20 Council of Great City Schools, "Condition of Great City Schools, 1980–1986" (Washington, D.C.: Council of Great City Schools, 1987), chart 3.

21 Ibid., chart 4.

22 Ibid., chart 5.

23 U.S. Department of Education, *Condition of Education, 1987*, p. 64; and Council of Great City Schools, "Condition of Great City Schools, 1980–1986" (Washington, D.C.: Council of Great City Schools, 1987), chart 5.

24 Gary Orfield, "School Segregation in the 1980s: Trends in the States and Metropolitan Areas," Metropolitan Opportunity Project (Chicago: University of Chicago, July 1987).

25 Ibid.

26 The Chicago Panel on Public School Policy and Finance, *Dropouts from the Chicago Public Schools* (Chicago: Chicago Panel on Public School Policy and Finance, 1987).

27 Gary Orfield, "Race Income and Educational Inequality: Students and Schools at Risk in the 1980s," a discussion paper prepared for the Council of Chief State School Officers: cited with permission of the council.

28 Aspects of this process have been described by several authors including John I. Goodlad in his book, *A Place Called School: Prospects for the Future* (New York: McGraw-Hill, 1984); Dolores Grayson and M. Martin, *Gender Expectations and Student Achievement: A Teachers Handbook* (Earlham, Iowa: The Graymill Foundation, 1986); and Jawanza Kunjufu, *Developing Positive Self-Images and Discipline in Black Children* (Chicago: African-American Images, 1984).

29 John I. Goodlad, *A Place Called School*; and Jeannie Oakes, *Keeping Track* (New Haven, Conn.: Yale University Press, 1985).

30 Ibid., p. 152.

31 See John Ogbu, "Schooling the Inner City," *Society*, November/December 1983 for a discussion of a court case brought by blacks against the San Francisco school district. Plaintiffs presented evidence that was accepted by the court in its favorable decision for the complainants, that black children who in 1976–77 made up only 31 percent of the total school enrollment constituted 53 percent of all children in educable, mentally retarded classes. In the twenty California school districts which enrolled 80 percent of all black children in the public schools, blacks composed only 27.5 percent of the schools' enrollment but constituted 62 percent of the educable, mentally retarded population. According to Ogbu the figures for San Francisco are similar to those for Chicago, Los Angeles, New York, Washington, D.C., and other large cities.

32 The National Coalition of Advocates for Students found that in 1982 blacks accounted for 16 percent of student enrollment but only 8 percent of placements in gifted and talented programs. Cited in Michelle Fine, "Deinstitutionalizing Educational Inequity: Contexts Which Constrict and Construct the Lives and Minds of Public School Adolescents," paper presented to the Council of Chief State School Officers, 1987, cited with permission of CCSSO.

33 Goodlad, *A Place Called School*; Henry Levin, "Accelerating Schooling," paper presented to the Council of Chief State School Officers, 1987, cited with permission of CCSSO; Jeannie Oakes, *Keeping Track*; and David Seeley, *Education Through Partnership* (Washington, D.C.: American Enterprise Institute, 1984).

34 Henry Levin, "Accelerating Schooling."

35 Suzanne Soo Hoo, "School Renewal: A Voice in Blocking the Barriers of Access, A Vision in Changing the Conditions in The School," working paper, 1988, Center for Educational Renewal, University of Washington and the College Board.

36 Henry Levin, "Accelerating Schooling."

37 Cited in Carol Ascher, *Trends and Issues in Urban and Minority Education, 1987*, Eric Clearinghouse on Urban Education, Teachers College, Columbia University.

38 Ibid.
39 Chicago Panel on Public School Policy and Finance, *Dropouts from the Chicago Public Schools.*
40 Michelle Fine, "Deinstitutionalizing Educational Inequity."
41 Ascher, *Trends and Issues*, p. 21.
42 Michelle Fine, "Deinstitutionalizing Educational Inequity."
43 John Ogbu, "Schooling the Inner City," *Society*, November/December, 1983.
44 Ibid.
45 Michelle Fine and Pearl Rosenberg, "Dropping Out of High School: The Ideology of School and Work," *Journal of Education*, vol. 165, no. 3, Summer, 1983.
46 Jean Anyon, "Social Class and the Hidden Curriculum of Work," *Journal of Education*, vol. 162, no. 1, Winter, 1980.
47 Ibid.
48 Michelle Fine, "Deinstitutionalizing Educational Inequity."
49 Ibid.
50 De Lone, Richard H., *Small Futures: Children, Inequality, and the Limits of Liberal Reform* (New York: Harcourt Brace Jovanovich, 1979).
51 The ideas presented here benefited from four meetings that ECS has sponsored. The first was the Working Party on Building Collaborative Strategies to Serve Youth At-Risk, chaired by Hillary Clinton and cosponsored by the Council of Chief State School Officers and the National Alliance of Business. The second was called "Youth 2000: The Leadership Team," and also was cosponsored by the Council of Chief State School Officers and the National Alliance of Business. The third major forum was the ECS National Forum for Youth At Risk, convened by Governor Bill Clinton and cosponsored by the Interstate Migrant Education Council. The fourth set of meetings brought interested foundation program officers together to discuss urban education.
52 For a related perspective on school reform and urban education, see Jeannie Oakes, *Improving Inner City Schools: Current Directions in Urban District Reform* (New Brunswick, N.J.: Center for Policy Research in Education, 1988).
53 National Governor's Association Task Force on Readiness, *Time for Results: The Governors' 1991 Report on Education* (August 1986); Grubb, W. Norton, *Young Children Face the States*, (Center for Policy Research in Education, May 1987); National Black Child Development Institute, *Safeguards: Guidelines for Establishing Programs for Four-Year-Olds in the Public Schools* (Washington, D.C.: National Black Child Development Institute, Inc.; 1987); and Cowhick, Timothy, *Early Intervention Efforts* summary of the ECS Survey of State Initiatives for Youth At Risk (Denver: Education Commission of the States, 1988).
54 Results gathered in the *ECS Survey of State Initiatives for Youth At Risk* (1987).
55 Epstein, Joyce L., "Parent Involvement: State Education Agencies Should Lead the Way," *Community Education Journal*, July, 1987; Education Commission of the States, "Drawing in the Family: Selected Readings" (Denver: Education Commission of the States, May 1988).
56 *Ibid*; and Barbara Lindner, *Parent Involvement* summary of the ECS Survey of State Initiatives for Youth at Risk (Denver: Education Commission of the States, 1987).

57 Margaret E. Mahoney quoted in "The President's Report: Mentors," the 1988 Annual Report of the Commonwealth Fund, Harkness House, 1 E. 75th Street, New York, N.Y.

58 Coalition of Essential Schools, "Prospectus: 1984 to 1994," (Providence, R.I.: Brown University, 1984); and Beverly Anderson, "The Re: Learning Project" (Denver: Education Commission of the States, 1988).

59 Rodriguez, Esther, Patrick McQuaid and Ruth Rosauer, *Community of Purpose: Promoting Collaboration Through State Action* (Denver: Education Commission of the States, February 1988).

60 For a thorough discussion of the role of community regeneration in school renewal in urban areas see Rona Wilensky and D. M. Kline III, *Renewing Urban Schools: The Community Connection* (Denver, Colo.: The Education Commission of the States, 1988).

61 Though not so long in Denver's case, see Susan Klein Marine, Rona Wilensky, and Cindi Yantz, *A Profile of Poverty in Metropolitan Denver* (Denver: The Piton Foundation, April 1987).

4 Urban Poverty: Where Do We Go from Here?

1 Bureau of the Census, U.S. Department of Commerce, "Money, Income, and Poverty Status in the United States; 1987," (Series P-60, no. 161, August 1988), pp. 1, 2, and 7.

2 Ibid., p. 7.

3 Ibid., p. 2.

4 Ibid.

5 Ibid.

6 Ibid., p. 8.

7 Ibid.

8 Ibid., p. 29.

9 Ibid., p. 30.

10 Ibid.

11 Ellwood, "Divide and Conquer: Responsible Security for America's Poor," Occasional Paper No. 1, Ford Foundation Project on Social Welfare and the American Future, (1987) p. 9.

12 Bureau of the Census, *supra* note 1, at p. 35.

13 Ibid.

14 Committee on Ways and Means, U.S. House of Representatives, *Background Material and Data on Programs Within the Jurisdiction of the Committee on Ways and Means,* (1988) pp. 408–10.

15 Center on Budget and Policy Priorities, "Analysis of Poverty in 1987," (August 31, 1987) p. 4.

16 Bureau of the Census, *supra* note 1, at p. 8.

17 Cuomo Task Force on Poverty and Welfare, "A New Social Contract" (1986), pp. 20–22.

6 Urban Infrastructure and City Budgeting: Elements of a National Urban Policy

Ideas and concepts presented in this chapter have been shaped by active debate with many individuals over several years. The author would like to acknowledge an intellectual debt in particular to William Barnes, Research Director at the National League of Cities. Others who have contributed include Douglas Peterson, Heywood Sanders, Frank Shafroth, John Bowman, Richard Mudge, Richard Moore, and Ann Bowman. Financial support for survey and other research work from the Lincoln Institute of Land Policy, the National League of Cities, and Miami University's Faculty Research Committee are gratefully acknowledged.

1 An opinion survey was administered to local officials selected from a random sample of 204 cities with populations greater than 25,000; another thirty cities with populations under 25,000 were randomly selected from a list of member cities of the National League of Cities. Three randomly selected *elected* officials from each of the 234 cities were then administered a survey. The survey was also sent to three *appointed* officials in each selected city who are responsible for, or knowledgeable about, city capital spending plans: the city manager or chief administrative officer and the chief budget officer were each sent a survey; and one other official was randomly selected from a list of department heads. This sampling procedure resulted in mailing 1,404 surveys to 234 cities in April 1986: 474 responses were received, a response rate of 34 percent.

2 This section draws heavily from my article, "Fiscal Disruptions and City Responses," in *Urban Affairs Quarterly* (September 1988).

3 Budget officers from the same 234 cities identified in note 1 responded to a separate questionnaire. The response rate from this group was 48 percent.

4 For a detailed examination of the capital spending impacts of total city revenue shifts on functional categories, see note 12.

5 We also assume that taxpayers are not sophisticated enough to link their federal tax bill to total grant costs.

6 Local commitment to capital spending is defined as local revenues for capital projects and debt retirement. It excludes expenditures for capital projects because expenditures do not always represent commitment, or sacrifice. For example, a bond issue of $10 million for repairing or constructing a capital facility would result in immediate community benefits. But because the issue is amortized over a number of years, the annual commitment or sacrifice borne by the taxpayers is only the amount of money needed to repay that debt in each year. *Local commitment* to capital spending is expected to change only marginally each year, although *capital expenditures*—which include federal grants—will be "lumpy," that is, high in some years and low in others.

7 The Census Bureau publishes total capital outlays and total current outlays, but it is impossible to identify revenue sources for either (except that debt cannot be used for current outlays). The volume of debt issuances (long-term and short-term) cannot be considered expenditure data for the year in which they are issued; so one cannot match "long-term debt issued" (revenue) with "capital outlays" (expenditure) and assume the difference is composed of local reve-

nues. There are two reasons for this. First, bond funds are usually spent over a number of years, while "capital outlays" refer only to annual outlays. Second, the "difference" includes not only local revenues (taxes and fees) but other revenues, usually intergovernmental (often federal) aid.

The author is indebted to Joe Tuss of Dayton's Office of Budget and Management for his help in explaining historical changes in city record-keeping and for access to the budgetary data.

8 A regression equation specifying local commitment as a function of last year's local commitment and federal aid availability produced a partial regression coefficient for the federal aid variable that was not statistically significant ($p = .218$). The coefficient for last year's local commitment was statistically significant ($p = .0001$). This result obtained when both constant and current dollars were employed. Following Larkey's (1979) Constant Proportion of Base model, local commitment was regressed against last year's local commitment. The resulting regression coefficient of determination was .54 (constant dollar equation) and .87 (current dollar equation). Other models, similar in design to Larkey's differencing regression models, were also employed and were not improvements over the simple model. For example, differencing federal aid did not significantly improve the model, and the t-ratio for the differenced federal aid variable was significant only at the unacceptable .214 level. Thus, these results raise serious questions about whether or not it is plausible to argue that federal grants compel cities to respond to either the availability or volume of federal aid.

9 See note 1 for survey data.

10 Development fees suffer much the same fate. They are successful revenue-raising devices in cities with high demand for residential or commercial development. Development fees, like impact fees, may actually inhibit development in low-demand cities (see Apogee, 1987).

11 An important federal strategy not pursued in this article is a change in the federal tax code. The 1986 Tax Reform Act made sweeping revisions in definitions of tax-exempt bonds, repealed arbitrage (except for "small" issuers —less than $5 million per year), and lowered the business and security test to 10 percent. A bill introduced in 1988 (H.R. 3806) to Congress by representatives James Howard and William Clinger would allow small-issue arbitrage to be increased from $5 million to $25 million and would raise the 10 percent limits to the pre-Tax Reform Act limits of 25 percent.

12 Responses by key local officials to a simulation question—see note 1—helped answer the questions on comparative valuations of city functions. The question asked officials, as knowledgeable observers of and participants in their city's budgetary process, was how they would expect their city to apportion a hypothetical revenue increase of 25 percent across traditional city functional categories. Only the responses from officials within cities which were responsible for the identified functional categories were tabulated.

Figure 6.4 graphically presents the responses to the scenario of a 25 percent *increase* in total revenues for capital purposes. The black bar represents no (or minimal) increase in capital spending for each of eight common city functions. Capital spending on water and sewer facilities would increase hardly at all,

Figure 6.4   Responses to Increase in Revenue By Function

Confronted with a 25 percent increase in revenue, the percentage of officials who
would adopt no increase, a moderate increase, or a significant increase in capital
spending for eight major functions is the following:

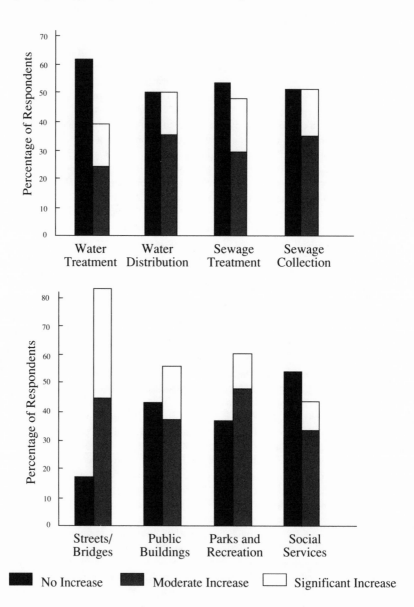

according to more than half the respondents. This response suggests capital spending for water and sewer facilities is very close to an optimum level. Local officials do not believe capital spending would increase much, if bequeathed a sizable sum. Provision of water and sewer is considered basic and inviolable: spending levels appear, in general, to be unaffected by a considerable revenue increase.

Local officials predict that revenue increases would not significantly alter capital spending levels for social service facilities (museums, senior citizen centers, libraries) much above current levels. In other words, capital spending levels in general should not be expected to increase for social service facilities because actual levels are considered adequate.

The three functional categories that are predicted by local officials to benefit the most are public buildings, street and bridge networks, and parks and recreation facilities. Streets and bridges would receive the largest increase, according to respondents. If total revenues for capital spending increased by 25 percent, more than four-fifths of local officials surveyed predicted that more revenues would be funneled to street and bridge projects than elsewhere, and, of those officials, almost half predicted an increase in capital spending of more than 25 percent.

13 This leads to a secondary argument: a national *capital budget* will not, as supporters argue, arrest the deteriorating condition of the nation's infrastructure. Facility condition can be improved or prevented from deteriorating only if the facility is maintained properly. For cities and states "maintenance activities" are funded not from the capital budget but from the operating budget. In fact, if a national capital budget could do all those wonders ascribed to it, one has to question why those wonders have been dashed at the state and local level, where capital budgets are commonplace.

Bibliography

Advisory Commission on Intergovernmental Relations [ACIR]. 1987. *Significant Features of Fiscal Federalism*. Washington, D.C.: U.S. Government Printing Office.

Apogee Research. 1986. "The Uses and Misuses of Infrastructure Needs Surveys and Inventories." Prepared for the National Council on Public Works Improvement, July.

Apogee Research. 1987. *Financing Infrastructure: Innovations at the Local Level*. Washington, D.C.: National League of Cities.

Bahl, Roy. 1984. *Financing State and Local Government in the 1980s*. New York: Oxford University Press.

Bradbury, Katherine L., and Helen F. Ladd. 1985. "Changes in the Revenue-Raising Capacity of U.S. Cities, 1970–1982." Discussion Paper D85-2, State, Local, and Intergovernmental Center, Harvard University.

Choate, Pat and Susan Walter. 1981. *America in Ruins: Beyond the Public Works Pork Barrel*. Washington, D.C.: Council of State Planning Agencies.

Congressional Budget Office. 1985. *Efficient Investment in Wastewater Treatment*

Plants. Washington, D.C.: U.S. Government Printing Office.

CONSAD Research Corporation. 1980. *A Study of Public Works Investment in the U.S.* 4 volumes. Prepared for the U.S. Department of Commerce. Pittsburgh: CONSAD Research Corporation.

Courant, Paul N., Edward M. Gramlich, and Daniel L. Rubinfeld. 1979. "The Stimulative Effects of Intergovernmental Grants; or Why Money Sticks Where It Hits." In Peter Mieszkowski and William H. Oakland, eds., *Fiscal Federalism and Grants-in-Aid*. Washington, D.C.: Urban Institute, pp. 5–21.

Cusack, Thomas. 1985. "Contention and Compromise: A Comparative Analysis of Budgetary Politics." *Journal of Public Policy* 5:4 (October): 497–519.

Ellwood, J. 1982. *Reductions in U.S. Domestic Spending*. New Brunswick, N.J.: Transaction Books.

Fischer, Gregory and Mark Kamlet. 1984. "Explaining Presidential Priorities." *American Political Science Review* 78:2 (June): 356–71.

Galper, Harvey, and Eric Toder. 1983. "Owning or Leasing: Bennington College, and the U.S. Tax System." *National Tax Journal* 36:2 (June): 257–61.

Gramlich, Edward, and Harvey Galper. 1973. "State and Local Fiscal Behavior and Federal Grant Policy." *Brookings Papers on Economic Activity* 1: 15–65.

Hamilton, Randy. 1983. "The World Turned Upside Down: The Contemporary Revolution in State and Local Government Capital Financing." *Public Administration Review* 43:1 (January/February): 22–31.

Inman, Robert. 1979. "Fiscal Performance of Local Governments." In Peter Mieszkowski and Mahlon Straszheim, eds., *Current Issues in Urban Economics*. Baltimore: Johns Hopkins University Press, pp. 270–321.

Keating, W. Dennis. 1986. "Linking Downtown Development to Broader Community Goals." *Journal of the American Planning Association* (Spring): 133–41.

Larkey, Patrick. 1979. *Evaluating Public Programs*. Princeton, N.J.: Princeton University Press.

Leonard, Herman. 1986. *Checks Unbalanced*. New York: Basic Books.

Levine, Charles H., and Irene Rubin, eds. 1980. *Fiscal Stress and Public Policy*. Beverly Hills: Sage.

Levine, Charles H.; Irene Rubin, and George Wolohojian. 1981. *The Politics of Retrenchment*. Beverly Hills: Sage.

Miller, Girard. 1986. *Investing Public Funds*. Chicago: Government Finance Officers Association.

Nathan, Richard, Fred Doolittle, and Associates. 1983. *The Consequences of Cuts: The Effects of the Reagan Domestic Program on State and Local Government*. Princeton, N.J.: Princeton Urban and Regional Research Center.

National Council on Public Works Improvement. 1988. *Fragile Foundations*. Washington, D.C.: National Council on Public Works Improvement.

National Infrastructure Advisory Committee. 1984. *Hard Choices: A Report on the Increasing Gap between America's Infrastructure Needs and Our Ability to Pay for Them*. Prepared for the U.S. Congress, Joint Economic Committee. Washington, D.C.: U.S. Government Printing Office.

Pagano, Michael A. 1984. "Notes on Capital Budgeting." *Public Budgeting and Finance* 4:3 (Autumn): 31–40.

———— . 1986. "Old Wine in New Bottles? An Analysis and Preliminary Appraisal of the Surface Transportation Assistance Act of 1982." *Publius* 16:1 (Winter).

Pagano, Michael A., and Richard J. T. Moore. 1985. *Cities and Fiscal Choices*. Durham, N.C.: Duke University Press.

Petersen, John E., and Wesley C. Hough, eds. 1983. *Creative Capital Financing*. Chicago: Government Finance Research Center, Municipal Finance Officers Association.

Peterson, George. 1978. "Capital Spending and Capital Obsolescence: The Outlook for Cities." In Roy Bahl, ed., *The Fiscal Outlook for Cities*. Syracuse, N.Y.: Syracuse University Press, pp. 49–74.

Peterson, George, ed. 1980–82. *The Future of America's Capital Plant*. 6 vols. Washington, D.C.: Urban Institute Press.

Peterson, George, Mary John Miller, Stephen R. Godwin, and Carol Shapiro. 1984. *Guide to Benchmarks of Urban Capital Condition*. Washington, D.C.: Urban Institute Press.

Porter, D. R. 1986. "The Rights and Wrongs of Impact Fees." *Urban Land* (July).

Reid, Gary. 1988. "California Cities and Proposition 13." *Public Budgeting and Finance* 8:1 (Spring): 20–37.

Snyder, Thomas P., and Michael A. Stegman. 1986. "Financing the Public Costs of Growth: Using Development Fees, Exactions and Special Districts to Finance Infrastructure." U.S. Department of Housing and Urban Development.

Stegman, Michael A. 1986. "Development Fees for Infrastructure." *Urban Land* (May): 2–5.

Stine, William F. 1985. "Estimating the Responsiveness of Local Revenue to Intergovernmental Aid." *National Tax Journal* 38:2 (June): 227–34.

Tarr, Joel. 1984. "The Evolution of the Urban Infrastructure in the Nineteenth and Twentieth Centuries." In Royce Hanson, ed., *Perspectives in Urban Infrastructure*. Washington, D.C.: National Academy Press, pp. 4–66.

U.S. Department of Commerce, Bureau of the Census. 1988, 1979. *City Government Finances in 1985–86 [1977–78]*. Washington, D.C.: USGPO.

Warren, Charles, ed. 1985. *Urban Policy in a Changing Federal System*. Washington, D.C.: National Academy Press.

Wolman, Harold. 1983. "Understanding Local Government Responses to Fiscal Pressure." *Journal of Public Policy* 3:3 (August): 245–64.

7 Boston

Note: This chapter is an amended version of the article "Is America's 'In' City Losing its Soul?" in *Bostonia* (September/October 1987).

8 National Urban Policy:
Where Are We Now? Where Are We Going?

1 This essay is a much amended and extended version of papers given at the Great Society Retrospect Conference hosted by the University of Colorado's Graduate School of Public Affairs in the spring of 1984 and a National Urban Policy Conference hosted by the school in honor of the late Secretary Patricia Roberts

Harris in 1986. The author wishes to acknowledge the helpful comments of Bernard Frieden and Anthony Downs, Jr.

2 Bernard J. Frieden and Marshall Kaplan. *The Politics of Neglect: Urban Aid for Model Cities to Revenue Sharing*. Cambridge, Mass.: MIT Press, 1975.

3 Frieden and Kaplan, *The Politics of Neglect*.

4 I was deputy assistant secretary for urban policy during the Carter administration.

5 John Palmer and Isabel Sawhill, eds. *The Reagan Record*. Cambridge, Mass.: Ballinger, 1984); George E. Peterson and Carol W. Lewis, eds., *Reagan and the Cities* (Washington, D.C.: Urban Institute, 1986).

6 See Henry J. Aaron, *Politics and the Professors: The Great Society in Perspective* (Washington, D.C.: Brookings Institution, 1978); Marshall Kaplan and Peggy Cuciti, eds. *The Great Society and Its Legacy* (Durham, N.C.: Duke University Press, 1988); Richard R. Nelson, *The Moon and the Ghetto: An Essay on Public Policy Analysis* (New York: Norton, 1977); Alice Rivlin, *Systematic Thinking for Social Action* (Washington, D.C.: Brookings Institution, 1971); Jane Jacobs, *Cities and the Wealth of Nations: Principles of Economic Life* (New York: Random House, 1984).

7 Marshall Kaplan and Franklin James, *Federal Housing Agencies and National Housing Policies* (Cambridge, Mass.: MIT Housing Project, 1988).

8 Charles Murray, *Losing Ground: American Social Policy 1950–1980* (New York: Basic Books, 1984).

9 John E. Schwarz, *America's Hidden Success: A Reassessment of Twenty Years of Public Policy* (New York: Norton, 1983).

9 Chasing Urban Policy:
A Critical Retrospect

1 *National Growth and Development*, Hearings before the Subcommittee on Housing and Community Development of the Committee on Banking, Currency and Housing, House of Representatives, September 4, 5, and 8, 1975 (Washington, D.C.: U.S. Government Printing Office, 1975), p. 587.

2 Ibid.

3 Ibid., p. 558.

4 Daniel P. Moynihan, "Toward a National Urban Policy," *The Public Interest*, no. 17 (Fall 1969), p. 8. The memorandum referred to was substantially similar to a speech delivered later at Syracuse University and published in *The Public Interest*.

5 Ibid., p. 14.

6 Ibid., p. 8.

7 "Statement by the President announcing the creation of the Council for Urban Affairs," *Weekly Compilation of Presidential Documents*, vol. 5., no. 4 (January 29, 1969), p. 161.

8 Moynihan, "Toward a National Urban Policy," p. 3.

9 *Toward Balanced Growth: Quantity With Quality*, Report of the National Goals Research Staff (Washington, D.C.: U.S. Government Printing Office, 1970), pp. 44–45.

10 Ibid., p. 42.

11 Ibid.

12 *Population and the American Future*, Report of the Commission on Population Growth and the American Future (Washington, D.C.: U.S. Government Printing Office, 1972), p. 37.

13 *Toward Balanced Growth*, p. 45.

14 Ibid.

15 President's State of the Union Message, January 22, 1970.

16 National Committee on Urban Growth Policy, *The New City* (New York: Frederick A. Praeger), 1969.

17 Ibid., pp. 19, 31.

18 *Toward Balanced Growth*, p. 219.

19 Ibid., p. 221.

20 William E. Finley, "A Fresh Start," in *The New City*, p. 163.

21 "Report of the National Committee on Urban Growth Policy," in *The New City*, p. 172.

22 Spiro T. Agnew, "Foreword," in *The New City*, p. 7.

23 Finley, "A Fresh Start," p. 167.

24 Ibid., pp. 163, 167.

25 "Council for Urban Affairs," *Weekly Compilation of Presidential Documents*, vol. 5, no. 4, January 27, 1969, p. 162.

26 "Memorandum for all Cabinet Members," The White House, June 2, 1969.

27 "Urban Affairs Council," a listing of UAC subcommittees and other Cabinet committees, September 29, 1969.

28 "Record of Action for the Fifteenth Meeting, Council for Urban Affairs," July 11, 1969.

29 Briefing Outline: Reorganization Plan—Executive Office of the President, p. 3 (undated).

30 "Domestic Council Study Memorandum 1," The White House, April 23, 1970.

31 "Domestic Council Study Memorandum 2," The White House, July 30, 1970.

32 "Domestic Council Study Memorandum 3," The White House, August 20, 1970.

33 "Domestic Council Study Memorandum 5," The White House, October 12, 1970.

34 "Memorandum for the President (Draft)," from Domestic Council Committee on National Growth Policy, November 20, 1970, pp. 13–35.

35 Ibid, p. 7.

36 "Memorandum for the President," via John Ehrlichman, from the Committee of the Domestic Council on National Growth Policy, December 9, 1970.

37 *The President's Proposals for Executive Reorganization*, Domestic Council (Washington, D.C.: U.S. Government Printing Office), 1971, p. 5.

38 "Memorandum for Committee on National Growth Policy," from John R. Price, The White House, June 28, 1971.

39 "Memorandum for the Honorable George Romney and Frederick McLaughlin," from Vicki Keller, The White House, October 22, 1971.

40 "Memorandum for Secretary George Romney," from Herbert Stein, Council of Economic Advisers, November 10, 1971.

41 *Report on National Growth, 1972* (Washington, D.C.: U.S. Government Printing Office, 1972), p. 31.

42 The President's State of the Union Message, January 30, 1974, in *Historic Documents* (Washington, D.C.: Congressional Quarterly, 1974), p. 45.

43 Letter, James T. Lynn to the President, December 3, 1974, Folder "National Growth Report 1974 (2)," Box 15, F. Lynn May Files, Gerald R. Ford Library.

44 *National Growth and Development*, p. 531.

45 Ibid., p. 570.

46 Ibid., pp. 34–35.

47 Ibid., p. 34.

48 Memorandum for the President, from William E. Simon, September 8, 1975. Folder "New York City, May–October 1975 (3)," Box 78, L. William Seidman Files, Gerald R. Ford Library.

49 Memorandum for the President, from Charles E. Walker, October 7, 1975, Folder "New York City, May–October 1975 (6)," Box 78, L. William Seidman Files, Gerald R. Ford Library.

50 Ibid.

51 Memorandum from Art Quern to Jim Cannon on "Urban Problems," March 8, 1976. Folder "Urban Policy: 7/1/75–4/8/76," Box 39, James Cannon Files, Gerald R. Ford Library.

52 *Interim Report of the President's Committee on Urban Development and Neighborhood Revitalization*, October 1976 (photocopy).

53 The Carter urban policy process and outcome is discussed in Charles J. Orlebeke, "Carter Renews Romance with National Urban Policy," *Planning*, vol. 44, no. 7, pp. 11–16.

54 *A New Partnership to Conserve America's Communities: A National Urban Policy*, The President's Urban and Regional Policy Report, March 1978.

55 For a review of the 1980 report, see Charles J. Orlebeke, *The President's National Urban Policy Report, Journal of the American Planning Association*, Winter 1982, p. 116.

56 *Urban America in the Eighties*, President's Commission for a National Agenda for the Eighties (Washington, D.C.: U.S. Government Printing Office), 1972, pp. 97–109.

57 *The President's National Urban Policy Report 1984*, (Washington, D.C.: U.S. Government Printing Office, 1984), p. vi.

58 George E. Peterson and Carol W. Lewis, eds., *Reagan and the Cities* (Washington, D.C.: The Urban Institute Press, 1986), p. 35.

59 Ibid., p. 24.

60 Ibid., p. 35.

61 Richard P. Nathan and Paul R. Dommel, "Needed—A Safety Net for Communities," statement to the U.S. Senate Committee on Governmental Affairs, Subcommittee on Intergovernmental Relations, June 25, 1987 (photocopy), p. 1.

62 Richard P. Nathan and Charles Adams, *Understanding Central City Hardship* (Washington, D.C.: The Brookings Institution, Technical Series Reprint T-012, 1976).

63 Nathan and Dommel, "Needed—A Safety Net for Communities," p. 5.

64 Ibid., pp. 9–11.

65 See Richard P. Nathan, Fred Doolittle, and Associates, *Reagan and the States* (Princeton, N.J.: Princeton University Press, 1987).

10 Policy Liberalism, National Community Liberalism, and the Prospects for National Urban Policy

1 Charles J. Orlebeke, "The President's National Urban Policy Report: 1980," *Journal of the American Planning Association*, Winter 1982, p. 116.
2 The President's Urban and Regional Policy Group, "A New Partnership to Conserve America's Communities," March 1978, p. III-3.
3 Ibid., p. III-5.
4 Ibid., p. II-8.
5 Harold L. Wolman and Astrid E. Merget, "The Presidency and Policy Formulation: President Carter and the Urban Policy," 10 *Presidential Studies Quarterly* 403 (Summer 1980), p. 411.
6 "Urban Policy," in Joseph Pechman, ed., *Setting National Priorities: The 1979 Budget* (Washington, D.C.: Brookings Institution, 1978), p. 187.
7 Charles J. Orlebeke, "Carter Renews the Romance with a National Urban Policy," 44 *Planning* 7 (August 1978), p. 14.
8 "Policy vs. Program in the '70s," *The Public Interest* 20 (Summer 1970).
9 "New Partnership," p. II-2.
10 Ibid., p. III-1.
11 "The Theory of Governance of the Reagan Administration," in Lester M. Salamon and Michael S. Lund, eds., *The Reagan Presidency and the Governing of America* (Washington, D.C.: Urban Institute, 1981), p. 62. This is a superb discussion of the problems Carter encountered with his policy approach.
12 "The Passionless Presidency," 243 *Atlantic Monthly* 5 (May 1979), p. 42.
13 Ceaser, "The Theory of Governance," p. 62.
14 *In the Absence of Power: Governing America* (New York: Viking Press, 1980), p. 296.
15 Fallows, "Passionless Presidency," p. 42.
16 Quoted in William A. Schambra, "Progressive Liberalism and American 'Community,'" *The Public Interest* 80 (Summer 1985), p. 32.
17 "Energy and National Goals," *Public Papers of the Presidents of the United States: Jimmy Carter (1979)*, 2 vols. (Washington, D.C.: U.S. Government Printing Office, 1980), II, pp. 1235–41.
18 Michael Malbin, "Rhetoric and Leadership: A Look Backward at the Carter National Energy Plan," in Anthony King, ed., *Both Ends of the Avenue* (Washington, D.C.: American Enterprise Institute, 1983), p. 245.
19 *Politics and the Professors: The Great Society in Perspective* (Washington, D.C.: Brookings Institution, 1978), p. 167.

11 American Neighborhood Policies: Mixed Results and Uneven Evaluations

1 According to HUD's recent Annual Housing Surveys, most Americans appear satisfied with their neighborhoods. But considerable variation exists. It appears

to relate in part to the distress level of the cities in which neighborhoods are located and to the income and color of neighborhood residents. Several housing analysts, among them William Apgar, Jr. (see pp. 101-130), have indicated that low-income renter households have been squeezed of late by a declining availability of units in cities, by the absence of purchase options, and by competition from younger buyers priced out of the ownership market. Their continued inability to pay increased housing costs likely will result in a visible increase in housing problems in central cities and their neighborhoods. Many inner-city poor neighborhoods remain subject to high concentrations of very low-income minority households. As William Wilson notes: "It is the growth of the high and extreme poverty areas that epitomizes the social transformation of the inner city, a transformation that represents a change in the class structure in many inner city neighborhoods as the non-poor black middle class and working classes tend to no longer reside in these neighborhoods, thereby increasing the proportion of truly disadvantaged individuals and families." William Julius Wilson, *The Truly Disadvantaged: The Inner City, The Underclass, and Public Policy* (Chicago: University of Chicago Press, 1987), p. 86.

2 Katharine Bradbury, Anthony Downs, and Kenneth Small, *Urban Decline and the Future of American Cities* (Washington, D.C.: Brookings Institution, 1982), pp. 165–66.

3 Michael H. Schill and Richard P. Nathan, *Revitalizing America's Cities: Neighborhood Reinvestment and Displacement* (Albany: State University of New York Press, 1983), pp. 14–15.

4 Ibid.

5 David P. Varady, *Revitalizing America's Cities: Neighborhood Reinvestment and Displacement* (Albany: State University of New York Press, 1986), p. 9.

12 The Rise and Fall of National Urban Policy: The Fiscal Dimension

1 U.S. Bureau of the Census, *Historical Statistics of the United States, Colonial Times to 1970*, Bicentennial Edition, part 2 (Washington, D.C.: U.S. Government Printing Office, 1975), p. 1133.

2 For a discussion of this issue, see James W. Fossett, *Federal Aid to Big Cities: The Politics of Dependence* (Washington, D.C.: Brookings Institution, 1983).

3 Advisory Commission on Intergovernmental Relations, *A Catalog of Federal Grant-in-Aid Programs to State and Local Governments: Grants Funded in FY 1984*, (Washington, D.C.: U.S. Government Printing Office, 1984), M-139; also editions for fiscal years 1978 and 1981 published in 1979 (A-72) and 1982 (M-133).

4 Advisory Commission on Intergovernmental Relations, *A Catalog of Federal Grant-in-Aid Programs for FY 1981* (1982), M-133, Appendix A.

5 The figures in this paragraph were calculated from data contained in Office of Management and Budget, *Budget of the United States Government, Fiscal Year 1989, Historical Tables* (Washington, D.C.: U.S. Government Printing Office, 1988).

13 A Nonurban Policy: Recent Public Policy Shifts
Affecting Cities

1 David Walker, "The Nature and Systemic Impact of Creative Federalism," in Marshall Kaplan and Peggy Cuciti, eds, *The Great Society and Its Legacy: Twenty Years of U.S. Social Policy* (Durham, N.C.: Duke University Press, 1986).

2 Royce Hansen, *Rethinking Urban Policy* (Washington D.C.: National Academy of Science 1982), p. 31

3 It now appears that some of the northeastern cities have made a transition to a services economy and are prospering. To some extent, this has eased their fiscal situation. Such cities, however, still face problems in ensuring that the benefits of economic growth accrue to their residents.

4 The President's Commission for a National Agenda for the Eighties, *A National Agenda for the Eighties* (Washington, D.C.: 1980). p. 65.

5 Ibid., p. 65.

6 See U.S. Department of Housing and Urban Development, *The 1984 President's National Urban Policy Report* (May 1984).

7 U.S. Executive Office of the President, *Budget of the United States Government, Fiscal Year 1987*, pp. 3–7.

8 The Economic Recovery Tax Act of 1981 also reduced progressivity by giving tremendous tax breaks to corporations. Corporate taxes were substantially increased, however, by the Tax Reform Act of 1986.

9 U.S. Congressional Budget Office, *The Economic and Budget Outlook: Fiscal Years 1989-1993* (Washington, D.C.: U.S. Government Printing Office, February 1988), p. 142.

10 We recognize there are several drawbacks to use of these data. Numerous limitations in program reporting have been identified by analysts using these data in the past. Over and beyond these limitations is the potential for noncomparable reporting as the responsibility for production and overall format changed between 1980 and 1985.

11 See Franklin James, "City Need and Distress in the United States: 1970 to the Mid-1980's," in this volume. The classification represents an update of work originally undertaken for the *1980 President's National Urban Policy Report*, HUD 583-1-CPD, August 1980.

12 U.S. Congress, Joint Economic Committee Hearings, *New Federalism: Its Impact to Date* (Washington D.C.: U.S. Government Printing Office, March 8, 1983).

13 For a detailing of changes at the state level, see U.S. Advisory Commission on Intergovernmental Relations, *State and Local Roles in the Federal System*, Report A-88, April 1982.

14 Coalition on Block Grants and Human Needs, *Briefing Book on Block Grants and the New Federalism* (April 1982), p. 72.

15 Joint Economic Committee, *New Federalism*.

16 U.S. General Accounting Office, *Maternal and Child Health Block Grant: Program Changes Emerging Under State Administration*, GAO/HRD-84-35, May 7, 1984; *States Have Made Few Changes in Implementing the Alcohol, Drug Abuse and Mental Health Services Block Grant*, GAO/HRD-84-52, June

6, 1984; *States Use Added Flexibility Offered by the Preventive Health and Health Services Block Grant*, GAO/HRD-84-41, May 1984.

17 Reported in Steven V. Roberts, "Budget Ax Becomes a Tool for Social Change," *New York Times*, June 21, 1981, cited in John L. Palmer and Isabel V. Sawhill *The Reagan Experiment* (Washington D.C.: Urban Institute Press, 1982).

18 Joint Economic Committee, *New Federalism*, pp. 412–13.

19 Richard Nathan, *The Consequences of Cuts: The Effects of the Reagan Domestic Program on State and Local Governments* (Princeton, N.J.: Princeton Urban and Regional Research Center, 1983), p. 92.

20 City of Seattle, *Impact of Proposed Federal Budget Reduction on the City of Seattle*, March 1982.

21 Nathan, *Consequences of Cuts*, p. 191.

22 Cited in Art Levine, "Easing of State-Local Regulatory Burden Leaves Some Pleased, Others Grumbling," *National Journal* (August 8, 1984), p. 1468.

23 Gary Walker, *An Independent Sector Assessment of the Job Training Partnership Act, Phase 1: The Initial Transition*, p. 48.

24 Ibid., pp. 130–31.

25 Joint Economic Committee, *New Federalism*, p. 418.

26 John Kirlin, Ruth Ross, and Cristy Jensen, "California: Impacts of the Reagan Program," prepared for conference on the Reagan Domestic Program, Princeton University, June 7–8, 1984.

27 David Lowery, Stanley D. Brunn, and Gerald Webster, "From Stable Disparity to Dynamic Equity: The Spatial Distribution of Federal Expenditures, 1971–1983" *Social Science Quarterly* 67, no. 1 (March 1985): 98–107

14 HUD in the Nineties: Doubt-Ability and Do-Ability

1 For a detailed and authoritative account of congressional consideration of HUD cabinet status and the interplay of forces in the internal organization of HUD which this section summarizes, see Emmette S. Redford and Marlan Blissett, *Organizing the Executive Branch: The Johnson Presidency* (Chicago: University of Chicago Press, 1981), chap. 2. See also Robert Wood, "Mayor Richard C. Lee: A National Vantage," *Journal of the New Haven Colony Historical Society* (Spring 1987).

2 The most authoritative accounts of HUD in the 1970s are Robert C. Weaver, "The First Twenty Years of HUD," *American Planning Association Journal* (1985), and Royce Hauson, *The Evolution of National Urban Policy, 1970–80* (Washington, D.C.: National Academy Press, 1982).

3 David C. Schwartz, Richard C. Ferlauto, and Daniel N. Hoffman, *A New Housing Policy for America* (Philadelphia: Temple University Press, 1988), p. 50.

4 Thomas E. Cronin, *The State of the Presidency* (Boston: Little, Brown, 1980), p. 276.

5 National Academy of Public Administration, *A Presidency for the 1980s: A Report on Presidential Management* (Washington, D.C., 1981).

6 Thomas E. Cronin, *The State of the Presidency* (Boston: Little, Brown, 1980), p. 276.

7 Interview with Robert Embry, former HUD assistant secretary of planning and community development during the Carter administration.

8 Stewart Alsop, *The Center* (New York: Harper and Row, 1968), p. 254.

9 Howard Kurtz, "HUD Secretary Defends Himself Against Critics of Low-Key Style," *Washington Post*, October 19, 1983, p. A3.

10 During interviews with Beverly Klimkowsky, Washington insiders characterized Lynn and Pierce as "ciphers" and "friendly undertakers."

11 Suzanne Farkas, *Urban Lobbying* (New York: New York University Press, 1971), p. 112.

12 Interview with Henry Reuss, former chairman, U.S. Congress, Subcommittee on Urban Affairs.

13 George C. Edwards III and Ira Sharkansky, *The Policy Predicament and Implementing Public Policy* (San Francisco: W. H. Freeman, 1978) p. 321.

14 Schwartz et al., *A New Housing Policy*, p. 47.

15 Ibid., p. 26.

16 Ibid.

17 Interview with Philip Brownstein, former HUD assistant secretary for mortgage finance during the Johnson administration.

18 Royce Hanson, *The Evolution of National Urban Policy, 1970–1980: Lessons from the Past.* (Washington, D.C.: National Academy Press, 1982), p. 51.

19 124 *Congressional Record* H6204 (daily ed., June 29, 1978).

20 Barbara Hinkson Craig, *The Legislative Veto: Congressional Control of Regulation* (Boulder: Westview Press, 1983), p. 60.

21 Ibid., p. 62.

22 Interview with Anthony Downs.

23 Ibid.

24 Hanson, *The Evolution of National Urban Policy*, see concluding section.

25 Schwartz et al., *A New Housing Policy*, pp. 7–11.

26 The policy objectives in quotes are from the Declaration of Purpose of PL 89–174.

27 U.S. Congress, House, Committee on Banking, Finance, and Urban Affairs, *Housing—A Reader*, Committee Print 98-5, pp. 6–7.

28 Herbert Kaufman, *Are Government Organizations Immortal?* (Washington, D.C.: Brookings Institution, 1976).

29 Interview with Henry Reuss.

30 Ibid.

31 John E. Mulford et al., *Housing Consumption in A Housing Allowance Program* (Santa Monica: Rand, 1982), and Stephen K. Mayo et al., *Housing Allowances and Other Rental Housing Assistance Demand Experiments* (Cambridge, Mass.: ABT Associates, 1980).

32 U.S. President's Commission on Housing, *Report* (Washington, D.C., 1982).

33 Interview with Ralph Taylor.

34 Schwartz et al., *A New Housing Policy*.

35 Interview with Robert Embry.

36 Interview with Anthony Downs.

15 Who Gets the Jobs in the New Downtown?

This chapter is based on a forthcoming book by Bernard J. Frieden and Lynne Sagalyn, *Behind the New Downtowns: Politics, Money, and Marketplaces*, which contains fuller citations and documentation.

1 U.S. Department of Housing and Urban Development, *The 1978 HUD Survey on the Quality of Community Life* (Washington, D.C.: Department of Housing and Urban Development, 1978).

2 Aaron S. Gurwitz and G. Thomas Kingsley, *The Metropolitan Cleveland Economy* (Santa Monica: Rand, 1982), p. 22; Ruth Eckdish Knack, "Pittsburgh's Glitter and Gloom," *Planning* 51 (December 1985): 4–11; John D. Kasarda, "Urban Change and Minority Opportunities," in Paul E. Peterson, ed., *The New Urban Reality* (Washington, D.C.: Brookings Institution, 1985), pp. 33–68, at p. 48.

3 Vincent P. Barabba, "The Demographic Future of the Cities of America," in Herrington J. Bryce, ed., *Cities and Firms* (Lexington, Mass.: Lexington Books, 1980), pp. 3–45.

4 The top ten cities, identified in Urban Investment and Development Company, "Downtown Office Construction in Major U.S. Cities" (1984), were New York, Chicago, Washington, D.C., Houston, San Francisco, Dallas, Los Angeles, Boston, Denver, and Philadelphia. Data on unemployment and poverty from U.S. Bureau of the Census, *County and City Data Book, 1972* (Washington, D.C.: U.S. Government Printing Office, 1973), table 6; and *County and City Data Book, 1983* (1983), table C; and *State and Metropolitan Area Data Book, 1986* (1986), table B. Poverty data for 1985 supplied by Sheldon Danziger, University of Wisconsin Institute for Research on Poverty, from 1986 *Current Population Survey* tapes.

5 National Urban Policy Advisory Committee, *Urban America 1984: A Report Card*, prepared for U.S. Congress, Joint Economic Committee, Subcommittee on Investment, Jobs, and Prices (1984).

6 Data on commuter shares of central-city employment from U.S. Census of 1980, reported in Samuel M. Ehrenhalt (New York regional commissioner of labor statistics), "Growth in the New York City Economy: Problems and Promise," paper presented to eighteenth annual institute on Challenges of the Changing Economy of New York City, New York City Council on Economic Education, May 8, 1985. Information for Boston from 1981 surveys reported in Boston Redevelopment Authority, *Boston Tomorrow: Background on Development* (Boston: Boston Redevelopment Authority, undated), table IX-5; and Jeffrey P. Brown, "Who Works in Boston?: Commuting Patterns in the Boston Metropolitan Area, 1980," Boston Redevelopment Authority Research Department, April 1984. Information for San Francisco from Chester Hartman, *The Transformation of San Francisco* (Totowa, N.J.: Rowman and Allenheld, 1984), pp. 261–62, 287.

7 Boston Redevelopment Authority, *Boston Tomorrow*; and U.S. Commission on Civil Rights, *Greater Baltimore Commitment* (Washington, D.C.: U.S. Commission on Civil Rights, 1983), pp. 56–57.

8 Norman Krumholz, "Recovery of Cities: An Alternate View," in Paul R. Porter

and David C. Sweet, eds., *Rebuilding America's Cities: Roads to Recovery* (New Brunswick, N.J.: Rutgers Center for Urban Policy Research, 1984), pp. 173–90; at p. 174.

9 Desmond Smith, "Info City," *New York* (February 9, 1981), cited in Michael C. D. Macdonald, *America's Cities* (New York: Simon and Schuster, 1984), p. 365.

10 Krumholz, "Recovery of Cities," p. 187.

11 Information on jobs and education from Daniel E. Chall, "New York City's 'Skills Mismatch,'" *Federal Reserve Bank of New York Quarterly Review* 10 (Spring 1985): 20–27; Manhattan share of New York jobs in Ehrenhalt, "Growth in the New York City Economy."

12 Alexander Reid, "Growth in Finance Jobs Slackens in Manhattan," *New York Times*, December 15, 1985, p. 59; tabulation of entry-level and knowledge-intensive jobs from Kasarda, "Urban Change and Minority Opportunity," p. 50.

13 Louis Jacobson, "Labor Mobility and Structural Change in Pittsburgh," *Journal of the American Planning Association* 53 (Autumn 1987): 438–48.

14 Samuel M. Ehrenhalt, "Insight and Outlook: The New York Experience as a Service Economy," paper presented at nineteenth annual institute on Challenges of the Changing Economy of New York City, May 14, 1986; and data from Massachusetts Division of Employment Security, Economic Research and Analysis Service, "Selected Occupational Wages in Manufacturing Industries" (May, June 1986) and "Selected Occupational Wages in Service Industries" (April, May 1987).

15 Ehrenhalt, "Insight and Outlook"; and wage distribution data for 1985 calculated by Bennett Harrison and Barry Bluestone, based on March 1985 *Current Population Survey*, reported in Bennett Harrison and Barry Bluestone, *The Great U-Turn* (New York: Basic Books, 1988).

16 Finance and business services data from Ehrenhalt, "Growth in the New York City Economy"; minority employment data from Samuel M. Ehrenhalt, "New York City's Labor Force: Change and Challenge," *City Almanac* 17 (December 1983): 1–12, at 9–10.

17 New York data from U.S. Census of 1980, reported in Ehrenhalt, "Growth in the New York City Economy"; and Matthew Drennan, "Economy," in Charles Brecher and Raymond D. Horton, eds., *Setting Municipal Priorities: 1982* (New York: Russell Sage, 1984), pp. 55–88, at p. 84. Data for other cities in U.S. Department of Labor, Bureau of Labor Statistics, *Geographic Profile of Employment and Unemployment, 1985* (Bulletin 2266, September 1986), table 25.

18 Elizabeth Neuffer, "Companies Cite Poor Skills in Entry-Level Applicants," *New York Times*, July 4, 1987, p. 29.

19 Labor force status of the poor from U.S. Census of 1980, reported in Ehrenhalt, "Growth in the New York City Economy"; and Louis Uchitelle, "America's Army of Non-Workers, *New York Times*, September 27, 1987, p. 1F.

20 Richard Child Hill, "Crisis in the Motor City," in Susan S. Fainstein, Norman I. Fainstein, Richard Child Hill, Dennis Judd, Michael Peter Smith, *Restructuring the City* (New York: Longman, 1983), pp. 80–125, at pp. 108–9.

21 Robert Mier, "Job Generation as a Road to Recovery," in Porter and Sweet, *Rebuilding America's Cities*, pp. 160–72, at p. 167; Robert Lindsey, "Oakland 'Renaissance' Is One of Many in the West," *New York Times*, November 17, 1985, p. 4E; and Susan E. Clarke, "More Autonomous Policy Orientations: An Analytic Framework," in Clarence N. Stone and Heywood T. Sanders, eds., *The Politics of Urban Development* (Lawrence: University Press of Kansas, 1987), pp. 105–24, at p. 117.

22 U.S. Commission on Civil Rights, *Urban Minority Economic Development: Hearing Held in Baltimore, Maryland, November 17–18, 1981*, testimony of James W. Rouse, p. 259.

23 U.S. Commission on Civil Rights, *Greater Baltimore Commitment*, pp. 56–57; U.S. Commission on Civil Rights, *Urban Minority Economic Development*, pp. 256–57.

24 Information on Copley Place from Keri Lung, "The Job Linkage Approach to Community Economic Development," unpublished M.A. thesis, MIT, Department of Urban Studies and Planning, June 1985.

25 Information from Hal Scott, economic development coordinator, Private Industry Council, San Diego, March 13, 1986.

26 Information on the Boston Compact from William S. Spring, "Commentary: Boston Compact Pays Off in Jobs," *Boston Globe*, September 29, 1985, p. B17; Rushworth M. Kidder, "The Boston Compact: Breaking the Stalemate in the Public Schools," *Christian Science Monitor*, September 30, 1982, p. B6; Neal R. Pierce, "The 'Boston Compact'—An '80s School Model," *National Journal*, February 1, 1986, p. 284; Boston Private Industry Council, "Boston Compact Placement Status Report," November 1985; Boston Private Industry Council, "An Update on the Boston Compact," August 1986.

27 "7 Cities Picked in Plan to Foster School Attendance," *New York Times*, April 18, 1987, p. 26.

28 Data on Boston dropouts from Eleanor Farrar and Anthony Cipollone, "After the Signing: The Boston Compact: 1982–1984" (Cambridge, Mass.: Huron Institute, 1985); Boston Private Industry Council, "An Update on the Boston Compact," August 1986; Jane Perlez, "Dropouts: Data Maze," *New York Times*, March 4, 1987, p. B24; Jane Perlez, "A Lag Cited in Finishing High School," *New York Times*, November 19, 1987, p. B1; and Patricia Wen, "Wilson Hails Lower Dropout Rate," *Boston Globe*, September 10, 1987, p. 1.

16 The Shifting Focus of Neighborhood Groups: The Massachusetts Experience

1 "A Decent Place to Live: The Report of the National Housing Task Force," March 1988, p. 2.

2 Ibid., pp. 2–3.

3 Ibid., p. 18.

4 "Agency Budget Request: F.Y. 1985," Massachusetts Executive Office of Communities and Development, p. 8.

5 Ibid.
6 "Agency Budget Request, F.Y. 1986," Massachusetts Executive Office of Communities and Development, p. 12.
7 Memo (xeroxed), Tierney to Ortiz, Executive Offices of Communities and Development, July 1983.

17 Building a New Low-Income Housing Industry:
A Growing Role for the Nonprofit Sector

The authors would like to thank James Pickman, vice president, MPC & Associates, a development, management, and consulting firm based in Washington, D.C. This chapter builds on many of the concepts in *Producing Lower Income Housing: Local Initiatives* by Pickman, Benson F. Roberts, et al., published in 1986 by the Bureau of National Affairs.
1 *Against All Odds: The Achievements of Community-Based Development Organizations* (Washington, D.C.: National Congress for Community Economic Development, 1989).
2 National Housing Task Force, *A Decent Place to Live* (Washington, D.C., 1988).

18 Has America Lost Its Social Conscience—
Can It Get It Back?

This chapter is an amended version of the article "Has America Lost Its Social Conscience and How Will It Get It Back?" in *Political Science Quarterly* (no. 4, 1986, vol. 101).
1 *Washington Post*, January 4, 1966.
2 Quoted by Robert Shogan, "Feeling Bad About Doing Good: The Great Society Conclave," *Public Opinion* (April/May 1985), p. 19.
3 *Public Opinion* (June/July 1985), p. 30.
4 I. A. Lewis and William Schneider, "Hard Times: The Public on Poverty," *Public Opinion* (June/July 1985), p. 2.
5 *New York Times*, December 17, 1979.
6 Interestingly, there is little difference in outlook on these matters between the general public and the poor themselves. Only 3 percent of people in poverty believe that giving money to the poor is the best form of help. Fifty-six percent chose education and training for jobs, and 32 percent preferred creating government jobs for the poor. *Los Angeles Times* survey, April 1985, reported in *Public Opinion* (June/July 1985).
7 *Public Opinion* (December/January 1982), p. 29.
8 Ibid.
9 Ibid.
10 *Public Opinion* (June/July 1985), pp. 6, 31.
11 "Politics in the 80's: An Electorate at Odds with Itself," *Public Opinion* (December/January 1983), p. 5.

19 Eliciting an Effective and Necessary
Urban Policy Response

1 *New York Times*, May 1, 1986, p. B-1.

2 Royce Hanson, ed., *Rethinking Urban Policy* (Washington, D.C.: National Academy Press, 1983).

3 *Minneapolis Star and Tribune*, May 27, 1986, p. 13A.

20 Urban Policy in the Nineties and Beyond:
The Need for New Approaches

1 Jane Jacobs, *Cities and the Wealth of Nations: Principles of Economic Life* (New York: Random House, 1984), p. 29.

2 William Schambra, "Policy Liberalism, National Community Liberalism, and the Prospects for National Urban Policy."

3 Arthur M. Schlesinger, Jr., *The Cycles of American History* (Boston: Houghton Mifflin, 1986), chap. 2.

4 Donald Mason, working paper prepared for the Urban Institute in 1983, is among the best.

5 Joint Economic Committee, *Trends in the Fiscal Condition of Cities, 1981–1983* (Washington, D.C.: U.S. Government Printing Office, 1983).

6 Subcommittee on the City, Committee on Banking, Finance, and Urban Affairs, U.S. House of Representatives, *How Cities Can Grow Old Gracefully* (Washington, D.C.: U.S. Government Printing Office, 1977).

7 Marshall Kaplan and Franklin James, "Federal Housing Agencies and National Housing Policies" (Cambridge, Mass.: MIT Housing Project, April 1988).

8 Charles Murray, *Losing Ground* (New York: Basic Books, 1984).

9 Lester C. Thurow, *The Zero-Sum Society* (New York: Basic Books, 1980), pp. 203–4.

10 National Commission on Excellence in Education, *A Nation at Risk: The Imperative for Education Reform* (Washington, D.C.: U.S. Government Printing Office, 1983).

11 M. Kaplan, P. Cuciti, F. Cesario, D. Donald, et al., "Hard Choices: A Report on the Increasing Gap Between America's Infrastructure Needs and Our Ability to Pay for Them," Study for the Subcommittee on Economic Goals and Intergovernmental Policy, Joint Economic Committee, U.S. Congress (Washington, D.C.: U.S. Government Printing Office, 1984).

Index

About the Editors and Contributors

Marshall Kaplan has been dean of the University of Colorado's Graduate School of Public Affairs since 1981. From 1977 to 1981 he was deputy assistant secretary for urban policy at the Department of Housing and Urban Development (HUD). His books include *The Politics of Neglect* (with Bernard Frieden, coeditor), MIT Press, 1975; *City Planning in the Sixties: A Design for Irrelevancy*, MIT Press, 1976; and *The Great Society and Its Legacy* (with Peggy Cuciti, coeditor), Duke University Press, 1986.

Franklin James was director of the urban policy staff at HUD from 1977 to 1981. Prior to that, he was senior policy analyst at the Urban Institute. He is now professor of public policy, University of Colorado, Graduate School of Public Affairs. His research and publications have covered a wide range of subjects related to urban policy and poverty. Some of his works are *Intra-Metropolitan Industry Location*, 1975; *Zoning for Sale*, 1976; and *Minorities in the Sunbelt*, 1984.

Contributors

William C. Apgar, Jr., is an associate professor at Harvard University's John F. Kennedy School of Government. He also has an appointment in the Joint Center for Housing Studies at Harvard.

Roy Bahl is professor of economics and director of the Policy Research Program at Georgia State University. From 1971 to 1988 he was Maxwell Professor of Political Economy and director of the Metropolitan Studies Program in the Maxwell School at Syracuse University.

Peggy L. Cuciti serves as associate director of the University of Colorado's GSPA's centers for applied research and policy analysis. She coedited with Marshall Kaplan the book *The Great Society and Its Legacy*, Duke University Press, 1986.

William Duncombe, a Ph.D. candidate in public administration at the Maxwell School, is a research assistant in Syracuse University's Metropolitan Studies Program.

Peter Edelman is professor of law at the Georgetown University Law Center. He was vice president of the University of Massachusetts from 1971 to 1975 and director of the New York State Division for Youth from 1975 to 1979.

Bernard J. Frieden is Class of 1942 Professor in the department of urban studies and planning at the Massachusetts Institute of Technology and chairman of the MIT faculty. He is also a member of the faculty committee of the MIT Center for Real Estate Development.

Langley Keyes, professor of urban studies and planning at MIT, was special assistant for policy development, Executive Office of Communities and Development, Commonwealth of Massachusetts.

Beverly M. Klimkowsky has written extensively on urban policy and pension policy. She has held positions at Wesleyan University, the Social Security Administration, and the U.S. Senate.

Ian Menzies, a national award-winning writer and former managing editor and associate editor of the *Boston Globe*, is currently a senior fellow at the John W. McCormack Institute of Public Affairs, University of Massachusetts at Boston.

Frank Newman is president of the Education Commission of the States (ECS). He is most widely known as the author of the Newman reports (*Report on Higher Education*, 1971; and *National Policy and Higher Education*, 1974).

Charles J. Orlebeke is professor and director, School of Urban Planning and Policy, University of Illinois at Chicago. During the Nixon and Ford administrations he served in policymaking positions at HUD.

Michael A. Pagano is associate professor of political science at Miami University, Oxford, Ohio. He is coauthor of *Cities and Fiscal Choices*, Duke University Press, 1985.

Robert Palaich is a senior policy analyst at the Education Commission of the States and director of the Youth at Risk project.

Fern C. Portnoy is president of Portnoy & Associates, Inc., a philanthropic management and advisory firm in Denver. From 1975 to 1987 she was chief executive officer of the Piton Foundation, which provides funding in the areas of housing, health, and social service issues.

Robert D. Reischauer has recently been appointed director of the Congressional Budget Office. A nationally recognized economist, he has written on federal budget policy, Congress, social welfare issues, poverty, and state and local fiscal problems.

Benson F. Roberts is special assistant for policy and program development at the Local Initiatives Support Corporation, a nonprofit organization that operates financial and technical support programs for community-based development corporations.

William A. Schambra has been a resident fellow at the American Enterprise Institute for Public Policy Research and has written extensively on public policy issues.

Wanda Schulman is a business analyst with American Management Systems in New York. She specializes in state and local government finance and business practices.

James L. Sundquist is Senior Fellow Emeritus, Governmental Studies Program, the Brookings Institution. A deputy undersecretary of agriculture from 1963 to 1965, he was adjunct professor at Smith College from 1975 to 1978.

Rona Wilensky is staff associate for the Kettering Foundation's project on community educational development. She is also a consultant to the Education Commission of the States.

Robert Wood is Henry R. Luce Professor of Democratic Institutions and the Social Order at Wesleyan University, Middletown, Connecticut. During the Johnson administration he was undersecretary and secretary of the Department of Housing and Urban Development.

Paul Ylvisaker is coordinator of the Alden Seminars on Higher Education. From 1972 to 1982 he was dean of the faculty and Charles William Eliot Professor of Education, Graduate School of Education, Harvard University.